French Legal Cultures

Law in Context

Below is a listing of the more recent publications in the Law in Context Series

Editors: William Twining (University College, London) and Christopher McCrudden (Lincoln College, Oxford)

Ashworth: *Sentencing and Criminal Justice*
Bercusson: *European Labour Law*
Birkinshaw: *Freedom of Information: The Law, the Practice and the Ideal*
Cane: *Atiyah's Accidents Compensation and the Law*
Collins: *The Law of Contract*
Scott and Black: *Cranston's Consumers and the Law*
Elworthy and Holder: *Environmental Protection: Text and Materials*
Fortin: *Children's Rights and the Developing Law*
Harlow and Rawlings: *Law and Administration: Text and Materials*
Harris: *An Introduction to Law*
Harvey: *Seeking Asylum in the UK: Problems and Prospects*
Lacey and Wells: *Reconstructing Criminal Law*
Moffat: *Trusts Law – Text and Materials*
Norrie: *Crime, Reason and History*
Oliver and Drewery: *The Law and Parliament*
Oliver: *Common Values and the Public-Private Divide*
O'Dair: *Legal Ethics Text and Materials*
Palmer and Roberts: *Dispute Processes: ADR and the Primary Forms of Decision Making*
Reed: *Internet Law – Text and Materials*
Turpin: *British Government and the Constitution: Text, Cases and Materials*
Twining: *Globalisation and Legal Theory*
Twining and Miers: *How to Do Things with Rules*
Ward: *Shakespeare and the Legal Imagination*
Zander: *Cases and Materials on the English Legal System*
Zander: *The Law Making Process*

French Legal Cultures

John Bell FBA
Professor of Public and Comparative Law, University of Leeds
Professor-Elect, University of Cambridge

Butterworths
London, Edinburgh, Dublin
2001

United Kingdom	Butterworths, a Division of Reed Elsevier (UK) Ltd, Halsbury House, 35 Chancery Lane, LONDON WC2A 1EL and 4 Hill Street, EDINBURGH EH2 3JZ
Australia	Butterworths, a Division of Reed International Books Australia Pty Ltd, CHATSWOOD, New South Wales
Canada	Butterworths Canada Ltd, MARKHAM, Ontario
Hong Kong	Butterworths Hong Kong, a division of Reed Elsevier (Greater China) Ltd, HONG KONG
India	Butterworths India, NEW DELHI
Ireland	Butterworth (Ireland) Ltd, DUBLIN
Malaysia	Malayan Law Journal Sdn Bhd, KUALA LUMPUR
New Zealand	Butterworths of New Zealand Ltd, WELLINGTON
Singapore	Butterworths Asia, SINGAPORE
South Africa	Butterworths Publishers (Pty) Ltd, DURBAN
USA	Lexis Law Publishing, CHARLOTTESVILLE, Virginia

A CIP Catalogue record for this book is available from the British Library.

ISBN 0 406 94303 6

Printed in Great Britain by Cromwell Press, Trowbridge, Wiltshire

Preface

The choice of the plural in the title of this book is deliberate. I wish to argue that French law has a number of distinct sub-cultures, which it is important to recognise.

The need for this kind of approach stems from the predominance of private lawyers among those who have written scholarly works in English on French law. Both French lawyers (eg David, Tallon and Tunc) and non-French writers (eg Gordley, Lawson, Nicholas, Von Mehren, Zweigert and Kötz, Legrand, Rudden and Samuel) have written insightful works in English very much from a private law perspective. These have been very important scholarly contributions to giving English-language readers a deep understanding of French law, from which I, for one, have benefited enormously. My opinion, however, is that French law viewed from the perspective and interests of a private lawyer is only part of the picture. By comparing private law with criminal, administrative and constitutional law in this book, I hope to convince the reader that the picture is more varied, and that some of the features which writers have emphasised as characteristic of French law have significantly different importance in other branches of the law. This work is too short to provide a definitive restatement of French legal culture in its different branches. It is, however, a beginning and may encourage further work in a similar direction.

A. THE CLAIMED DISTINCTIVE FEATURES OF FRENCH LAW

Let me start with the insights into French law which private law comparatists have presented. Among the features which are identified as distinctive by various writers, I would select seven as central: (1) the primacy of loi and the droit écrit; (2) the systematic and principled nature of codified law; (3) the relative importance of la jurisprudence and of la doctrine as legal authorities and influences in developing the law; (4) the use of some distinctive concepts to organise legal thought; (5) the focus on individual rights, rather than remedies; (6) the existence of a career judiciary and the dominance of the profession of avocat; and (7) distinctive court structures. Each of these will be discussed at length in subsequent chapters, but it will be useful here to sketch some of the main lines of the traditional picture of French law.

Zweigert and Kötz argue that the 'style' of a legal system can be identified from its historical background, 'its predominant and characteristic mode of thought in legal matters', its particularly distinctive concepts or institutions, which legal sources it uses and how it handles them, and its ideology.[1] The features listed above relate predominantly to sources of law and legal concepts from which a way of thinking or 'mentality' emerges. It is this structure for thinking or mental map which forms the basis of Pierre Legrand's argument that there is a distinctive French law mentality, compared, for example, with that of English law.[2] This is offered as a holistic analysis of which the individual features listed form a part. The history provides an explanation for these features and is a constant point of reference. The ideology is understated and implicit. The existence of a capitalist market economy and liberal democratic political institutions is taken as part of the background, and is, in any case, common to western countries with different legal traditions. But in a more detailed study, one would want to identify the different pre-occupations of different branches of law which certainly merit being given the label.

(1) The primacy of *loi*

Nicholas argues, in France 'law is primarily and characteristically a body of rules enacted by the state, to be found in the codes and, in ever-increasing measure, in legislation supplementing the codes'.[3] This is a constitutional statement of principle, as well as a starting point for the hierarchy of sources of law. This provides a focal conception of the law and shapes legal reasoning. David suggested:

> In a very broad sense, legislation plays the same role in France as judicial decisions play in common law countries. Legislative rules provide the starting point from which lawyers and judges work toward their goal, the most just solution for the problem at hand.[4]

David also suggests that law is regarded primarily as a body of substantive rules of organisation and conduct, and that procedure and the administration of justice take second place.[5] This contrasts with the importance of procedure in the development of the common law, and the place of remedies as a focus for legal thinking.

(2) Codified law

Zweigert and Kötz single out the Code civil of 1804 as the heart of private law in France and its major contribution to legal development in other countries.[6] As Nicholas puts it, Roman law from 532 AD was the 'law of the book', the *Corpus Iuris Civilis*, and this

1 K Zweigert and H Kötz, *An Introduction to Comparative Law* (3rd edn trans T Weir, Oxford 1998), p 68.
2 P Legrand, 'European Legal Systems are not Converging' (1996) 45 ICLQ 52; see below, p 15. B Nicholas in D Harris and D Tallon, *Contract Law Today* (Oxford 1989), p 385 also talks of a difference in 'fundamental mental attitudes' between English and French lawyers.
3 B Nicholas, *The French Law of Contract* (2nd edn, Oxford 1992), p 5.
4 R David, *French Law* (1959, English trans by M Kindred, Baton Rouge 1972), p xiii.
5 Ibid, p ix; also David, op cit, p vi.
6 Op cit, p 74 and Ch 8 on the reception of the Code civil.

continues, though the 'book' is now the Code civil.[7] The characteristic of the Code is not just that it is written law, but that it is systematic, complete, and principled. There is an attempt to state the whole of the relevant area of law and all legal reasoning works from the basis of that structure. The fact that the law is stated in a principled fashion enables it to develop to meet new circumstances. Medieval and renaissance lawyers were used to working with a fixed and unalterable text in the *Corpus Iuris*, but they adapted its principles to life over 1,000 years later. French lawyers have had to reason with the Code civil in a similar way.

The drafting of the law and the more teleological approach to interpretation are identified by Nicholas as significant differences from the common law.[8] Certainly many texts of the Code civil and of *lois* are brief, without the detailed provision for possible eventualities found in common law statutes. The Code civil arts 1156 to 1164 are normally taken to set out principles for the interpretation of legislation, as well as of contracts.

(3) Legal authorities: la jurisprudence and la doctrine

This hierarchy of sources reflects a political and historical background. The parlements of the Ancien Regime were considered to have blocked reform, and the Revolution sought to impose the will of the legislator as the way forward. The loi of 16-24 August 1790, reaffirmed in art 5 of the Code civil, prohibits judges from making general or regulatory pronouncements on the law. They are to decide cases, not to take the opportunity of cases to declare general rules for the future, as the parlements had done. But, should the law be unclear or inadequate, then the courts are still required by art 4 to come to a decision in the case before them. This is traditionally seen as giving only a low authority to judicial decisions. In theory, they are interpretations of the written law, not an authority in their own right.[9] Of course, in practice, writers acknowledge that, over the past 200 years of interpretation, large areas of French private law have effectively moved from droit écrit into a form of case law system.[10] But French writers have used many curious theoretical constructions in order to explain how judicial development of the law can take place without judicial decisions being a source of law.[11] There is not a cult of precedent, as in the common law.[12] Lower courts can and do refuse to follow the decisions of the Cour de cassation, and this conflict between courts often forces the higher court to change its mind.[13] Naturally, this

7 *French Law of Contract*, p 4.
8 Ibid, pp 5-6.
9 M Troper, C Grzegorczyk and J-L Gardies, in DN MacCormick and RS Summers, *Interpreting Statutes* (Aldershot 1991), p 177: 'Judges do not use the concept of 'gap' at all. They follow a formal (decisionist) point of view – to use all possible interpretative techniques and arguments to avoid the appearance of gaps in the law, even if there are some in particular texts ... French judges tend to disguise the filling of gaps as interpretation'.
10 See Ripert quoted by Zweigert and Kötz op cit, p 96.
11 The arguments are best summarised and analysed in S Belaid, *Le pouvoir créateur et normatif du juge* (Paris 1974). Selections are provided in O Kahn-Freund, C Lévy and B Rudden, *A Source-book on French Law* (2nd edn, Oxford 1979), pp 116-152.
12 See M Troper and C Grzegorczyk, in DN MacCormick and RS Summers, *Interpreting Precedents* (Aldershot 1997), Ch 4.
13 See below, p 78.

constitutional principle of the separation of powers has an impact on the status of judges. The instrumental image given by Montesquieu that they are the 'mouth of the law' (bouches de la loi) does not convey the idea that they have a major autonomous power of decision-making.[14]

The low place accorded to case law and its focus on interpretation of the law in individual cases leaves a gap which is filled by *la doctrine*, doctrinal legal writers, predominantly from the universities. As Nicholas points out, this is a continuity with Roman law where the jurists performed a major role in advice and in systematising the law, a role which was continued after the rediscovery of Roman law in the eleventh century:

> In France *doctrine* has inherited the authority enjoyed by the universities in the period of the *ius commune*, an authority which is augmented by the relatively subordinate position which is, as we have seen, accorded to the judiciary in the constitutional scheme.[15]

The standard forms of literature are the treatise, the student manual, and the note d'arrêt, the commentary on judicial decisions published alongside the case in the law reviews. For David, this legal science is viewed as an essential, but not an exclusive source of insights into the kinds of rule required to achieve justice.[16] But , apart from such a critical role in relation to the law, the doctrinal writer provides a systematic account of the law, piecing together the results fragmentary legislative reforms and of interpretations made by the courts.

The importance of these different authorities is also linked to a more conceptual approach to the law, which reflects an academic influence. Lawson suggests:

> The civilian likes to be able to see clearly the shape and limits of the abstract concepts and doctrines with which he has to work before he starts to work with them...The common lawyer is much more inclined to use a concept of half-known outline as soon as he knows it is capable of performing the actual limited task he wants it to perform, leaving for further consideration what its other possibilities may be.[17]

Nicholas also points to a contrast between reasoning with broad concepts and principles in French law, rather than a more pragmatic approach in the common law.[18] I will wish to discuss in this book how far the contrast between a conceptualist and a pragmatic or incremental approach to law is a contrast between French law and the common law, or how far it is really a difference between academic and doctrinal reasoning on the one hand and judicial and practitioner reasoning on the other.

(4) Legal concepts

All legal systems have their distinctive legal concepts. They provide a kind of mental map of the legal world into which particular problems have to be located. English

14 See generally, JP Dawson, *The Oracles of the Law* (1968).
15 Op cit, p 20.
16 Op cit, p xii.
17 H Lawson, *A Common Lawyer looks at the Civil Law* (Ann Arbor 1953), p 66.

lawyers will use the trust and fiduciary duties, when civilian lawyers would use totally different concepts. Lawson suggested:

> … the leading differences between [the Civil Law] and the Common Law world are not differences of method or in ways of handling source materials, but the concepts themselves; and again that, although the concepts often differ in their general character, the most significant difference lies just in the simple fact that the two sets of concepts are not the same.[19]

For Zweigert and Kötz, as well as for Samuel and Legrand, the distinctive legal concepts reflected in the Code civil are important for legal thinking. Private law relationships must be analysed in terms of the concepts used by the Code, because the Code provides the complete framework for private law. For example, the totality of a person's property is discussed as his patrimoine, including debts he owes, in a way which is unfamiliar to the English lawyer (except in fields such as succession and insolvency). There are a whole range of other distinctive concepts which even lawyers from other civilian systems do not use.

(5) Rights and remedies

David and Samuel[20] argue that French lawyers differ from common lawyers in their focus on rights (le droit subjectif), rather than remedies. English law developed through the writ system – it was necessary to fit a claim into one of the permitted remedies which the courts could use. French private law was restructured in terms of principle in the 17th and 18th century. French law identifies rights and then tries to work out appropriate protection. By contrast, the common law established strong remedies to protect certain identified and important interests.[1] Accordingly, the Code civil sets out the entitlements of an individual and the procedures by which they are enforced are in a totally distinct code, the Nouveau Code de procédure civile. The flavour of this approach can be seen in art 1382 of the Code civil: 'Any human act whatever which causes damage to another obliges him by whose fault it occurred to make reparation.' By contrast, an English text would start by saying that 'a person can bring an action in negligence if …' The two approaches are different, and lead to different ways of dealing with new situations. The common lawyer must find a remedy within which to deal with a new situation. The French lawyer must decide, in principle, if a right should be recognised, and then can provide a remedy. On the whole, this difference in thinking separates common lawyers from civilian lawyers, and is not claimed to be peculiar to French lawyers.

(6) Legal professions: judges and avocats

The French have distinctive legal professions, which will be discussed in Chapter 2. Among the features noted by leading authors is the career judiciary. From leaving

18 B Nicholas in D Harris and D Tallon, *Contract Law Today*, p 13.
19 Op cit, p 209.
20 See David, op cit, p ix; G Samuel, ' "*Le droit subjectif*" and English Law' [1987] CLJ 264.
1 Samuel, ibid, p 273.

university, a law graduate can seek to enter the judicial college, the Ecole Nationale de la Magistrature, and progress to becoming a judge, a career which can last for 40 years or more. The judge is a civil servant and paid accordingly. Thus the age, status and character of the professional judiciary is different from that in the common law. The jury is used in very few cases, but lay participation as judges is very significant in juvenile criminal justice, as well as in commercial and labour law. Lay participation is also different in France, not only from the common law, but also from many civil law countries.

Zweigert and Kötz suggest that 'One may throw some light on the characteristic style of a legal system by asking which *type of lawyer* it regards as representative.'[2] For them, in France, the avocat is the representative figure. He is most in the public eye because of 'his brilliant oratory and his special prestige'.[3] This model of the avocat contrasts with the more retiring and modest function of the judge, who decides often collegially and impersonally, with no dissenting judgments. All the same, both legal professions aspire to certain legal virtues of 'clarity, brevity of expression, eloquence, style , effect, and form'.[4]

(7) Distinctive court structures

The French system of courts is distinctive, though it is a model that has been exported to other countries.[5] The major features identified are the fact that there is only one national court, the Cour de cassation. This corrects the judgments of the lower courts, but does not typically decide individual cases on their merits. Decisions on the merits are decided by regional courts, both at first instance and at appeal level. There are specialist first instance courts in commercial and labour matters. There is also a distinction between administrative and civil courts, which belong to different hierarchies with different supreme courts. The Conseil constitutionnel is, as we shall see, not strictly a court and is not integrated into the judicial hierarchy. Many of these features are not found in other western European legal systems, and they do make the French system distinctive.

A further feature mentioned by Zweigert and Kötz, among others, is the distinctive judicial style. The classic judgment of the Cour de cassation is brief, laconic and often uninformative. It tells you at best the solution to the case, but not the reasons for it. It lacks the personal and literary qualities, as well as the length, of the common law judgment, and it is much briefer than judgments in many other European legal systems.

B. THE STRUCTURE OF THIS BOOK

The features just mentioned build together to create a setting out of which a distinct mentality arises, a distinctive way of understanding and operating the law. This would suggest that there is a distinct French legal culture. This book tries to examine the

2 Op cit, Ch 9, esp p 129.
3 Ibid.
4 Ibid, p 130.
5 Ibid, pp 119-124.

extent to which the features identified by private lawyers are found also in other branches of the law. The book will also have to take on board the dynamic aspect of legal culture. It seems to me that some of the rhetoric deployed by Legrand and others suggests that legal culture is fixed and unalterable. If the French can adapt to MacDonalds, Coca-Cola and the Internet, then their legal culture can also adapt to the external environment and appropriate elements from it, thereby changing the French way of doing law.[6] In particular, the European dimension of the current legal context is causing major changes in the French legal culture. If this book identifies certain features of legal cultures, I would want to stress that each is open to change from both inside and outside the French legal order.

In one sense, this book has two introductions, and readers can make use of this according to their needs. I deliberately start in Chapter 1 with a general, theoretical chapter on the nature of legal culture. This is a controversial subject, but one of some importance in contemporary comparative law debates. This chapter will be of particular interest to postgraduate students. Undergraduates may prefer to start with the more concrete topics in Chapter 2, where I describe the institutional setting of French law – the courts, legal professions and key legal concepts and ideas. The next four chapters deal with different branches of French law. The choice of branches of law to be studied in this work reflects not only major divisions of French law: civil law, criminal law, administrative and constitutional law, but also the location of different dynamics between professional legal actors. There are different corps of judges in the different areas, and they relate differently to the various avocats and doctrinal legal writers in their fields. Since the paradigm used for English-language writing on French law has been civil law, it seems sensible to start with describing that culture in Chapter 3. Chapter 4 deals with criminal law. French criminal law procedure, notably the juge d'instruction, is also well known in English-language circles, both in academic writing and in the media. This already forms a contrast with civil law, even though many of the same legal actors are involved in both branches of law. Chapter 5 deals with administrative law, which is distinctive in terms of legal sources, its personnel and its principles. It is obviously different from civil law, and has long established the paradigm for public law, not only in France, but elsewhere. In Chapter 6, I deal with the newest of the branches of law, constitutional law, which has now become established in a very distinctive way. Compared with most constitutional courts in Europe, it is odd in being neither formally a court with court procedure, nor being integrated into the hierarchy of the judicial system. Neither civil nor criminal nor administrative courts can refer questions of law to it. In a final chapter, I review the traditional picture of French law which private lawyers have developed and ask how far it is right to see a common French legal culture among the distinct French legal sub-cultures I have identified.

This book is not setting out anything startlingly new. Most of the private law writers acknowledge that, although they entitle their sections 'French law', they are speaking specifically about 'French private law'.[7] David remarked that:

6 For example, some writers, such as D Soulez-Larivière, talk of and practice the 'Americanisation of law' in France: see *Lettre à un jeune avocat* (Paris 1999), esp p 14 where he suggests 'le biculturalisme est l'avenir' (biculturalism is the future).

7 For example, Zweigert and Kötz start their chapter on the 'History of French Law' with a discussion of the Code civil as the heart of 'private law in France' and proceed to discuss private law explicitly throughout: op cit, p 74.

> Although French law is unquestionably a single whole, its various branches often claim a certain independence of each other. Each asserts its own particularity … Their attitudes towards interpreting legal rules are not necessarily the same, and their instincts will not affect them in the same way. One has to be retuned before moving from one area of the law to another. As a result of legal classification, lawyers within a single legal system often feel like strangers when dealing with each other. When they abandon their area of specialization, they will at least experience the same uncertainty and reservation that any lawyer experiences when he gives a client advice on a question of foreign law.[8]

The question discussed in Chapter 7 is whether the differences identified in Chapters 3 to 6 are simply between different legal specialisms, such as might be encountered in any legal system, or whether the differences are great enough to describe as different legal cultures.

C. ACKNOWLEDGEMENTS

This book would not have been written without the award of a British Academy Readership and of funding for study visits again from the British Academy. In conducting the research, I owe a debt of gratitude to the many judges and practitioners whom I interviewed or who have assisted me in other ways. I would like to mention, in particular, Antoine Garapon and Jacques Debû-Carbonnier who assisted in arranging meetings in Paris and Bordeaux. Antoine Garapon also was very helpful in reading early drafts of my ideas and suggesting lines of resesearch. I am also grateful to John Spencer, Adam Crawford and Jacqueline Hodgson who read and commented upon Chapter 4. I owe many debts of gratitude for inspiration in this field, but it will suffice to single out André Tunc who first interested me in French law while I was a student in Cambridge and who died at the beginning of the research period for this book.

8 Op cit, pp 95 and 97.

Contents

Abbreviations

AJDA	*Acutalité juridique – droit administratif*
Bell, 'Reflections'	J Bell, 'Reflections on the procedure of the Conseil d'Etat' in G Hand and J McBride, *Droit sans frontières* (Birmingham 1991)
Brown and Bell	LN Brown and J Bell, *French Administrative Law* (5th edn 1998)
Bourdieu	P Bourdieu, *La noblesse d'Etat. Grandes Ecoles et esprit de corps* (Paris 1989)
C proc pén	Code de procédure pénale
D	Recueil Dalloz (-Sirey)
DDHC	Declaration of the Rights of Man and of the Citizen of 1789
Deguergue	M Deguergue, *Jurisprudence et doctrine dans l'élaboration du droit de la responsabilité administrative* (Paris 1994)
EDCE	*Etudes et Documents du Conseil d'Etat*
Fortsakis	T Fortsakis, *Conceptualisme et empiricisme en droit administratif français* (Paris 1987)
Garapon 1993	A Garapon, unpublished ENM course 22-26 November 1993
GD	L Favoreu and L Philip, *Les grandes décisions du Conseil constitutionnel* (10th edn, Paris 1999)
L Greilsamer and D Schneidermann	L Greilsamer and D Schneidermann, *Les juges parlent* (Paris 1992)
Jan	P Jan, *La Saisine du Conseil constitutionnel* (Paris 1999)
Karpik	L Karpik, *French Lawyers* (Oxford 1999)
Le Berre	H Le Berre, *Les revirements de jurisprudence en droit administratif de l'an VIII à 1998 (Conseil d'Etat et Tribunal des Conflits)* (Paris 1999)
Legal Cultures	D Nelken (ed), *Legal Cultures* (Aldershot 1997)

Livre Jubilaire	*Le Conseil d'Etat. Livre Jubilaire* (Paris 1952)
Massot and Girardot	J Massot and T Girardot, *Conseil d'Etat* (Paris 1999)
Massot Report	*Groupe d'étude sur la responsabilité pénale des décideurs publics* (Report to Minister of Justice, 16 December 1999)
Merryman Collection	DS Clark (ed), *Comparative and Private International Law: Essays in Honor of John Henry Merryman on his Seventieth Birthday* (Berlin 1990)
NCPCiv	Nouveau code de procédure civile
RDP	*Revue de Droit Public*
Rfda	*Revue française de droit administratif*
RFDC	*Revue française de droit constitutionnel*
RTDCiv	*Revue trimestrielle de droit civil*
Stone	A Stone, *The Birth of Constitutional Politics in France* (New York 1992)
Stone Sweet	A Stone Sweet, *Governing with Judges* (Oxford 2000)
Truche Commission	*Rapport de la commission de réflexion sur la Justice* (Paris 1997)
Vedel and Delvolvé	*Droit administratif* (12th edn, Paris 1992), vol 1
Viala	A Viala, *Les réserves d'interprétation dans la jurisprudence du Conseil constitutionnel* (Paris 1999)
Zweigert and Kötz	K Zweigert and H Kötz, *An Introduction to Comparative Law* (3rd edn, Oxford 1998)

Table of cases

French cases are usually cited by date and this table reflects that convention

Chapter 1

Legal culture

> A living body of law is not a collection of doctrines, rules, terms and phrases. It is not a dictionary, but a culture; and it has to be apprehended as such.[1]

Friedman's argument is important for the study of any legal system. Walk into any French tribunal correctionnel and you will see a number of people. There is the policeman who tells you to turn off your mobile phone before coming in and who keeps order in the courtroom. There is the greffier in robe who calls the cases and discusses their order with the avocats who are there. There is the judge in robe, the ministère public acting as prosecutor at the same level and in similar clothing to the judge. There are the defendants and the civil parties. To a foreigner, the way these individuals interact may seem strange. For example, the judge may just read information out to the defendant from the file and ask for reactions. She may well call no witnesses, even when the accused contests their version of the facts. The prosecutor does not lead the evidence, but is invited by the judge to comment and then to propose a sentence. The civil party will be requesting damages in the same hearing that the prosecution takes place. Indeed, it may happen that neither the civil party nor the accused is legally represented. Quite often, there is not much doubt about the facts. Such examples of routine criminal justice reveal much about a legal system. They give insights into the law that cannot just be grasped from looking at the legal rules as set out in the Code pénal or in the Code de procédure pénale. The relationships between the rules, the people and the procedures taken together make it possible to understand what the law is trying to achieve and how it works.

Again, look along any French street. 'Défense d'afficher: loi du 29 juillet 1881'. Compare that with a typical English notice: 'No billposting. By order.' Both are commands and authoritative, yet the law is more prominent in the French injunction. This gives us an insight into the place of law in the two societies

The purpose of this work is to try to go beyond the legal rules and doctrines and to set out the context of some different aspects of the French legal system. By spending

1 LM Friedman, in DS Clark (ed), *Comparative and Private International Law: Essays in Honor of John Henry Merryman on his Seventieth Birthday* (Berlin 1990) (hereafter 'Merryman Collection'), at p 47.

time on a few major branches of law, I will try to move beyond the anecdotes, which first strike the English lawyer, to a more systematic study.

We can try to understand law in a variety of ways. This work tries to explain how the French legal system works at an official level. My focus of attention is deliberately on the institutional features of the legal system and thus on its claims to shape action and society, rather than on how it is perceived and has actual effects on citizens in society. To that extent, my research is about an 'official culture' of the legal system. Since individuals have a range of social roles and activities, one must recognise that a single individual will belong to more than one culture and also has a number of different relationships to the law. A Catholic, Socialist judge active in his quartier in Paris will belong to specific gender, religious, political and local cultures, as well as belonging to the legal community. To that extent, his profile will differ from a woman, Protestant, right-wing judge from the provinces. This judge will, in her turn, relate to the law differently in her judicial work, as a taxpayer, as a member of a voluntary association, or as the recipient of a parking ticket. By choosing to focus on the official legal culture, this study is necessarily limited, even if it does try to go beyond the study of legal rules and doctrines.

In this chapter, I want to set out my understanding of 'legal culture'. The idea of 'culture' is used in a variety of disciplines and in a first section, I will try to outline how my conception relates to ideas current in these other disciplines. Since 'legal culture' has become a major topic among sociologists of law and comparative lawyers, in a second section I will try to relate my ideas to these current debates. In a third section, I will outline the methodology to be adopted.

A. WHAT COUNTS AS 'CULTURE'?

A classic definition of culture comes from Kroeber and Kluckhohn:[2]

> Culture consists of patterns, explicit and implict, of and for behaviour acquired and transmitted by symbols, constituting the distinctive achievements of a human group, including their embodiment in artifacts; the essential core of culture consists of traditional (ie historically derived and selected) ideas and especially their attached values; cultural systems may, on the one hand, be considered as products of action, on the other hand as conditioning elements of further action.

This definition contains two elements. On the one hand, culture is a pattern of behaviour or an activity, which Bauman would describe as 'praxis' or cultural acts.[3] On the other hand, there is a set of ideas and values, which are communicated through language and signs that express attitudes and values towards the activity.[4] In this book, I will argue that a study of legal culture needs to pay attention to both aspects.

2 AL Kroeber and C Kluckhohn, in *Culture. A Critical Review of Concepts and Definitions* (Chicago 1952), p 181.

3 Z Bauman, *Culture as Praxis* (London 1973).

4 See also C Geertz, *The Interpretation of Cultures* (1973, Basic Books edn, London 1993) p 5; R Williams, *Culture* (London 1981), pp 11-12.

(1) Culture as ideology

The best presentation of the current legal debate on culture is contained in David Nelken's collection, *Legal Cultures*.[5] In it, Friedman argues that culture is best defined as the ideas and state of mind of the public towards the law.[6] Cotterell accepts this orientation, but suggests that the concept of 'culture' is not the most appropriate term and that 'ideology' would fit this function better.[7] A similar approach is adopted in the study of political culture. In studying France, Bernstein describes a political culture as 'a totality of representations, bearing norms and values, which constitute the identity of the great political families'.[8] This emphasises the ideological attachment that is at the heart of political parties. For Bernstein, such a vision relates not only to the future, but also to an interpretation of the past, particularly the country's past. That vision provides an account of the political tradition of the country which it is seeking to re-shape.[9] There is then a clear connection between the intellectual representation or vision (*l'imaginaire*) and the organisation realisation of the project in a party or a governmental regime.[10] On this approach, the practical is the expression of the ideological. In Friedman's words, 'culture' is measured directly by what people think and, indirectly and consequentially, about what they do in the light of those perceptions.[11]

Much of the study of legal cultures has focused on this idea of culture as symbolic representation. Thus in her studies of the transmission of legal cultures, Kourilsky tries to identify the *significance* which attach to concepts, ideas and institutions in different countries. In interviews with young people, she seeks to discover their ways of understanding the phenomena of law in their society. In particular, she is concerned to identify how the young people come to develop their ideas. The people questioned have not had a particular close exposure to the law, and so she identifies conversations overheard in the family as major influences in perceptions of law, rather than direct experience.[12] On this account of 'culture', individuals acquire a specific way of looking at the phenomena of law as a major part of socialisation, and so there would be much to be said for Cotterell's observation that the term 'ideology' might be appropriate.

5 D Nelken (ed), *Legal Cultures* (Aldershot 1997) (hereafter '*Legal Cultures*').

6 LM Friedman in *Legal Cultures*, p 35 and in Merryman Collection, p 53, where he talks of 'legal consciousness', ie the ideas, attitudes, values and opinions about law, the legal system and legal institutions in some given population'.

7 R Cotterell in *Legal Cultures*, at pp 22-23 and 29.

8 S Bernstein, *Les cultures politiques en France* (1999), p 10.

9 Ibid, p 13. Cf R Cotterell in I Loveland (ed), *A Special Relationship. American Influences on Public Law in the United Kingdom* (Oxford 1995) (hereafter 'Loveland'), p 25 who argues that constitutional thought proclaims certain cultural characteristics of a society which favour the establishment and maintenance of political authority.

10 Bernstein, *Les cultures politiques*, p 15.

11 LM Friedman, 'Is there a Modern Legal Culture?' (1994) 7 Ratio Juris 117 at p 119.

12 See C Kourilsky-Augeven, 'Sociologie juridique et modèle culturel. L'image du droit en Russie et en France' *Droit et Société* No 18 (Paris 1996), p 19, though she notes that this is modified by other influences, eg what is learned through lessons and encounters at school. See also C Kourilsky, 'Socialisation juridique et identité du sujet' (1991) 19 *Droit et Société* 259 where a similar study was conducted in relation to Poland.

Bauman is right, however, to criticise this 'idealist' description as too far removed from the practice, since culture shapes the practice of human beings and not just their attitudes towards it.[13]. To understand a culture it is necessary not only to understand a set of beliefs and attitudes, but also the context in which those arise and are carried out. As Bernstein points out in relation to politics, a culture arises as an engagement with a concrete set of events, an attempt to offer solutions, often in relation to some key, catalytic moment or event.[14] Praxis is not merely the initial cause or occasion of the development of an ideology. Legal or political actions continue to be carried out, and this leads to the development and the revision of ideas in the light of the realities of experience. A set of ideas has to be rooted in a practical situation. A person could hold an ideology almost whatever the particular legal system in which the person finds him- or herself. But the reality of practice is central in shaping the context in which a person makes sense of a legal system.

(2) Culture as praxis

More empirical scholars suggest that behaviour or institutions are the appropriate focus of culture. Blankenburg argues that, although the 'law-in the books' between two countries such as Germany and the Netherlands may be similar, the differences are accounted for by the actions of professions and legal institutions.[15] King also argues for a focus on social institutions in order to avoid stereotypes which idealist descriptions of law may suggest.[16] Of course, one cannot simply describe a set of empirical phenomena and treat them as constituting the culture.[17] Facts may be evidence for culture, but a study of culture has to give an account of the significance that the actors give to these externally observed events. In Geertz's terms, cultural analysis is concerned with guesses at meaning, rather than description of events.[18] But this is not to deny that the events and social institutions are significant.

Culture is thus a reflexive phenomenon. In the context of law, an individual's own values are constrained by the external practice of a legal culture. It is taken for granted that, in law, the individual judge cannot give effect to his personal opinions, but must judge according to law.[19] The culture of the legal system is there a constraint on individual action. But, in a very important way, the legal task in the first place defines the individual as a legal actor and assigns her a role as 'lawyer', 'judge', 'litigant', 'victim of crime' and so on. Such categorisation depends on what the various legal actors think is happening in a legal situation. The position is similar to Searle's analysis of the cocktail party. The gathering of individuals drinking wine in a common location

13 Z Bauman, op cit, pp 91, 105, 172-173.

14 Bernstein, *Les cultures politiques*, pp. 21-22. But in ch 10 he notes the importance of change as well.

15 *Legal Cultures*, ch 3; also E Blankenburg, 'Patterns of Legal Culture. The Netherlands Compared to Neighbouring Germany' (1998) 46 Am Jo Comp Law 1 at p 39.

16 Nelken, *Legal Cultures*, p 122.

17 C Geertz, *The Interpretation of Cultures*, p 9.

18 Ibid, p 20.

19 Cf The 'Magneaud Phenomenon' where a judge applied his own sense of fairness, rather than the law in dealing with a poor woman caught stealing bread to feed her child: Amiens, 22 April 1898, DP 1899.2.329, note Josserand; F Gény, *Méthodes d'interprétation et sources du droit positif* (2nd edn, Paris 1919), vol 2, pp 287-307.

is only 'a cocktail party' because participants have a common intention to treat it as such an event.[20] Without the common intention, there would be just a group of individuals drinking in the same place. In law, agreed perceptions constitute a set of facts as a 'trial' – the situation in which one person sits on a raised platform while another person stands silently in front of him and yet two others argue facing the person seated. The role that an individual occupies, and the role of other actors, arise from perceptions of the task and from the cultural traditions associated with it. Furthermore, the regularity of any such practice gives rise to professions, which in turn develop their own understandings. A culture thus shapes the task and the implicit and explicit assumptions related to it, as an organisational culture. Although the participant has a personal perspective on legal events, culture is a collective phenomenon where groups use the same language and have a common identity despite other differences.[1] There is a genuine reflexive quality to the relationship of praxis and ideas that needs to be captured in a definition of legal culture.[2]

(3) Institutional facts

The most helpful way to consider the relationship between the ideological and practical aspects of culture is to use Searle's conception of 'institutional fact'. An 'institutional fact' is a fact, which we invest with meaning within a particular set of social relations because it performs a particular function. Thus a green piece of paper having the right design may count as a 'dollar' in money. The paper has no intrinsic worth, but rules arising from social convention confer on it the value of money.[3] The same is true with law, for law is an institutional system. As Weinberger and MacCormick point out,[4] law is not a set of 'natural facts' that can be inspected directly. Rather it is an interpretative reality under which certain physical events take on a special significance. A visitor to England might observe one person sitting on a raised platform and wearing robes who is talking to another person in a box surrounded by two men in uniform. That is a set of brute facts we can see with our eyes. But to describe this as the sitting of a 'court' is to appeal to a set of institutional rules, which confer a specific meaning on the events and legitimate them. The description that this is a 'court' in which a 'judge' 'sentences' an 'accused' in the 'dock' surrounded by 'prison warders' requires an ability to participate in an institutional system, here the English legal system. That assignment of meaning to natural facts depends on collective intentionality, not just the wishes or views of a particular individual observer or actor.[5] The community acting creates the institutional reality, which individuals can then use to explain events. But it is clear that this institutional system and practice precedes them.

As Searle points out, this operation by which one thing counts as another occurs only within language and thus in the minds of individuals.[6] For example, a non-legal,

20 See JR Searle, *The Social Construction of Reality* (London 1995), p 26.
1 Op cit, p 29.
2 See AJ Arnaud, *Pour une pensée juridique européenne* (Paris 1991), p 27.
3 JR Searle, *The Social Construction of Reality* (London 1995), p 47.
4 N MacCormick and O Weinberger, *An Institutional Theory of Law* (Dordrecht 1986), ch 3.
5 Searle, *The Social Construction of Reality*, p 46. See further below, p 9.
6 Ibid, pp 68-69.

empirical observation might identify that one person has killed another. But it requires legal institutional language to establish this event as 'murder' and then to have processes by which the killer is labelled a 'murderer' and, as such, liable to 'punishment'.[7] Such institutional facts are necessarily embedded within the language of a particular community. This requires the observer to relate law to a specific community, which develops the social conventions. That community has the collective intention to treat a person wearing certain clothes, speaking in a certain setting and in a certain context as 'acting as a judge'. In that way, the law is both a set of activities and a set of attitudes towards those activities. I consider it important to view the issue of legal culture not as a matter of how the individual interfaces with a culture, but rather as a version of organisational culture: how do individual roles become defined and operate within an overall corporate culture.

(4) Law as tradition

Tradition is an important part of culture, and especially within the law. Law is a body of norms and practices which is handed down. The practice of preserving and developing a tradition gives rise to a legal community. Taking part in the tradition is the way one comes to understand the law from the legal point of view.[8] A tradition connects norms, practices and people.

(a) A body of received knowledge and practices (the traditum*)*

Hazareesingh suggests that 'a tradition is characteristically defined as the transmission of a relatively coherent body of knowledge or thought from one generation to the next'.[9] Legal writers such as Krygier and Gerber[10] concentrate on authoritative texts (statutes, reported cases and key doctrinal writings) as central to the legal tradition. Texts are handed on and become the focus of legal activity. The particular style and influences of the texts and the way these texts are treated and interpreted, are also important features of the legal tradition and make it distinctive. But it is also important to see both procedures and rituals as part of what is handed on. The way lawyers dress and perform legal acts helps to create the law as a way of life. The role of the notary in drawing up wills or marriage contracts in France, the layout of the courtroom and the roles which the different lawyers, avocats, greffiers and judges, perform in court is as much part of the French legal tradition as the Code civil or other received texts. Certainly both a body of principles and a set of practices form the basis for how continuity is preserved within the legal community.[11]

7 Ibid, p 50.
8 J Bell, 'Comparative Law and Legal Theory' in W Krawietz, *Festschrift for RS Summers* (Berlin 1994) 19 at p 29. See also M Krygier, 'Law as Tradition' (1986) 5 *Law and Philosophy* 237 at p 255.
9 S Hazareesingh, *Political Traditions in Modern* France (Oxford 1994), p 5.
10 M Krygier, 'Law as Tradition' (1986) 5 *Law and Philosophy* 237, note 25; DJ Gerber, 'System Dynamics: Towards a Language of Comparative Law?' (1998) 46 Am Jo Comp Law 719, 731.
11 See AWB Simpson, 'The Common Law and Legal Theory', in ibid (ed), *Oxford Essays in Jurisprudence* (2nd series, Oxford 1973), 79.

Grosso suggests that we should examine the 'experienced tradition', a substantive and continuing body of attitudes and activities which is not only handed on, but is lived out and serves a basis for renewal. This is in contrast to the 'tradition as myth' or the 'sentimental tradition' which is a set of sentiments and attachments to a 'grand past' and aspirations for the future.[12] The focus, as he suggests is on the experience *from the legal point of view*, which perceives legal activity as a unity and as developing organically.[13]

(b) A process by which the tradition is handed on and received

A tradition has to be transmitted and made accessible to each generation of participants. As a result, there has to be processes of conservation, of authenticating what is handed on and of interpretation. There is also a process of induction is the way by which new participants are formed to be able to make use of the tradition in a way that counts as legitimate. By all means, there is a legitimate activity of external criticism and interpretation, eg a Marxist critique of the civil code as the expression of bourgeois social values.[14] But we are concerned here, for example, to explain the internal process of making sense of the Code as part of a legal argument. For this purpose, there are established ways in which interpretations can be accepted as valid. There are conventions within the legal community about what are appropriate arguments which support an interpretation – whether cases can be cited and from which courts, whether doctrinal legal writers can be cited as appropriate authorities. Education has an important role in the socialisation of participants into a culture.

Conservation and education are only part of the picture. A living tradition has to renew itself as it is applied to new situations. For this reason, we have to see the process of interpretation as a way in which the tradition is brought up to date and developed. As Grosso points out, the experience of continuity within a tradition provides a way for assimilating innovations.[15]

(c) A body of guardians of the tradition

Certain individuals will have a special status as a reference group for the interpretation of the tradition. The guardians of the tradition may not be the whole community, but may be key actors within it who serve as reference points. In early Roman law, these were the priests and in later Roman law the praetor and the jurisconsults. In more recent times, the bodies are more diffuse and we will talk of the relationships of distinct legal groups, judges, avocats, doctrinal legal writers and so on.

In describing a legal community within which decisions take place or advice is given, we need to map the roles which different individuals occupy, particularly the leading guardians and developers of a tradition. Outside that community, there are the other communities and reference groups who constitute the environment within which a legal community works and with whom it enters into dialogue about both its role and

12 G Grosso, *Tradizione e misura umana del diritto* (Milan 1976), pp 26-27 and 37-39.
13 Ibid, p 41.
14 See A-J Arnaud, *Les origines doctrinales du Code civil* (Paris 1978).
15 G Grosso, *Tradizione e misura umana*, p 41.

what it is trying to achieve.

In rapidly changing societies, legal systems increasingly face similar problems and are influenced by political, business and administrative trends in ideas which cut across jurisdictional boundaries. While open to outside influences, they retain certain distinctive characteristics and values. Systems are often searching for ideas, rather than authorities in the other systems, and engage in their own selection.[16] The argument of this work will be that it remains important to see what is distinctive in individual legal systems, as well as to focus on the more general, global trends.

(5) Culture as the basis for legal thinking

Because law is an institutional fact, becoming part of a culture makes it possible to understand and describe what is happening from the appropriate point of view. Whatever individuals may think privately, to describe and to participate in a legal activity, it is necessary to adopt a legal point of view. Hart labels this as an 'internal' point of view.[17] To do this it is necessary to act as part of a tradition.

My argument has two aspects. First, as a general feature, understanding requires insertion in a tradition in which a text or idea becomes accessible. We cannot just listen to a talk or pick up a legal text and expect to be able to understand it and make a valid comment on it. We have to situate ourselves as part of the tradition out of which the speaker or writer is expounding. The second, more specific, feature of law is that reasoning develops by analogy, such that one needs to be part of the tradition before one can operate in this way. Although this approach essentially argues for the importance of an intellectual culture of which the reader or listener has to become part, I would argue that the distinctive feature of law is that the intellectual community is very closely bound up with a social community that provides for its continuity.[18]

Gadamer explains that we do not come to read a text cold or by chance.[19] We come with questions or a focus of interest which we expect to have illuminated, if not resolved, by our reading. This 'pre-understanding' (*Vorverständnis*) directs our attention and helps us to approach the text in the appropriate way. When reading a piece of literature, we will come with an understanding of the different literary forms of poetry, novel, and so on. The understanding of the genre will help us to know what to expect to gain from the work and the appropriate method of interpretation to adopt. Thus the communication which is involved in the text operates within a broader setting of expectations.

Our expectations are set typically by a tradition. That tradition establishes the meaning of core concepts, the values and ideas to which the writer may only make implicit reference or allusion. It also establishes the method by which one should

16 See V Gessner, 'Global Legal Interaction and Legal Cultures' (1994) 7 *Ratio Juris* 132; W Twining, *Globalisation and Legal Theory* (London 2000), pp 189-193, 252-253; Loveland, pp 13-15

17 HLA Hart, *The Concept of Law* (2nd edn, Oxford 1994), pp 89-91, 254-258 and N MacCormick, *HLA Hart* (London 1981), pp 37-40 on the hermeneutic point of view.

18 On the importance of experience transmitted through tradition, see G Grosso,*Tradizione e misura umana*, p 43.

19 HG Gadamer, *Truth and Method* (London 1975).

approach the text in order to understand it properly. On the basis of the explicit and implicit language and references in the text, the reader will be able to engage with it in an appropriate manner. Take the example of a statute. Words are chosen by the draftsman for their meaning and resonance within a body of existing law, and the reader is then involved in making that body of law live in a particular situation. In order to achieve this, the interpreter has to connect the text with the current corpus of the law, in order to distil its meaning. It is not just a matter of learning the meaning of concepts, there is also a method of interpretation which has to be acquired. As Watson puts it, 'to know a legal system is not just to have learned its rules but to understand how the rules are put together, how the system is structured, how the rules are interpreted'.[20] This enables one to work out which texts one should be reading and how to connect the individual parts. Law is thus a process of using and interpreting a received tradition of texts. As Betti put it:

> It is precisely by living in the tradition of the case law that jurists realise in themselves the continuity in the life of the law, blend in coherent harmony the data of the tradition with the new acquisitions, point out the links between the letter of the law and the thought handed down.[1]

In brief, the idea of pre-interpretation explains both the possibility of interpretation for the reader separated in time from the origins of the text, and the importance of the legal tradition and community.

Bourdieu emphasises more generally this *constitutive* function of culture – that it makes it possible for a person to be able to interpret reality and to act:[2]

> It may be assumed that every individual owes to the type of schooling he has received a set of basic, deeply interiorized master-patterns on the basis of which he subsequently acquires other patterns, so that the system of patterns by which his thought is organized owes its specific character not only to the nature of the patterns constituting it but also to the frequency with which these are used and the level of consciousness at which they operate …
>
> It is primarily through the cultural unconscious which he owes to his intellectual training and, more particularly, to his scholastic training, that a thinker belongs to his society and age …[3]

This analysis is in accord with the analysis of comparative lawyers such as Rudden who suggest that there are a range of features about the judiciary (which might apply to any lawyer) which have an impact on the kinds of assumptions that underlie judicial reasoning. For him, training and recruitment and even the location of work 'create a corpus of professional habits and assumptions which affects the judicial

20 A Watson, *The Making of the Civil Law* (Cambridge Mass 1981), p 14.

1 E Betti, *Interpretazione della legge e degli atti giuridici* (Milan 1971), p 66 (my translation); H-G. Gadamer, *Truth and Method*, p 250. See also JWF Sundberg, 'Civil Law, Common Law and the Scandinavians' (1969) 13 Scandinavian Studies in Law 179 at 182: 'legal training teaches us not only what to do but also, and even more, what not to do. The result of this is to block some of our ways of thinking and lead us to proceed along others.'

2 P Bourdieu in MFD Young (ed), *Knowledge and Control* (London 1971), 189 at p 193; also Williams, op cit, p 13.

3 P Bourdieu, op cit, pp 192-193.

method and, through it, the legal order, and does so all the more strongly for being so rarely made explicit'.[4]

Because law is institutionalised, it is easier to identify the specific language, concepts and assumptions which mark out the tradition. This is the intellectual tradition with which participants of the visible legal community are engaged. There is an important difference between law and activities such as literature. Literature or historical documents are located in the past, but are made to speak in the present. They can be read as artefacts of their period or as distinct texts having a message for the present. By contrast, as Gadamer points out, legal and religious texts are inherently normative. Although the product of a particular moment in the past, they form part of a normative order which, as a whole, has force for the present moment.[5] The result is that law has what Martin Krygier calls an 'authoritative presence'.[6] In this process, the original author becomes less important. The law adopts an 'ambulatory' or 'updating' approach which asks what the text means in the present, rather than what it meant when it was enacted.[7] It may well be, as Krygier suggests, that since the legal tradition as a whole is subject to 'glacial change', the individual can only have a limited impact upon it.[8] All the same, he is right to argue that the interpreter is not the passive recipient of the past, but is able to offer new interpretations, which fit with the law as a whole at the moment of decision.[9]

Tradition has a particularly important role in law because of the importance of analogy in legal reasoning. Of its own motion, law proceeds incrementally, showing similarity between the established situation and the current one.

(6) Individual and organisation

Sapir argued that the *locus* for culture is always the individual. The individual does the thinking and adopts attitudes, and if there is a group perspective then it is located in specific individuals who can be identified.[10] In this work, however, I am concerned less with what makes individuals different from each other than with the way individuals work within organisations. Derné argues that understanding social organisations and movements enables us to explain how the sets of ideas are developed and perpetuated.[11]

Attitudes individuals share from their activity on a common task form the basis for ascribing a culture to an organisation. At the same time, individuals develop their attitudes within a particular context. The context of the activity in which they are

4 B Rudden, 'Courts and Codes in England, France and Soviet Russia' (1974) 48 *Tulane Law Review* 1010 at 1014.
5 See J Bell, 'Comparative Law and Legal Theory', at p 27.
6 'Law as Tradition, at pp 245-246.
7 See J Bell, 'Interpreting Statutes over Time' in F Ost and M Van Hoecke, *Time and Law. Is it the Nature of Law to Last?* (Brussels 1998) and below, p 133.
8 M. Krygier, 'Law as Tradition', p 248.
9 Ibid, p 254; Bell, 'Comparative Law and Legal Theory', p 25; WM Gordon, 'Legal tradition, with particular reference to Roman Law.' in DN MacCormick and P Birks (eds), *The Legal Mind* (Oxford 1986), 279 at p 291.
10 See E Sapir, *The Psychology of Culture. A Course of Lectures* (reconstructed and edited by Judith T Irvine, Berlin 1994), p 141.
11 S Derné, 'Cultural Conceptions of Human Motivation' in D Crane (ed), *The Sociology of Culture* (Oxford 1994), 267 at p 282.

engaged is given by the organisation with which they are involved. All the same, within the organisation, there will be diversity. Individuals have a variety of opinions, so that the ascription of a particular culture to an organisation is really to take a point along the spectrum as 'typical' or representative. One is trying to identify a recurrent or pervasive set of characteristics.[12]

As Trompenaars and Hampden-Turner suggest:

> ... a specific organisational culture or functional culture is nothing more than the way in which groups have organised themselves over the years to solve the problems and challenges presented to them.[13]

This approach, it seems to me, rightly places the task at the heart of organisational culture. Within a purposive institution such as the law, the roles and meaning arise out of the way individuals perform the tasks which their role assigns them.

I do not claim, however, that culture is the same as the institutional or organisational structure. The concept of culture identifies the shared beliefs, interests and ideologies which people have with regard to their activity within an institution or organisation. Such beliefs help to legitimate their activity and give it purpose.[14] Explaining the physical phenomena in terms of their cultural significance provides a richer or 'thick' description of what is happening – it combines description of events with the significance attributed to them by the participants.[15]

We have to hold in tension two features of the institution: an object which is shaped by the culture of society, and a framework within which the activity of the community takes place and by which that activity is shaped. The first is a genetic question about how a culture came to be as it is, and the second is an impact question about how it now operates.

B. LEGAL CULTURE IN CURRENT DEBATE

I would argue that my proposed focus on organisational culture represents an advance in the existing literature on legal culture. Comparative lawyers are agreed that it is not sufficient just to look at legal texts and rules to explain why legal systems are different. Cappelletti, Merryman and Perillo argued:

> ... a principal source of ... differences lies quite outside the formal legal order. It is found in the pervading assumptions and attitudes, lay and professional, about law, in the generally accepted view of what law is, of what the legal process in the society should be, of how the legal process should be divided up among various official and unofficial agencies for making and administering the law. In a phrase, what gives the legal order character, individuality, a style of its own, is the prevailing legal outlook in the culture of which that legal order is an integral part.[16]

12 GER Lloyd, *Demystifying Mentalities* (Cambridge 1990), p 5; Derné,op cit, pp 284-285.
13 F Trompenaars and C Hampden-Turner, *Riding the Waves of Culture* (2nd edn, London 1997), p 23.
14 See C Jenks, *Culture* (London 1993), ch 2.
15 C Geertz, op cit, p 5.
16 M Cappelletti, JH Merryman, and JM Perillo, *The Italian Legal System. An Introduction* (Stanford 1967), p 165.

Even if there is agreement to go beyond the 'law in the books' for explanation, there is no agreement on how the concept of 'legal culture' can offer an explanatory framework.

(1) Whose culture?

In his seminal study, *Law and Society: an Introduction*,[17] Friedman distinguishes two different aspects of legal culture:

> … legal culture refers to two rather different sets of attitudes and values: that of the general public (we can call this *lay* legal culture) and that of lawyers, judges and other professionals (we can call this *internal* legal culture).

In his view, comparative lawyers tend to study this internal culture of a legal system, a lawyer's or a jurist's culture, rather than a general or social culture, the culture of the 'living law'.[18] This he considers to be 'the marginal and arcane culture of lawyers in their formal training', the official law, which is the wrong focus of study for legal culture:

> Legal systems are not museums; they are tools, instruments, mechanisms; and those who use them are living people and living entities, grimly determined to float bonds, collect damages for auto accidents, merge with another company, avoid or minimize taxes, avoid or minimize prison, start or end a marriage, vindicate a reputation, go bankrupt, adopt a baby, or do any of the thousand things that people and institutions do by and through the law.[19]

This radical contextual approach focuses on the social setting within which law operates and has its impact on the behaviour of individuals. For him, 'the best evidence of legal culture would mix behavioural indicators with careful surveys of attitudes [of those who use the law].'[20]

In my view, this draws too sharp a distinction between the culture of the officials of the system and the general public who are affected by law. A more sophisticated analysis is presented by Varga.[1] He suggests that to go beyond the study of rules and of legal science or doctrine, which interprets and systematises legal norms, one needs to pay attention to two further layers of a legal order, each of which involves particular social groups. Closely connected to the legal norms and doctrine, one has the *institutional legal actors* whose principal role it is to interpret and apply these standards. Thus the administration, the courts and, I would argue, the legal professions have an important role in shaping the reality of the law. These official actors have their own approach to the law. As Cotterell points out:

> The popular will or reason of the community does not make law. Law is the 'artificial reason' of professional lawyers given force by the institutions of the monarchical state.[2]

17 Englewood Cliffs, New Jersey 1977, ch 7 at p 76.
18 Merryman Collection, p 51.
19 Ibid.
20 Ibid, pp 53-55; AJ Arnaud, *Pour une pensée juridique européenne*, p 23.
1 In V Gessner, A Hoeland and C Varga, *European Legal Cultures* (Aldershot 1996), pp 245ff.
2 R Cotterell in Loveland, p 41.

Varga then identifies a further group of 'non-institutional actors', individuals, associations and business enterprises who are the subjects of the law. In their life 'from the legal point of view', they are influenced by the law in various ways.[3] From this point of view, the law offers a set of directions in much the same way as it offers to institutional actors:

> Legal action involves an active 'navigation' of circumstances via predefined cultural 'maps', the use of which gives social actors their bearings and purposeful orientation towards all institutional, interpersonal and professional contexts.[4]

Studied in this way, the non-institutional actors are *legal actors* who occupy a different position within the legal system. The extent to which the non-legal actors adopt this official perspective or prefer some other point of view is often the subject of research, and is the focus that Friedman recommends. In his definition of legal culture, Friedman focuses on the lay legal culture, which adopts much more an external perspective on law – a strategic perspective of someone affected by the law and interested in what he can get out of the law:[5]

> We define legal culture to mean attitudes, values, and opinions held in society, with regard to law, the legal system, and its various parts. So defined, it is the legal culture which determined when, why, and where people use law, legal institutions, or legal process; and when they use other institutions, or do nothing. In other words, cultural factors are essential ingredients in turning a static structure and a static collection of norm into a body of living law.[6]

The concern here in talking about views 'held in society' is the reality of law's impact in society. But this does not give enough scope to the normative, and thus ideal character of law.[7] As Attwooll points out, 'What is significant about the law is that it provides a set of understandings and expectations in which [subjects of the law] are expected to share, even if in practice they do not.'[8]

If in this work I focus on legal culture as described from the legal point of view, I do not thereby deny that very interesting studies of law can be undertaken by adopting Friedman's focus on the lay participants in a legal system. Such studies draw attention to the social environment – the political, religious, economic and social setting of the legal community. I am content to develop one important aspect of legal culture in this work and to leave others to add further and alternative perspectives according to their abilities and resources.

I would, however, contest the view that the 'popular legal culture' approach is the only alternative to the 'law in the books' kind of comparative law. 'Law in the books' research in relation to legal doctrine and case law has a valuable place in explaining the coherence of rules and principles adopted as normative standards within a legal system

3 Loc cit.
4 M Salter, 'A Dialectic Despite Itself? Over the Phenomenology of Legal Culture' (1995) 4 *Social and Legal Studies* 453 at p 459.
5 This is not unrelated to what OW Holmes described as the point of view of the 'bad man': 'The Path of Law' (1897) 10 Harvard Law Review 461.
6 *Law and Society*, p 76.
7 On the importance of the normative character of law, see HLA Hart, *The Concept of Law*.
8 E Attwooll, *The Tapestry of Law* (Kluwer, Dordrecht 1997), p 36.

and whether the law in force, as applied by official institutions, conforms to them.[9] A more contextual approach is necessary both to explain how those rules and principles came into being and how they develop. It is in this perspective that the present work is conceived. If the purpose is to understand the ideas which lie behind a foreign legal system and make it work from the official point(s) of view, then I agree with Ewald that neither sociological data nor the rule-books are able to provide us with what we want, an understanding, from the inside, of the reasons, principles and concepts which are deployed by foreign lawyers.[10]

Such a picture of 'official law' lies outside the formal legal order as described in legal textbooks, but retains as important the framework of describing the law.[11] If this form of contextualism is seen as narrow or marginal, so be it. It may, however, help towards building the broader contextualism which Friedman wants. Understanding the culture of the official system has some value in terms of explaining what officials and other legal actors are trying to achieve, even if it does not help to explain the strategic use of law by institutions and individuals who are supposedly subject to that law.

In a book on French legal culture, there is an additional reason for being content with a focus on the internal legal culture, rather than the lay legal culture. From a practical point of view, there is simply not the kind of empirical evidential information produced on French citizens and practitioners which would enable the writing of a study of popular legal culture. Apart from the various opinion polls which have been conducted, and which are referred to during the course of this work, French researchers have not studied what French people think about the law to any great extent. An exception would be the work of Chantal Kourilsky-Augeven mentioned earlier.[12] These studies, comparing France with Russia and Poland, are concerned with images of law, but do not study how the French young people act in relation to the law. There have been very few studies of the practice of French lawyers, and the excellent work of Karpik[13] provides predominantly statistical evidence about the range of transactions and activities in which lawyers engage. The kind of transaction- and observation-based research which Friedman suggests is not readily available, and certainly not in relation to the range of aspects of French law which I wish to cover.

(2) Legal culture and legal mentality

The concept of 'mentality' as an explanation of differences in cultural practices has become popular, particularly in France since the work of Lévy-Bruhl. It is associated with a pre-logical set of perspectives on the world that shape action. Mentality offers

9 For a clear defence of this kind of approach, see J Gordley, 'Is Comparative Law a Distinct Discipline?' (1998) 46 Am Jo Comp Law 607.

10 W Ewald, 'The Jurisprudential Approach to Comparative Law: A Field Guide to "Rats"' (1998) 46 Am Jo Comp Law 701 at pp 703-704, 705.

11 Cf the comparative law approaches suggested by M Cappelletti, JH Merryman, and JM Perillo, *The Italian Legal System*, p 165, cited above, p 11. See also G Tarello, *Cultura giuridica e politica del diritto* (Bologna 1988), esp. the Introduction by R Guastini and G Rebuffa at p 24 which talks of the 'class of jurists' and how the grid of formal law demonstrates their focus of interest in law.

12 Above, p 3.

a core explanation for ideas and practices. The concept has been much used by comparative lawyers. Zweigert and Kötz consider that a significant hallmark of a difference in a legal system is 'a distinctive mode of legal thinking' which they also characterise as a 'mentality'.[14] The concept has been developed further by Pierre Legrand. For him, a 'mentalité' is the 'collective mental programme' which contains the 'assumptions, attitudes, aspirations and antipathies' which provide the 'deep structures of legal rationality'.[15]

Legrand focuses on the difference between common law and civil law, which he describes as a *primordial cleavage* in ways law is understood. There are radical differences in the nature of legal reasoning, the significance of systematisation, the character of rules, the role of facts, and the meaning of rights.[16] Taken together, these represent a mapping of the world under the sway of culture. Such ideas shape the individual lawyer's mentalité.[17] He considers that a particular mentality is so fundamental to the approach of civilian lawyers to law, that it constitutes a barrier to real harmonisation with common lawyers, even on the basis of common texts. Common lawyers just think differently about law. In this approach, mentalité describes a set of beliefs and interpretative ideas which shape an approach to action:

> I understand the notion of 'culture' to mean the framework of intangibles within which an interpretative community operates, which has normative force for this community (even though not completely and coherently instantiated) and which, over the *longue durée*, determines the identity of a community as *community*.[18]

But there are voices which argue that such a single, macro explanation is unnecessary. Lloyd[19] studied the scientific arguments of ancient Greece and ancient China, their styles of argument, their concepts and their products. He concludes that there are certain features that are common to all societies, such as the pursuit of logic, but there are other features of scientific argument that arise in a specific set of circumstances. Thus within a full set of beliefs, some features of a particular society are held in common with others, and some are specific. Lloyd's concern is how far there is a real difference in beliefs, and how far there are simply differences in the way those beliefs are presented and defended. Presentation depends on the availability of linguistic terms, and defence requires certain paradigms of convincing argument to be used more widely in society. He certainly notes a difference between Greece and China in the presentation of scientific argument. Chinese argument appealed to tradition and used a metaphorical form of language, while Greeks appealed to adversarial and legal

13 L Karpik, *French Lawyers* (Oxford 1999).

14 K Zweigert and H Kötz, *An Introduction to Comparative Law* (3rd edn trans T Weir, Oxford 1998), pp 69-70.

15 P Legrand, 'European legal Systems are not Converging' (1996) 45 ICLQ 52 at pp 60-61.

16 Ibid, p 63.

17 P Legrand, *Fragments on Law-as-Culture* (Deventer 1999), pp 74-75.

18 Ibid, p 27.

19 GER Lloyd, *Demystifying Mentalities* (Cambridge 1990). For a study which also argues for radical differences in style of justification between the Greek and Chinese traditions, see F Jullien, *Le détour et l'accès. Stratégies du sens en Chine, en Grèce* (Paris 1995). In this he argues that myth and discourse try to *explain* what is happening, while in China *allusion* makes the link between the said and unsaid and to indicate the justification.

forms of proof. But he does not think that the difference in presentation of reasoning demonstrates a difference in the form of scientific thought, since this can be explained by differences in the available and acceptable paradigms of argument and concepts in the two societies. He concludes that differences are best explained not in terms of some grand difference in scientific mentalities, but in the combination of more specific detailed differences of styles of inquiry and interpersonal exchanges.[20] He concludes:

> … the appropriate framework within which we have to tackle the problems of interpretation that such examples [of diverse forms of investigation] present is provided by the complex interactions and tensions between a variety of competing ideas and assumptions on the aims, methods and subject-matter of those investigations. It is those ideas and assumptions, together with the contexts of communication in which they are embedded, that define what I have been calling divergent styles of inquiry, and nothing is to be gained from resorting to an appeal to one or more supposed underlying mentalities.[1]

Lloyd essentially argues that the concept of 'mentality' is too general. It fails to pay adequate attention to the complexity of the diverse individual approaches within a single society and to the way in which the situations of people in one society diverge from another society.[2] His preference is for specific case-studies. Furthermore, he is concerned to explain the environmental conditions which facilitate the development and spread of certain views, rather than just to talk about a shared and global 'mentality' among a group of people.

In part, the methodology of this work responds to such careful criticism of the concept of mentality by trying to focus on a number of case-studies. Rather than discussing the 'French legal mentality' as a single phenomenon, the object of investigation is to identify some discrete parts of what might be considered French legal culture and see how far they are the same. By comparing these, it will be possible to draw conclusions about the utility of the general concept.

(3) Culture and 'style'

Lloyd's own reductivist approach to mentality still talks of 'style' of inquiry and reasoning. For Zweigert and Kötz, the notion of 'style' is central to a distinction between legal systems, because it identifies not one single trait, but 'a congeries of particular features which the most diverse objects of study may possess' and which mark them out as belonging together.[3] But again, this notion focuses attention on the

20 Op cit, p 134.
1 Ibid, p 144.
2 A similar view is shared by Sperber who argues that you need to analyse micro-situations and mechanisms to explain the ideas and attitudes of individual actors, rather than some grandiose concept of 'mentality': D Sperber, *Explaining Culture. A Naturalistic Approach* (Oxford 1996), pp 50-55.To be fair, these points are not lost on the protagonists of 'mentality' study, but they consider that there is still a 'representative common core' which has a strong explanatory force: Legrand 'Legal Systems are not Converging', p 63.
3 Op cit, p 68. See also W Ewald, 'The Jurisprudential Approach to Comparative Law: A Field Guide to "Rats"' (1998) 46 Am Jo Comp Law 701 at 703-704 who argues that sociological data and rule books need supplementing by 'a grasp, from the inside, of the conscious reasons and principles and concepts that are employed by the foreign lawyers – a grasp of the styles of legal *thought*.'

ideological elements of a legal system – the key factors to be studied are the historical background of the legal system, its predominant mode of legal thought, its distinctive institutions, the kinds of legal sources it acknowledges, and its ideology.[4] In other words, one is looking at a set of ideas and how they are conditioned. 'Style' is used by Markesinis to be essentially about presentation and ways of doing things, a superstructure, rather than something which defines the task in hand, hence his discussion of the style of judgments.[5] I would want to go further and look at mentality and style as ways of describing more deeply rooted activities. The existence of particular styles of presentation may serve as evidence of difference in either a deep level of legal thought, or different traditions about how legal argumentation is presented. It can serve as an indicator that there is a different legal culture in operation.

(4) Is law self-contained?

It is clear that law is only one manifestation of a broader social culture. Legrand argues that those who make and apply the law are also shaped by their society.[6] In his view, one needs to look beyond a common legal text and examine the culture of legal actors, to which legal culture relates, and which is fashioned by their society. One needs also to explain of the context in which they are operated.[7] By contrast, others argue that law is semi-autonomous from its social setting. Mattei argues that legal principles offer themselves as competing ideas to be adopted by legal systems.[8] Similarly, Watson has made a long study of legal transplants and legal evolution. In his view, legal transplants have been a most fertile source of change, but these have happened somewhat independently of economic and social conditions. The key lies in the legal professions who, for their own purposes and to support their own authority, adopt concepts and institutions from abroad.[9]

To explain the self-contained nature of law, some legal theorists have drawn analogies from science. Luhmann draws from cybernetics to suggest that law is like a communicative system in which the different parts speak to each other in a language of their own.[10] The problem with such a model is the inherent rigidity of the concept. A computer programme is limited and inflexible. If you don't conform to the language and its ways of saying things, nothing will happen. Law is, of course, not really like that. It has soft concepts and is open to a range of external values and references. Interpretation is an important feature, which the model of the cybernetic system does not really capture. Law is not what Luhmann described as a 'programmed' situation in

4 Ibid.

5 B Markesinis, A Matter of Style' (1994) 110 LQR 607.

6 *Fragments*, p 74; also E Banakas, 'The Method of Comparative Law and the Question of Legal Culture' (1994) 3 Tilburg Foreign Law Review 113, 127. O Kahn Freund, 'On Uses and Misuses of Comparative Law' (1974) 37 MLR 1 and Ewald, 43 Am Jo Comp Law at 496 also emphasise the embeddedness of legal rules in a culture.

7 Blankenurg, op cit; A Allott., *The Limits of Law* (London 1971), ch 2.

8 U Mattei, *Comparative Law and Economics* (Ann Arbor 1997), ch 4.

9 A Watson, *Legal Transplants: an Approach to Comparative Law* (London 1974); R Post, *Law and the Order of Culture* (Berkeley 1991), pp vii-viii.

10 N Luhmann, *Essays on Self-Reference* (New York 1990); also *A Sociological Theory of Law* (London 1985), pp 174-183.

which an activity will only work if the rules are adhered to. Teubner draws the analogy from biology. Cells have a life of their own, but react to an environment. The cell undergoes internal change in response to changed conditions, but it remains somewhat self-contained and reproduces itself as it grows.[11] The metaphor suggests both that law is self-contained and that it adapts in response to changes in the environment. Now this approach is richer than Luhmann, but ultimately it stresses too much the self-contained nature of law. Teubner accepts that the system evolves, but in a hypercycle by which the law chooses its own pace of development. It is self-reproducing, but it is not causally independent, ie free from the indirect effect of events occurring outside it.[12] Teubner's analysis suggests significant self-contained activity. I think this fails to give enough weight to the instrumental function of law. Law is intended to achieve social purposes which are set by political and social institutions. Lawyers play their part in formulating these social objectives and determining how they will be realised. The model of the biological cell lacks this intentional, purposive direction.

It does not seem to me that this work has to choose between the idea of legal culture as a subset of social culture and the view that legal culture is in some sense independent. It is a commonplace that the culture of the legal system has an important role as part of the cultural heritage of society,[13] and that, as an instrument of social policy, legal ideas and practices are related to political and social culture more generally. But this does not commit one to accepting the view that law is merely a mirror of forces within the economy or society.[14]

Rather than either of these concepts, I think the metaphor of a game, proposed by Van de Kerchove and Ost is more suitable.[15] A game is a system, which has defined rules, and these regulate both the activity and the players. The rules constitute the activity as a game and the participants as players, and the rules also identify the objective of them all. In this sense, the rules define the game and are also defined by it. Yet, there is much unsaid in the rules, particularly about strategy and interpretation of the rules. A game is self-contained in some respects, but is not fully self-organising. Its purpose relates to the outside as well as to the motives of the players. At the same time, it has its own purposes.

The study of legal cultures proposed here will contribute to an assessment of the 'insulation thesis'. Contemporary comparative law suggests that legal systems are only self-contained to limited and varying degrees. Goldberg and Attwooll[16] suggest that legal systems fit along a spectrum of dimensions, among which are whether the system is unified or pluralist in its sources of law, whether it draws its inspiration for legal developments from within the system or from outside, whether its standards are open or closed. Örücü argues that there are no pure legal systems. Almost all systems

11 G Teubner, *Law as an Autopoeitic System* (Oxford 1993), esp ch 3.
12 Ibid, pp 35 and 49.
13 M Cappelletti in Merryman Collection, p 2; A Edel and E Flower in SA Vojcanin, *Law, Culture and Values* (New Brunswick, 1978), pp 37-38.
14 Cf L Friedman., 'Is there a Modern Legal Culture?' (1994) 7 *Ratio Juris* 117.
15 M Van de Kerchove and F Ost, *Legal System between Order and Disorder* (Oxford 1994), p 92.
16 D Goldberg and E Attwooll, 'Legal Orders, Systematic Relationships and Cultural Characteristics: Towards Spectral Jurisprudence' in E Örücü, E Attwooll and S Coyle, *Studies in Legal Systems: Mixed and Mixing* (Hague 1996), 313 at pp 329ff.

are mixed to some degree, though some mixtures will be well integrated (as in a purée) and some will remain distinct and separate (like in a salad bowl)[17] This idea of mixity and pluralism offers a way of understanding legal systems which is apposite for this work. My argument will be that the different branches of French law have their own distinct dynamics and mixtures of ideas. They also draw on ideas and practices from other branches of French law and beyond. The French legal system is made up of these different parts which can co-exist without being harmonised into a homogeneous 'French legal culture', even if there are many resemblances between them.

C. METHODOLOGY

(1) The proposed method

This work will study the task or role which individuals undertake *as legal actors*. I will work from an 'official' description of that legal role. The subject matter of research into legal cultures is not what might be described as 'brute facts', physical phenomena which can be observed through classical empirical observation. Institutional facts, as described by Searle and Weinberger, involve a particular significance which attaches to certain actions and which make them into 'acts-in-law'.[18] To capture this feature, we need a 'thick' description of the norms and values of the legal community, which captures the attitudes and intentions of the actors involved. This involves the description of the institutional facts – how certain facts become a 'trial' or 'lawmaking' depends on the use of the sets of values and institutional rules which are conventional in that particular legal community. These generic features in each area of law will be discussed in a section on *institutional setting*. We also need to examine the particular perspectives of the different legal actors. These actors may have a variety of formal and informal roles and interact in a variety of ways within a legal setting. The more specific features of legal actors and their relationships will be discussed both specifically in relation to *legal actors*. The beliefs described are held by individuals to a greater or lesser degree, and interact in each case with their other belief systems. All the same, it is possible to talk of a 'typical' or 'representative' pattern of beliefs.[19]

As Friedman argues, 'A culture, including a legal culture, is always embedded in a mosaic of micro contexts'.[20] At the same time, there is a danger of losing the plot in a description of a plethora of micro-situations.[1] The description adopted tries to present branches of law which are sufficiently precise to capture their distinctive relationships to their social setting, but are large enough to be coherent. For that reason, the conventional legal categories of criminal, civil, administrative and constitutional law were chosen as most appropriate.

17 See ibid, pp 343-345.
18 See above, p 6 and N MacCormick and O Weinberger, *An Institutional Theory of Law* (Dordrecht 1986), ch 3 at pp 82-84.
19 See Trompenaars and Hampden-Turner, op cit, pp 24-25.
20 *The Republic of Choice*, p 200.
1 See Bauman, op cit, p 35.

(2) Evidence

(a) What counts as evidence of culture?

The evidence for legal culture is rather difficult to pin down. As Garapon remarks:

> ... the concept of legal culture is at the same time stimulating and disappointing. It is stimulating because it raises the expectation that it will lead us directly to the root of the differences between legal systems, but disappointing because claims about legal culture are so often forced to remain impressionistic. One cannot talk 'scientifically' because so little that is important is quantifiable, and the use of numbers only serves to reassure the researcher.[2]

One of the foremost theorists, Friedman argues that 'The legal culture rests on certain basic social norms that are not easy to map out or measure. These norms are vague and variable, and the evidence for them is distressingly "soft".'[3] The basic evidence will include evidence of attitudes, but Friedman would argue that these are not susceptible of opinion polls. Rather one has to engage in inference from conduct and statements, plus some questioning of participants. Essentially, one is trying to match up the observer's analysis and the participants' perspectives and making a judicious balance between them.

The evidence inevitably must combine description of activity and the operation of physical institutions with analysis of attitudes. The study of culture in this context can explain the agenda of the institution.[4] The analysis of attitudes will rely heavily on what parties say about themselves or the stories they recount about the legal process,[5] but will also make use of analysis of the fundamental structures of thinking[6] and the assumptions which lie behind what is expressed and done. There is not only a linguistic dimension to the activity of law. Courtroom architecture, procedure and dress are vivid ways of communicating the majesty and distinctiveness of the law.[7]

(b) A constructivist approach

Culture involve a set of beliefs and attitudes that give shared meaning to an activity. Ewald suggests that the focus is on the *conscious* and explicit views of the participants which can be documented and recorded.[8] This is, however, too narrow. I would rather adopt the view of Garapon that one must include some unconscious features of the culture which explain why actions take place:

2 A Garapon, 'French Legal Culture and the Shock of 'Globalisation' (1995) 4 Social and Legal Studies 493 at p 495.
3 *The Republic of Choice*, p 95. He suggests that survey research is not a reliable guide: "I can only estimate, interpret, and infer": ibid, p 198.
4 C Guarnieri in D Nelken, *Legal Culture*, p 188.
5 See Friedman, *The Republic of Choice*, ch 10.
6 See G Samuel, *The Foundations of Legal Reasoning* (Antwerp 1994), esp ch 3; also Legrand, *Fragments*, chs 5 and 6.
7 R Jacob, *Images de la Justice* (Paris 1994); A Garapon, *Bien Juger. Essai sur le rituel judiciaire* (Paris 1997); R Wasserman, *Justizreform* (Neuwied 1970), ch 2; D McBarnet, *Conviction* (London 1979).
8 'The Jurisprudential Approach to Comparative Law', p 705.

> To grasp a culture thus involves one in trying to formulate what is so obvious for the members that 'it goes without saying'. The best way of abstracting oneself from one's own culture is to look at it from the outside in confronting it with other cultures.[9]

The analysis of these implicit attitudes is a matter of interpretation. It has to be recognised that such analysis is a construction of the author.[10] The reality of such an analysis depends on the degree of correspondence between it and the perception of the actors. Because these may be implicit rather than explicit, there is no suggestion that the actors would use the author's concepts to describe themselves and how they perceive what they are doing. All the same, there needs to be sufficient evidence that they could recognise themselves in the presentation without distortion.

The research has therefore been structured both to bring out the implicit features of French legal culture and to check the reliability of the interpretations presented. In the first place, the practice of French law in terms of lawmaking, judicial decisions, other processes (often reported in the media) and statistics are combined with direct observations, which I or others have conducted, some of which are published. These different pieces of evidence go beyond many French accounts of their own system. But secondly, I have tried to corroborate the inferences made from practice by considering French accounts of their own system. The works consulted are frequently popular rather than academic works. Many are written as high-level journalism, reporting interviews or recording opinions of controversialists in the typical French intellectual tradition. These works contain reflections on the French legal system which either express or allude to features of the legal culture. A further feature of the research was a number of semi-structured interviews conducted with the objective of checking out my own observations with informant practitioners of the system. The interviews were conducted over a number of years, but particularly during two periods. The first interviews were in 1986 when I was in Paris for a year and had regular contact with the Conseil d'Etat and the Conseil constitutionnel, as well as some tribunaux administratifs. The second interviews were in 2000 when I made a number of visits funded by the British Academy to Bordeaux and Paris. In these interviews, I was able to confirm and complement the findings of the 1986 interviews, and to conduct observations and interviews relating to criminal and civil procedure. There were no questionnaires and the role of the interviewees was as informants on the processes, rather than providing specifically quantifiable information.

(3) A framework for analysis

My framework of analysis is set out in Figure 1. In broad terms, the concept of culture has at its centre an action learning cycle typical of any reflective practitioner.[11] There

9 A Garapon, *Bien juger*, p 150. Also Jenks, op cit, p 128: 'Culture is a conventional, yet deep structural practice, the rules of which may be only part of the unconscious of its members. Cultural symbols and representations are the surface structure.'

10 C Geertz, p 15: 'In the study of culture, analysis penetrates the very body of the object – that is, we begin with our own interpretations of what our informants are up to, or think they are up to, and then systematise those – the line between (Moroccan) culture as a natural fact and (Moroccan) culture as a theoretical entity tends to get blurred.'

11 See I McGill and L Beaty, *Action Learning* (2nd edn, 1995), pp 30-32.

is an *activity* leading to *outputs*. These give rise to *reflection* by the *professional legal actors* who adjust the *constitutive norms and values* which re-define the *activity*. To this action learning cycle of the professional legal actors, I have added the reflection and input of external legal actors, particularly the legislator and the executive who can have a direct input both into the *constitutive norms and values*, but also into the *institutional setting* which also influences the way the activity is performed. A final element of the picture is that *history* also defines the institutional setting. The way the institutions of law operate is partly the result of deliberate choice, but also the result of history, which no-one seeks to alter or challenge. The picture is more complex that that presented by Trompenaars and Hampden-Turner in which they identify three layers: an external output, informed by the explicit attitudes and perspectives of the actors, and at the core, some implicit basic attitudes. [12] I do not deny the importance of these three elements, but have sought to present them in a different way. Attitudes have a place both in defining the activity (the constitutive norms and values) and in the reflection on the output.

Figure 1: A map of legal culture

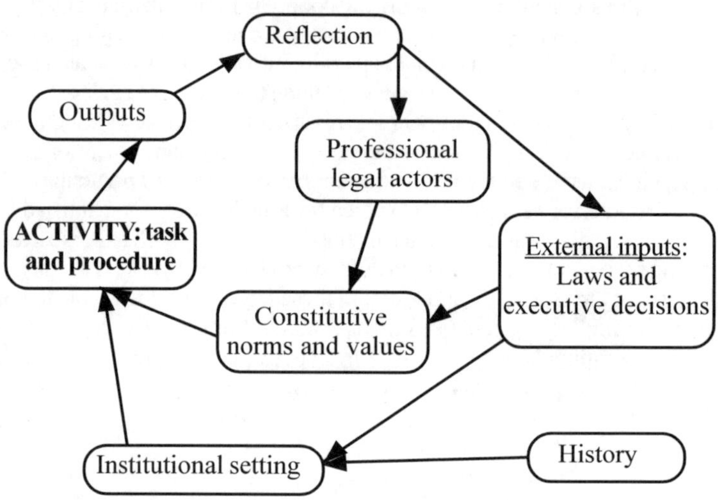

(a) Activity and outputs

The central feature of the culture of a branch of law is thus an ACTIVITY. An activity involves both a task and a procedure by which it is carried out. I argue in this book that the core activities differ from one branch of the law to another, and so it is important to identify the core activities related to each branch studied. The activity is described in terms of both the observable phenomena – court processes, lawmaking and the like – and the ideas and attitudes that legal actors have towards it. The area of lawmaking will be an especial focus of attention since this will show up relationships between

12 Op cit, pp 20ff.

different professional legal actors and also between these and external legal actors, as well as the wider world. Any identification of an 'activity' is necessarily a construct, a chunk of reality that has been separated out from the continuum of physical actions in society for special attention. The identification of such a public activity should primarily rest on the perceptions of the participants, who not only perform roles, but have a shared understanding of what is involved. That perception makes the activity what it is and creates it as an institutional fact.

Each activity is defined by the legal rules which establish its character as 'an activity-in-law'. Those constitutive rules are related to various legal values which need to be observed if the activity is to carry out its legal purpose. For that reason, the description of the activity needs to bring out the *norms and values* that constitute and shape the activity in question. But these norms and values also involve shared perceptions of the nature and significance of an activity held by the legal actors, both express attitudes and implicit understandings.[13] These attitudes and understandings relate to the following elements: how the task is defined: what are its constitutive rules, how the task ought to be performed, and what are the reference groups to whom the legal actor relates as part of its performance.

The other principal conditioning feature of the legal activity is the *institutional setting* within which it occurs. The activity takes place as part of a legal system and the participants will assume that other parts of the system are operating when they engage in a task. A criminal investigation assumes the existence of various professions, such as the police, procureur and juge d'instruction, as well as a system of courts and procedures. More widely, there will be setting of other institutions, governmental or otherwise, to which the activity relates. The institutional setting is shaped directly by actions of the executive and legislature, but is also the product of history in a more gradual way, which affects particularly some of the implicit assumptions on which actors operate. To avoid repetition, the issue of institutional setting will be handled at two levels. Chapter 2 will describe the broad outline of the legal institutions and professions in France as part of the general institutional setting. Each specific chapter will then have a section focused on additional features of the institutional setting for that branch of law, which has a special impact on its operation.

The activity will generate *outputs* of two forms. First, there will be decisions or actions, such as a judgment. Second, there will be the impact on attitudes institutional and non-institutional actors to them. This will give rise to critical reflection on how the activity has operated and what its role in the future should be.

(b) *Reflection and legal professional actors*

In taking an 'official' perspective on the legal culture of different branches of law, it is necessary to discuss the roles of legal professionals in the activity of each branch. I use the term 'legal professionals' here predominantly to describe those who have a regular and official role within the legal system. It goes further than legal professions, and would include both the police and parliamentarians, as well as doctrinal legal writers. Strictly, the people described are legal actors who are part of the institution

13 See further, M Van Hoecke and M Warrington, 'Legal Cultures and Legal Paradigms: Towards a New Model for Comparative Law' (1998) 47 ICLQ 495 at pp 514-515.

and who perform their legal role on a regular basis. It is this latter feature which distinguishes them from the non-institutional actors, the subjects of the law.

Although the main legal professions will be described for convenience in Chapter 2, more specific aspects of the legal actors will be described in the chapters on the individual branches of law. A particular interest will be the relations between the legal actors and who exercises dominance among them. Although we have seen that there is a classical picture of the dominance of doctrinal writers and the weak role of the judiciary, this work will suggest that the picture is more varied among the different branches of law.

As will be seen from Figure 1, I conceive a reflexive relationship between the activity and legal professionals. The 'internal point of view', which is necessary to constitute the activity,[14] will be adopted by the legal professionals. They make the system work and have to conceive themselves as performing the legal role (as opposed to any other social activity) and conform to the constitutive norms and values. At the same time, the existence of the activity gives rise to institutional roles, and its operation will generate reflection, which may alter attitudes towards the activity or even the activity itself. This model of reflective practitioners applies both to the legal professions and to other institutional actors, such as the executive and the legislators. It may be that the non-institutional actors, citizens as subjects of the law and the like, cannot directly influence the institutional setting or the activity. But they can have an impact through the legislature or the executive. There are, therefore, a series of reflections carried on, each of which may have different impacts on both the activity and the climate of institutional arrangements and expectations within which it takes place.

14 See Searle, op cit, p 98.

Chapter 2

The institutional setting

A. INTRODUCTION

Before examining our four specific branches of French law, it is useful to understand some general features of the French legal system. The activities of each branch of law take place within an institutional setting, some of which is specific and some of which is part of the more general context of French law. In this chapter, I want to examine a few of these general features. Court institutions and legal actors (especially judges and avocats) will obviously recur throughout the discussion of particular branches of law. But it will also be important to understand certain key legal values and concepts that shape both legal institutions and attitudes among legal actors. I will also consider certain aspects of the evolving European dimension of French law.

B. COURT INSTITUTIONS

Court institutions are described more fully in other works.[1] Here, it is sufficient to give the broad outline of court institutions and their principles of organisation, as they affect the branches of law discussed in subsequent chapters.

French court institutions are structured according to four basic principles, the first two of which are structural, while the last two are more operational in character. First, in terms of subject-matter, courts are *specialist* to varying degrees. Certain specialisms are fundamental to the structure of the French court system (and to its substantive law), others result more from convenience than legal principle. Three distinctions are of fundamental importance: between public law and private law, between civil law and criminal law, and between these ordinary courts and the Conseil constitutionnel. There is no court that has even residual jurisdiction over all branches of law. The civil and criminal courts and the administrative courts have both courts of general jurisdiction (juridictions de droit commun) and also specialist courts, described as exceptional courts (juridictions d'exception) or as courts of limited jurisdiction (juridictions d'attribution). Second, in terms of territorial jurisdiction, French courts are *local or*

1 J Bell, S Boyron and S Whittaker, *Principles of French Law* (Oxford 1998), ch 2.

regional. Only at the highest point in the hierarchy is there a national court in any branch of law (with the obvious exception of constitutional law). Third, in terms of levels of court, the French adhere to the principle of the *right to an appeal* (double degré de juridiction), which entitles the litigant to a hearing at first instance and then on appeal. This right of appeal on law and fact means that there is no leave required for an appeal.[2] There are restrictions on access to the Conseil d'Etat and the Cour de cassation, the national courts at the pinnacle of the public and private law systems, but their functions are primarily to review the legal basis of decisions reached by lower courts, rather than to act as a third level of appeal on the merits. As we will see, constitutional law is an exception in that the Conseil constitutionnel is a court of first and last instance. Finally, in terms of *composition*, French courts are traditionally collegial and professional, viz they are composed of a bench of professional judges. As will be seen, there are in fact numerous instances where there is a single judge and where non-professional judges are used.

(1) Civil and criminal courts

Private law judges sit in both criminal and civil courts, which carry distinct names depending on whether its functions are civil or criminal, but are typically co-located. The judges involved are drawn from the corps of private law judges. This combination of functions and personnel makes it appropriate to call these courts the 'ordinary courts' for many purposes.

(a) First instance civil courts

There are two general first instance civil courts, the tribunal d'instance and the tribunal de grande instance. Cases are assigned to one or other of these courts depending on their seriousness.

Until 1958, the tribunal d'instance was known as the court of the juge de paix (justice of the peace). It has long been a single-judge court hearing small civil cases. Since 1958, the judges have formed part of the corps of the ordinary judiciary. The 473 courts are located in the main towns of départements, arrondissements and important cantons. They have jurisdiction for all claims under 30,000F (and in personal and movable property actions up to 50,000F). In very small claims (under 13,000F), there is no right of appeal against decisions of this court. In other cases, appeal lies to the cour d'appel. In 1998, the tribunaux d'instance handed down 452,646 judgments on the merits and 69,034 decisions en référé.[3]

More important civil cases are heard by the 181 tribunaux de grande instance, located in each département. Some are very large – Paris has over 300 judges, and where this occurs the courts may, in practice, have specialist sections. The tribunal de grande instance deals with family matters (marriage, divorce, affiliation and nationality),

2 No right of appeal exists from many decisions of the tribunal d'instance because of the small sums involved, though cassation remains possible.

3 In addition, they issued 661,439 injonctions de payer as well as large numbers of administrative decisions, such as providing certificates of nationality.

as well as cases beyond the jurisdictional limits for the tribunaux d'instance. The tribunaux de grande instance decided 635,340 cases on the merits in 1998, as well as 118,785 cases en référé.

The tribunal de grande instance is, by tradition, a collegial court, but there have been sufficient derogations in recent years that, in practice, much of its important civil work is carried on by single judges. The importance of single judges is reinforced by their role in preliminary decisions. The référé is a rapid procedure before a designated judge (the president of the court or his delegate) who can make orders to protect the status quo pending hearing of the case, and can order either the payment of provisional damages or even the performance of contractual or other obligations.[4] Since bringing the case to trial will be expensive and time-consuming, the decision of the juge des référés is often in practice the definitive solution. The single juge de la mise en état takes decisions to order expertise or to request further information before the judgment hearing.

(b) First instance criminal courts

As will be seen in Chapter 4,[5] the French distinguish between three categories of offences according to their seriousness: in ascending order of seriousness they are contraventions, délits and crimes. This categorisation is matched by the jurisdiction of criminal courts.

At the lowest level, the tribunal de police deals with the minor offences, the contraventions. Such offences carry a fine of less than 20,000F and imprisonment of up to three months. There are 454 located in the chief town of an arrondissment or département. Cases will be tried by a single judge. The tribunal de police tried some 746,155 cases in 1998, of which 97.8% were convictions.[6]

More serious cases, involving heavy fines or imprisonment, are tried by the tribunal correctionnel. These 181 courts are located in the main town of a département and the judges are the same as those for the tribunal de grande instance. In some cases, a juge d'instruction will prepare the case for trial. In the tribunal correctionnel, trial will be before a panel of three professional judges in most cases, though some specific offences (eg in the financial fraud field) are subject to special procedures. In 1998, the tribunaux correctionnels decided some 412,090 cases (95.15% of which were convictions).

A small number of very serious cases, eg involving murder, are tried by the cour d'assises. This is located with the Cour d'appel and at least the presiding judge is drawn from that court. There are 99 cours d'assises, which decided 3,364 cases in 1998 of which 95.4% were convictions. The first stage is the commital hearing before the Chambre d'accusation which is before three judges. The trial is heard by three judges sitting with nine jurors.

Young persons are tried in specialist courts. Juvenile offenders between 16 and 18 charged with a crime are tried by a special formation of the cour d'assises, which has two juges des enfants in place of the normal assessor judges. In 1998, this court tried

4 See article 809 C pr civ on the powers of the president of the tribunal de grand instance.

5 Below, p 112.

6 This figure is a marked drop from 1994 because of the use of fixed penalty fines and the decriminalisation of certain activities, such as signing cheques without sufficient resources.

268 cases. Most young offenders, however, are tried by one of the 134 tribunaux pour enfants or by the juge des enfants. Their competence is the same: serious contraventions and délits by minors and crimes committed by those under 16. In 1998, the tribunal des enfants handed down 17,194 convictions and the juge des enfants 16,746. These courts are staffed by a judge and two lay assessors. Lay assessors are appointed by the Minister of Justice for four year periods on account of their expertise in relation to children. The criminal jurisdiction of the juge des enfants is an adjunct to his or her main function of intervening when the health, safety or moral situation of the child is threatened.

(c) *Specialist first instance courts*[7]

There are a number of specialist courts which are spread across the French regions, which will not be discussed in this book, but which are significant within the French legal system viewed as a whole.

A system of commercial courts has existed since 1563, and has survived with little change. The Code de commerce of 1807 entrusted the decision on litigation on commercial matters to these tribunaux commerciaux. Commercial matters are those which arise between commercial people (commerçants), or on commercial matters (eg commercial leases or companies), or about commercial things (eg patents). There are 227 commercial courts of varying sizes in France outside Alsace,[8] and are staffed only by non-professional or 'consular' judges elected indirectly by the members of the local chamber of commerce.[9] In 1998, these courts decided 168,038 cases on their merits and 40,083 decisions by way of référé and also oversaw 68,056 insolvency cases.

Labour courts (Conseils des prud'hommes) also pre-date the Revolution. Napoleon generalised the system to deal with employment issues. There are now 270 Conseils across France, and they are staffed essentially by lay people. The court is paritaire, that is to say it has equal numbers of employer and employees, at least four from each side. In the event of a tie, a professional judge from the tribunal de grande instance will act as the juge départiteur. In 1998, these courts decided 165,947 cases on their merits and 48,680 decisions by way of référé

A similar *paritaire* court exists in relation to rural leases (3,680 cases on their merits and 270 decisions by way of référé in 1998), although it is always presided over by a juge d'instance. Representation of employers and employees also exists on the tribunaux des affaires de sécurité sociale (129,312 cases in 1998).

(d) *The cour d'appel*

Appeals on both civil and criminal cases lie to the cour d'appel. The only exceptions are the decisions of the cour d'assises which, until 2001 could not be appealed. The loi of 15 June 2000 has created a right of appeal to a differently constituted cour d'assises.[10]

7 See J Bell, S Boyron and S Whittaker, *Principles of French Law*, pp 48-50.
8 There are also 23 tribunaux de grande instance which have jurisdiction in commercial matters.
9 A reform of this system is in progress, see below, p 43.
10 See below, p 113.

There are 33 cours located often where the pre-revolutionary Parlements sat, maintaining a significant element of continuity in the French legal tradition.[11] Apart from urgent matters, the cour d'appel is collegial with a minimum of three members, though, as we will see, civil cases are often heard before a single rapporteur. A typical cour d'appel will have a number of specialist chambers, dealing with civil, social, criminal and juvenile matters. Appeal lies on law and fact. Because there is a file on the case containing all the elements of the evidence reduced to writing produced by the lower civil and criminal courts, it is easy to conduct such an appeal on fact as well as law. Although it is usually sufficient to review the file as presented by the lower court, the court may order such additional investigations as might seem necessary. In 1998, the cours d'appel heard 209,839 civil appeals and 28,361 criminal cases.[12]

(e) The Cour de cassation

A litigant may make a pourvoi en cassation against a decision of the cour d'appel to the Cour de cassation, created in 1790, which is the only national court in France on civil or criminal matters. As its name implies, it is not strictly an appeal court, but merely a body that quashes the rulings of appeal courts for error of law.[13] The normal cassation procedure is that the Cour de cassation merely decides the disputed question of law and then refers it to a different cour d'appel for decision on the merits in the light of its ruling. In 1998, the Cour de cassation decided 19,815 civil matters (resulting in cassation in 19.15% of cases) and 7,335 criminal matters (resulting in cassation in only 5.5% of cases).

The Cour de cassation is made up of six chambers, five civil chambers and the sixth dealing with criminal law. It has nearly 200 members, of whom over a hundred are conseillers or presidents of chambers or avocats-généraux. The Cour sits normally in panels of five judges, though the president of the chamber may order a case to be heard by merely three judges in an appropriate case. More important cases may be heard by a larger panel of judges within a chamber. To resolve divergences of interpretation and case law, a chambre mixte composed of the Premier President of the Cour together with the president and three senior members of each chambre concerned (anything between 13 and 25 people in total). The Cour sits in plenary session (Assemblée plénière) where a case is appealed from a cour d'appel to which it has been remitted after cassation or where the premier président considers a matter to be of major importance. In such cases, the premier président sits with four members from each of the six chambers (the president, oldest conseiller and two others), a total of 25 judges.

Since 1991, the Cour de cassation gives a ruling (technically an opinion) on a point of law on a preliminary reference from a lower court.[14] This saisine pour avis applies where a case raises a novel legal issue of serious difficulty relevant to a number of cases. An opinion is issued within three months. The Cour sits in a particularly solemn formation to

11 For this reason, the location of the cour d'appel does not always match the major cities of modern France. For example, the cour in the Nord is sited in Douai and not Lille.

12 This does not include the 34,206 decisions of the Chambre d'accusation.

13 The nature of cassation is discussed in J Bell, S Boyron, and S Whittaker, *Principles of French Law*, pp 3-4, 85.

14 Art 151-1 of the *Code de l'organisation judiciaire*.

deliver such opinions, being presided over by the First president and attended by the president and oldest conseiller and two other members of each chamber concerned.

In recent times, two measures have been taken to reduce the time taken to decide cases submitted to the Cour de cassation. In the first place, summary decision procedures have been introduced to deal with appeals which lack merit. Since 1981 and where the solution was obvious, the premier président or the president of chamber has discretion to refer a case to a formation restreinte composed of three judges, provided neither party objects. Second, in 1979 the Cour de cassation was given power to decide cases without referring them back to another court (cassation sans renvoi). The Cour may enter a definitive judgment where the facts as found by the lower court enable it to apply the correct legal rule or where quashing the decision of the lower court does not require further inquiry into the facts of the case. Only in a very limited way does this procedure turn the Cour de cassation into a trier of fact. The procedure is used frequently in criminal matters, but is rarely used in civil cases.[15]

(2) Administrative courts[16]

(a) Public law and private law

Administrative law is the branch of law that is concerned with the powers and organisation of governmental bodies, notably the State. Its central characteristic is the presence of the administration as one of the parties to the dispute. The notion of the 'administration' here covers not only national government, but also local authorities, public agencies and public services, ranging from universities to utilities or the regulatory agencies such as the Conseil supérieur de l'audiovisuel. Public law has special rules governing not only the use of powers, but also the rules of contract, the liability of public authorities and employment. By contrast, a private law dispute is one between two individuals or companies.

The precise allocation of disputes to either public law or to private law does pose some difficulties and there is a special court, the Tribunal des Conflits, which exists to resolve them. It is made up of equal numbers of judges from the highest public and private law courts, and the Minister of Justice (Garde des Sceaux) has the casting vote.[17] In 1998, it decided 47 cases. One illustration captures the problem of distinguishing public law from private law. In some regions of France, blood transfusions are provided by public hospitals and so liability for infected blood lies in public law. In other (even neighbouring regions), blood transfusions are carried out by private associations, and so the liability to the patient lies in private law.[18]

15 *Annuaire statistique de la justice 2000*, p 18.

16 See generally LN Brown and J Bell, *French Administrative Law* (5th edn 1998) (hereafter 'Brown and Bell'), chs 3 and 4.

17 His casting vote is rarely required, but was used recently in TC 12 May 1997, *Préfet de Police de Paris*, D 1997, 567. For a critical comment, see the letter of Pierre Sargos, *Le Monde*, 16 May 1997, p 15.

18 The rules on liability in such cases are different: see Cass 1re civ, 12 April 1995, below, p 87 (obligation de résultat owed by a private blood transfusion centre in contract to the victim); CE Ass, 10 April 1992, *V*, AJDA 1992, 355; CE Ass, 9 March 1993, *MG*, RFDA 1993, 583 (fault liability of the administration for circulation of contaminated blood).

The consequence of the distinction between public and private law is two-fold: first, the rules of law applicable to a contract or a wrong or to the use of powers are not the same for public bodies as for private bodies; second, any litigation is tried by different courts according to different procedures by different groups of judges, whose background is distinct from that of private law judges. This radical separation between public and private law courts, in its present form, is a feature of the French republican tradition. It was set out in a loi of 16-24 August 1790 and by Napoleon's creation of the Conseil d'Etat in 1799, and was restated by decisions of the Tribunal des Conflits at the beginning of the Third Republic. More recently, it has been declared a fundamental principle recognised by the laws of the Republic by the Conseil constitutionnel. In its decision of 23 January 1987, the Conseil constitutionnel declared that this principle stipulated that the quashing of administrative decisions should be a matter for the administrative courts, though this is much narrower than the separation which currently exists.[19]

(b) The Conseil d'Etat

The oldest of the public law courts is the Conseil d'Etat, set up by Napoleon in 1799, which had many similarities to the King's Privy Council. It was originally a court of first and last instance, but since the creation of the tribunaux administratifs in 1953 and the cours administratives d'appel in 1987, it has increasingly become a supervisory court, with a role as an appeal court in a small number of areas. Its jurisdiction is typically to review the decisions of the lower administrative courts and to quash them where the law has been wrongly applied. Since 1989, it also gives advisory opinions on the law during litigation when requested to do so on a reference from those courts.[20] It retains some matters as a court of first and last instance.[1]

Its judges are drawn from a distinct corps of the administration[2] around 300 members who have distinguished administrative and judicial careers (of whom about 100 are on secondment to other duties at any one time). The Conseil is not only a judicial body, it is a major advisor to the government. Accordingly, it is organised into six sections, only one of which is concerned with litigation (the Section du contentieux).[3] This Section du contentieux is then further divided into sous-sections which both prepare cases for decision (the work of instruction) and decide most of the routine cases either their own (a sous-section jugeant seule) or jointly with another sous-section (sous-sections réunies). Important cases of principle or where there are conflicts of case law between different sous-sections will be decided by the whole Section du contentieux. Very important cases are reserved to the Assemblée du contentieux, presided over by

19 CC decision No 86-224 DC of 23 January 1987, *Competition Council*, Rec 8.

20 Brown and Bell, pp 79-86.

1 For a summary of the current jurisdiction of the Conseil d'Etat, see Brown and Bell, pp 54-55. In 1998, the jurisdiction in first and last instance was still significant at 2,047 cases: *Rapport Public 1999*; *Etudes et Documents du Conseil d'Etat*, No 50, p 20.

2 The term 'administration' is preferred to 'civil service' since the latter is much narrower in meaning than the French term 'fonctionnaire'.

3 The other sections are Finances, Intérieur, Travaux Publics, Sociale and the Section du Rapport et des Etudes: see Brown and Bell, pp 64-78.

the Vice-President and involving the presidents of all the Sections of the Conseil. In 1998, the Conseil d'Etat decided some 10,540 cases.[4]

There have been attempts to deal expeditiously with unmeritorious cases. The reforms of 1987 provided for a commission des pourvois en cassation to review pourvois against the decisions of the Cours administratives d'appel and decide the unmeritorious cases quickly. This proved cumbersome and slow, and the procedure was abolished in 1997. Instead, the cases are reviewed quickly within the Section du contentieux and about 50% to 55% of cases are then sent on for a detailed process of *instruction*.[5]

(c) *The tribunaux administratifs and the Cours administratives d'appel*

The tribunaux administratifs and the Cours administratives d'appel are staffed by a separate corps of judges from the Conseil d'Etat. These are drawn from the administration and, to an increasing extent, from private practice. As we will see, they are very much more like the civil courts in their activities.

At the bottom of the pyramid of courts are the tribunaux administratifs. They originate in Napoleon's conseils de préfecture which advised the Prefect. There are now 36 spread across France. Each court is made up of a minimum of a president and three or four judges, though some, such as Paris are very large. They have jurisdiction on most matters arising in their area: contracts, liability, illegal municipal elections or decisions. They now have jurisdiction to enforce their own decisions by way of ordonnance to the administration. In 1998, the tribunaux administratifs decided 110,966 cases.

Above these are the cours administratives d'appel, created in 1987. These seven cours are located in Bordeaux, Douai, Lyon, Marseilles, Nancy, Nantes, and Paris, and deal with appeals on points of law and fact from the tribunaux administratifs. They are staffed by the same corps of judges, but are presided over by members of the Conseil d'Etat. In 1998, they decided 11,651 cases.[6]

(d) *Specialist administrative courts*

In addition to the ordinary generalist administrative courts, there are a number of specialist public law courts, each with their own staff of judges. These are often called *commissions* and have competence only in respect of particular issues. Such *commissions* are usually chaired by administrative judges. Among the most important of these *commissions* is the Commission des réfugiés.[7] Another major group of administrative courts deal with public finances. Whereas in Britain, public finances are supervised by public agencies (the National Audit Office and the Audit Commission) under the control of parliamentary committees, in France (as elsewhere in Europe and

4 The *Rapport Public 1999* p 56 indicates that of these cases 55 were decided by the Assemblée du contentieux and 47 by the Section du contentieux, 2,328 by sous-sections réunies and 3,390 by a sous-section jugeant seule.

5 *Rapport Public 1999* p 20.

6 On the statistics of the tribunaux administratifs and the Cours administratives d'appel, see Brown and Bell, Appendix F.

7 On the commissions, see Brown and Bell, Appendix D.

in the European Union), the supervision of public finances is undertaken by courts.[8] For central government, the Cour des Comptes investigates the management of public accounts and may criticise the government, eg for the way in which it has tried to mask a budget surplus by its presentation of accounts. The Cour de discipline budgétaire deals with failures of control or misdemeanours of the finance officers of government departments and agencies. At the level of local government, similar tasks are performed by the Chambres régionales des comptes from which appeal lies to the Cour des comptes.

(3) The Conseil constitutionnel[9]

Technically, the Conseil constitutionnel is not a court, but a 'council'. It was not originally envisaged as playing the role of a court, striking down legislation and protecting civil liberties. It was a body to which disputes on the boundaries between the legislative competence of the executive and Parliament could be referred, and which decided issues concerning disputed parliamentary elections. As will be seen in Chapter 6, the actual role of the Conseil has changed markedly from that original brief, but neither the structure nor the procedure has changed to make it more like a court. Only in election issues, does the procedure resemble that of a court, rather than an administrative inquiry.

There is only one national Conseil constitutionnel. It does not hear applications from individual citizens concerning the constitutionality of lois passed by Parliament in relation to concrete fact situations, nor can it receive references on constitutional issues from the administrative or civil and criminal courts. Rather it reviews the constitutionality of lois before they are signed by the President in abstract on a reference from either the President of the Republic, the Prime Minister, the President of the National Assembly or the President of the Senate, or, more commonly, from 60 deputies or senators (usually from opposition parties). In this way it does not deal with 'cases', but rather reaches 'decisions' about the constitutionality of the loi taken as a whole. As will be seen later, the members of the court do not need to have legal qualifications and are not drawn necessarily from the ranks of the various judiciaries.

Although not integrated into the hierarchy of courts, the Conseil does carry authority in its interpretations of the Constitution. Its rulings on the constitutionality of a loi must be followed by the ordinary private law and public law courts, and its interpretations of provisions of the loi are respected by them and are typically followed as authoritative statements.

In the matter of national elections (for the President of the Republic, for the National Assembly or for a referendum), the Conseil constitutionnel is both the overseer of the election and adjudicates on disputes. It declares the results, though the Ministry of the Interior organises the practical arrangements. Through a court-like procedure, it deals with petitions concerning irregularities in the electoral process and comes to individual decisions (often several hundred in relation to parliamentary elections). But this is not the principal focus of its work.

8 See Brown and Bell, p 59.
9 See generally, J Bell, *French Constitutional Law* (Oxford 1992), pp 48-56.

C. LEGAL ACTORS

Subsequent chapters will deal with ways in which the media and others become important interlocutors of the legal process. This chapter will seek in a more limited way to give an account of some of the principal actors who occupy specifically legal roles in the ways in which the various branches of law operate. It is convenient to distinguish professional judges, non-professionals as judges and avocats. There are other legal professions, such as huissiers and greffiers, who are involved in litigation.[10] These roles are important, though predominantly administrative within the litigation process and have, therefore, not been the focus of attention in this study. Furthermore, there are legal professions such as notaires who have a very important role outside litigation.[11] In the areas chosen for this study, they do not play a significant role. As a preliminary, however, I will try to situate the legal professions within the wider context of professions in France, particularly the administration.

(1) The importance of corps in France

Both Bourdieu and Crozier have noted the high priority placed on competitive processes and educational achievement in the selection of members of the administration. Bourdieu describes these bureaucrats as the new nobility, the nobility of the State, products of the educational process, which has, in some ways come to replace the nobility of blood of the Ancien Régime.[12] His studies of the grandes écoles show how each of these institutions of professional higher education select individuals and form them into 'homogeneous classes of habits', sorting them out and conferring on them their distinctive identity.[13] These grandes écoles cover a wide range of disciplines, including engineering, the civil service (both general and technical), the judiciary, teaching, and management. The competitive entrance examinations (the concours) limit entry and then there is a high quality training, which compares favourably with the mass education in universities. At the end, there are usually further competitive tests producing a ranking (classement) which aids obtaining future employment or postings. Each élite group or corps has its own distinctive identity, often dating back to the special preparatory classes immediately after school or university, which precede the entrance examination. As Bourdieu notes:

> Of all social groups, the corps founded on educational achievement which are created by the conferring of a diploma or a common identity on individuals brought together by very strong social resemblance, which is thereby recognised and legitimated, are, no doubt, those which are closest to a family. In fact, the intense and enduring emotional bonds of fraternity which are created inevitably between adolescents, who are so similar that everything predisposes

10 These professions are discussed in J Bell, S Boyron and S Whittaker, *Principles of French Law*, ch 3.

11 Ibid, pp 73-74.

12 See P Bourdieu, *La noblesse d'Etat. Grandes Ecoles et esprit de corps* (Paris 1989).

13 Bourdieu, p 254. On the grandes écoles see J Ardagh, *France in the New Century* (London 1999), pp 566-570.

> them to 'get on', makes the solidarity of the corps appear natural, just as family feelings for the domestic group.[14]

Within the bureaucracy, Crozier notes the importance of the range of groups, each with its own sense of 'the one best way' and he argued consistently that this was a weakness in governmental planning, even though he did note the importance of the grands corps of the civil service (inspection des finances, Conseil d'Etat, Cour des comptes, and corps diplomatique) as mediators between the bureaucracy and the social environment.[15] Conflicts between corps, each seeking to preserve its territory and influence are a normal part of administrative life.[16]

This phenomenon is not confined to the public service. The private sector too has its different corps of managers, various skilled workers, and so on, who operate in a similar fashion. Crozier argued that, in relations between managers and workers, there is not a straightforward hierarchical relationship. The managers may dictate rules, but these have to recognise both the status and independence of the relevant groups of workers:

> ... the independence of the workers makes it impossible to coerce them directly; they are completely protected as long as they obey the rules. They need, however, stability and due process, ie peace and order; they also need some sense of purpose and recognition. Formal authority is, therefore, indispensable to them, but they would like it to be their servant and to acknowledge their status.[17]

The rules of the factory or office have their place, and they ensure that no one can interfere with the affairs of the immediately inferior category of staff.[18] While Crozier studied private sector office workers, the analysis has been developed by Philippe D'Iribarne's studies of industrial organisations. Within factories, he discovered distinct corps among managers, professional engineers, skilled technicians, and unskilled staff. Hierarchy has to operate within the setting of these different corps, each of which has a strong self-respect and sense of identity:

> Each 'status' is marked by a demanding conception of responsibilities, which the mere fact of belonging to [the corps] imposes on the members, without waiting for any superior to give them the task. It is rich with duties required to be completed beyond any legal or contractual obligation or any formal sanction threatening anyone who fails to comply.[19]

14 Ibid, p 257. His analysis of the background of entrants to the grandes écoles shows how much they come from a similar social stratum and are often children of members of the same or similar corps to which they are applying: see also EN Suleiman, *Politics, Power and Bureaucracy in France. The Administrative Elite* (Princeton 1974). On how homogeneity within these corps engenders mutual confidence, but can create conformism and lack of innovation, see M Crozier, *Strategies for Change. The Future of French Society* (trans WR Beer, Cambridge, Mass. 1982), ch 6. For a similar critique, see V Wright, *The Government and Politics of France* (3rd edn, London 1989), pp 119-124.

15 See M Crozier, *The Bureaucratic Phenomenon* (London 1964), pp 303ff. For a discussion of the coherence of élites, see also his *Strategies for Change*, pp 49-53.

16 V Wright, *the Government and Politics of France*, p 124.

17 *The Bureaucratic Phenomenon*, pp 87-88.

18 Ibid, p 55.

19 P D'Iribarne, *La logique de l'honneur* (Paris 1989), p 58.

There is a pride in a job well done, and the manager must not attack this self-respect, for example of skilled workers.[20] Jesse Pitts identified the concept of 'prowess' as an important value in French culture, an act by which an individual achieves the highest ideals to which a human action could aspire in their particular circumstances.[1] The sense of responsibility arising from status is important because it affects both what an individual does and how relationships are established. In terms of what is done, the responsibilities (and not just privileges) of belonging to the corps define what one should do and how one should perform the tasks. The requirements are those of professionalism. In a setting where an individual's duties are thus largely fixed by the custom of his professional group, he is not tolerant of the superior fixing objectives for him in an authoritarian way.[2] D'Iribane argues that, as a result, American-style 'management by objectives' is not compatible with that culture.

Beyond the point at which responsibilities are fixed by the duties of one's status, other actions contributing to the collective good are affected by the quality of personal relationships.[3] Establishing appropriate working relationships thus obeys what D'Iribarne describes as 'the logic of honour'. This concept was identified by Montesquieu who suggested that each rank in society had a fear of losing prestige and tried to avoid actions which would make it appear that a person was satisfied with acting below their rank.[4] In D'Iribarne's words 'Honour commands above all that one does not lower oneself, does not "demean oneself", does not "submit".'[5] Organisations have to operate acknowledging the sense of honour or self-respect of the different corps:

> In France there are several models of authority relationships. Unless one knows how to use these with skill, one runs a great risk of arousing indignation and demoralisation. A French person in authority has an interest in knowing well which notion of honour the different categories which he has the task of directing have, what that honour accepts and what offends it. ... The guiding principles of the French style of management are, no doubt, easy to understand. It has to make use of the intensity with which each devotes himself to *his* work, provided that he feels it is respected, whilst leading him to act in relation to objectives which go beyond his direct interest.[6]

This formality, which is traditionally important in French society, involves both putting each rank in its place and individualism, which involves each person finding their place within the hierarchy.[7] This is not to suggest that the French are not profoundly individualist in their ways of working. An individualist way of working, encouraged by

20 Ibid, p 27.
1 JR Pitts. 'Continuité et changement au sein de la France bourgeoise' in S Hoffman et al, *A la recherche de la France* (Paris 1963), 265 at p 273.
2 D'Iribarne, p 96.
3 Ibid, p 52.
4 Ibid, p 59.
5 Ibid, p 79, also p 258 where he describes France as 'the country of honour'.
6 Ibid, pp. 98-99. See also JR Pitts, op cit, p 279: 'It is in part thanks to the universality of the aristocratic values of prowess in the field of achievement and thanks to their relative accessibility that the French find it hard to defer to any superior who does not know how to seduce them and, in a certain sense, associate them with him.'
7 JR Pitts, p 271.

the competitive education system, and the decisive role of the corps in one's career path and in defining what is good work are simultaneously operating variables.[8]

The analysis of professions just outlined is a curious combination between what Trompenaars and Hampden-Turner identify as the 'Eiffel Tower', hierarchical model where individuals have roles, assigned by rules, and change comes through changing those rules, and the 'family model' in which hierarchy exists, but within strong personal relationships of an affective character.[9]

This analysis has important consequences for the study of law. The various professional legal actors discussed in subsequent chapters belong to different corps. There are various corps of judges in the civil and administrative fields. There are various corps of avocats. There are various corps of the police. Their internal senses of responsibility, their internal sense of solidarity, and thus their exclusion of others and of external dictation are important features of the dynamics of different branches of law. If the analysis of Crozier and D'Iribarne is replicated in relation to law, then one would expect important differences in the sense of justice and serving the public interest among the different corps of legal actors. Subsequent chapters will examine how far the legal cultures identified are really a feature of the various branches of law studied, and how far of the specific corps of legal actors.

(2) Professional judges

Unlike most European countries, France does not have a single body of professional judges. There are several corps of judges, which makes it easier to establish that there are different legal cultures within France. If anything, the distinction of the corps has been accentuated in recent years, although the origins of many differences pre-date the Revolution of 1789. Among the professional judges, there is a major distinction between the magistrats judiciaires, dealing with civil and criminal law, on the one hand, and the two main corps of administrative judges on the other. Both these groups of judges are civil servants and, therefore there are similarities in the way they are recruited, even if there are also significant differences. To these must be added a body of judges who are not strictly speaking professional judges, the members of the Conseil constitutionnel, who are appointed for a non-renewable period of nine years.

(a) The magistrats judiciaires

The civil and criminal judges are the successors of the Parlements of the Ancien Régime. Indeed some were often the same people.[10] The distinction between judges and avocats is of very long standing.[11] As we will see shortly, the distinction between the members of the Parlement and those of the Conseil privé du Roi has a parallel in

8 See L Rouban, 'The Senior Civil Service in France', in EC Page and V Wright, *Bureaucratic Elites* (Oxford 1999), ch 4.

9 See *Riding the Waves of Culture*, pp 158-172.

10 See A Bancaud, *La haute magistrature judiciaire entre politique et sacerdoce* (Paris 1993), pp 22-24, 85.

11 L Karpik, *French Lawyers* (Oxford 1999), pp 32-35.

the distinction between civil and administrative judges. Although until modern times those recruited as judges had to have already completed a two-year period of traineeship in a *cabinet* of an avocat, since 1959 the career has normally begun in the judicial college (called the Ecole Nationale de la Magistrature since 1970) after a law graduate has passed the entrance examination. A gradual feminisation of the profession has occurred since the 1960s.[12] Boigeol attributes this to a view that 'The judiciary appeared ... as a respectable position for the daughters of the middle classes who were more hesitant to place their sons in it'.[13] In November 2000, there were 6,882 judges of whom 3,413 (49%) were women.[14] The long and distinctive corporate identity of the civil judiciary is fostered and sustained in a number of ways: through initial and subsequent training, through career paths, and through the structures by which promotions are achieved.

The basic career pattern since the 1960s has been that a judge is trained through the professional college (ENM) based in Bordeaux which involves not only courses, but also placements in different organs involved with the law, including in a cabinet d'avocat, and the prefecture (and even possibly abroad). There are also a number of practical exercises. Such a period of training over two years, often with group work, socialises the year group (*promotion*) with each other, as well as with the judicial world. ENM also serves to prepare the judges for their initial posting, following the exit examinations. As an organisation involved with continual professional development, it offers courses that are taken up by a significant number of judges. (Some events can involve several hundred judges.) The activities of the ENM can thus be opportunities for both formal and informal dialogue among judges from different parts of France.

Recruitment takes place through three concours.[15] The first concours is designed for those leaving university. Of the 3,948 people admitted to this concours in 1998, only 156 candidates were successful, of whom 74.38% were women.[16] The second concours is for civil servants of at least four years' standing who are aged over 46 years and 5 months. For the 214 people admitted to the competition, there were only 34 places available in 1998. The third concours is for those of at least eight years' standing in a private sector profession (including being an avocat) and who are over 40. Of the 84 people admitted to the competition, there were only 10 places available in 1998. Finally, there can be a secondment à tour extérieur for a number of years where individuals are recruited often for their expertise. For example, some members of the Cour de cassation might be drawn from among university professors.

The multiplicity of recruitment routes enables a certain balance of age and experience. Not all judges belong to the cohort of life-long judges. That said, the experience of the ENM is meant to provide an element of initial socialisation for the majority of judges.

12 See A Boigeol, 'La magistrature française au féminin: entre spécificité et banalisation' (1993) 25 *Droit et Société* 489.

13 Ibid, p 492.

14 Speech of Mme Lebranchu, Minister of Justice, Senate 22 November 2000 from Ministry of Justice website.

15 The concours is seen as increasing the democratic character of the judiciary: see H Dalle, 'Le recrutement et la formation des magistrats: une question de légitimité' (1991) 57 Revue de l'administration publique 53.

16 Statistics from ENM website. This figure compares favourably with other professions. Women occupy 34% of places in French managerial and higher intellectual professions: see *Le Monde*, 18 December 2000.

Initial socialisation is assisted by the familiarity with the career that many recruits already have because of their family background. According to Bodiguel's research:

> One judge in ten is from a family of judges, one in five is from a family of lawyers, and one in two is from a family in the public service.[17]

In addition, nearly half in his survey (43.6%) were married to another judge. He concludes that family links are an important influence in the choice of this profession. Women now constitute the majority of the profession, above all at lower levels, though they are less strongly represented as yet at the most senior levels.[18] The recruitment of women has actually increased the number of recruits from the Paris region and from bourgeois families.[19]

The diversity of recruitment is reinforced by the different activities that the judges can undertake during the course of their career. The classical judicial career can involve any of three activities. First, the most traditional activity is for the judge to adjudicate on individual cases (as a magistrat de siège). A number of judges will devote themselves to this task for all their career. (Bodiguel estimates the number at about half.[20]) Naturally, a judge will have a number of postings, both geographical and in terms of task. The work as an adjudicating judge at first instance can include work as a juge des enfants, or as a judge of civil or of criminal matters. Women are over-represented among the magistrats de siège in part because this offers the possibility of a relatively solitary work with limited numbers of fixed appointments, thus permitting flexible working patterns.[1]

Second, a substantial number of judges will choose to become members of the parquet whose role is essentially as public prosecutor. More than half of these will return to become adjudicating judges.[2] Equally, those who start in the parquet will typically go to the siège (only 11% did not), and just over 40% of these return to the parquet.[3] Traditionally, this second route has been taken by those who attain the highest places in the Cour de cassation. A posting in the parquet ensures that one is known. The 1999 report of the CSM notes that fewer people are applying for this route. In part, the reason lies in the greater responsibilities with local associations and others

17 J-L Bodiguel, *Les magistrats, un corps sans âme* (Paris 1991), p 139. But, according to Bancaud, 26.2% of top posts in Cour de cassation in the period 1945-85 went to children of judges and the figure rises to 47.7% if one includes all who have a family connection with the judiciary. This last figure is similar to the figure for members of the Cour de cassation with a family member in the judiciary in 1901 (44.6%): see A Bancaud, *La haute magistrature judiciaire entre politique et sacerdoce*, pp 21-22.

18 The *Rapport Annuel d'activité 1999* of the Conseil supérieur de la magistrature (CSM)(Paris 2000) p. 186 reports that women constituted 52.17% of candidates for posts at grade II (the lowest grade), but men constituted 84.92% of candidates for the most senior grade (*hors hiérarchie*) and made up 70.83% of those who were appointed.

19 Ibid, p 166. See also V Roussel, 'Scandales politiques et transformation des rapports entre magistrature et politique' (2000) 44/45 *Droit et société* 13 at pp 17-22.

20 Bodiguel, p 110.

1 A Boigeol, (1993) 25 *Droit et Société*, pp 501 and 522.

2 Ibid, p 111.

3 CSM, *Rapport 1999*, p 182 reports that from 1 June 1998 to 31 August 1999, 96 individuals moved from parquet to siège and 83 moved in the opposite direction out of a total of 2,093 appointments made.

which has changed the legal aspect of work, and has made it perhaps less flexible.[4] In part this is due to proposed changes to the career which would make it less attractive. Until 1994, posts in the parquet were decided by political authorities and they were essentially part of the political spoils system.

A third frequent posting is an administrative role within the Ministry of Justice (the Chancellerie). Since all the posts in this ministry are held by judges, rather than by ordinary civil servants, there are significant opportunities to be placed here and to influence the formulation and implementation of policy. It is argued that, to gain advancement, it is necessary to be known by those in authority. A posting in the Ministry of Justice ensures this. The top third of ENM candidates choose this as their first post. This is seen as the 'royal route' to a higher judicial career. Certainly a very substantial number of the senior judiciary have spent at least some time in the Ministry during their careers. In contrast to members of the Conseil d'Etat, members of the private law judiciary do not tend to be seconded to other parts of government or the public sector.[5] There are exceptions, such as the small number who become members of parliament or even of the government.

Overall, there is no set pattern for a judicial career. The 2,881 judges studied by Bodiguel had followed 683 different career paths!

The promotion of private law judges is secured through a single framework. Before 1946, political influence and recommendation was particularly important.[6] The Conseil Supérieur de la Magistrature (CSM) was created in 1946 to ensure the independence of the judiciary. Initially it had a power of recommendation over the promotions of the lower judicial grades, but it became gradually less effective in this role and, when reconstituted in 1958, it was given only an advisory role. Gradually this has been increased, and so, since a constitutional amendment of 1993, it has two roles. In relation to the ordinary grades of judge, it is required to give a favourable opinion on promotions to postings in the siège or the parquet which are recommended by the Chancellerie. In the cases of the highest postings, such as procureur, president or member of the Cour de cassation, the CSM makes proposals. The CSM is made up of a number of external members, together with judges elected onto one of two panels, either the siège or the parquet. (There is one member of the parquet on the siège panel and similar cross-membership on the parquet panel.) Promotion is first determined by a person being placed on the tableau d'avancement, where seniority is the principal determinant, although recommendations on performance are also included. This degree of self-government is important for the character of the judiciary. In November 2000, there were over 800 judges on the tableau d'avancement, who would take years to be promoted, and for this reason reforms of the promotion system were being presented to Parliament (even if the quid pro quo is that judges will have to move, since they will not be able to be promoted in their present location if they have been there for more than five years).

4 CSM, *Rapport 1999*, p 77.

5 See A Boigeol, 'Les magistrats "hors murs" ' (2000) 44/45 *Droit et société* 225. She notes that their most frequent external posting is to be a sous-préfet: ibid, pp 241-242. Secondment was rejected at the beginning of the century for the ordinary judiciary (though allowed for the Conseil d'Etat and the Cour des Comptes), but has become more frequent in the Fifth Republic and was facilitated by a loi of 1992.

6 Bodiguel, p 113. For an example of the process, see A Bancaud, 'Une nomination judiciaire sous la IIIe République' (1997) 26 *Genèses* 154.

But it has to be acknowledged that the promotion for most judges is recommended by the Chancellerie. There are usually only sufficient recommendations made to fill the places. This means that the Conseil is not called upon to select, but to approve or disapprove. The Conseil does reject proposals, even if they are not contested by the individual or by others who consider they have a better claim.[7] Candidates make their requests known to the Ministry and the CSM and this will typically trigger the promotion process.

Elections to the CSM tend to be the opportunity for the judicial unions to play a role. They are able to ensure that their candidates occupy key positions. Certainly the research conducted by Bancaud into the Mitterand period of the 1980s suggests political manoeuvres by judicial unions and political figures has not altogether disappeared from the judicial appointment process.[8] Judicial unions also organise strikes, such as the strike against inadequate funding of the judicial system, which coincided with the special session of the Cour de cassation to mark its bicentenary.[9]

Ordinary judges have a mixed reputation among the public. In 1997, an opinion poll found that, while 71% of those questioned thought them to be competent, and 57% thought they were courageous in their work, and even 77% thought they were overworked, only 21% thought they were independent of economic influence and 17% independent of political influence. They had a higher score for honesty than avocats (47%), but only 39% of those questioned thought they were fair. The survey concluded that the judges 'lack credibility'. The survey also noted that left-wing supporters had markedly less confidence in the judiciary than right-wing voters.[10]

(b) *The administrative judges*[11]

As will be seen in Chapter 5, administrative judges have a different background to private law judges. They are essentially administrators trained at the Ecole Nationale de l'Administration (ENA). They are recruited predominantly among those who have been through the various concours to enter ENA, and they have chosen the tasks of administrative judge as their posting. Administrative judges belong, however, to two distinct corps.

On the one hand, some 300 judges belong to the grand corps of the Conseil d'Etat, which is one of the élite groups of administrators. As will be seen later, these highly talented individuals are likely to have a variety of postings within government and in the public administration during the course of their career. By contrast, the judges of the tribunaux administratifs fit the more classical model of a judiciary and will have predominantly judicial functions once they enter the corps, although a few may spend some time on secondment to various branches of the administration. Some members of

7 CSM, *Rapport 1999*, p 15.

8 A Bancaud, 'Le paradoxe de la gauche française au pouvoir: développement des libertés judiciaires et continuité de la dépendance de la Justice' (2000) 44/45 *Droit et société* 61.

9 See RL Jones, *Justice of the Peace*, December 29 1990.

10 CSA survey, 'Les Français et la justice' (1997) published on the GIP Mission de Recherche Droit et Justice website, p 6.

11 See Brown and Bell, pp 79-88; J Bell, S Boyron, and S Whittaker, *Principles of French Law*, pp 57, 63 and 65.

this corps will be promoted to the Cours administratives d'appel, though the president of each Cour is a member of the Conseil d'Etat.

Members of corps of the tribunaux administratifs and the Cours administratives d'appel enjoy similar status to private law judges in that, since 1986, they cannot be moved against their will and their promotions are organised by the Conseil Supérieur des tribunaux administratifs et des Cours administratives d'appel. This body is presided over by the Vice-President of the Conseil d'Etat and administered by a secretary-general adjoint from the Conseil d'Etat. Substantial networking and visiting occurs to ensure that the Conseil d'Etat is well aware of the career aspirations and situations of candidates for promotion, and the corps of the lower judges is still small enough (nearly 800) to rely on personal knowledge, compared with the more formal procedures for promotion and career development that exist among the 7,000 and more magistrats.

Initial training and continuing education for such administrative judges is run by the Bureau de formation of the Conseil d'Etat, drawing on the expertise of administrative judges from the different courts. Initial training involves four elements: a number of special lectures, training in the functions of being a rapporteur within a sous-section of the Conseil d'Etat through work on selected (past) files, attendance at judicial hearings, and a general familiarisation with the working of the administrative sections of the Conseil d'Etat. This process of inculturation serves to achieve some kind of standardisation of expectations for the judicial role.

No such formal procedures or protections exist for members of the Conseil d'Etat. Promotion is based on seniority and the interests of members, and is managed within the corps. New recruits are trained on the job within the Conseil, with few formal training events. The small number of recruits is like that of an English provincial law firm, and much of the training is handled by way of individual mentoring.

(c) Members of the Conseil constitutionnel

Members of the Conseil constitutionnel are not formally judges. They do not belong to any career structure, for they are appointed for a non-renewable term of nine years. But they are not really lay judges either. Although there are no formal criteria for such an office, it is well understood that the body of judges should contain legal, parliamentary, and government expertise, though not every individual will have all three. Members are appointed by the President of the Republic, the President of the National Assembly and the President of the Senate. There is, thus, a clear political judgement made about their suitability, which will include their political affiliation. But the absence of formal criteria makes it difficult to say much about what is required for the role. Certainly no formal training is provided. Since nearly all members of the Conseil are of retirement age once they leave the Conseil (if they were not already when they were appointed), career development and promotion have not been considered relevant features of this fixed-term appointment. More will be said on such appointments in Chapter 6.

(3) Lay judges

France has a long tradition of lay involvement in the judicial process. Apart from the minor role played by the criminal jury, this has not taken the form of popular representation in the decision-making panel. Rather, it has taken the form of the engagement of the social partners in the operation of key areas of justice which affect them. In many cases, there are conflicting social groups and, rather than the judiciary arbitrating between them on their own, the system has sought to involve the groups in the decision-making and involve the judge much more as the ultimate (but infrequently used) tie-breaker.

(a) Commercial judges

Commercial judges are elected indirectly by their peers every four years through the chamber of commerce. Courts have anything from 5 to 170 judges, who are unpaid. In these courts, the judges, elected by the Chambers of Commerce, sit in panels hearing contract and company cases, including insolvency issues. The 1999 report has raised concerns about the way in which this system places local businessmen as judges over issues such as the winding up of other businessmen in their locality, who may even be trade rivals.[12] Accordingly, it proposed reforms to introduce a professional judge as president of commercial court panels concerned with insolvency and other such sensitive issues. These are likely to be introduced in 2001.[13] The result will be to reduce the status of the commercial judges and this has already led to the resignation of 700 of the 3,200 commercial judges.[14]

(b) Conseillers des prud'hommes

Employee members of the Conseil des prud'hommes are not appointed by trade unions, but are elected by workers registered in the appropriate employment categories. Employers are elected similarly from those in the appropriate employer categories. They are elected for five years and may be renewed. They undertake some training in the law, and the employer must allow a conseiller to be off work for up to six weeks a year for this purpose.

(c) Other lay judges

Election by appropriate peers characterises a number of other lay judge appointments, in particular the assessors of the tribunal paritaire des baux ruraux. Others are appointed, especially the assessors for the tribunal des enfants. In these latter cases, the legal system is not seeking representatives of conflicting social interests, but wishes to appoint people with experience who can offer a view which enables the court to represent the opinion of society. It is in this latter category that the jurés of the cour d'assises belong. Chosen by lot from the electoral register, these citizens are intended to introduce popular common sense into the judgments of facts and sentence.[15]

12 See *La mixité dans les juridictions commerciales* (Report to Ministry of Justice, 2 April 1999).
13 See Martine Orange, *Le Monde*, 18 July 2000.
14 Ibid.
15 See further, below, p 139.

(4) Lawyers[16]

As indicated above, this chapter will not discuss all legal professions. I will, however, discuss the main legal professions involved in litigation and advice.

(a) Avocats

The French profession of avocat can be traced back to at least 1274, and its clear separation from the judiciary was reinforced in the 16th century when Francis I introduced the sale of offices such as member of the Parlement.[17] With the introduction of the investigating judge and the separate parquet during the same period, the role of the avocat has long been confined to criminal defence and private client work. Although some avocats do seek to enter the judiciary by one of the concours or even by nomination by the tour extérieur, this is not the typical career structure.

Becoming an avocat involves both passing university examinations and undertaking a training period. The idea of a bar examination is modern and dates only from 1941. Thus nowadays a law student would take the CAPA after a law degree as a prelude to a *stage*. As a liberal profession, there is no ceiling on membership, nor is there the need to purchase an office, as is the case with the notary profession. The profession has gradually taken centre stage. In 1971, it merged with the avoué which was responsible for preparing and filing papers in litigation, though this function is still performed by avoués at the level of the cour d'appel. In 1990, the profession merged with the conseils juridique to provide a single profession covering legal advice and representation.

The profession is organised into regional bars attached to each cour d'appel or tribunal de grande instance, rather than as a unified national profession. There are 181 bars.[18] Until the 1990 reforms, it was not possible to set up an office in more than one bar area, nor to have salaried lawyers. The result has been the slow growth of large law firms. In 1998, of the 30,277 qualified avocats, 13,044 (43%) were in single practice, 10,307 (34%) were in partnership (associés), 4,725 (15.6%) were collaborators (self-employed lawyers working in the office of another lawyer), and only 2,201 (6.6%) were salaried.[19] In many large towns, for example Bordeaux, there are no partnerships as large as ten partners. In 1998, there were also 4,993 trainee avocats.

In most civil matters of any significance, the litigant is obliged to be represented by an avocat. A duty avocat system exists in criminal law. As a result, avocats are involved in most litigation. Much of the bar is generalist. In 1998, only 13,457 (44%) advertised any specialism, nearly half of whom specialised in tax or commercial law. Karpik's study shows that the bar was not traditionally involved in commercial work, and this gave rise to the separate profession of the conseil juridique. Even before the merger of the professions in 1990, there had been an increasing growth of commercial work. In Karpik's research, there was a close connection in the minds of lawyers between income, complexity and prestige of legal work.[20] In all these aspects, non-litigious,

16 J Bell, S Boyron, and S Whittaker, *Principles of French Law*, pp 69-73.
17 See L Karpik, *French Lawyers* (Oxford 1999), p 34.
18 Ibid, p 231.
19 *Annuaire Statistique de la Justice*, 2000, p 273.
20 L Karpik, p 197.

commercial work had a higher prestige. Personal client work is more likely to involve litigation, in criminal and family matters. In commercial law, there is likely to an ongoing relationship with the client, and many in this field have family connections in business.[1] By contrast, private client work will frequently be supported by aide judiciaire, and will not involve a continuing relationship over several pieces of litigation. General work is thus a substantial part of the avocats. It is not surprising that at the end of 2000, there was a 'work to rule' by the bars of France in protest against the levels of funding for legal aid.[2]

The bar had a very important part in the creation of liberal political society.[3] In the period of 1875-1920, one in four deputies was an avocat, and those who had held the leading post of secretary of the training conference of the bar constituted 10% of the holders of political office. But its role as the champion of liberal causes faded after the Dreyfus affair in the 1890s. The commercial law has tended to replace this as in economic importance, but the political dimension has remained as part of the status of the profession.[4]

The public opinion of avocats is mixed. In a survey conducted in 1997, 78% of those questioned considered them to be competent and 76% thought they were welcoming. On the other hand, only 39% thought they were honest and 93% thought they cost too much. The suspicion of avocats was greatest among those who had been involved in litigation.[5]

(b) Avocats au Conseil d'Etat et à la Cour de cassation

Since Napoleon, there has been a specialist bar with rights of audience before the two supreme courts based in Paris. Apart from criminal cases,[6] it is necessary for a pourvoi en cassation or a request to the Conseil d'Etat to be presented by an avocat au Conseil d'Etat et à la Cour de cassation. This specialism is to ensure that cases are properly presented and that the courts are able to work efficiently. There are only 90 such avocats, 30 individuals and 60 associations, dealing with about 30,000 cases a year. Since they hold an office ministeriel, a public office which can be sold, entry to the profession is limited to those who can buy or inherit an étude from an existing holder. Unlike the profession of avocat, it is not possible just to pass the bar examinations and set oneself up. Of course, the case-load before the supreme courts entails that the avocats au Conseil d'Etat et à la Cour de cassation cannot do all the work themselves. They have teams of highly able lawyers working for them (including young academics) who will prepare cases under their supervision. These avocats act as heads of offices, but only they can appear before the courts. This small group regularly files cases with the supreme courts and develops an understanding of them, as well as a relationship

1 Ibid, p 213; see also D Le Guilledoux, 'Dans les "niches" du droit des petits gens', *Le Monde*, 18 May 2000.
2 See *Le Monde*, 13 December 2000.
3 L Karpik, pp 78ff.
4 Ibid, ch 7.
5 CSA survey, 'Les Français et la justice' (1997) published on the GIP Mission de Recherche Droit et Justice website, p 5.
6 Where there is no obligation to be represented by an avocat à la Cour, then any avocat may be used to prepare the litigant's pourvoi.

with the members of the courts, particularly the commissaire du gouvernement in the Conseil d'Etat and the avocat-général in the Cour de cassation. They have a particular opportunity to influence the highest courts and will constitute a particular audience for the decisions rendered by these courts.

(c) Avoués

The avoué is now confined to preparing papers for filing in the cour d'appel. There are 410 avoués, 79 in individual practice and 331 in associations. Although these are important for the efficiency of the cours d'appel, the avoués have little influence on the arguments put before the courts, since this is done by the avocat. Nor do they really influence markedly the selection of cases which are submitted to the courts. As a result, this work will not discuss their role to any great extent.

(5) The academy

The universities have existed in France since the 13th century. But, as in England, the teaching of law was confined to the teaching of Roman and canon law for a long period. France was a major centre for the study of Roman law, especially at Orléans and Bourges, and of natural law under Domat.[7] The intellectual energy which went into Roman law and developing general principles from it was applied to the ordering of French customary law by Dumoulin and Coquille in the 16th century and more famously by Pothier in the 18th century.[8] French law was only taught in the universities after the decree of St.Germain-en-Laye of 1679, as a final year subject.[9] The law faculties were closed in 1793 and reopened in 1804. But the programme was set out by decree and the number of subjects was limited (droit civil, droit public, and législation criminelle et procédure), and the civil law had to be taught in the order of the Code. Academic freedom in teaching was really only fully established in 1895.[10]

Universities were thus the institution where basic legal education was given. Even then, the status according to university education was limited. Karpik argues that the university *licence* represented only a general certification of basic legal knowledge and this was of little influence in the professions where priority was accorded to practical knowledge.[11] But professional training schools for the Bar and for the judiciary

7 P Stein, *Roman Law in European History* (Cambridge 1999) pp 67-68, 77-81, and 109; more generally, A Watson, *The Making of the Civil Law Tradition.*

8 Stein, op cit, pp 83-85, 114-115.

9 J-P Royer, *Histoire de la justice en France* (Paris 1995), p 135, suggests that the magistrat 'would only have listened to [French law] distractedly in at least two different lessons a day, when he did not have the money to appoint one of his poor (even illiterate) classmates to take the notes and produce the exercises'. For the avocats, training within the profession was more important than the poor quality education at many universities: L Karpik, *French Lawyers*, pp 46-47 and 49-51.

10 See A Perrot, 'La doctrine et l'hypothèse du déclin du droit' in Y Poirmeur et al., *La doctrine juridique* (Paris 1993) 181 at p 191.

11 Karpik, *French Lawyers*, p 111. Karpik suggests that higher level university degrees did not count for much before the 1970s among avocats.

are a phenomenon only of the post-1945 period. For the Bar, the training for the CAPA is conducted by universities, rather than by separate schools run by the professions (unlike the training of judges).

There are some factors that reciprocally influence the development of doctrinal legal writing:

1. The existence of a body of writers who conceive themselves as specialists in the field.
2. This results from a set of means both to pay for the activity and to distribute it (thus a form of market for the ideas must exist): the writers need some form of economic insertion, publication, and a market for their product. The existence of a law programme creates the need for teachers and a market, the students, and so we get the *cours*, the *manuels* and *précis* for students and the *traités* for academics and practitioners.
3. The writers need to have some standing which is independent of the quality of the product: hence the authority of being a judge or a leading lawyer or a professor.
4. All the same, the doctrinal writing needs to carry authority in its own right and thus exercise some influence.

The narrowness of the academic programme in the universities produced an exegetical tradition in civil law, with works in multiple volumes following the order of the Code.[12] A more critical approach developed in the mid-19th century with the founding of reviews and the writing of the note d'arrêt as a commentary on case law. Such works gave more scope for individual and critical opinion which might influence the development of the law. The quality of doctrine improved with writing of textbooks in the second half of the 19th century and critical approaches to law developed with Gény and Duguit, whose interests were sociological and theoretical. Published lecture courses and textbooks remain the major forms of doctrinal writing in most branches of law, and many are cited as sources of individual opinions by leading scholars. Monographs by established professors are relatively rare. Since the 1970s, there has been an increase in the number of legal journals, which has coincided with the increase in the number of universities and academics. Some of these journals have been more theoretical, covering philosophical and sociological perspectives on law.

Senior academic posts are acquired by the agrégation, a competitive examination for those who had obtained a doctorate in law. The doctoral thesis has been a major work of doctrinal writing since the 19th century. The breadth of subjects chosen for doctorates and the specialisation of young academics has not been helped by the limitation of the agrégation to four areas of law (public, private, history and criminal) since 1895 (previously it was fewer). This has not helped the development of legal philosophy or new legal subjects. Some individuals undertake pure research careers in research institutes or centres funded by the Centre national de la recherche scientifique, which are situated outside the university career system. The work undertaken there includes comparative law and sociology of law. The breadth of university research has been expanded since 1980 by the founding of a number of research centres within universities.

12 Troplong's commentary is in 27 volumes and Demolombe in 31 volumes.

The pay of academic staff is considered low, especially by those living in Paris. As a result, many academics find work as avocats. The practice of giving consultancies to members of the profession (and to government) has long been part of the role of the legal academic. As will be noted later, these relationships with practice influence both the time for scholarly writing and the kinds of topic which are chosen, particularly in civil and commercial law.

D. KEY LEGAL IDEAS

(1) The Etatiste tradition

The State is a cultural phenomenon in France of primordial importance. It embodies the cohesion of society through the concept of the public or general interest.[13] If 'the Nation' (rather than 'the community') represents the population as a whole, the State represents the political collectivity. There is therefore a tension between the concepts of the 'social' and the 'political'.[14] In his study of political traditions in France, Hazareesingh identifies étatisme as an important feature.[15] The concept involves two aspects. On the one hand, there is the expectation that the State will be involved in a wide range of areas. If the area is important for the public interest, the State will be involved in some way, either as provider of a service or as guardian.[16] On the other hand, and consequentially, there is a significant power that is exercised by the higher civil service. The core idea, which binds the two aspects together, is the notion of the public interest. The State is seen as the guardian of the long-term interests of the Nation, and the civil servants have the institutional vocation to defend and serve the public interest. In consequence, the performance of the administration is measured according to distinctive measures, rather than by generalised measures applicable to the performance of any service.[17] The notion of the public interest will be discussed further in the chapter on administrative law. But it is important to stress that the administration of justice is one of the pouvoirs régaliens (prerogative powers) which are seen as essential to the nature of the State. It thus fits into this core idea of the functions of the State and of civil servants, amongst whom the various judges are typically classed. The juge d'instruction in criminal cases is carrying out these roles of the State as much as other fonctionnaires.

The relationship between the administration and politics is well captured by Hazareesingh when he suggests that, in the eyes of the civil service, its role is instrumental:

13 See HS Jones, *The French State in Question: Public Law and Political Argument in the Third Republic* (Cambridge 1993), ch 1, esp pp 10-12.

14 Ibid, pp 78-79. In Kourilsky's 1987 study, French 16-18 year-olds related the concept of the State to political institutions, whereas Poles of a similar age related it to a social and linguistic community: 19 *Droit et Société* 259 at p 265.

15 S Hazareesingh, *Political Traditions in Modern France* (Oxford 1994), ch 6.

16 This idea is undergoing change, see J Ardagh, *France in the New Century*, pp 70ff.

17 See EC Page and V Wright (eds), *Bureaucratic Elites in Western European States*, pp 272-273.

> In their eyes the good society was a matter for definition by politicians, not administrators: the role of civil servants in furthering its achievement was nothing more than instrumental. The institution which appeared to bear this paradigm almost to perfection was the Conseil d'Etat (Council of State) which discreetly performed its advisory role in the sphere of legislative codification and administrative regulation without overtly impinging on the leadership functions of political élites.[18]

We will see that this apparently passive and instrumental function needs much qualification, especially in relation to the Conseil d'Etat. All the same, the importance of a demarcation line between the administrators and politicians is important.

The broad state tradition[19] expresses itself, therefore, through both the concepts of the State and the public interest, as well as through the institutions and personnel of the public service. The institution and personnel of la fonction publique, a notion wider than the British term 'the civil service', is a major vehicle through which the public interest is both determined and implemented. The judiciaries, both civil and administrative, are part of the fonction publique which carries out the public service of justice in the public interest.

(2) Law and non-law

The State tradition is a tradition of action by the State and state officials (including judges). A major vehicle for such action is the law. But there are also areas of 'non-law' where the law does not intervene. Jean Carbonnier defines 'non-law' as the absence of law in a number of human relations where one would expect it, in theory, to be present.[20] But such a concept depends on certain assumptions about the areas in which law ought to intervene. The kind of situations in which law is or is expected to be involved is indicative of a legal culture. By and large, it would be fair to suggest that French culture gives a significant place to law, and expects the State to use it to intervene and regulate many social situations in which other legal systems might not use the law.

The most important aspect of this phenomenon is the use of law to achieve social objectives. An illustration would be the regulation of the press. By the 1930s, improved production and distribution systems made possible the widespread distribution of newspapers and periodicals. But, in addition, the investment needed to maintain quality and to keep down costs was also important. Furthermore, in increasingly literate societies, the press was a major vehicle for influencing public opinion either in consumer markets or in politics. The tendencies seen in the 1930s were for rich individuals to acquire ownership of a range of national and local newspapers. The danger emerged that this concentration of press ownership in few hands would threaten the freedom of expressing opinion. Unlike in the 18th and 19th centuries, the key question was no longer censorship of publication by the government, but reduction in the private outlets through which individuals could express opinions.

18 Op cit, p 153.
19 See K Dyson, *The State Tradition* (Oxford 1980), pp 122-123.
20 J Carbonnier, *Flexible droit: pour une sociologie sans rigeur* (7th edn, Paris 1992), p 23.

In France, the Liberation Government passed an ordonnance of 26 August 1944 regulating publicity about press ownership and management. In addition a loi of 11 May 1946 created a public body, the Société national des Entreprises de Presse which was charged to distribute funds acquired through the confiscation of property of collaborators to fund the creation of new newspapers.[1] The job of the law here was to ensure transparency and to promote pluralism in the press. The trend continued with legislation in 1984 and in 1986,which imposed further restrictions on press ownership and created an authority charged with the regulation of the press and to handle complaints about the performance of the press. The French Criminal Code and the loi of 29 July 1881 on the freedom of the press have regulated deficiencies in what is published. Some publications, eg suicide of minors or interference with privacy, are punished by the Criminal Code. Other publications will give rise to a right of reply (art 13 of 1881 loi) and the right of rectification (art 14 of the same law). The law has the role here of being the organisation to punish abuses of press freedom as they affect the individual or the State.

There is a strong contrast with the United Kingdom. Since 1945, the issues of press ownership and the abuse of press freedom have been the subject of a number of official commissions.[2] But these commissions have not resulted in legislation. Even if their analysis of the social problems involved have been accepted, much as in France, the way of achieving change has been different. Industry self-regulation, albeit established under the threat of legislation, has been the route. A Press Council was instituted in 1949, composed of representatives of editors and external people nominated by the industry to examine issues of press concentration. In the absence of a formal common-law protection of privacy, the Calcutt Committee of 1990 suggested that there should be statutory protection. But the government preferred to use the report to make the Press agree to create a *Press Complaints Commission* which produces a range of codes of practice. The legal form of this self-regulation is contract, not statute. The role of the commissions is to make a determination according to contemporary opinions of what is appropriate, not to judge on the basis of precise legal norms.

In both countries, the regulation of the press is important. In the French framework, the law takes a central role, standing above the actors and imposing norms on them in the name of society. The solution is *le droit de la presse*. In England, the central feature of the framework is the self-regulation of the industry under pressure from the government and public opinion, essentially *le non-droit de la presse*.[3]

A further example would be the role of the criminal law, which is more frequently used to deal with professional and administrative failings. For example, prosecutors and judges have worked together in the mountain regions by using the criminal law

1 See J Rivero, *Les Libertés publiques*, (3rd edn 1983), vol 2, pp 206-207: whereas there were 402 daily newspapers in France in 1901, there were 239 in 1938, merely 142 in 1950 and 89 in 1973.

2 See *Royal Commission on the Press* (1949; Cm 7700); *Royal Commission on the Press* (1962; Cmnd. 1811); *Royal Commission on the Press* (1977; Cmnd 6810); *Report of the Committee on Privacy and Related Matters* (1990; Cm 1102). See generally, J Bell, (1998) 33 Rfdc 173-177.

3 See also J Bell, 'English Law and French Law – Not so different?' [1995] *Current Legal Problems* at pp 90-95, where I suggest that there has been a non-droit de la fonction publique in English law, and that issues of political corruption are dealt with by political rather than legal standards. In both areas, this contrasts with the use of the law in France.

(and to some extent civil liability) to force the local political and commercial interests to take action to protect skiers against the risk of avalanches. Somewhat controversially, they have intervened to suggest good practice as well as to sanction failings. In this, their actions have worked in parallel with the prefects who have also being trying to impose national standards on the local mayors and interests. Analysing this kind of intervention, Caille comments:

> One might question the appropriateness of the use of legal norms to regulate the tensions relating very largely to the mechanisms of the most usual politico-administrative collaboration, which exist in abundance in the mountain area. [But] one has to recognise that, in the minds of the relatives of the victims, ... the action of the judiciary accelerates and supports the reconfiguration of relationships between actors which have long been dominated by power.[4]

This use of the criminal law is seen also in relation to medical negligence. It is not uncommon for doctors to be prosecuted for medical negligence in cases that would, in England, give rise at most to professional disciplinary action.[5]

(3) French perceptions of law

French has three terms which are translated into English by 'law' – le droit, a total set of standards which can include notions of justice, la justice, meaning the legal system, and la loi, which more specifically means the legislation enacted by Parliament.

There are few studies into French popular legal culture, what the French citizen thinks of the law and how he or she acts towards it. The studies by Kourilsky have focused on associations between ideas among French adolescents. In her 1993 study, the association of the word 'la justice' among the French was overwhelmingly with the institutions of justice (courts, police etc) than with justice as a moral value, whereas the situation was reversed among the Russian adolescents.[6] In part, this reflects a scepticism that the institutions of justice actually achieve justice in France. The other images, more commonly shared with the Poles and Russians, are that law is associated with authority and power, and, to a lesser extent, with rights. Indeed, the three commonest associations with the word justice were the institutions of justice, judicial activity and loi, and all these represent authority.[7] If the researchers are right that these images are strongly influenced by discussion in families, then this provides some evidence of dominant images among the French.

Garapon[8] also suggests that the French conception of law is associated with authority. He contrasts the origins of the common law in spontaneous norms, growing up from customs among a community, with the continental conception of law as the

4 F Caille, 'L'action des magistrats dans la régulation des risques collectifs: l'exemple des sports de montagne' (2000) 44/45 *Droit et Société* 179.

5 See J Pennau, *La responsabilité du médecin* (Paris 1992), pp 99-103.

6 'Socialisation juridique et modèle culturel', p 221. The association with justice institutions ranged from 37% among the highest social class to 43% among the working class in France, but from 2% to 0% among the equivalent Russians. By contrast, the moral ideal of justice featured in 8% of responses from among the highest social class to 16% among the working class in France, but from 26% to 31% among the equivalent Russians.

7 Ibid.

8 A Garapon, 'Cultures judiciaires', unpublished manuscript, IHEJ, Paris 1999.

edicts of authority, be it the Prince or the State. Whatever the validity of this analysis of the history of the common law, the model is of interest for what it reveals as an insider's perception of the French system of law. Law is not about the protection of self-government, but about the provision by authority of justice. In such a model, there are reciprocal expectations – of justice for the citizen, and of respect for the State.

If the loi is supposed to be supreme as the authoritative source of norms within society, then it, and case law interpreting it, is meant to shape les moeurs (manners, moral opinions).[9] This gives law and the lawyer a major role in setting a climate for society, though this is a role which, traditionally at least, fell to the intellectual. In relation to a whole range of political and social problems, judges are being invited to lay down standards and the law is acting as the regulator of such issues.[10] In such cases, they are creatively interpreting the texts of loi.

But this traditional model of the law and the State is under challenge from changes in society. The Conseil constitutionnel has become the supervisor of the legislature and thus is, in some sense, superior to the organs of the State. It has stated clearly that the 'a voted loi ... only expresses the general will in respecting the Constitution'.[11] The Constitution, of which it is the guardian, now stands above the political game, and thus sets limits to decisions as to what constitutes the public interest. In Minc's phrase, the State has undergone *capitis diminutio*.[12] In addition, judges in this field, as elsewhere, are seen to be making the law, and thus rivalling the legislature and the political process as sources of authority. As will also be seen later, the politicians and administrators have become the subjects of judicial investigation, which has reinforced the image of la justice as a power.[13] Wright, among others, talked of the 'juridification' of the State and of the political process.[14] With the advent of European integration, traditional national élites and activities are having to adapt to the new context.[15] As we will see in the chapters on specific branches of law, the traditional model of the role of law in French society is undergoing change and, with it, the roles of the professional legal actors. This merely reinforces the idea that there is a dynamic and re-interpretative feature of tradition, and that notions of legal culture cannot be mothballed and preserved as museum exhibits. What is said about the French legal culture represents a snapshot which has a long history and, in some no doubt altered form, a long future.

9 See Jones, op cit, pp 42-43, citing Saleilles. I am grateful to Michel Troper for pointing out that the emphasis on loi is important here, even if one might also say that le droit has to adapt to social morality.

10 See B Joubert, 'Les nouveaux usages du droit dans la régulation politique' in J Comaille, L Dumoulin and C Robert (eds), *La juridicisation du politique. Leçons scientifiques* (Paris 2000) ch VII.

11 CC decision No 85-197 DC of 23 August 1985, *Elections in New Caledonia*, Rec 70 at p 76.

12 A Minc, *Au nom de la* loi (Paris 1998), p 25. For similar comments on the decline of the importance of the State, see Bernstein, op cit, ch 10 and E Suleiman, 'Change and Stability in French Elites' in G Flynn (ed), *Remaking the Hexagon. The New France in the New Europe* (Boulder 1995), pp 161-166.

13 Ibid, pp 31-36.

14 V Wright, 'The Fifth Republic: From *Droit de l'Etat* to the *Etat de droit*' (1999) 22 West European Politics 92.

15 See M-C Kessler, in F d'Arcy and L Rouban, *De la Ve République à l'Europe* (Paris 1996), pp 188-192.

(4) La loi

The Declaration of the Rights of Man and of the Citizen of 1789 gives a high status to loi. In art 6, it proclaims that 'Loi is the expression of the general will. All citizens have the right to participate in its creation, either personally or through their representatives.' The Declaration then continues by setting out a number of restrictions on freedoms which must be sanctioned by a loi. Symbolically, loi represents two ideas: democracy and national sovereignty. In art 3 of the Declaration, the principle of democracy is set out by the statement that 'The source of all sovereignty lies ultimately in the nation.' This principle is repeated in art 3 of the 1958 Constitution. In both cases, the idea of 'nation' appears as an associated idea. The body which exercises democratic power is the nation through the Constitution and through the organs granted legislative power.

French writers draw a distinction between the formal and the material meanings of loi. In a formal sense, a loi is a measure that has been passed by Parliament according to the procedures set out in the Constitution and in parliamentary standing orders. But in a material sense, 'one calls a loi any norm whose content has certain characteristics: for example to be general (that is to say to prescribe the conduct not of individuals identified by name, but of categories of individuals described abstractly) or to relate to certain subject-matter.'[16] On the whole, the French remain attached to a formal and organic conception, though with some changes since 1958.[17] In terms of legal culture, it is necessary not only to look to the definition, but also to the authority of loi and thus, as Malaurie and Aynès point out, it is necessary to recognise that 'It also has a moral character (it imposes, exposes or proposes a hierarchy of values on which it is based), is political (it is an exercise of power) and technical (it expresses itself by language and by concepts)'.[18]

Much of French constitutional and private-law thinking pre-dates the Constitution of 1958. The step change introduced by the Declaration of 1789 was to move the centre of power (and legitimacy) from the King and the Parlements to the legislature. Republican constitutions did not impose blocks on the exercise of the sovereign will of Parliament. There has been an elision in the status accorded to the product (la loi) and that of its creator (Parliament). Thus Hamon still argued in 1987 that 'The conflict between parliamentary sovereignty and popular sovereignty in France since the Liberation ... remained settled in favour of parliamentary sovereignty.'[19] The core of this was the identification of Parliament with the volonté générale.[20] The process of change in the recent period which Hamon identifies lies in the way the role of the State and the role of the protection of fundamental rights has been fitted into this. For leading writers like

16 G Burdeau, F Hamon and M Troper, *Droit constitutionnel* (26th edn, Paris 1999), p 115. In the 19th century, there was a strong tradition of thinking that believed in a higher principle of law than the loi of Parlement: see J Bonnecase, *La notion de droit en France au dix-neuvième siècle* (Paris 1920), esp p 41.

17 Ibid, pp 116-117; P Malaurie and L Aynès, *Droit civil – Introduction générale* (Paris 1994), pp 181-183.

18 Ibid, p 183.

19 L Hamon, *Les juges de la* loi (Paris 1987), p 73.

20 For an authoritative explanation of this point of view, see R Carré de Malberg, *La loi, expression de la volonté générale* (Paris 1931), esp p 115: 'Parliament ... is the qualified, habitual and permanent representative of the will of the national community.'

Jèze between the Wars, the greater status given to individual rights was a way in which the propertied classes could resist the general will expressed through Parliament.[1] For others, the sovereignty of loi was accepted, but all institutions which created the loi were subject to the limits on their constitutional powers and had to keep within them. Thus for Duguit and Eisenmann, judicial control of the constitutionality of legislation was a control over the institution which created it, rather than over the popular will.[2]

The Constitution of 1958 has established three important changes in the conception of loi. The first is that it has made clear that legislative power (in a material sense) is shared. Parliament has only competence to legislate on the areas specified in art 34 and the Executive has inherent power under art 37, as well as power delegated by parliament under art 38. The equation of Parliament and the volonté générale is further weakened by the occasional use of referenda under art 11 to approve lois or constitutional amendments. Second, under art 55 and the provision of title XIV on the European Union, France accepts that it must make duly ratified treaties and provisions of EC law prevail over a national loi. Thus, in a real sense, loi is restricted by the status of European and international agreements. National sovereignty has been restricted (as art 88-1 makes clear in relation to the EU) and with it the scope of national lois. The third restriction is the importance of fundamental rights as set out in the Declaration of the Rights of Man and of the Citizen of 1789 and the Preamble to the 1946 Constitution, as well as in the European Convention. These rights are now considered to restrict the domain of loi, rather than just to be matters that good legislator has in mind when exercising his powers.[3]

Despite these changes, the authority of loi remains very important both symbolically and in legal status. The concern of Carbonnier with the flood of lois in recent years has been the reduction in the role of loi as a solemn act to endorse a policy after reflection and debate.[4]

The status of loi may help to explain the suspicion which doctrinal writers show towards notions of *fairness* (l'équité) as the basis for judicial decisions. As a general notion, it is associated with judicial arbitrariness and the undermining the authority of the legislator.[5] Unlike justice (le juste) which is an external standard for judging the law[6] Unlike in German law, French law has not developed any general principle of 'fairness' or 'good faith'. Instead, 'équité' in art 1134 § 3 and art 1135 of the Civil Code

1 Hamon, p 75.

2 See L Duguit, *Traité de droit constitutionnel* (2nd edn, Paris 1923), t III, p 553; C Eisenmann, D 1938.3.1 at p 4.

3 Cf F Gény, 'De l'inconstitutionnalité des lois' JCP 1947. I. 613 at §4.

4 J Carbonnier, *Droit et passion de droit*, pp 107-113.

5 See E Agostini, 'L'équité' D 1978 Chr 7. The classic example, typically cited and criticised is the decision of juge Magneaud to acquit a poor woman stealing bread for her child on grounds of 'necessity': Amiens 22 April 1898, D.P. 1899.2.329 note Josserand. But see the *conclusions* of Premier avocat-général Cabannes to Cass ass plén 12 May 1989, D 1989, 377:

> You are judges, you are not legislators. Whether the statute seems to you to be just or unjust, you must ensure it is respected – that is your highest law!
>
> I do not claim in any way that you have not to concern yourselves with fairness, and your most developed legal techique, at the instigation of the authors of the Civil Code itself, often permits you to reconcile in harmony the scruples of a lawyer and the impulses of the heart.

serves as an open-ended concept that is filled in rather specific ways in particular areas of law. For instance, it serves as a point of reference for determining the obligations of the carrier of persons towards passengers.

A similar approach is seen in relation to 'public policy' (ordre public) in arts. 6 and 1134 of the Civil Code. In Malaurie's view, the legal concept of public policy is concerned with protecting the essential foundations of existing society, rather than developing society in new directions as the legislator seeks to do.[7] Now, the court may well have to decide issues on which no public authority has taken a formal decision about where the public interest lies. This was the case in the late 1980s on the topic of surrogate motherhood. The legality of associations set up to promote services in this area was the subject of decisions in both the Conseil d'Etat and the Cour de cassation at a time when there was no legislation.[8] Both courts sought to identify an emerging consensus among social institutions, especially the 1984 report of the National Consultative Committee on Ethics. The *conclusions* and *rapport* in the cases demonstrate clear awareness of divisions in social opinion, but judicial and doctrinal opinion were the main points of reference other than that 1984 report. The French decisions demonstrate a concern of the French courts to identify and formalise a consensus among social institutions about controversial social and moral questions.[9] This ensures that the courts do not appear idiosyncratic and usurping the legislator's role, but also reinforces their role within 'the establishment'.

These two areas of équité and ordre public illustrate that the French legal system is not self-contained. However detailed and numerous are the lois and règlements, the Civil Code (and other rules of French law) recognise the need for the law to be open to social normative orders more generally. This is for two reasons. In the first place, there is a need to supplement established legal prescriptions to cover new or undecided issues, and so open ended concepts such as équité and ordre public direct the judge or lawyer to other normative standards.[10] In the second place, as Alexy points out, legal reasoning is only a special case of general practical reasoning.[11] Although a legal argument does not have to be justified in absolute terms, but only in relation to the framework of the prevailing legal order, it does have to be tested against wider social norms, especially when the legal issue is novel or unclear.[12]

Although French doctrinal writing in modern times has adopted a model of the hierarchy of norms in which loi stands as the highest internal source of law, this model really needs revising given the plurality of normative and influential sources which now exist and which are depicted in Figure 2 overleaf. The Constitution, EU Law and

6 See *L'Utile et le juste* (1981) 26 *Archives de philosophie du droit.*

7 P Malaurie, *Les contrats contraires à l'ordre public* (Paris 1953), pp 38-41 and 52. See generally J Bell, 'Conceptions of Public Policy' in P Cane and J Stapleton, *Essays for Patrick Atiyah* (Oxford 1991), 87 at pp 89-91.

8 See CE Ass 22 Jan 1988, *Association les Cigones*, AJDA 1988, 163; Cass 1re civ, 13 Dec 1989, *Association Alma Mater c Procureur-général d'Aix en Provence* D 1990, 273, rapport Massip; Bell, 'Conceptions of Public Policy', pp 106-109.

9 Bell, 'Conceptions of Public Policy', p 110.

10 See more generally, C Perelman and R Vander Elst (eds), *Les notions à contenu variable en droit* (Brussels 1984), esp J Carbonnier, pp 99ff, J Ghestin pp 77ff and N MacCormick, pp 132ff.

11 R Alexy, *A Theory of Legal Argumentation* (Oxford 1989), pp 279 and 284-286.

12 See J Bell in Z Bankowski, I White and U Hahn, *Informatics and the Foundations of Legal Reasoning* (Dordrecht 1995), at pp 76-78.

Figure 2: The network of norms and the legal decisions

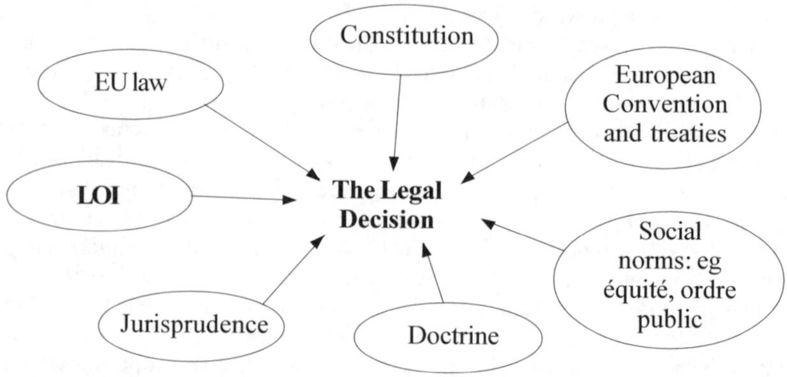

the European Convention are all obligatory sources, but the relationship between these norms and loi is not fully worked out, nor is it the same for all courts. Doctrine and social norms, such as équité and ordre public, are influential in different ways. Jurisprudence lies in between the obligatory sources and influential sources, since it is an authoritative interpreter of the former.[13] For this reason, some commentators now speak of a 'network' of norms, rather than a 'hierarchy'.[14] This feature of legal pluralism is often associated with the impact of globalisation.[15]

(5) Codes and codification

As was noted in the Preface, it is typically suggested that the spirit of codification has affected much of its attitude to law.[16] Malaurie has written:

> Codification – above all our Civil Code – has permeated deep into our national culture. The Civil Code is part of our national heritage, just like French-style gardens, the Palais of Versailles, Philippe de Champaigne or General de Gaulle. At stake in codification is our culture and our identity. The Civil Code has been more than the symbol of national unity ... The Civil Code is at the same time the cause, the witness and the consequence of our cultural unity.[17]

Inspiring and picturesque as a statement, this is only partly true. While interpretation of codes is a major part of the work of civil and criminal lawyers, the picture of the whole of the law is more complex. France has at least three types of provision which

13 See J Bell, S Boyron, and S Whittaker, *Principles of French Law*, ch 1.
14 See F Ost and M van de Kerchove, 'De la pyramide au réseau? Vers un nouveau mode de production du droit?' (2000) 44 *Revue interdisciplinaire d'études juridiques* 1.
15 See W Twining, *Globalisation and Legal Theory* (London 2000), pp 82-88 and 224-233.
16 Above, pp vi-vii.
17 P Malaurie, 'Les enjeux de la codification' AJDA 1997, 642.

are labelled 'codes'. In the first place, there are the original Napoleonic codes. These provided a synthesis of ideas from Romanist and customary traditions in France, rationalised by writers in the 17th and 18th centuries, with some Enlightenment principles adopted at the French Revolution.[18] Only the Code civil (1804) survives, though some provisions have been amended substantially. The second set of codes is similar in that they constitute a serious review and restatement of the law in a systematic and principled fashion. The best example is the new Code pénal of 1994, which was the product of many years in a ministerial committee and then in Parliament. The Nouvel code de procédure civil (1976), the Code de procédure pénal (1958) and the Code de commerce (1999) are similar, though criminal procedure is frequently amended. Thirdly, there are a number of consolidations of legislation which are labelled 'codes'. The Commission supérieure de codification was created in 1989 and has produced a number of systematic and coherently organised texts that restate existing provisions in a usable fashion. A good example is the Code de justice administrative (1999) which sets out the rules governing procedure in the administrative courts. But such administrative restatement has no power to change the substance of the law.

Although each of these kinds of codes provides a systematic and coherent structure to the law, only the first two represent a refashioning of the law at a single point in time, which can serve as a new departure for the law. It is this idea of a code as self-contained and a new departure that has been an important feature of the idea of codification. The other aspect to the idea of a code is a certain style of legislation. The provisions of the Code civil of 1804 and the Code pénal of 1994 deliberately state principles in short phrases, rather than the more detailed provisions which are found in administrative regulations. The style is to be succinct and inspiring, rather than to cover every eventuality. The point is made by comparing the provisions of the French Code pénal of 1994 on the criminal liability of corporations (art 121-2) with those of articles 30 and 31 of the English Law Commission's Draft Criminal code of 1989. The French provision is 105 words long (after the addition of a long section on the liability of local authorities). By contrast, the English provision is 594 words long. As has been pointed out by Dale, in England there is an attempt to make the text the sole point of reference for all issues. which might arise.[19] By contrast, the tradition stated by Portalis in 1799 was that:

> The task of legislation is to determine the general maxims of the law, taking a large view of the matter. It must establish principles rich in implications rather than descend into the details of every question which might possibly arise. The application of the law belongs to the judge and the lawyer, steeped in the general spirit of the legislation.

That style is not found even in all provisions of the Code civil,[20] nor in much more modern legislation. As a consequence, it cannot be stated that the French have a legislative style that permeates all legislation. Rather the systematic codes have a style of their own

18 See especially, J-L Halperin, *L'impossible code civil* (Paris 1992); A-J Arnaud, *Les origines doctrinales du code civil français* (Paris 1969); J Gordley, 'Myths of the French Civil Code' (1994) 42 Am Jo Comp Law 459.

19 On drafting style, see especially W Dale, *Legislative drafting: A new approach* (London 1977), ch 14; W Dale (ed), *British and French Statutory Drafting* (London 1988).

20 See, for example, the provisions on the rights of the usufructuary, such as in art 590.

that tries to return to basic principles. All the same, Codes are now divided according to the legislative competence of Parliament – legislative provisions (L) – and that of the government – regulatory provisions (R). The legislature has competence to lay down the principles of several branches of law, including the civil law. It can therefore leave the detail to be worked out by the administration The simplicity of some legislative provisions needs, therefore to be placed in the context of the more detailed provisions of regulatory law. For example, art R 39 of the Electoral Code contains detailed provisions on the size and weight of election material that is distributed free!

The more important feature is, therefore, the attitude to codification that French lawyers adopt. Nicholas observes:[1]

> Because French law, at least as presented in the *Code civil*, is a complete and internally coherent system, any part of which may ... illuminate any other part, and because the principles or rules are broadly formulated and therefore call for more elaborate ratiocination when they are applied, the French lawyer undoubtedly sets greater store by the intellectual coherence of his system and by the elegant manipulation of large-scale concepts than does his English counterpart.

This perspective is important, but one also has to bear in mind the importance of both case-law and standards outside the Code (such as ordre public and équité) which make the law less self-contained. Furthermore, the whole context of French law is now changing to embrace a greater variety of sources for legal norms.

(6) Forces for change in French law: European laws

In relation to the administration, Kessler argues that Europe has become a factor in breaking down the barriers between different parts of the civil service and in creating homogeneity as they work together on European agendas an in European institutions.[2] The same is even more the case in law, where Europe has changed the landscape and has set an agenda embraced fervently (if not by Gaullists).[3]

(a) The law of the European Union

Membership of the European Community was already agreed before the 1958 Constitution, but it was conspicuously silent on the matter and gave it no special status. The status of European Community law, especially the doctrine of direct effect developed in *Van Gend en Loos*[4] was based essentially on art 55 of the Constitution which gives ratified treaties a status higher than loi. The French government was for a long time ambivalent about the European Community. The Gaullists had opposed the Treaty of Rome in 1957 and had made provision in art 54 of the Constitution that a treaty could be referred to the Conseil constitutionnel to judge whether it was compatible with the Constitution. This was explicitly to prevent further encroachments on national sovereignty. In the post-De

1 B Nicholas, *The French Law of Contract* (2nd edn 1992), p 13.
2 In F d'Arcy (ed), *De la Ve République à l'Europe* (Paris 1996), p 188.
3 J Ardagh, *France in the New Century*, pp 678-679.
4 Case 26/62 [1963] ECR 1.

Gaulle era and especially with the election of the pro-European, non-Gaullist President Giscard d'Estaing in May 1974, the political mood changed. This readier acceptance of being fully in Europe was reflected in the decision of the Cour de cassation in 1975 which explicitly gave priority to a provision of the Treaty of Rome over a later French loi in the field of customs duties.[5] This 'internationalist ethic' which the avocat-général attributed to the writers of the 1946 and 1958 Constitution was not shared by the Conseil d'Etat. In a decision of 1968, it had given priority to a national loi over contrary EEC legislation.[6] This was reinforced more solemnly in 1978 when the Conseil quashed a reference to the ECJ made by the lower court to determine whether a decision taken in application of clear French law was compatible with the EEC Treaty.[7] This was contrary to established case-law of the European Court of Justice on the rights of individuals to challenge administrative decisions conflicting with EC directives in the courts of Member States. But with a change of generation among the senior personnel of the Conseil and a clear political consensus emerging on Europe among the main political parties, a sea-change in attitude occurred in 1989. In *Compagnie Alitalia*,[8] the Conseil d'Etat laid down the principle that the Prime Minister had a duty to withdraw règlements that were contrary to EC directives. Subsequently in *Nicolo*,[9] the Conseil d'Etat decided that it was willing to accept an argument that the provisions of the EC Treaty prevailed over subsequent and contrary national loi (even though it did not have to apply it in that case). It did hold in cases in the following few years that EC regulations and directives prevailed over subsequently enacted national lois.[10] In reaching its decision, the Conseil d'Etat was influenced by the change of position by the Conseil constitutionnel which decided in 1988 that it would give priority to EC law over national law in an election case.[11]

The position was settled by the constitutional amendment of 1992, made to give effect to the Treaty of Maastricht. Article 88-1 of the Constitution now provides that the Republic shall participate in the European Communities and the European Union and exercise its competence according to the treaties. Article 88-2 specifically accepts a limitation of sovereignty. All the same, the separateness of the European legal order is not explicitly accepted.[12] Given the alignment of the national courts to the priority of EU Law over national lois, this outcome is actually quite secure. Only the Conseil constitutionnel will not test the validity of lois passed by Parliament against treaties, only against the Constitution.

The more interesting question is not whether the French courts will apply EC legislation, but whether they will seek inspiration from it. Well, in the first place, the

5 Ch mixte 24 May 1975, *Société Cafés Jacques Vabre*, D 1975, 497 concl Touffait.

6 CE 1 March 1968, *Syndicat général des fabricants de semoules de France*, D 1968, 285, note M-L, concl Questiaux.

7 CE Ass 22 December 1978, *Cohn-Bendit* D 1979, 155, conl Genevois, note Pacteau.

8 CE Ass 3 February 1989, RFDA 1989, 391 concl Chahid-Nourai, note Beaud and Dubois.

9 CE Ass 20 October 1989, RFDA 1989, 824 concl Frydman, note Genevois; AFT Tatham. 'Effects of European Community Directives in France: the Development of the Cohn-Bendit Jurisprudence' (1991) 40 ICLQ 907.

10 CE 24 September 1990, *Boisdet*, AJDA 1990, 863; CE Ass 28 February 1992 *SA Rothmans* and *SA Philip Morris*, AJDA 1992, 210. See also CE Ass 30 October 1996, *SA Cabinet Revert et Badelon*, RFDA 1997, 1056, conc Goulard.

11 Decision of 21 October 1988, *5e circonscription du Val d'Oise*, AJDA 1989, 128.

12 See S Boyron, 'The Maastricht Treaty and the Revision of the French Constitution' (1993-94) 16 Hold LR 62.

avis procedure, which the Cour de cassation and the Conseil d'Etat have adopted, has been modelled in part on the reference procedure used in relation to EC law under art 234 of the TEU. But there is limited evidence of the influence of EC principles in reshaping French law outside the areas in which it is directly applicable.[13]

(b) The European Convention on Human Rights

The European Convention on Human Rights and Fundamental Freedoms has been described by Braconnier as 'a legal earthquake' because of its focus on individual rights, which will cause the French to reassess both their conceptual structures and values in public law.[14] In his speech at the beginning of 2000, the President of the Cour de cassation remarked similarly that:

> Within the judicial order, it is under the impetus of [the higher law] and by a mechanism of law creation identical to the method of development in the Common Law, that the Cour de cassation as national judge reconstructs internal law on the basis of community law or the law of the Convention by changing it profoundly.[15]

In 1995 there were 1,620 applications against France and, in 1996, 2,175, only 128 of which were referred to the French government for comment.[16]

(i) Impact on the judicial role Judges are given a greater role through the European Convention. The current hierarchy of norms is not the same for all judges. For the Conseil constitutionnel, the national constitution takes priority over treaties, and it refuses to judge national legislation to be incompatible with treaties, including the Convention. Compatibility with the constitution is sufficient. By contrast, civil and administrative judges apply article 55 of the Constitution under which they have to give priority to ratified treaties over national law. This gives the civil judge has a new status.

In *Zielinsky v France*,[17] the Strasbourg court declared as contrary to the Convention a loi voted to validate what the courts had declared unlawful. In this case 36 employees successfully brought actions against the Strasbourg region's social security authorities for having reduced an allowance due to them. While the appeal from the lower courts to the Cour de cassation was pending, Parliament voted a law validating the actions of the social security authorities and the employees lost the case before the Cour de cassation. The Conseil constitutionnel[18] had considered that the legislator had justified the retrospective legislation by reference to the public interest – the economic impact

13 See J-C Bonichot, 'Le droit communautaire et le droit administratif français' AJDA, *Special Issue*, 20 June 1996, 15.

14 S Braconnier, *Jurisprudence de la Cour européenne des droits de l'homme et droit administratif français* (Brussels 1997), p 505.

15 Guy Canivet, Audience de rentrée, 6 January 2000, from Cour de cassation website, Annual Report for 1999.

16 R de Gouttes, 'La Convention européenne des droits de l'homme et le juge français' (1999) 51 RIDC 7 at p 8.

17 ECHR 28 October 1999, RFDA 2000, 289.

18 Cf CC decision No 93-332DC of 13 January 1994, Rec 21, considérants 13 and 14 which notes that the bill did not deprive people of rights where judgments had been given but was a legitimate exercise of power to take decisions in the public interest to deal with divergences in the case law of courts which could disturb the balance of the social security budget,

of the lower courts decisions, and the potential divergence in the case law of lower courts. The Conseil did not go behind the assessment of the public interest by the legislator, but was essentially deferential to the separation of powers. By contrast, the Strasbourg court did not consider that the public interests in question were sufficient to deprive the litigants of their vested rights.

Now, in theory, this approach of the ECHR, frees the civil and administrative courts to challenge the validity of legislation and even of the Constitution. So far, neither the Conseil d'Etat nor the Cour de cassation has been willing to go down this road.[19]

(ii) Impetus for legal reform In criminal law and procedure, perhaps more than in other branches of French law, it is important to recognise that the law is no longer a purely national matter. Especially in the last 10–15 years, criminal procedure has been reshaped in the light of the European Convention. This was precisely the mission conferred on the Delmas-Marty commission. As Pradel suggests, the 'wind from Strasbourg is blowing increasingly strongly' and the Cour de cassation is increasingly basing decisions on it.[20]

As will be seen in Chapter 4, the reforms of criminal procedure in June 2000 represent a strong influence of the European Convention on the treatment of the suspect under investigation. The Convention appears in the reports which preceded them and in the introductions made by the Minister of Justice, Elisabeth Guigou. But, when one digs deeper, one sees that the Convention is useful support for what one might describe as the 'liberal' wing of French opinion, and is used to resist the views of the traditionally strong authoritarian wing of political opinion. Many of the reforms which have finally seen the light of day in the 2000 loi were proposed by the Donnedieu de Vabres report in 1949 – for example, the separation of the juge de l'instruction and the juge des libertés. Some were even voted by the Socialist Parliament in 1993, only to be overturned by the conservative majority later in the same year.[1] The Convention serves as a way of closing the political options in internal debate.

(iii) Judicial case developments Both supreme courts have taken the European Convention increasingly seriously.The Conseil d'Etat only referred to the Convention in 24 cases between 1981 and 1983, but in 1996 alone it referred to it in 851 decisions. The Cour de cassation has appointed an academic, Mme Koering-Julien to the Chambre criminelle in order to improve its understanding of the Convention. From observation, the Convention and its implications are a normal and natural part of everyday legal procedures throughout the French legal system. There has been a change in emphasis from the Jacobin state of the past.[2]

As will be seen in Chapter 5, the Conseil d'Etat has applied the Convention as a ground for changing the existing law and it has been the guiding influence in developing

19 CE Ass.30 October 1998, *Sarran* RDP 1999,919; Cass ass plén 2 June 2000, *Fraisse*, D 2000, 865 note Mathieu and Verpeaux; X Prétot, 'La Cour de cassation, la Constitution et les traités' RDP 2000, 1037.

20 J Pradel, 'La procédure pénale française à l'aube du troisième millénaire' D 2000 Chr 1.

1 See below, pp 126-128. The same was done by Mitterand in relation to the death penalty. His internal abolition of the death penalty was sealed by signing up to the protocol to the European Convention before the right-wing could get back into power.

2 See D Salas, *Le tiers pouvoir. vers une autre justice* (Paris 1998), part 1.

some general principles of law.[3] Similarly, the Cour de cassation has relied on it, particularly in criminal matters.[4] But there are sometimes divergences between the interpretations of the Convention offered by the two supreme courts.[5] The Conseil constitutionnel had also been influenced by the Convention to develop the right of freedom of expression into a right of the recipients of information to transparency and pluralism in the media.[6]

In a number of important cases, it has been the conduct of the police that has been the subject of censure from the Strasbourg court.[7] But a much larger number of cases involve delay in the handling of cases through the courts. In this area, France has been forced to undertake reforms, often through judicial initiative to speed up justice, for example by using single judge courts. More controversially, the procedure of the highest courts has come under attack from Strasbourg.

The advocate-general in French procedures is a member of the judiciary and is considered part of the judicial team. In preparing decisions for hearing, the advocate-general will be at the preliminary hearing within the court (séance d'instruction) where several judges discuss the file. The advocate-general has to speak in the name of the law and will be responsible for regrouping similar cases to ensure that the law is advanced by the judicial decision. He will speak in open court at the end of the speeches by the parties or their lawyers. He does not remain for the deliberation.[8] Another judge will be reporter on the file and will produce the draft judgment as well as a commentary. This is only read to the court in private session as it deliberates. There are thus three parts to the judicial team – the rapporteur, who has researched the file and drawn up the draft decision, the advocate-general who presents arguments from the public interest to advance the law, and then the rest of the court who deliberate and vote.

The European Court of Human Rights adopted a different analysis of the proceedings. In its view, there are three parties (as at Luxembourg): plaintiff, defendant and the public interest. In some recent decisions, the ECHR seemed to undermine

3 See Brown and Bell, pp 225-227; J-P Flauss, in J Schwarze, *Administrative Law under European Influence* (London 1996), pp 31ff. See generally below, p 179.

4 See below, p 130.

5 A good example of the use of the Convention is CE 18 October 2000 *Terrail* AJDA 2001, 288. In this case, the Conseil d'Etat held that a quango – the Conseil supérieur de la Magistrature – was not a 'court' within art 6 §1 and was not dealing with civil or criminal matters when it was disciplining a judge who had published anti-semitic statements in an article. This contrasts with the Cour de cassation's decision in relation to the disciplinary functions of the Conseil de l'ordre des avocats: Cass 1re civ, 23 May 2000, AJDA 2000, 762 obs Sargos. But in general the courts try to adopt similar positions: compare their views on the application of art 6 § 1 of the Convention to regulatory quangos: CE Sect 20 October 2000, *Sté Habib Bank Ltd*, AJDA 2000, 1071 which comes into line with the views of the Cour de cassation: Cass ass plén, 5 February 1999, *Commission des opérations de Bourse c Oury* D 1999 Somm 249.

6 See below, p 232.

7 ECHR 28 July 1999 *Selmouni v France*, D 2000 Somm. 179 (torture); ECHR 27 Aug. 1992 *Tomasi v France*, D 1993 Somm. 383 (police brutality).

8 Where there are no parties present and the judges do not wish to separate the hearing from the deliberation, the avocat-général may well be invited to remain in the room during the deliberation, but he takes no part in the discussion or decision. This procedure is in marked contrast to the role of the commissaire du gouvernement in the administrative courts who is present and takes part in deliberation, but has no vote in the decision.

fundamentally the basis on which the Cour de cassation and the Conseil d'Etat have organised their procedures for the last 200 years. In two decisions, *Slimane Kaïd v France* in 1998 and 2000,[9] the ECHR condemned France for a failure by the advocate-general and the rapporteur to communicate their arguments to the avocat of the defendant before the hearing. There had developed an informal practice of avocats ringing up the advocate-general and asking for some hint of the line of argument he will pursue before the court. But there was no formal requirement that these are communicated. The practice that the rapporteur's note had been communicated to the advocate-general, but not to the avocat of the party was considered by the Strasbourg court as against the equality of arms. In a further case, it was held that the unrepresented appellant must be treated the same as the avocat à la Cour de cassation in terms of notification and access to the arguments of the avocat-général.[10] In the face of this case law, the Conseil d'Etat has dug in its heals and argued that the commissaire du gouvernement is completely independent and is a judge like all the other members of the court, and so is, in material respects, different from the avocat-général in the Cour de cassation.[11] By contrast, the Cour de cassation has reformed some of its procedures. But there is a sense of grievance that the 'exception française' has not been recognised as achieving equal justice as other legal systems.

Similarly, some well-established legal principles have been overturned.[12] Thus, for the legal system as a branch of government, it is arguable that the European Convention poses the greatest threat as well as the greatest opportunity for an enhanced status for judicial power.

9 ECHR 31 March 1998, *Reinhardt and Slimane Kaïd v France*, D. 1999, 281. ECHR 25 January 2000 *Slimane Kaïd v France*, D 2000 Somm 186.

10 ECHR 8 February 2000, *Voisine v France*, D 2000, 651 note Thierry; but see Cass 1re civ, 10 May 2000, D 2000, 645 where the Cour de cassation upheld the rules on requiring representation by avocat.

11 See CE 29 July 1998, *Esclatine*, D 1999, 85 concl. Chauvaux; V Haïm, 'Le commissaire du gouvernement et le respect du contradictoire' D 1999 Chr 201.

12 See ECHR 23 November 1993, *Poitrimol v France* and ECHR 29 July 1998, *Omar and Guérin v France*; De Gouttes, p 18.

Chapter 3

Civil law

Civil law ('droit civil') covers the relations between individuals. But it has an importance within French law, which Malaurie articulates well:[1]

> What gives the civil law its importance is not only its continuity [with Roman law], but the scope of its application and above all its perfection.
>
> The scope of its application: the civil law has as its subject-matter all the daily relationships of human beings, the relationships which individuals have with each other.
>
> Above all, what confers its value is its perfection, to such an extent that it is the common law ... That the civil law is the common law signifies that all other branches are exceptions, that is to say a body of derogations from the civil law. Commercial law or maritime law are defined by their subject matter; they only apply within the limits of their field. The civil law applies, in principle, to all relationships of private law; for it to be otherwise, a special law must be enacted for the subject in question. Even then, if the special law does not contain any specific rule on a particular question, the civil law must apply ... The civil law is thus a very important law, because it provides the general principles which inspire all the other branches of private law and even of public law: it is the common trunk of all branches of law.

A. CORE ACTIVITIES

As Malaurie states, the civil law is concerned with relationships between private individuals. By contrast administrative law and criminal law are concerned with relationships between individuals and the State. Now, unlike in constitutional law and administrative law, the subjects of civil law are not typically creatures of the law. The dynamics of personal and business relationships does not depend primarily upon the law. Cohabitation provides an excellent example of a situation created by individual initiative that the law then subsequently tries both to regulate and to redress problems arising from it. The same is true of contract. That said, there is in France often a plethora of administrative and legislative rules and regulations that govern economic

1 P Malaurie and L Aynès, *Droit civil – Introduction générale* (by P Malaurie 1994-95 edn, Paris 1994), p 51.

and other relationships. For example, the research by Sayag on car distribution demonstrated that there was more legal regulation compared with English law, but that this resulted mainly from public law regulation.[2] In these sorts of situation, the role of civil law can be seen as twofold – it can provide a structure within which people can organise their affairs and it can provide a set of remedies when the deal goes wrong. But there is a clear hierarchy. As described by one member of the Cour de cassation, litigation is 'pathological', it represents the extreme case of failure. For the most part, the civil law does not produce its effects in court, but in the offices of the avocat or the notaire, if not in society at large.

In terms of structuring relationships, as Hart described it, the law sets out a set of power-conferring rules.[3] Perhaps best described by MacCormick as 'institutions',[4] the law offers a set of optional frameworks (contract, gift, sale, lease etc) with some predetermined rules. If you want to make a sale, then you must agree on the subject-matter to be transferred in return for the price, and the law will impose a certain number of obligations, eg as to title or hidden defects. The individual can be guided through these well-established frameworks by legal advisers or can work it out for himself.

The function of the law in this context is to establish the rules that can be used by the citizens and their lawyers in order to plan activities to take advantage of the options which the law creates or avoid those it precludes. The functions of lawmaking and authoritative interpretation of the law become central to achieving this. Although, in theory, the primary responsibility for establishing these frameworks lies with the legislator, this presupposes a far greater level of intervention than actually exists. As will be seen in the case study below, significant aspects of the law can continue for decades without legislative intervention. Even in areas where the legislator has acted, there will only be the basic statement of principles, which need to be fleshed out by interpretation. The roles of doctrinal legal writing (*la doctrine*) and case law (*la jurisprudence*) are critical to the elaboration and development of the rules which create and regulate the legal institutions of private law.

The judge also has to perform the task of resolving disputes that arise. Many disputes are brought to the civil courts. Sayag demonstrated that in car distribution, recourse to the courts (and thus reporting of decisions) was more frequent than in England.[5] Recourse to the courts was not an activity after a relationship had come to an end, but could be a way of sorting out an ongoing relationship. Obtaining a ruling, especially by way of référé, is seen as a tactic for taking the relationship forward, as well as for obtaining a remedy to a particular grievance. That suggests that the judge is invoked frequently to resolve civil law disputes. If one looks at the numbers of cases arising before the courts, then it is clear that most of their time is spent as a registration board in formalising outcomes which the parties do not contest. For example, over half the divorces are uncontested, [6] many decisions at the tribunal d'instance deal with the management of the affairs of adults or children incapable of managing their own affairs,[7]

2 See D Harris and D Tallon, *Contract Law Today* (Oxford 1989), p 336, 350-355, 373.
3 HLA Hart, *The Concept of Law* (2nd edn, Oxford 1994), pp 27-28, 283-285.
4 DN MacCormick and O Weinberger, *Law as Institutional Fact* (Dordrecht 1986), ch 2, esp pp 64-67.
5 Harris and Tallon, pp 371-373, 392-393.
6 About 55%: see *Annuaire statistique de la Justice 2000*, pp 79 and 80.
7 In 1998, some 121,998 cases: ibid, pp 37 and 39.

most cases of sale or lease are about non-payment of the price or rent.[8] In these cases, there is little that the court has to decide except to give judgment as requested. Similarly, there are many cases of référé. Disputed cases remain a significant number, and most of these will turn on facts which are submitted to the judge and which do not require guidance on the law. If we compare the number of decisions of the Cour de cassation compared with those at first instance,[9] we can see that significant rulings on a point of law are small – less than 1 decision of the Cour de cassation for every 100 heard at first instance.

In terms of remedies, the courts are far less active than in criminal or administrative law. The judicial role in France is reactive in civil matters. There is no investigation conducted into the facts, as by the criminal or administrative judge. The judge does control the process by deciding whether the case is *en état* and by setting the case down for hearing when (s)he considers that it is ready. But the activity is really in the field of case-management, rather than in the field of dispute resolution. The parties bring the case and its issues to the judge, who will decide on the basis of what they have included in the file. Of course she will investigate the law, but interviews make it clear that the judicial role is to decide the issues that the parties want deciding. The lawyers will attempt to reach a solution, and there will be conciliators on hand at first instance to intervene, if the parties want. Of course, where parties are unassisted by lawyers, then the judge may have to take an active role in the management of the hearing and in clarifying the claims of the parties. But, observation and discussion with judges and lawyers would suggest that civil law judges are less happy to restructure the application than their criminal law brethren.

B. INSTITUTIONAL SETTING

(1) The authority of case law[10]

(a) Formally, not an authority

The status of case law is ambiguous in civil matters. Formally, following the experience with the parlements, judges were forbidden from making arrêts de règlement (general rules)[11] As a result, the decisions are not formally binding, except in the case of decisions of the Assemblée plénière which decides in a case which has been the subject of divergence between the Cour de cassation and the cour d'appel to which the case was remitted, or in conflicts among the lower courts. But even this arrangement, which has existed since 1837, does not formally make the ruling binding in subsequent cases. For that reason, case law is described as 'une autorité' (albeit a privileged authority), but not binding.[12]

8 Before the tribunal d'instance 72.6% of sale cases and 61.9% of lease cases fall into this category: ibid, p 49.

9 Above, pp 26-27 and 29.

10 See generally, M Troper and C Grzegorczyk, in D Neil MacCormick and Robert S Summers, *Interpreting Precedents* (Aldershot 1997), ch 4 (hereafter 'Troper and Grzegorczyk').

11 Art 12, loi 16-24 August 1790; art 5 Civil Code.

12 See J Carbonnier in J Dainow (ed), *The Role of Judicial Decisions and Doctrine in the Civil Law* (Notre Dame UP 1971), 91 at p 97.

According to many, the golden age of case law is in the past, particular in the period 1910 to 1940.[13] A major role of the Cour de cassation is to ensure the consistency of judicial decisions across the country. Being the only national court, it has a role of imposing a degree of uniformity among the lower courts.[14]

(b) An authority in fact

Doctrinal literature has always struggled to state the legitimacy of case law development. In the end, it has had to admit that policy decisions have to be made to keep the law up to date, but that the judges have to work within the conceptual structure which they inherit from the Code.[15] To this extent, there is an important distinction between original interpretation, which implies an ability to lay down rules, and derived interpretation, which tries to apply them to new circumstances. Though not a tight distinction, this does offer some limits to judicial development of the law.[16] Boulanger notes that the institutional continuity of the judiciary facilitates some form of judicial development of the law.[17] Certainly, as he remarks, the reality is that judges (and commentators) will frequently use the words of a judicial decision as if it were the text of a loi and interpret it in a similar way.[18] Carbonnier notes the importance of judicial habits and the meeting of citizens' expectations.[19] There is a natural tendency to refer back to decisions made in the past. But there is, more importantly, a desire not to disappoint the expectations of practitioners and litigants based on previous decisions. Such expectations are particularly important in private law where people are likely to plan their affairs in the light of the law.

All the same, it is clear that the decisions of the Cour de cassation have come to acquire a status of an authority within the legal community. As Serverin points out, the writings of academics at the end of the 19th century and especially the commentaire d'arrêt served to treat the decisions of courts as a source of legal norms and to reinforce a very normative conception of law.[20] Furthermore this is reinforced by the practitioners of the law. Although cases are only, at least formally, illustrations of the Code, in practice, even in civil law, there is an acceptance of the concept of 'a leading case', such that particular lines of legal principle are commonly described by reference to the leading case which established them.[1] A multiplicity of indicators are used by the informed reader to determine the importance given to its decision by the Cour de cassation.[2] Thus the formation of the Cour matters.

13 P Malaurie, 'Droit civil' (1980) *Travaux de l'Association Henri Capitant*, 81.

14 J Ghestin and G Goubeaux, *Traité de droit civil – Introduction* (Paris 1977), § 445.

15 See generally S Belaid, *Essai sur le pouvoir créateur du juge* (Paris 1974).

16 See A-J Arnaud, 'Le médium et le savant: singification politique de l'interprétation juridique' (1972) Archives de philosophie du droit 165.

17 J Boulanger, 'Notations sur le pouvoir créateur de la jurisprudence civile' (1961) 59 RTDCiv 417.

18 Ibid, p 426.

19 J Carbonnier, *Droit et passion de droit sous la Ve République*, p 57; Troper and Grzegorczyk, p 118.

20 See E Serverin, *De la jurisprudence en droit privé. Théorie d'une pratique* (Lyon 1985), pp 171-173; Troper and Grzegorczyk, pp 123 and 129.

1 Troper and Grzegorczyk, pp 131-132.

2 For a full discussion in a framework which makes comparison possible with other legal systems, see Troper and Grzegorczyk, pp 119-125.

The Assemblée plénière is called upon when there is a matter of principle to decide, and the chambre mixte resolves conflicts between different Chambers of the Cour. But there will also be an importance attached to decisions of a full Chamber, as opposed to a section. In other words, the internal practices of the Cour select out important decisions for resolution by the more solemn formations of the Cour (and the same is true for the lower courts). A second feature which serves as a signal is the basis of the appeal. If the complaint is about the misinterpretation of the law or the failure to give facts the right legal classification, this provides the Cour with an opportunity to state a rule. On the other hand, merely to sanction the lower court for failure to respond to a ground relied upon by one of the parties is only an act of discipline of the judges below. The formulation of the statement of law will also be a key to the significance of a decision. If the ruling is general and abstract, this will be taken as an attempt to lay down the law in a way that a more specific analysis of the facts of the case will not.[3] The Cour de cassation also engages in the selection of its own decisions for publication. On the basis of their 'legal interest', the more significant decisions of each Chamber are published in the *Bulletin de la Cour de cassation*.[4] Private law reports also operate their own selection between decisions to be published in full, and those only in summary. The former amount to about 100 decisions of the Cour de cassation a year in each journal, with perhaps a further 50 civil and criminal cases from other courts. This provides a significant selection undertaken by a combination of the judges and the editors of law reports (often assisted by academics and practitioners).[5] The important cases are identified and published, while the rest will, at best, appear as summaries or in databases. There are thus ways of the leading cases becoming identified. Once identified, they come into wide circulation and discussion.

(c) *Relations with the legislator*

In more recent years, the Cour de cassation has used its annual report both to highlight its major decisions (perhaps 20 a year) and to recommend to the government some desirable changes in the law.[6] But there are instances where the court uses its judicial functions to make changes itself[7] and to force the hand of the legislator.[8] The best example of the latter was the *Desmares* decision of 1982. There had been discussion since the 1960s about the need for a no-fault scheme for motor vehicle accidents. The legislator had not acted, but the courts gradually developed no-fault liability for things under art 1384 § 1 of the Civil Code to provide a regime for vehicle accidents. In the *Desmares* case in 1982,[9] the Cour de

3 Ibid, pp 275-279.
4 Ibid, p 329.
5 Ibid, pp 341-350.
6 Discussed in J Déprez, 'A propos du Rapport Annuel de la Cour de cassation, «sois juge et tais-toi»' (1978) 77 RTDCiv 503.
7 Boulanger describes the law on liability for things based on art 1384 § 1 as 'a real skyscraper built on a pinhead': op cit, p 431.
8 Déprez, p 354 sees this as inevitable, but there have been criticisms from others: see , for example, O Dupeyroux, 'La jurisprudence, source abusive du droit' *Mélanges Maury* (Paris 1960), vol II, 349 at p 377.
9 Cass 2ème civ, 21 July 1982, D 1982, 449 concl. Charbonnier, note Larroumet. See generally A Tunc, 'It is wise not to take the Civil Codes too seriously. Traffic accident compensation in France' in P Wallington and RM Merkin (eds), *Essays in memory of Professor FH Lawson* (London 1986), 71.

cassation held that the driver could not be exonerated by the fault of the victim unless this amounted to force majeure. So pedestrians who were not looking where they were going were not to be treated as contributing to their own loss. The case forced the hand of the legislator who produced a loi on road traffic accidents in 1985.[10] Given the difficulty of finding either the time or political will to achieve reform of the civil law through Parliament, the courts are often forced into partial solutions. As avocat-général Charbonnier argued in this case:

> The fact that you cannot reform the whole law of delict in one go is no reason for not improving it as far as you can without further delay. In fact you will perhaps facilitate the task of the legislator.[11]

Similarly, judicial refusal to act can be the trigger for legislation. In 1997, the Cour de cassation refused to treat a homosexual partner as a spouse for the purpose of succession to a tenancy, despite the arguments of the avocat-général Weber. The latter argued that it was for the courts to achieve the desirable state of the law by an imaginative interpretation. The Cour de cassation, supported by some members of la doctrine, argued that this was a step too far. As a reaction, the government was forced to bring about legislation to cover the issue that was more wide-ranging (especially in regard to the administrative procedures involved) and introduced the pacte civil de solidarité (PACS).[12] In both the *conclusions* and the *note* to the case, there is a wide-ranging discussion of social developments, not limited to legislative texts and judicial decisions, but including reference to comparative law and to internet sites operated by associations promoting homosexual rights. There was also a recognition that the sections of the legislature (mainly Socialists) were keen to act to achieve the rights of homosexuals, but that this had been unsuccessful in 1993 because the Conseil constitutionnel had struck down the provision for breach of parliamentary procedure. As a result, the avocat-général suggested that a failure of the judges to act would bring about legislative reform.[13] All the same, he argued in favour of developing the law by interpreting the term 'concubin notoire' to include homosexuals by refusing to insist on a restriction to heterosexuals which was not specifically mentioned in the text of the 1989 loi. Such an approach ran contrary to what Weber himself described as the 'quasi-unanimity' of judicial opinion and part of doctrinal opinion for whom 'concubine' referred linguistically and traditionally only to unmarried, heterosexual relationships. But he argued that 'one of the most noble missions of our Court is to interpret texts in relation to the development of the society to whom they apply'. Furthermore, the impact would be limited since the decision came from a formation of the Cour de cassation concerned with leases, rather than from a higher formation.[14] All the same, the Cour de cassation itself preferred to apply the established approach and to refuse to extend legal protection to homosexuals in the absence of express provisions, as it had done in 1989 when considering the regulations of Air France and social security

10 See J Bell, S Boyron, and S Whittaker, *Principles of French Law*, pp 382-386.
11 D 1982, at p 451 (trans. D. Pugsley, *The Strange Case of the Exploding Motorbike* (Tiverton 1991), p 10).
12 Cass. 3e civ, 17 December 1997, *Vilela c Mme Weil*, D 1998, 111 concl Weber, note Aubert.
13 See D 1998 at p 113.
14 Ibid, right-hand column.

law.[15] There was thus a clear view about the appropriate scope of judicial legal development in areas of social controversy in which Parliament took an active interest and was only prevented from acting by divergence of political opinion.

(d) The style of judgments

The idea of the impersonal judge who does not give transparent reasons has been criticised for most of the 20th century.[16] Judges have been required to give reasons for their decisions since the loi of 20 April 1810. But the style adopted combines the traditional medieval recital of 'attendus' with a brief summary of the facts.[17] There is a recourse to tradition in the approach. The result is that the decision hides many of the contentious arguments which have been considered by the judges and which lead them to their solution. As Touffait and Tunc argued, legal reasoning which sought to be convincing would have to engage with the economic and social consequences of the decision taken and the rule laid down.[18] In more recent years, the lower courts have been empowered to make their decisions even more uninformative in order to enable them to deliver more decisions. Since 1999, art 455 NCPCiv (as amended) permits the summary of the arguments of the parties to be replaced by a simple reference to the documents filed with the court (but to which the reader of the judgment has no access). This makes it even harder for lawyers to make use of previous cases as guides for the future. There is, however, a much fuller expression of opinion during the private deliberation between the judges, where a much wider range of opinions appear.[19]

(e) Limitations on lawmaking by civil judges

The law-making role of case law is, however, limited. To begin with, the parties define the issues to be raised and the judge only has freedom of manoeuvre in categorising the facts or in (rare) situations in which she can raise an issue of law *ex officio* (and that only after hearing both sides). More importantly, many of the cases presented to the lower courts are référé decisions where there is an *ex parte* application for a remedy, rather than a discussion of a disputed point of law. In relation to the Cour de cassation, one has to distinguish between *discipline*, sanctioning the failure by the lower court to apply established rules of law, and *jurisprudence* where the court is creating new rules or changing old ones to deal with deficiencies in the law. As Severin points out, the courts are also limited by the choices of editors in the publicity that they give to decisions.[20]

15 Cass soc 11 July 1989, *Rapport Annuel de la Cour de cassation 1990* (Paris 1990), pp 96ff.
16 See E Lambert, 'Codified law and case law' in E Bruncken and LB Register, *Science of Legal Method* (New York 1921) at p 273.
17 On the style of judgments before the revolution, see R Jacob, 'La décision judiciaire en Europe dans la perspective de l'histoire comparée. Eléments de synthèse' (1996) 17 *Droit et Société* 397 at pp 408-410.
18 A Toufait and A Tunc, 'Pour une motivation plus explicite des décisions de justice', RTDCiv 1974,487, at p 503.
19 See 'La méthodologie du délibéré', a conference in 1994 on the ENM website.
20 See above, p 68.

In a 1993 colloquium, members of the Cour de cassation and other lawyers considered explicitly that these roles required the court to develop its own legal doctrine.[1] The role is explicitly to develop their own idea of the law. But this does not create binding precedents in the common-law sense. That same colloquium contains a discussion about the 'legitimate resistance' of the lower courts to the rulings of the higher courts. It is acknowledged that the refusal of the lower courts to follow a ruling of the Cour de cassation has led the latter to reconsider its views and to come up with a different solution.[2] As is said by the judges of both the Cour de cassation and the cour d'appel of Lyon, the role of the lower court judge is to be a rebel, but not too often.[3] This authority accorded to the case law of higher courts is confirmed by interviews with judges. On the one hand, they are very respectful of decisions of the Cour de cassation and seek them out as the first point of reference (as far as they can be known). The Cour de cassation produces a bulletin of decisions through its Service de documentation and this supports what can be known through databases and law reports. It will be rare that a judge in a lower court (even in the cour d'appel) will consider expressly going against the established case law of the Cour de cassation. In interviews, judges suggest they will often only do so where they think that the Cour de cassation might well reverse its case law or where other courts are moving in the same direction. In other words, they seek out evidence of criticism from practitioners, academics or other courts to support their personal opinion that the Cour de cassation was wrong.

Lower courts are less concerned with the decisions of courts of co-ordinate jurisdiction. To begin with, these have no authority. In the second place, they have less knowledge of what these other courts have decided. The bulletin produced by the Cour de cassation does contain information provided by local correspondents about the salient decisions of the cours d'appel. But this is in no way systematic or complete. *Avocats* may also provide copies of decisions from other cours d'appel, but these will only include cases which are favourable to their cause. Finally, there may be regional collections of case law produced by local universities. Although there are a number of these, they are by no means complete, nor do they cover every region. At least until there is a much greater use of information technology, most of what is decided at levels below the Cour de cassation is unknown, unless the judges or lawyers involved draw the attention of editors of reports to it.

(f) Conflicting images of the civil judge

Based on his reading of court files and the opinions of reporter judges and the ministère public, Lasser remarks 'I have not found a single conclusion or rapport that does not provide citations of previous cases – ie of jurisprudence.'[4] He contrasts this with the official portrait of the judge who is not authorised to make law through arrêts de règlement under art 5 of the Civil Code. The limited authority officially recognised to

1 *L'image doctrinale de la Cour de cassation* (Paris 1994).

2 For example, on the civil liability of children (Cass ass plén, 9 May 1984, D 1984, 525 note Chabas), liability for things (Cass ch réunies 13 Feb 1930, *Jand'heur*, below, p 85), on the dismissal of teachers in religious schools (Cass ass plén, 19 May 1978, JCP 1978 II 19009).

3 *L'image doctrinale*, 188-190, 191.

4 M Lasser, 'Judicial (Self-)Portraits: Judicial Discourse in the French Legal System' (1995) 104 Yale LJ 1325 at p 1376.

the civil courts contrasts with the reality of their position, almost a schizophrenia, which has long been recognised. Portalis recognised that, once drafted, laws were fixed while human beings were constantly changing, such that one could not regulate all that might occur.[5] Thus, 'to simplify everything is something on which we must agree; to foresee everything is a goal which is impossible to achieve'.[6] Accordingly, 'the function of statute is to establish through a broad view the general maxims of the law; to establish principles rich in consequences and not to descend into the detail of questions which could arise on every question. It is up to the judge and the jurist, imbued with the general spirit of the laws, to direct their application'.[7] This role included deciding issues which were not regulated by a statute such as the Code. This reality was reinforced by Gény writing in 1899 who considered that, except where there was an imperative rule, the interpreter is left to find solutions to changing situations. His sources of inspiration are the same as the legislator, if faced by the similar situation.[8]

Thus, although case law is not authoritative in the sense of a binding precedent, decisions of the Cour de cassation are a major authority to which judges refer and are expected to follow.

(2) The authority of doctrinal legal writing

Civil law is the field *par excellence* in which doctrine (*la doctrine*) is credited with a strong influence. French law was not taught in the French universities until the Edict of St Germain-en Laye of 1679. The tradition was of teaching Roman law. But a major function of doctrinal writing in the late 17th and 18th centuries was to consolidate and systematise the customs of French regions.[9] In the codification process, doctrine was influential in offering the mix between Roman, customary, and natural law that became the Code civil. Although la doctrine is not a formal authority, it is a strong influence in shaping the law.

(a) Functions of la doctrine

Doctrinal writing is expected to perform three main functions: to explain and describe, to construct and systematise, and to evaluate and criticise.

(i) Explain and describe A major function of doctrine has been to describe the law and to explain legal developments. The treatise and the manuel have served to provide both practitioner and student audiences with a clear presentation of the state of French law. From the systematic commentaries of the immediate post-Code period, dominated by l'Ecole de l'exégèse to the modern student manuel, there has been an important market for the description of the law, typically connected to the educational function of doctrinal writing. These have been traditionally produced by academics.

5 Discours préliminaire in F Ewald (ed), *Naissance du Code civil* (Paris 1989), 41.
6 Ibid, 39.
7 Ibid, 41-42.
8 F Gény, *Méthode de l'interprétation* (Paris 1919), vol I, p 207; vol II, pp 77-78.
9 See J-L Thireau in Y Poirmeur et al, *La doctrine juridique* (Paris 1993), pp 34-40.

In the larger, encyclopaedic works destined for practitioner use, such as the *Encyclopédie Dalloz* and the *Répertoire Dalloz*, practitioners also often write entries.

The laconic character of French judicial decisions has given rise to the *note d'arrêt*. Since these first appeared in the Dalloz reports of 1845 as editorial commentaries, they have served to situate a decision in its broader legal context (and often to render it comprehensible to the legal community). Jestaz has argued that these notes have become increasingly technical, as academics or others present something relevant either to a case they are working on or a half-finished article.[10] But it would be fair to say that commentaries have been of variable quality in the past, especially in the 19th century. Judges, avocats and academics have all contributed, often with essentially expository ambitions in mind. The role of la doctrine can be illustrated by two examples from the cases which will be discussed in section C. In the first case decided by the Cour de cassation in 1989,[11] the situation of fact concerned an exploding television manufactured by the appellant. The Cour d'appel of Paris held the manufacturer liable for breach of its obligation not to put onto the market a product whose internal dynamism did not present any danger. The Cour de cassation quashed the decision on the ground that the obligation was merely to sell a product without defect. It also held that the liability towards the other owners of flats in the building could only be delictual. The key points are stated in 80 words covering nine lines. It is for the commentator to situate not only liability in relation to televisions in previous cases, but also the general rules of liability of the manufacturer-seller, as well as to third parties. In his commentary, Malaurie cites 13 precedents and six works of doctrinal writing, not including casenotes on 6 of the precedents. In a second case of 1995,[12] the Cour de cassation laid down two major new principles. Under the first, the professional seller was liable both to a contracting party and to third parties to deliver goods that were not defective. In this way, the EC Product Liability Directive of 1985 could be brought into French law, despite the failure of Parliament to enact the relevant legislation. Second, there was an obligation of security on the providers of services for the damage caused by things used to perform the contract. In this way, a uniformity between contractual and delictual liability was achieved. Both were stated in 105 words, but are discussed in a note of three-and-a half pages. The note situates these major legal developments, explains their justification, and draws out the implications for precedent decisions that now appear to be overruled. It also criticised the solution adopted. Even from the most limited practical point of view, the decisions here are incomprehensible without the notes.

(ii) Construct and structure Picard argues that the job of doctrinal writing is a matter of finding and grounding the law in principle, not simply interpreting a given body of norms.[13] Jestaz and Jamin have argued that making doctrine is like making a cherry cake:

10 P Jestaz, 'Déclin de la doctrine?' in *Droits 20: Doctrine et recherche en droit* (Paris 1994) 85 at p 87.

11 Cass 1re civ 20 March 1989, D 1989, 381 note Malaurie.

12 Cass 1re civ 17 January 1995, D 1995, 350 note Jourdain.

13 E Picard, '"Science du droit" ou "Doctrine juridique"', in *L'unité du droit. Mélanges en hommage à Roland Drago* (Paris 1996), 119 at p 170.

> Once and for all, Parliament creates the law, the Administration the regulations and our three great jurisdictions the case law. However, 'doctrine' makes the system ... On the one hand, it washes and takes the stones out of the cherries, after removing the stalks: in other words, it eliminates the contradictions, obscurities or insufficiencies of the law in its crude state. Moreover, it makes the pastry (a dogmatics) to cover the cherries (to categorise the prescriptive solutions) in order to create from all this the cherry cake (the system).[14]

The systematising function of legal doctrine (called 'legal dogmatics' in German) is its essential role. It performs this role through the interpretation of law (often by extrapolation from enacted laws or decided statutes), through definition and through classification.[15] It has its own style and logic of argumentation with an emphasis on rightness as systematic coherence and consistency, rather than based on authority like case law.[16] This systematic function was precisely the contribution made by Domat and Pothier before the Revolution and was restarted by Auby and Rau in the middle of the nineteenth century. Unlike natural science, the system is not discovered by the legal scientist, but constructed.[17] There are thus multiple ways of viewing the system according to the philosophy proposed by particular authors. In civil liability, there were thus those who supported individual liability based on fault and these contrasted with those who supported strict liability based on risk or social solidarity. As Nicholas observes, intellectual coherence matters to the doctrinal writer.[18]

(iii) Evaluate and criticise Mazeaud argued that;

> Jurists should not be content to study the law, revealing it as written reason: *ratio scripta*. They have the duty to seek out its faults, to show to the legislator the failing which could separate it from morals or social and economic needs. Inspired by the works of comparative law and of history, they should propose the best rules, most adapted to our civilisation.'[19]

Saleilles also argued that doctrine and jurisprudence had the task of achieving justice.[20] As such the role of doctrine is to criticise to ensure that this ambition is achieved.

(b) Place of doctrine

The place of doctrinal writing is explained by the narrow ambitions of judgment writing in the French system. Thus Pierre Mimin wrote:

> The art of discussion does not apply in the same way in pleading as in a judgment. Given a particular interest to defend, the *avocat* resorts to any argument that has a chance of being

14 P Jestaz and C Jamin, 'The entity of French doctrine: some thoughts on the community of French legal writers' (1998) 18 LS 415, 426.
15 See M Van de Kerchove and F Ost, *Legal System between Order and Disorder* (Oxford 1994),pp 77-83; M Van Hoecke,*What is Legal Theory?* (Leuven 1985), p 43: 'legal doctrine can be defined as the branch of legal science which, from a prescriptive point of view, places into systematic order and describes the positive law which prevails in a certain society at a certain time'.
16 See especially, R Alexy, *A Theory of Legal Argumentation*, pp 257-266.
17 E Picard, p 123.
18 Quotation cited above, p viii.
19 HL and J Mazeaud, *Leçons de droit civil* vol 1 (6th edn by F Chabas, Paris 1980), p 134.
20 See Y Poirmeur, *La doctrine juridique*, p 137.

> accepted. The judge, tasked with pronouncing the law only relies on correct arguments. If the former therefore needs eloquence (the more so where his case is bad), the latter only needs logic. The *avocat* who seeks to move uses the techniques of rhetoric and makes play of every oratorical passion. The judge who, in deciding, seeks also to convince only sets out propositions which are useful, relevant and clearly organised.[1]

If the judge seeks to write in a style marked by its 'brièveté vigoreuse' and avoiding 'puerile reflections', then the more extended form of justification can only be found in other sources. The *conclusions* and the occasionally published *rapport* become an indirect source of the reasons that justified the solution reached. Of course, the court may well have refused to follow the arguments presented to it, but a picture of the potential reasons does emerge. The arguments serve to influence subsequent submissions to the court. But simply examining the judgments (to which is only what the academic or practitioner often has access) is often very difficult. Changes in the case law are announced by subtle changes in the formulation of the statement of the law or in the way the facts are stated and only someone well versed in that case law will spot what has been done. As Nicholas points out, 'the interpretation of *arrêts* calls therefore for skill, experience, and an eye for the nuances of language. The application of these qualities is, again, a function of doctrine.'[2]

The influence of doctrinal writing in creating new doctrines is abundantly noted elsewhere. The classic examples are the enrichissement sans cause and liability for things. In the former, a decision of 1892[3] was based on a principle of restitution set out by Auby and Rau in 1873. In the latter area, the principles were announced by a small group of the doctrine but were extensively developed once the Cour de cassation made its breakthrough in 1897. In his work on principles in private law, Morvan[4] argues that the case of the *actio de in rem verso* is both exceptional and limited as an example of the influence of doctrine. It is exceptional that doctrine has the idea first. It is limited in that, thereafter, the detail of the limits of the principle were worked out by case law, a fact acknowledged by the fact that later editions of Auby and Rau replaced the original doctrinal statement of the principle with a summary of the case law developed since 1892. In the other cases, he argues that case law both takes the initial step to set out a decision and then develops the detail, often with the support of doctrinal writing. For him, 'principles exceptionally receive an *impetus* from doctrine, but they do not result from a doctrinal *elaboration*. Doctrine is commonly reduced to the role of greffier of principles discovered by the judge'.[5] Morvan argues that the principles discovered by case law develop in a process of 'legal sedimentation', a gradual accumulation of decisions on aspects which are then brought together in a declaration that a principle exists.[6] This helps to support the view that the judge is not making up a new rule, but is 'discovering' by construction. Certainly, what is being argued is that the interpretative function of case law and doctrine support each other in the development of the law. There is a constructive work in which judges are engaged.

1 P Mimin, *Le style des jugements* (4th edn Paris 1970), p 207.
2 B Nicholas in D Harris and D Tallon, *Contract Law Today*, p 11.
3 Cass req 19 June 1892, *Patureau-Milan c Boudier*, DP 1892.1.596; S 1893.1.281 note Labbé.
4 P Morvan, *Le principe en droit privé* (Paris 1999), pp 522-523.
5 Ibid, p 524.
6 Ibid, pp 452-462.

It is clear from reading published *conclusions* and rapports in the Cour de cassation that judges of this court are impressed by the reactions of lower court judges. If there is a groundswell of reaction against the present state of the law, then this seems to act as a trigger. The doctrinal arguments may well have been there for many years, but there needs to be a sense among the judiciary that this is the right moment to change. Thus, for example, in the *Desmares* case, the avocat-général Charbonnier notes the attempt by the lower judges to evade the rules on contributory fault of the victim:

> Why this reaction? No doubt because they thought it fair to ensure for the victims of this accident full compensation and that to take account of the defence objection would have led them, in the present state of the law, only to partial compensation. Such an attitude, already observed many times, should retain our attention.
>
> Is it not a sign of a distortion, at the level of the application of the rule of law, between the content of this rule and the requirements of justice, such as they are really perceived? And if this is the case, if the legal principle does not result in a just solution, because, in this case, the principle comes from case law, because you have laid it down, you are the masters and you can change it.[7]

He then goes on to quote extensively from doctrinal legal writing to document a change in the social situation and in social attitudes, as well as to offer a coherent solution and assess the consequences of any change in the law. The balance seems to be between doctrinal writing as the source of solutions and reflections and judicial attitudes to individual fact situations as the barometer of the fairness of the law and the need for change. Commentators such as Carbonnier note this phenomenon. If the common opinion of the doctors of the law creates a doctrine, its influence is essentially intellectual and persuasive. But 'among the judges, doctrinal writing does not have the same authority as case law, which imposes itself by the hierarchical weight of the higher courts'[8]

Interviews with judges would suggest that they are essentially pragmatic in the researches they conduct. They will only resort to reading doctrinal writing when this is necessary. There are at least four levels of work that may be consulted. Most commonly, the encyclopaedias will suffice. Written by academics and practitioners for an essentially practitioner audience, they distil academic knowledge into brief and accessible statements. A second source would be textbooks. A third source would be case-notes and short doctrinal pieces in law reviews, especially the comments in the law reports. A final (and less frequently used) source would be theses and other monographs. The importance of doctrinal writing to the judicial decision-maker will depend on the difficulty of the case.

In relation to the legislator, there is a distinction to be drawn between the influence of doctrinal writers and that of doctrinal writing. Whereas, as will be seen in section D, the former may serve as advisers or members of committees in making formal recommendations for legislation and even in producing draft laws, doctrinal writing serves more to create a climate of opinion which is favourable to certain outcomes. It serves as a repository of ideas and arguments in favour of them.

7 D 1982, at p 449.
8 J Carbonnier, *Droit et passion de droit*, p 71.

(3) The conceptual structure of civil law

As was seen in the Preface, in writings about French law, it is a common-place for authors to stress the distinctiveness of the conceptual structure of private law.[9] Samuel presents the argument most clearly.[10] He suggests that there is a distinctive epistemological structure to the civil law tradition that arises out of the distinctive institutional framework within which it operates. The available conceptual structure, inherited from Roman law and imprinted on the Civil Code, shapes the way in which French lawyers think. In the first place, there is the focus on rights and interests, rather than remedies. In the second place, there is the relationship between persons, things and actions. 'Persons' and 'things' and the 'legal bond (*vinculum iuris*)' between them become the points of reference for thinking and legal argumentation.[11] This framework of legal institutions and the relationship between them becomes a 'meta-language' for legal actors within the system. It affects not only the structure and content of rules, but also how facts-in-law are described and classified.[12] Because legal situations have to be classified within the available legal categories, it is inevitable that lawyers will use these in thinking about problems. From the legal point of view, this is expected. The Code Civil has specific categories such as contract and delict set out in terms of the rights of the parties. A French lawyer would think through a problem in terms of the categories which are within the Code. But Samuel's argument goes deeper in that the application of categories can be seen as the lawyer searching to identify the fundamental pattern which the civil law expects: the relationship between persons, things and actions. The basic legal relationships are between people or between people and things. In the law of obligations and persons, the relationships are between people. In the law of property, the relationship is between things and people. (By contrast, the common law is focused around the law of actions or remedies, which tend to be ultimately relationships between people.) Facts fit these patterns. These categories also serve as *topoi* from which justification must be offered.[13] It is the apparent 'naturalness' of this fundamental pattern to those who are educated in and have to operate the system which constructs a 'mentalité'.[14] Thus, he argues that civil law has both the surface structure of the categories and institutions of the Civil Code, and the fundamental structure, or meta-language, of core institutions into which the more specific categories and rules of the Civil Code, and the facts-in-law with which civil lawyers deal, have to be situated.

9 Above, p ix.

10 G Samuel, *The Foundations of Legal Reasoning* (Antwerp 1994), ch 9.

11 Ibid, pp 172-178.

12 G Samuel, 'Classification of obligations and the impact of constructivist epistemologies' (1998) 18 LS 448 at pp 464471; G Samuel, 'Comparative Law and Jurisprudence' (1998) 47 ICLQ 817 at pp 827-833; D MacCormick and O Weinberger, *Law as Institutional Fact*, ch 3.

13 On *topoi*, see T Viehweg, *Topik und Jurisprudenz* (5th edn, Munich 1974); R Alexy, *A Theory of Legal Argumentation* (Oxford 1989), pp 20-24.

14 Samuel, 47 ICLQ at 833-6. I find this analysis more developed and plausible than that presented by P Legrand, 'European Legal Systems are not Converging' (1996) 45 ICLQ 52 at pp 74-79.

C. ILLUSTRATION OF ACTIVITIES

(1) Lawmaking

It is generally asserted that doctrinal legal writing influences the development of civil law in a marked way. Indeed, it has been described as a 'law of the professors'. But the evidence of influence is not always easy to establish. As Jestaz and Jamin suggest:

> ... the fact that the French *Cour de cassation* at times borrows an idea or an expression from an author proves at most an open-mindedness on the part of the former and pragmatic intelligence on the part of the latter, but in no case does it provide the proof or the criteria of doctrinal power.[15]

Of course there are famous instances where the Cour de cassation has overturned its decisions in the light of doctrinal criticism (but also of resistance from the lower courts). Thus in the case of liability of car owners for accidents caused when their vehicle was being driven by a thief, the Cour de cassation had at first found against the car owner, but in the light of doctrinal criticism from Capitant, the Cour d'appel of Besançon resisted the superior court and the Chambres réunies climbed down and found the owner not liable.[16] In his review of the Cour de cassation in the 20th century, Malaurie suggests that there has been an increasing exchange between doctrinal writing and the Cour de cassation, with reciprocal influence.[17]

It is the critical and analytical doctrine of the late 19th and early 20th centuries which has been seen as the classical age of doctrinal writing in civil law.[18] To demonstrate this, one must go further. In this chapter, I try to suggest ways in which this might work through a sample of law reports and through a case study.

(a) *Sample of law reports*

Judgments of the highest courts contain effectively summaries of conclusions reached, rather than the justifications which lie behind them. Perdriau captures the purpose well in his guidance on the writing of judgments in the Cour de cassation – we do not give reasons for the reasons.[19] But my own observation of judicial discussions and that of others (notably Lasser) suggests the style of the published rapports and *conclusions* is a good guide to the forms of justification used in the court, even though the formal justification is more truncated. In order to have a sense of the place of both doctrinal

15 18 LS at p 421.

16 See Cass civ 30 March 1936, *Connot c Franck*, D 1936.1.81 note Capitant; Besançon 21 February 1937, DC 1937, 182; Ch réunies 2 December 1941, DC 1942, 25 note Ripert.

17 Cour de cassation, *Rapport annuel 1999*, p 8.

18 Carbonnier, above, p 66, note 12, at pp 106-107.

19 A Perdriau, *La pratique des arrêts civils de la Cour de cassation: principes et méthodes de rédaction* (Paris 1993), § 1274 : 'We consider ... that it is important to refrain from 'giving reasons for the reasons', meaning by thereby that, whereas in a judicial decision the inclusion of reasons corresponds to an absolute necessity, the explanation of these reasons moves away from the sphere of law by bringing out considerations of a more or less subjective or contingent kind, and this should therefore not be done'.

legal writing and precedent in legal argumentation, I have taken at random the *rapports* and conclusions published in the *Recueil Dalloz-Sirey* for two years, 1989 and 1997. There were 12 rapports and conclusions published in 1989 and 13 in 1997, though the balance between the two types of submission to the court was different in the two years: there was only one rapport and 11 conclusions in 1989, but 9 rapports and 4 conclusions in 1997. There is thus a reasonable number of each in the sample. The range of cases is varied. In only one set of conclusions is neither precedent nor doctrinal writing discussed.[20] A further 11 cited only case law. Thus doctrinal writing was discussed in only half these documents. It is noticeable that of eight decisions of the administrative courts or the Tribunal des Conflits for which there are published conclusions, doctrinal writing is only discussed in two of them. By contrast in the 17 rapports and conclusions from the civil and criminal courts, only 5 fail to discuss doctrine, though one of the remaining cases only discusses as doctrinal writing a case-note written by a member of the Cour de cassation in 1934. There would thus appear to be a higher place for doctrinal writing in civil case law and this writing has a bearing on the outcome of decisions. In a number of cases, doctrinal writing appears to have been particularly influential.[1] Clearly such a small sample can only give an impression, but from other works, this does not appear to be misleading. Doctrine is cited where it exists (and this is not on all topics) and where it is seen as useful (if only to suggest that there are several respectable answers).

(b) Case study: liability of the seller for defective goods

The influence of doctrinal legal writing and case law on the development of a branch of private law can be illustrated by the development of the law on defective goods.

Article 1641 of the Civil Code provides that, in a contract of sale, the seller is held to guarantee against hidden defects in the object sold where the defect makes it unsuitable for its intended use or so reduces its suitability that the buyer would not have bought it. The provision goes back to the principles of Roman law.[2] Developments since 1804 demonstrate how the Code has been adapted to changes in the market through judicial and doctrinal interpretation, rather than by legislative intervention. The 1993 Consumer Code has restated the law suitable to modern conditions, but certainly until the 1970s, legislation was limited to specific instances, and did not seek to revise the Code in any systematic way. Malinvaud described the development of the case law as an attempt to protect consumers:

> Guided by the desire to compensate as much as possible the victim, that is to say the consumer of the product, the case law has created a new positive law whilst respecting the texts, at least in appearance.[3]

20 Concl L Carbonnier in Cass 1re civ, 5 July 1988, D 1989, 398.

1 See Cass com 20 June 1995, D 1997, 1 rapport Rémery; Cass 1re civ 3 December 1996, D 1997, 151 rapport Chartier; Cass 3e civ, 22 May 1997, D 1997, 565 concl Weber; Ass plén, 22 December 1988, D 1989, 105 concl Monnet.

2 The provision is to be found in J Domat, *Loix civiles*, Livre I, titre II, sections XI, vi-xii, and in R Pothier, *Traité des obligations* (Paris 1761), No 231.

3 Ph Malinvaud, 'La responsabilité civile du fabricant en droit français', GP 1973.2.463.

It is essential to remember the setting of the early 19th century. France was a rural, pre-industrial country and so the sales involved typically agricultural produce and the leasing of buildings.[4] For example, cases concerned seeds sold which did not germinate[5] or the unusability of the building[6] Since the protection was against *hidden* defects, then the buyer was expected to take care in examining the products and in obtaining express stipulations.[7] The possibility of inspection in these kinds of sales would usually mean that a defect could not be considered 'hidden' at the time of sale.[8] Of course, the prudent buyer might, in some cases, be expected to be assisted by his own expert, eg an architect for the purchase of a building.[9]

The position began to change with the development of mechanical tools and vehicles. As the products became more complicated, so there was less expectation that the buyer could detect defects by inspection and so reliance on the seller became more accepted. The purchaser was often no longer buying in a market in which he had some expertise, nor would the normal visual inspection reveal the defect. For instance, in the case of a machine assembled by the seller, the mechanism was too complicated for the buyer to inspect sufficiently to detect the defect.[10] The sale of second-hand vehicles became a standard area for the application of this case law.[11] Judicial interpretation of the concept of what is a 'hidden' defect adjusted to what could reasonably have been expected from buyers in the market.

The concern to protect the victim focused in the early period on the compensation which the victim should receive. Articles 1644 provides that, in the case of a hidden defect, the buyer has the choice of returning the thing and obtaining reimbursement of the price (the Roman *actio rehibitoria*), or keeping the thing and having a reimbursement of part of the price (the Roman *action aestimatoria*). Articles 1645 and 1646 provide for additional payments in two different circumstances:

> *Art 1645*: If the seller knew of the defects in the thing, he is liable, over and above the restitution of the price which he has received, for full damages to the buyer.

4 Ibid. This is reflected in contemporary studies of this branch of law: see, for example, Th de Bernon, *Des vice rédhibitoire ou cachés dans les différents contrats en droit romain et en droit français* (Thesis Paris 1887), pp 125ff; Th Mouret, *Des vices cachés ou rédhibitoires dans les ventes de meubles et d'immeubles et dans les autres contrats* (Thesis Toulouse 1893).

5 Cass civ 22 March 1853, S 1853.1.481.

6 Montpellier, 23 February 1807, S 1807.2.298.

7 For example, the buyer can't complain that wine was adulterated or had too much tartar, unless there was an express provision for pure wine: Paris 18 March 1870, D 1871.2.31, Bordeaux, 25 July 1843, S 1844.2.254. By contrast, if there was a provision that wine had to have a specific degree of alcohol, then it did not matter that the buyer had not detected the defect in tasting: Paris 24 July 1879, D 1879.2.214. (Cf defects which could have been so discovered: Trib com Nantes, 19 January 1859; DP 1859.3.69).

8 See art 1642: 'The seller is not liable for apparent defects of which the buyer could have examined himself.' Req 1 March 1876, S 1876.1.318 (sale of a quarry).

9 Eg Bordeaux, 10 December 1928, D 1929.2.82.

10 Lyon, 18 August 1858, DP 1859.2.102; Trib com Gand, 18 February 1865, DP 1865.3.63 (rope); Bourges 27 June 1893, DP 1894.2.573 (bicycle).

11 See Seine 22 November 1907, D 1908.5.21; Req 31 July 1905, D 1908.1.148; Civ com 11 June 1954, D 1954, 697. See generally A Sudaka, 'Où en est la théorie des vices cachés dans la vente des véhicules d'occasion?' GP 1966.1. Doct 61.

Art 1646: If the seller did not know of the defects in the thing, he is only liable for the restitution of the price and to reimburse the buyer for the expenses incurred in the sale.

The case law developed in two phases, both of which demonstrated radically expansive interpretations of these provisions.

In the case of the good faith seller, the buyer could only recover the price (eg of seeds sown)[12] and expenses incurred during the sale, eg the cost of improvements to the building bought, but only to the extent that these increased its value.[13] All the same, the category of 'expenses incurred in the sale' was interpreted to become a broad heading of damages. For example, in a decision of 1858, the Cour d'appel of Lyons held that the buyer of a defective steam engine could claim damages to cover both the expenses necessary to make the machine conform to the contract requirements and for the losses caused by the mills being out of action.[14] All the same, loss of profit on crops resulting from seeds which could not germinate were not recoverable.[15] The line between 'expenses incurred in the sale' owed by the good faith seller and 'full damages' for which the bad faith seller was liable seemed to be drawn at the point of claiming for loss of profits. Reinstatement costs seemed to be broadly interpreted and included, for example, repairing a boat damaged by a defective boiler sold under the contract.[16] This idea that 'expenses' really covered any reinstatement was initially stated by the Chambre des Requêtes of the Cour de Cassation in 1847[17] and was confirmed by it in 1925. Here, the defective spring in a car broke and caused an accident. The victim sued and the buyer of the car was able to recover the damages paid to the victim as 'expenses incurred in the sale'.[18] In its judgment, the Chambres des Requêtes argued 'that it is wrong to claim, as the pourvoi does, that the good faith seller of a thing affected by a hidden defect is only liable to the buyer for the reimbursement of the price and the expenses of the contract; as the rescission of the sale should, as far as possible, put the buyer in the same position as if the contract had never taken place'. In his conclusions, avocat-général Célice argued that, contrary to the view of Pothier, it was necessary to include not only expenses relating to the thing, but also any expenses incurred by the buyer's patrimoine. Those conclusions cite, in particular, decisions of the Chambre des Requêtes of 1847 and 1898. In the former, it had held the seller liable for damages paid out by the buyer to subsequent buyers to whom he had resold the animal fat. In that case, the rapporteur was Troplong, author of the principal treatise on sale, had supported this, but he also confirmed the view of the Cour d'appel that an award of damages in addition had to be refused. For the most part, Célice's conclusions justify his argument by reference to case law and to pre-Code authors

12 Cass 22 March 1853, S 1853.1.480.
13 Cass 29 March 1852, S 1852. 1.321.
14 Lyon, 18 August 1858, DP 1859.2.102.
15 Amiens 16 January 1862, S 1862.2.156; cf in case of bad faith, loss of profit was recoverable: Req 10 May 1909, DP 1912.1.16.
16 Rennes, 13 June 1903, DP 1903.2.447, overturning the narrower view of the first instance court.
17 Req 29 June 1847, DP 1848.1.187, rapport Troplong; see also Req 28 March 1898, reported in a note DP 1903.2.447.
18 Req 21 October 1925, *Soc des automobiles Rolland-Pilain c Berchet* DP 1926.1.9, concl Célice.

such as Loysel, while noting his departure from Pothier. His discussion of la doctrine is predominantly to counter criticism that this approach departs too much from the Code or treats the seller in good faith the same as the seller in bad faith. Following the 1925 decision, the approach continued to be applied, for example the case of the *Poisoning at Pont St-Esprit* concerned the sale of toxic bread which affected 117 people, some fatally. In this case of 1960, the Cour d'appel of Nîmes applied the concept of 'expenses incurred in the sale' to include the funeral expenses and other losses which the heirs of victims sustained as a result of the poisoning.

This line of reasoning was criticised as departing too much from the letter of the Code in extending the liability of the good faith seller. In an aside at the end of his rapport in the 1847 decision, Troplong argued that, although the seller was in good faith in the sense that he genuinely believed his goods were without defect, as a merchant producing his own product he promised the skill of his art and this takes him outside the scope of the good faith seller.[19] In his note on the 1925 decision, Josserand also argued for a similar approach. Simply imposing the burden of loss on any seller was unjust and contrary to the law of obligations. By contrast, the idea of treating the *professional* seller as in bad faith was justified by the fact that 'the exercise of a profession naturally brings with it a responsibility and the risks from which the accidental author of an isolated act ought to escape'.[20] The judicial interpretation of art 1646 was reversed by the Première Chambre civile of the Cour de Cassation in 1963. On very similar facts to the 1925 decision, the Cour de cassation quashed a decision of the Cour d'appel based on art 1646 and compensating a sub-buyer for the damages paid out to the family of a victim of an accident caused by a defect in a car based on the idea that these were 'expenses incurred in the sale'. It held that, under art 1646, 'the seller who is unaware of the existence of a defect in the thing is only bound to reimburse the price and the costs of the sale, without having to guarantee the buyer against the consequences of damage caused by the defect'.[1] The court preferred to rely on a direct action of the sub-buyer based on the assignment of the guarantee along with the car, and the idea that a professional seller was to be treated as in bad faith. This combination of techniques avoided problems of the very short time limit within which art 1648 requires the buyer to bring an action for defects. This new reasoning was then applied to the *Poisoning of Pont St-Esprit* when it was heard on cassation by the Cour de cassation in 1965.[2] It limited the application of art 1646 to expenses of the sale, but then awarded the same damages by applying art 1645 and the concept that the professional seller is to be treated as in bad faith.

The early courts had been reluctant to consider that, the mere status of merchant sufficed to treat him as a bad faith seller, at least where natural products, rather than manufactured goods were being sold.[3] There was some doctrinal support for the view that a professional seller should be treated as being in bad faith. Troplong applied the Roman law adage (repeated in Pothier) that the workman is liable for incompetence in

19 DP 1848.1.48.

20 DP 1925.1.9 at p 11.

1 Cass 1re civ, 4 February 1963, *Entreprise moderne de canalisation et de travaux publics c consorts Ravaille*, JCP 1963. II. 13159 note Savatier.

2 Cass 1re civ, 19 January 1965, D 1965, 389.

3 Amiens 16 January 1862, S 1862.2.156 (non-germination of seeds).

his art as an example of a seller being in bad faith.[4] As we have seen, he then repeated this in his judicial role in 1847,[5] but this did not represent established case law for some time and was not the basis of that decision. The idea that the seller ought to know the quality of his goods was applied in 1905 to the sale of gas motors for use in a biscuit factory. The Cour de cassation held that the seller could not claim to be unaware that their motors were unsuitable for this use and so could not rely on a limitation of liability clause.[6] Similarly, in 1929 the professional seller of a motor car was held unable to rely on clause limiting liability for a defect, on the ground that as a professional he could not have been unaware of its defect. In an earlier decision, the manufacturer of a gun was liable for injuries caused by defects on the ground that lack of skill is equivalent to fault.[7] This technique of treating the professional seller to be aware of defects and thus of bad faith in selling the goods was designed mainly to establishing liability for injury or to remove exclusion clauses. It required a further jump in the case law to establish that the professional seller would always be held as in bad faith for the purposes of art 1645. In 1954, the Première Chambre civile of the Cour de cassation held that:

> ... it follows ... from the provisions of article 1645 of the Code that the seller who knew of the defects, to whom it is appropriate to assimilate he who by his profession could not have been unaware of them, is liable, over and above the reimbursement of the price which he has received, for all damages towards the buyer.[8]

In this way, it was able to award damages for the non-pecuniary loss of the heirs of a buyer killed when a gas container exploded. Followed, for example in the 1963 and 1965 decisions, there became established a new orthodoxy that the basis of liability was the deeming of the professional seller as of bad faith. By contrast, the non-professional seller was only to be liable under art 1646.[9] It is clear from judicial and academic commentary that the immediate cause of this judicial change of heart was attributable to the work of H Mazeaud, both in his treatise and in an article of 1955.[10]

The doctrinal basis for these developments is both specific and general. In terms of the specific basis of liability for hidden defects. Pothier justified the guarantee on the basis of ensuring that the intention of the parties, the economic basis of the contract, was respected.[11] The idea that the professional seller is deemed to know the quality of his products relies on the social expectation that Domat and Pothier articulated with the maxim that he 'promises the skill of his art'. But this became reinterpreted after the Second World War to reflect a more general principle of risk. Thus Savatier suggested that the principle was that 'he who introduces a defective thing into the circulation of

4 Troplong, *De la vente*, t II, No 574 (Paris 1835).
5 Rapport under Req 29 June 1847, DP 1848.1.187.
6 Req 31 July 1905, S 1907.1.437.
7 Aix, 4 January 1872, D 1873.2.55.
8 Cass 1re civ, 24 November 1954, *Gaz et Electricité de France c Etablissements Jacob Holtzer et Albert*, JCP 1955 II 8565. See also Cass 1re civ, 10 February 1959, D 1959, 117.
9 See, for example, Com 11 June 1958, *Philippon c Garçon*, Bull cass 1958 III p 202, No 247.
10 See the note of R Savatier, D 1960, 725 at p 729; R Meurisse, note D 1963, 193 at p 195.
11 Pothier, *Traité du contrat de la vente* , t III, IIe partie, ch 1, sect iv, p 161ff. See also L Fubini, 'La nature juridique de la responsabilité du vendeur pour les vices cachés' RTDCiv 1903, 279 at p 285.

goods should be liable for the damage which it causes'.[12] The drafters of the Civil Code were concerned to compensate a party for the economic losses sustained by defects in the goods. The writers in the 20th century became increasingly concerned to protect the victim against personal and property damage, and so the specifically *contractual* justification was eclipsed by ideas of security.[13]

The basis of compensation was connected to fault. In the absence of fault, the two innocent parties would be put back where they were. The professional seller, however, took the risk of his activity. But this became increasingly artificial in a situation where the seller (even a professional) was much more a distributor of goods, rather than the artisan-manufacturer or merchant of agricultural products envisaged in 1804. As Tunc argued in 1961:

> ... it is artificial to consider that a professional seller, even if he were the manufacturer, necessarily knows the defects in the thing which he sells: not only might he be unaware of them, but there are numerous cases in which his ignorance implies no fault on his part.[14]

As a result, the assimilation of the professional seller to the seller in bad faith 'can only be justified by purely policy considerations, of strategy, of adjusting social relations, which are the foundation of obligations of guarantee, not by a presumption of fault which often is contrary to the facts'.[15] This view of Mazeaud and Tunc argued for a basis in an obligation of security, which is more flexible than the obligation of guarantee against defects, particularly in relation to ultimate users. This movement of doctrinal writing reflected in articles by Mazeaud in 1955 and Malinvaud in 1973[16] was to prepare the way for the acceptance of a general legislative scheme on product liability in the 1990s. In part, Overstake argued that 'the non-manufacturing seller presents himself in reality more as an ally of the consumer against the manufacturer, rather than as the consumer's adversary'.[17] The manufacturer is the person who attracts consumers through publicity and is the person who is insured, or can insure himself, against all the risks.[18] Developing earlier work, doctrinal writing in the 1950s and 1960s was already preparing the way for an enlargement of contractual obligations from the guarantee against hidden defects to a more general obligation of security.

In general terms, the move to assimilate the professional seller to a seller in bad faith is part of a generalised movement from an understanding of fault as moral blameworthiness to a view of liability as a mechanism for providing compensation to victims. At the end of the 19th century, there was a move to establish the liability for

12 Note in JCP 1963 II 13159; also Ph Malinvaud, 'La responsabilité civile du fabricant en droit français' GP 1973.2. Doct 463; G Viney, *Le déclin de la responsabilité individuelle* (Paris 1963), nos 251ff.

13 See H Mazeaud, 'La responsabilité civile du vendeur-fabricant' Rfdc 1955, 611.

14 A Tunc, RTDCiv 1961, 116.

15 H and L Mazeaud and A Tunc, *Traité théorique et pratique de la responsabilité civile* (6th edn, Paris 1965), vol 1, No 705, note 5.

16 See above, notes 13 and 12. The view was also supported by Sudaka and Viney, above, p 80 note 11 and this page note 12.

17 J-F Overstake, 'Responsabilité du fabricant de produits dangéreux' RTDCiv 1972, 485, 517, No 78.

18 Ibid, p 518, No 84.

the custodians of things based not on fault, but on risk, especially in the area of accidents at work.[19] This liability was essentially non-contractual and involved, in private law, a move in the basis of liability from fault under arts 1382 and 1383 of the Civil Code to no-fault under a radically revised interpretation of art 1384 § 1. In administrative law, the move in the basis was from fault to equality before public burdens. Doctrinal legal writing was divided on this approach with some leading authors (such as A Esmein, Planiol, Ripert and Capitant) favouring fault, and others (Saleilles, Josserand, Demogue and Savatier) favouring the newer developments. Liability for accidents on trains and motor vehicles finally pushed the civil law towards a strong basis in risk. Following the case law and important currents of doctrinal writing, the legislator of 1898 had based the liability of the industrial employer on professional risk and this was expanded over the following 25 years to most other employers. But the post-War legislator of 1946 moved this compensation to an insurance-based, social security system.[20] The extension of this case law to motor vehicles followed a similar logic. The decision of the Cour de cassation in *Jand'heur*[1] firmly established liability without fault by omitting all reference to fault from its interpretation of art 1384 § 1, creating instead a presumption of liability.[2] Although proposals for legislation to this effect had been made in 1906, nothing had come from them. Compulsory insurance for drivers only came in 1958.[3] A parallel development occurred in contract law. In the area of transport, from 1911, the passenger was offered an obligation de résultat to be transported safe and sound to destination and this was a move away from fault-based liability.[4] In 1947, Starck proposed a general theory of 'garantie', under which certain basic qualities of security were assured through the civil law.[5] For him, the liability for hidden defects was based not on fault, but on a proper understanding of the responsibilities which the parties had undertaken in the contract.[6] Although his focus was predominantly delict, it fitted into discussions about consumer protection in contract and a similar approach was suggested by

19 See CE 21 June 1895, *Cames*, S 1897.3.333 concl Romieu, note Hauriou; Cass civ, 16 June 1896, DP 1897.1.433, note Saleilles; loi 9 April 1898 on liability of employers for work accidents. R Saleilles, *Les accidents du travail et la responsabilité civile* (Paris 1897) and L Josserand, *De la responsabilité du fait des choses inanimées* (Paris 1897). See generally F Leduc et al, *La responsabilité du fait des choses. Réflexions autour d'un centenaire* (Paris 1997).

20 Loi 30 October 1946; see generally J-L Gazzaniga, *Introduction historique au droit des obligations* (Paris 1992), No 220, 224-5.

1 Cass ch réunies, 13 February 1930, DP 1930.1.57, rapport Le Marc'hadour, concl Matter, note Ripert.

2 On the continuing importance of this interpretation of delictual liability, see Carbonnier, *Droit et passion du droit*, Part II, ch 2; A Tunc, above, p 84 note 14.

3 See Gazzaniga, nos 222 and 227, AT von Mehren and JR Gordley, *The Civil Law System* (2nd edn. Boston 1977), pp 632-639.

4 See Cass civ, 21 November 1911, S 1912.1 73 note Ch Lyon-Caen. This decision was a reversal of Cass civ, 10 November 1884, S 1885.1.129, against which Lyon-Caen had written a critical note. Cass civ, 6 December 1932, *Cie des chemins de fer de Paris à Orléans c Noblet*, D 1933.1.137 note Josserand. The distinction between *obligations de moyens* and *obligations de résultat* comes from R Demogue, *Traité des obligations en général*, vol V No 1237 and vol VI, No 599 (Paris 1925).

5 B Starck, *Essai d'une théorie générale de la responsabilité civile considérée en sa double fonction de garantie et de peine privée* (Thesis, Paris 1947).

6 Ibid, pp 334-342.

Gross[7] to be the basis for contract law. Thus from 1880 in major areas of injury in an increasingly industrialised society doctrine and case law (often ahead of the legislator) was creating instances of no-fault liability in relation to accidents at work, on the roads, and on public transport. The creation of similar liability towards consumers was part of the same trend.

The final part of the story goes beyond liability for hidden defects. The provisions on sale envisage the liability of the seller to the buyer. But, of course, the category of consumer is much wider – it includes not only subsequent purchasers, but also ultimate users of a product. Many of the cases on articles 1645 and 1646 involved a situation in which the ultimate consumer had recovered in delict for injuries sustained against a sub-buyer who was then suing in contract on the assigned guarantee against the initial vendor (often the manufacturer). All the same, the guarantee against hidden defects requires an action to be started within a brief time. This also places consumers in different positions. The ultimate consumer might rely on art 1384 § 1, and recover on the basis of strict liability for the action of the thing. His action would normally be against the current guardian of the thing. The seller only guarantees in relation to uses which are either normal or have been stipulated in the contract, and which the initial purchaser could not have discovered. The chain of contracts might not necessarily enable the buyer to claim against the manufacturer, as opposed to a distributor further down the chain. There was thus a potential difference in the treatment of the consumer as (ultimate) buyer and the consumer who was merely ultimate user of the product. Both the Council of Europe and the European Community proposed that there should be a basic system that enabled the consumer to have a basic protection against unsafe products directly against the manufacturer. The Council of Europe Resolution on a Consumer Protection Charter (Resolution 543 of 1973) already expressed this climate of opinion, but the EC Directive on Product Liability of 25 July 1985 gave it legislative force.

Now, in France and despite an early attempt to produce draft legislation, it was not found to be politically possible to bring the Directive into national law until 1997 (and that only after the substantial litigation on contaminated blood).[8] Instead, the Cour de cassation moved to fill the gap and in a series of decisions beginning in 1989, it gave a new and broader legal basis to the contractual protection of the consumer. In a decision of 20 March 1989,[9] the Première Chambre civile held that the vendor was bound 'to

7 B Gross, *La notion de l'obligation de garantie dans le droit des contrats* (Thesis Nancy 1962), p 39: 'there exists in French law an almost general obligation to guarantee against defects in the thing imposed either on the "custodian" of the thing, or on he who sells it, repairs it or uses it towards the performance of a contract'.

8 The issue of whether to include 'development risks' within the ambit of the legislation divided political opinion.

9 Cass 1re civ, 20 March 1989, D 1989, 381 note P Malaurie. In this case, the Cour de cassation overturned the cour d'appel of Paris which had required an even stronger duty – not to put on the market any product containing a mechanism which offered a danger to the consumer. The Cour de cassation limited the requirement to defects causing danger (in this case and exploding television)

On these developments see generally F Leduc et al, *La responsabilité du fait des choses. Réflexions autour d'un centenaire*, pp 75-108, and Cass 1re civ, 11 June 1991, D 1993 Somm 241, JCP 1992.I.3572 obs Viney. Note some earlier expressions of the idea of an obligation de sécurité: see Paris 14 December 1961, JCP 1962.II.12547 note Savatier; GP 1962.1.135 note Tunc: 'Whereas there arises from the contract imposed on him who provides the service an obligation of security which, by its generality and force dominates and exceeds just the guarantee against hidden defects and non-performance of which entails the liability of him who owes it, unless he can prove that it was due to an external cause which could not be imputed to him'.

deliver products free from any defect or manufacturing fault which was likely to create dangers for persons or property' and based this not on art 1641, but on art 1135, under which the contract is deemed to include any terms which custom or justice requires. Unlike the duty under art 1641, it is a rule which is thus broader than simply the contract of sale. In a further decision of 17 January 1995,[10] the Cour de cassation further held that this liability extended not only to the subsequent purchaser, but also to third parties. There was thus a contractual obligation of security imposed on the professional seller (often the manufacturer) towards consumers. The decision of 17 January 1995 also confirmed that the obligation was independent of the guarantee against hidden defects under art 1641, a view which was confirmed in relation to the liability of blood transfusion centres who had given contaminated blood to patients.[11] It is accepted by all that these solutions were inspired by the European Directive which had wished to establish a strict obligation of security for all consumers.[12] Indeed, in later decisions, the text of the Directive was cited and used to interpret existing articles of the Code.[13]

The original draft of the amendments to the Civil Code to incorporate the Directive was drawn up by a specialist group, led by an academic, Ghestin. In 1983, Ghestin himself had written that doctrinal writing had been unable to offer an adequate justification based on existing texts for a direct action by the ultimate acquirer of goods against the manufacturer, and certainly not for an independent action for the victim against the manufacturer. The case law also was not reaching this kind of result. As a result, an intervention by the legislator was necessary.[14] Indeed, the differences between the contractual and delictual regimes in this area were very artificial and needed 'a complete reconstruction'.[15] In his view, 'any product put into circulation by a professional should, *a priori*, correspond the legitimate expectation of the public to which it is intended, whether this is the consumers, in a specific sense of the term, or of professional users.' But such a wide reform would exceed even consumer law and would require a revision of the law of contract.[16] Accordingly, the draft bill to incorporate the Directive included provisions to revise the law on guarantees in sale and to make other changes to the law of contracts, thereby creating a new framework for this field. But the draft proved too contentious. Under threats of fines from the Commission, the French Parliament passed the loi of 14 May 1998 which essentially copied out the provisions of the Directive and left existing forms of liability intact under the new art 1386-18.[17] Thus the doctrinally inspired solution was dropped in favour of a more piecemeal and pragmatic solution.

The relationship between doctrinal writing, judicial development of the law and legislation is complex. In a field in which the legislator has intervened little, except in

10 Cass 1re civ, 17 January 1995, D 1995, 350 note P Jourdain. See F Leduc et al, pp 87-108.
11 Cass 1re civ, 12 April 1995, F Leduc, p 96.
12 See F Leduc, op cit, p 97 (Viney), p 100, (Sargos) citing the *Rapport annuel* of the Cour de cassation for 1995, p 311.
13 Cass 1re civ, 28 April 1998, D 1998 IR 142 (citing the Directive explicitly), and Cass 1re civ, 3 March 1998, D 1998 IR 96.
14 J Ghestin, *Conformité et garantie dans la vente* (Paris 1983), p 352.
15 Ibid, p 353.
16 Ibid, p 354.
17 See C Larroumet, 'La responsabilité du fait des produits défectueux après la loi du 14 mai 1998' D 1998 Chr 311; also G Viney, 'L'introduction en droit français de la directive européenne du 25 juillet 1985 à la responsabilité du fait des produits défectueux' D 1998 Chr 291.

rather a specific way, until the 1990s, the primary locus for adapting the law to the needs of modern times has been the judicial decision. But the influences on this decision are multiple. Doctrinal legal writing is clearly an important source of persuasive ideas. Arguments by writers such as Mazeaud were influential in encouraging turning points in case law on defective goods. But they are clearly not enough. After all, similar arguments were being made by Troplong a century earlier and by Josserand thirty years before to little avail. There needs also to be a certain context of opinion which doctrine is expressing. A general movement in favour of more protection and social solidarity made it easier to depart from a fault-based conception of 'bad faith' and establish a stricter liability for the professional seller of defective goods. The general movement of delict and contract made it possible to move towards a concept of an obligation of security towards the ultimate consumer. Doctrine may articulate ideas, but it is not the sole source. General changes in the social expectations for consumer protection and trends generally in Western states (shown by the Council of Europe resolution) or more specifically in the European Community were potent influences on the judges (as well as on doctrine). But, the short saga shows that judges have their own views on how the law should develop. The unwillingness to depart from a fault-based idea of 'bad faith' and a willingness to stand up against doctrinal argument is seen in the decisions of the Chambre des Requêtes of 1847 and 1925, especially in the conclusions of Célice. The momentum for change comes not just from the higher courts in civil law. The lower courts are judges of fact and are confronted first with the situations in which it is necessary to determine whether goods should be treated as 'defective', whether the seller was 'in bad faith' and which expenses are connected with the sale. Most of the early reported decisions are from the cours d'appel or lower courts. In these decisions, faced with the problems of particular situations of fact, the lower courts tried to interpret the law to achieve a fair result. It is in the context of the pressure of the lower courts that the Cour de cassation responds by its steering of the law through key decisions. Thus the Cour de cassation has to mediate external demands on the law, more specific trends of opinion within the judiciary, and the views of legal doctrine to achieve its own decision. Legislative trends have to be analysed, but also anticipated. It is clear that the Cour de cassation is not a passive institution.

(2) Resolving disputes

Not all civil disputes are resolved by the civil courts. On the one hand, there is an important role for mediation, conciliation and arbitration in resolving civil law disputes. On the other hand, civil disputes are resolved in criminal and commercial courts. Delict cases will be started by the partie civile in criminal cases and will be resolved by the criminal courts, both at first instance and on appeal. Significant numbers of contract disputes will fall within the jurisdiction of the commercial courts. As a result, the province of the ordinary civil courts lies typically in the areas of family law, consumer contract and property law.

Resolving disputes is the bulk of the work of the lower courts. As one judge suggested in interview, no more than 0.5% of cases involve innovation on legal rules. Most issues are ones of fact. Garapon identifies a contrast between what he describes as the traditional 'ritual' character of civil justice and 'bureaucratic' justice. In the former, a dispute is resolved through a process of authoritative decision taken as part of a public ritual process in which different parties have their roles. In the latter, a decision is taken in the judge's chambers often with the judge sitting alongside other professionals. As a result, instead of resolving a dispute according to fixed rules, the judge is involved in taking decisions of imprecise standing in the lives of individuals with imprecise guidance.[18] The decisions of the juge des enfants are run as part of an educational service often with agreement from the family matters. The judge ceases to be the imperious arbiter and becomes more of a professional struggling with others to deal with the complex questions which life throws up. It has thus to be recognised that these more bureaucratic interventions in social life offer distinct social roles for the judge compared with the classic role of deciding disputes. It is the sense that the judge has to follow up interventions in a repeated way that makes this kind of role distinctive, since it requires a range of other people to become involved.

The civil court is classically involved in making a narrowly specific decision in a dispute between parties. But in matters such as référé or in divorce the issues will return to the court several times and the court follows the progress of the case. Such situations fall in between the bureaucratic, hands-on involvement of the judge (with other professionals) in the management of a social situation, and the classical one-off decision where the parties bring a dispute to court and have it resolved.

(a) The passive civil judge

The essential character of a civil dispute is that the parties decide the issues that they want to bring before the judge. Unlike in constitutional and criminal law (and, to a lesser extent, administrative law), there is not an investigation of the situation of fact. As Bartin commented, the judge:

> ... is to decide the claims that the parties submit to him, and, consequently, to decide these claims as they are submitted to him. It is not his task to seek out himself the facts, documents or [other written] evidence which may support or weaken these claims. Any initiative on his part in this respect violates the fundamental rule that no fact may be invoked against a party except insofar as it has been submitted to him in advance and he has had an opportunity to challenge it.[19]

There is a tension between the requirements of the law and the requirements of the parties. As Jolowicz has pointed out:

> If ... it is the function of civil litigation to decide what are the legal rights and obligations of the parties in the circumstances that have arise, then, as a general rule and to the extent that human frailty allows, the decision should be based on the dictates of the law as a whole, not merely upon those of that particular part of the law or 'rule of law' that the parties and their legal advisers actually invoke.[20]

18 A Garapon, *Bien juger. Essai sur le rituel judiciaire*, pp 256-258.

19 Bartin, in his 5th edition of Aubry et Rau, *Cours de droit civil pratique français* (1922) cited in J Beardsley, 'Proof of Fact in French Civil Procedure' (1986) 34 Am Jo Comp Law 459 at pp 460-461.

20 JA Jolowicz, *On Civil Procedure* (Cambridge 2000), at p 186.

But the French civil law draws a distinction between the accidental failure to invoke the right legal rule, and the deliberate narrowing by the parties of the issues that the judge is asked to resolve. Under the New Code of Civil Procedure, all the parties have to specify is the subject-matter (objet) of the litigation. They do not have to specify a legal cause of action based on a specific legal rule as under the previous law.[1] If the parties set out the facts of the case, then the judge has to determine the appropriate legal classification. Under art 12 NCPCiv, 'The judge resolves the dispute according to the rules of law which are applicable to it. He has to give or restore the correct classification of the facts and events at issue without limiting himself to the characterisation that the parties have put forward.' Of course, the way in which the facts are written up in the pleadings will already be strongly influenced by a particular conception of the appropriate legal basis for the action. But the judge can re-classify the facts as appropriate; for example, she can decide that the situation of an exploding television gives rise to contractual liability for breach of warranty in sale, rather than delictual liability under art 1382. This power over the law fits with the requirement on the judge to research the law. The parties may draw attention to legal rules, but the judge is expected to undertake research, where necessary, to find the appropriate legal authorities. In practice, the lawyers on each side will draw attention to authorities which favour their client's case. But such presentation of the law is neither exhaustive nor balanced. Under art 13 NCPCiv., the judge can invite the parties to provide her with arguments on the law. The judge can therefore find this material useful, but cannot trust it to be sufficient to decide the case.

Where the parties have deliberately narrowed the focus of the dispute to a particular classification of the facts or to specific issues of law, the judge is not entitled to depart from these.[2] In this significant way, the parties are masters of the process. In addition, as a matter of public policy, the judge is entitled to raise *ex officio* 'grounds of pure law',[3] provided that these have been drawn to the attention of the parties so that they could make their observations on them. This power of judicial initiative is, however, of very limited application. The scope of ordre public in private law is far less significant than in administrative or criminal law.

Despite this broad power of the judge over the law, she is constrained by the facts that the parties present. The parties have the incentive to present all the facts available to them, because they cannot rely on facts which are not placed on file.[4] The parties have in this sense constructed the case, which the judge cannot go behind. As Bartin suggested, the role of the judge is essentially passive with regard to fact-finding. The rules of civil procedure give priority to written evidence, often pre-constituted proof, ie documents produced in advance of any dispute arising, eg a notarial act or a sales receipt. The oral hearing of witnesses is much less frequent than in English civil procedure and will be a separate proceeding in its own right, often before a juge de la mise en état, who may not ultimately decide the case.[5] This separation gives the

1 Ibid, pp 187-189; Serverin, p 229.
2 See art 12 § 3 NCPCiv.
3 See art 16 § 2 NCPCiv.
4 Beardsley, p 475.
5 The juge de la mise en état may well be the same judge who eventually tries the case. But with the time-lag between the orders made at the first stage and the eventual judgment hearing, personnel changes or workloads may well lead to a different judge hearing the case. Because of this, the content of the file is very significant.

parties more scope to comment on what emerges from this.[6] The result of this enquête will form part of the written file which the juge de l'audience will use as the basis of her decision. The French civil judge will not typically have to evaluate facts because it is usual to refer any disputed facts to the opinion of a court expert. The juge de la mise en état has the power to decide if an expert is needed and will appoint him and determine his brief. The judge will then make use of the report as part of the decision-making. In theory, the expert merely expresses opinions that do not bind the judge. The expert must not make any legal assessment or attempt to pre-judge the case. 'He is a technician, not a lawyer.'[7] In practice, the judge will almost always base her findings on the report of the expert. As Beardsley remarks, 'the impression is widespread that the courts are ready to deal with every case that is at all complex by the appointment of an *expert*'.[8] The lawyers for each side will often be involved in the enquiries that the expert makes and, for this reason, Beardsley describes the parties' involvement with the expert as a 'mini-trial'.[9] This approach, shared with administrative and criminal judges, involves a respect for specialist professionals. The judge is a professional on the law and on procedure, the expert is a professional on technical issues of fact. This deference to professionalism reduces the juge de l'audience to a very passive role in respect of the facts. The facts come pre-constituted from the parties or pre-digested by the expert. The job of the judge is to assemble the materials into a narrative of the chain of events and to apply a legal classification to them. It is the *audience* at which the avocats or parties will propose a narrative to the judge which links the facts on file and the law, and then the judge will go away and deliberate.

In this account of the civil procedure at first instance (accentuated in higher courts), the judge is a decision-maker, not an investigator. At the fact-finding stages, she may indicate that there are issues to be resolved and set in train mechanisms to find answers, but she does not engage in fact-finding herself and does not have to resolve conflicts between expert testimony. The judge's professionalism lies in the knowledge of the law. Of course, in the conduct of the hearings, the judge may assist unrepresented parties to present their arguments, and make them understand what is a sensible claim. But this is a style of approach to the task, rather than a definition of the task.

(b) Conciliation

Where the law is called upon to resolve a civil dispute, a decision by a judge is the most common outcome. As in most countries, lawyers do not seek a court decision as a preferred solution. They will seek some form of compromise without recourse to the courts. Even where this fails, in commercial disputes, lawyers will prefer to resort to arbitration or conciliation. Indeed, the role of arbitrator may well be undertaken by a law professor or by a registered expert.[10] All the same, as was noted by Sayag, French

6 See Beardsley, pp 478-480.
7 See C Rollot, 'Entre juge et parties', *Le Monde*, 24 May 2000, Supplement, discussing the work of an information technology expert.
8 Beardsley, p 484. See also CN Ngwasiri, 'Some problems of expertise in French civil proceedings' (1989) 8 CJQ 168.
9 Beardsley, pp 480-485.
10 Thus it could well be that on one day the expert is acting at the instance of the judge, and the next day is spent as an arbitrator: see C Rollot, op cit.

business people seem more willing to resort to the commercial courts than businessmen in common law countries.[11] There are no reliable figures on the number of disputes that are resolved in this way before the need for a judge, but the number is likely to be substantial.

In some fields, such as divorce and adoption, parties are required to come to court. Since 1975, some form of attempt at conciliation has become part of the process. Although initially desired as a way of encouraging reconciliation between couples, conciliation now functions primarily to encourage divorcing partners to reach an agreement on issues of property, maintenance and arrangements for the children.[12] In this way, the judge can be asked to approve an agreement between the parties, rather than being required to make a decision of her own.

Outside the field of divorce law, conciliation has a more limited place within the civil court system. Art. 21 NCPCiv states that 'It is part of the mission of the judge to conciliate the parties.' This role has been strengthened in 1995 by a power for the judge to suspend proceedings and to order mediation to be attempted. Art 127 reinforces the desirability of conciliation by stating that the parties are entitled to reach an agreement at any point in the proceedings. The system of conciliators (since 1996 called concilateurs de justice) in the lower courts was set up by the loi of 20 March 1978. The parties can approach a conciliator both within and outside any formal legal dispute. In practice, parties will be encouraged to refer their case to a conciliator either by the greffier of the court when they come to file their action or by the judge at trial. The conciliator is often present at the *audience* and goes off to an adjoining room with any parties to see whether a conciliation can be effective. If it can, the judge can then endorse the agreement, when the parties come back into court.

The quantity of official conciliation is rather limited. In the tribunaux d'instance during 1998, 452,646 cases were filed for decision and 354,407 decisions were reached of which only 3,967 were reached by conciliation. Similarly in référé cases, there were 69,034 decisions of which 353 were by conciliation. Figures for the tribunaux de grande instance are much the same. In 1998 there were 635,340 cases filed for final decision and 484,267 decisions of which 1,619 were reached by conciliation. Similarly among the 118,785 applications for a *référé* judgment, there were only 622 conciliations. The total number of cases referred to conciliators in 1998 was 85, 452 and they had a 46.8% success rate in reaching a settlement. In part the explanation will lie in the attempts by lawyers to reach a settlement. By the time the case has become a lawsuit, positions have been hardened. A further explanation lies in the relatively small number of conciliators. There were 1,614 for the whole of France in 1998, an average of 2.3 per 100,000 inhabitants, but these are very unevenly distribued across the country.[13] There has been an increased professionalisation of conciliation and mediation during the past 20 years as a result of the increased activity in France.[14] But the position outside family law and criminal law is still rather limited.

In brief then, the role of the law continues to be focused on the decision of the judge, rather than through the intervention of the mediator or conciliator. As one judge

11 See above, p 65.

12 See J Dahen, 'La médiation en matière familiale', in J-P Bonafé-Schmitt, *Les médiations, la médiation* (Ramonville St-Agnès 1999), 81.

13 See *Annuaire statistique de la Justice 2000*, p 25 and the map on that page.

14 See J-P Bonafé-Schmitt, *Les médiations, la médiation*, pp 128-132.

put it, there are many individuals who come to court because they want a judge to demonstrate them to be right. Often they have not thought through the cost-effectiveness of litigation. The broken fridge may be worth only 2,500F, and yet the cost of the *expertise* to determine the cause of the defect may be 5,000F. It is the role of the judge to introduce a sense of realism in the expectations of the parties and to encourage them to come to a reasonable settlement. This approach to the conduct of the hearing involves a pragmatic engagement by the judge with the parties and their lawyers, rather than just a reliance on a formalistic approach which might limit itself to deciding the case as presented in the formal documentation by reference to the legal rules.

D. LEGAL PERSONNEL

(1) Doctrinal writers

Doctrinal writers are typically members of the academic profession. Some may also be *avocats* or judges, but their interest in going beyond the individual case persuades them to produce reflections on legal developments and on the law in general.

The body of writers who constitute civil law doctrine is relatively narrow. The authors are predominantly academics, particularly professeurs agrégés.[15] Both leading textbooks and commentaries are provided by them. Of course, younger academics (particularly through their theses) and some notes by judges or avocats do also contribute to the body of doctrine, but the authoritative writing comes from certain established names. The agrégation serves to confirm the status of the academic as a recognised authority.[16] The economic position that this status gives enables the function to be performed. As Tunc reflected:

> The judge (of course, he can also be an author or teacher) goes from case to case, usually in most diverse matters. Conversely, the author stands well back and concentrates on a certain subject, perhaps a narrow one. By spending the necessary time to study its statutory, judicial, practical, and doctrinal aspects, he is in a much better position to arrive at a synthetic view of the matter.[17]

What Tunc says about the judge could equally apply to the avocat. The increasing number of agrégés in civil and commercial law who are also avocats is often cited as a reason for the decline in the status of doctrinal writing.[18] Few monographs are produced after the thesis in these fields, and much writing concentrates on rather technical case-notes, rather than the more generalist and reflective writing of previous generations.[19] The leisure for that broader study is not available to the avocat agrégés. On the other

15 Jestaz and Jamin, 18 LS at p 429, estimate that 90% of doctrinal writers are professors or maîtres-assistants, and the remaining 10% of judges and avocats are usually occasional lecturers
16 Ibid, pp 430 and 434.
17 A Tunc, 'The Methodology of the Civil Law in France' (1976) 50 Tulane L Rev 459 at p 469.
18 J Carbonnier, *Droit et passion de droit*, p 72. On agrégés and doctorate graduates in general see J Ardagh, *France in the New Century*, pp 561-562.
19 See P Jestaz, 'Déclin de la doctrine?' in *Droits 20: Doctrine et recherche en droit* (Paris 1994), 85 esp pp 87-88 and 96.

hand, Carbonnier notes that the cost of printing for an essentially national audience makes it difficult to publish some intellectually good theses, and this can help explain the emphasis on manuals and treatises for student and practitioner audiences among the established doctrinal writers in civil law and the small number of monographs.

In his study of law reviews, Wiederkehr notes that the reviews have served predominantly to serve the need of practitioners and this has reinforced a technicality in the study of civil law.[20] Certainly he notes a decline in generalist articles in the leading review, the *Revue trimestrielle de droit civil* (founded in 1902).[1]

Dezelay sees significant changes in the production of doctrine because of the globalisation of law and the rise of the large law firms. The Anglo-Saxon model of the 'knowledge entrepreneur' is replacing the 'pure jurist' and the involvement of professors in this new activity is changing the character of doctrine.[2] It is no longer possible to limit doctrinal writing to those who have been authenticated through the agrégation process. But, it does not seem to me that this necessarily represents a decline in the status of doctrine, but rather a displacement. The activity of alerting practitioners and academics to current developments was the role of the reports of Dalloz and Sirey and of the law reviews. Much of this is now being performed well by professional alerting systems and by databases. This still leaves a significant space for the more reflective consideration of legal developments, but the issue is how far this aspect remains the intellectual ambition of those who traditionally have performed the role of writing.

Others offer different reasons for the decline in the quality of doctrine. One argument would be that the number of writers has increased very substantially and so the authority of writers and the unanimity of doctrine are less easy to achieve.[3] Tunc argued in 1976 that the judges have less leisure to read the doctrine, although there are more assistants now available in courts.[4]

Some doctrinal writers are recruited as either temporary or permanent members of the Cour de cassation. At the time of writing there are three, which is fairly usual. Such members of the Cour continue academic writing and also bring to bear their expertise on decisions of the Cour.

The tradition of professors giving *consultations* provides a different form of influence of academic writers on the development of case law. But this form of intervention is seen as too partisan, too applied and too dependent to play a significant role in developing doctrine generally.[5]

But the picture presented by current commentators within France is not all gloom. Some of the most serious reflective work on current legal issues takes place in committees established by government which reflect on major issues of the day. A good example is the *Comité consultatif national d'éthique pour les sciences de vie et de la santé*. Its publications on bioethical issues have been influential in stimulating debate and legislation. Its president was invited by the Cour de cassation to present arguments to

20 G Wiederkehr, 'La culture des revues françaises de droit privé' in A-J Arnaud (ed) (1988) 29 *Quaderni fiorentini per la storia del pensiero giuridico* 9 at p 23.
1 Ibid, p 28.
2 Y Dezelay, 'La production doctrinale comme objet et terrain de luttes politiques et professionnelles' in Y Poirmeur (ed), *La doctrine*, 230.
3 Ibid.
4 Tunc, 50 Tulane L Rev at p 472.
5 See JD Bredin cited in Y Poirmeur, *La doctrine juridique*, p 154 and see generally pp 151-155.

it during the case on surrogate mothers.[6] A similar role is played by other leading academics on bodies dealing with consumer protection and so on.[7] The extent of contributions in these situations is difficult to assess, because it is typically not made public. In this area, and in the field of private consultations, there is thus a distinction to be drawn between the status of professors as acknowledged experts on the law and the influence of their published doctrinal writing.

While doctrinal writing is clearly situated within the realm of general interpretation of law and reflection on future developments, the role of the legal writers themselves is more diffuse. As knowledge experts, they play roles as consultants to government and to practitioners in resolving practical problems (or even practical disputes). There is a clear connection between their status acquired as a result of their writing, and their acceptability to perform the wider role.

(2) Judges

The civil judges are a substantial corps distinct from administrative judges, but will often be involved in judging criminal cases (or as procureur or juge d'instruction) at other stages in their career. The civil judicial career offers both generalist roles and specialist functions. As a specialist, a judge may be involved in family work, in the execution of judgments, and so on. As a generalist, a judge may serve as a juge de la mise en état, a trial judge, or as avocat-général. In a smaller court, the judge will necessarily be fairly generalist; whereas in larger courts, the judge will perform broader roles. In larger courts and cour d'appel with several chambers, a judge is likely to be a specialist in some particular areas of civil law. Within such a specialist area, with a substantial number of decisions to make, then the judge will have more scope to build up rule-making.

Informal, as well as formal contacts with the local bar enable the presidents of courts and chambers to let it be known how they wish cases to be presented. There are inevitable trade-offs between giving scope for the avocats to have their say and speed of decision-making (which also involves the rights of others to have their say). Local agreements on how long arguments should be often establish ground rules that can enable all to achieve their objectives.

In my interviews with judges at all levels within the French civil court system, the common analogy for the judge was the 'referee' (*arbitre*). In the view of one judge, the role of the civil law is to pacify, so the parties are masters of the proceedings and the judge does not normally challenge this, unless some public interest issue so requires.

The balance between dispute settlement and rule-making is very marked between the different levels of the system. In brief, the latter function is not significant until one reaches the Cour de cassation. At the level of the Cour de cassation, as one judge put it, the judge is called upon to 'judge the [lower court's] decision and not the case'. By contrast at first instance, people have come (with or without a lawyer) wanting a judge to give a decision and declare them to be in the right. Their interest is often as much symbolic as material. Now this may be unrealistic, given the cost of full legal proceedings.

6 See JCP 1991 II 21752 note Terré; J-C Galloux, in Y Poirmeur, op cit, 240.
7 This point was reinforced by interviews with a range of academics and judges.

So, especially where parties are unrepresented, the judge has to engage in both explanation and bargaining with the parties as to the way forward. The dynamics of a hearing at the tribunal d'instance, even in open court, focuses on the judge trying to encourage the parties to take the case forward in an appropriate way. The judge may well seek to clarify the precise details of their request or of the facts of the case. This may lead to suggestions about how the pleadings might be amended or which documents need adding. As a result, there is not the same expectation of a very detailed preparation by the judge before a hearing (and this would be impossible given the number of cases which have to be heard in a single session). The judge at first instance may be involved at various stages – as juge des référés (giving interim orders), as juge de la mise en état (organising the processing of more complex cases, eg by having an expert's report), as juge de l'audience (coming to decisions on the merits after a hearing), or as juge de l'exécution (ensuring the enforcement of decisions). These roles require engagement with parties and their lawyers to differing degrees. But interviews with judges suggest similar preoccupations, both to come to a socially satisfactory result, and to make those involved understand why decisions are being taken. The traditional long recital of the arguments of the parties in the lower court judgment[8] is a recognition that they have been taken seriously by the court.

The work of the judge at first instance is varied. In some cases, the judge works on her own, in others she will work with others. For example, the juge de la mise en état will work closely with experts and the juge de l'exécution with auctioneers and valuers. Judges dealing with adults incapable of managing their own affairs will deal with another group of professionals. In these cases, the judge is a leader of a team.

Of course, a large number of decisions have to be handed down, and the format of the judgments produced is both laconic and formalistic. But it is not in the formal judgment, handed down weeks after the hearing, that the real justification takes place. Faced with litigants, present with or without lawyers, the judge tries to 'gain the adherence' of the parties, and perhaps to find a form of words in describing the facts which will not exacerbate relations between them.

The cour d'appel falls in between. Frequently, courts now work with a single juge rapporteur holding a hearing and then the case being formally decided by the chamber, perhaps after further work has been done. The hearing is a mid-point in the process where information is gathered. Lawyers will present final arguments in the file handed in at the end of the oral hearing, and then research has to be undertaken.

In the lower courts, the issue of the efficient dispatch of a large number of cases is significant. The management role, which many judges undertake, is very much focused on the dispute resolution function.

Relations among judges of different courts remain structured in a pyramidal fashion. When talking to judges at regional level, it becomes clear that their lines of contact with other regional courts pass through Paris, especially the *Service de documentation* of the Cour de cassation. That court also holds annual events for the presidents of the cours d'appel which enables a certain comparison of experience. Within a region, there will be informal meetings arranged between the cour d'appel and the lower courts or at least among their presidents to ensure a degree of coordination. In major centres, the

8 Now replaced with a reference to the submissions of the parties: art 455 NCPCiv discussed above, p 70.

cour d'appel is located together with a tribunal de grande instance and a tribunal d'instance, so that informal contacts (eg over lunch in the canteen) are possible. But there are less formal ways in which civil judges meet each other. The continuing education programme of the ENM brings together often large numbers of judges from different parts of the country and different specialisms. This offers opportunities to exchange views.

(3) Lawyers

French *avocats* typically draw a distinction between two types of work – le juridique and le judiciaire.[9] Le juridique is concerned with legal advice and the conclusion of deals. It is the work which, until 1990, was largely the province of the conseil juridique. Le judiciaire is litigation and involves regular appearances in court, although there will also be written pleadings and the attempt to achieve out-of-court settlements. This was the traditional work of the avocat before 1990. In many places, including substantial sized cities such as Bordeaux and Montpellier, the formal union of the two professions has not induced a marked change in the work undertaken by lawyers as individuals or firms. Thus, to a substantial extent, the two functions of the civil law map onto the roles of different individuals. The hierarchy of esteem has passed in recent years to commercial work, both because of its inherent complexity and of the economic benefits arising from such work.[10] Other civil law work will typically be undertaken by generalist avocats. Unlike in the common law world, at least outside Paris, this difference between the people undertaking the work will not be reflected in a marked difference in the size of firms or lawyer's *cabinets* dealing with cases.

In the area of managing cases in court, then the lawyers develop understandings with their local court. This will cover the way cases are to be presented and the typical length of argument. Such understandings establish ground rules useful both for their relations with the bench and with their own colleagues. In civil cases, the art of advocacy is different from criminal law. The avocat is not trying to portray the character of his client, his personality and social setting. In civil cases, the avocat is trying to explain a file about a situation of fact. The principal work will have been done in ensuring that the file is complete. The *audience* is a chance to give an overview of the file, and then to hand in the final submissions (which will usually be much longer). In the words of several judges interviewed, they want the avocat to 'step back from the file' (sortir du dossier) and give the judge the key points and arguments, not a summary of the entire file. As a result, the submissions at the audience are typically brief, but can be effective. The avocat who adopts the criminal law method of pleading at length and presenting the whole case will both bore the judge and annoy his colleagues waiting for their case to come on. In this regard, pleading before the civil courts has much in common with pleading before the administrative courts. All the same, there is more of a tradition of pleading before the civil courts and more of a dialogue between bar and bench. The absence of the avocat-général in most cases below the Cour de cassation results in the parties having full control over the case, unlike in administrative and criminal law.

9 See L Karpik, *French Lawyers*, p 208.
10 Ibid, pp 197-199.

In interview with avocats and judges, it is clear that lawyers have a number of interests to please in a case. They have their clients, who may wish particular arguments to be pressed, even if they are unlikely to succeed. For instance, the legal service of a particular bank may have developed a policy of claiming interest and will instruct its lawyers to raise the claim against the defendant, even though the individual lawyer thinks it is a bad argument in this particular case. There is no sense that the avocat is an officer of the court. By contrast, the avoué and the avocat à la Cour de cassation are both officiers ministériels, holders of public offices and so have duties to assist the higher courts by their preparation of cases which come before them. They are supposed to ensure cases are put in proper form and, perhaps, to dissuade the would-be appellant of a hopeless case.

(4) Media

The civil law does not attract the same media attention as criminal and constitutional law. Civil cases are most usually reported when they involve a well-known individual or a subject of public concern, such as compensation for the victims of asbestos dust at work.[11] Such reporting will cover very few cases in a year. As a result, neither judges nor avocats will have many dealings with the media. This preserves the essentially private character of litigation. It creates a space where, although there is a public involvement through the judge, there is usually little public pressure. The public are rarely present at civil court hearings (unlike in the criminal courts).

Civil courts have no press service and do not seek out the press. Occasionally, an individual decision will attract public or media comment. By way of reaction, the judge may call in the press to explain the process which the court adopted and to counter mis-reporting. But the judge will not seek to defend his decision to the press.

E. THE CULTURE OF THE CIVIL LAW

(1) Lawmaking

The argument in this chapter has been that the development civil law involves both collaboration and independent action by a number of bodies. The legislature is far less active in classical civil law than in criminal or public law. In those areas, the legislature (or the legislative function of the executive) is necessary in order to authorise the actions of the state and of state officials. In private law, the law intervenes as facilitator or regulator. In some areas, such as family law, there is a clear community interest in dealing with a social problem. In other areas, the need for the state to intervene is less pressing. In these areas, the initiative for legal change is likely to be taken by the courts. In some cases, as has been seen,[12] the role of judicial decisions or the annual report of the Cour de cassation is to encourage legislative action in order to remedy a

11 See *Le Monde*, 5 June 2000, p 8 for a long discussion of such cases.
12 Above, pp 68-69.

clearly unsatisfactory state of the law. In many other situations, as in the issue of defective goods, the reform will be undertaken by the courts. That example illustrates the complex influences on reform. Doctrinal writing will offer both a critique of the existing law and a range of possible solutions. As Serverin points out, although doctrinal writers present arguments based on perceptions of social change, their evidence is indirect. The French tradition of sociology is rarely empirical. Doctrinal writers therefore use case law or general knowledge to demonstrate that social situations or needs have changed and that the law also needs to change.[13] Judges have more direct experience of social situations, as these are presented to them. Of course, especially in the higher courts, these situations will be mediated through the case file, rather than be directly perceived by the judges. It would, however, be wrong to portray doctrinal writers as totally remote. In the civil law, many are avocats dealing directly with clients, or they give consultations in individual cases. They thus have a knowledge of what is happening among actual or potential litigants. Particularly influential will be the opinion of the avocats au Conseil d'Etat et à la Cour de cassation who have regular dealings with the highest court and who are able to present substantial numbers of cases in a year and thus to generate a climate of opinion towards its decisions.[14] But avocats are treated by public opinion as particularly partisan. In some cases, the doctrinal writer may also be a judge or member of Parliament. In addition, doctrinal writers are members of commissions. If the dominant voice in identifying the perceived need is the judge, the source of solutions is more shared. The judges look for support for particular directions either to analogy with the legislator or to acceptance among doctrine (as well as from the lower courts). If the locus of decision-making remains the appellate courts, the responsibility for creating the climate of opinion is more shared.

(2) Conceptualism or pragmatism[15]

As noted in the Preface, French civil law is often criticised as overly conceptual.[16] A contrast is often drawn between the conceptual or dogmatic approach to thinking in the civil law and the more pragmatic approach of the common law. Nicholas wrote that 'the French lawyer undoubtedly sets great store by the intellectual coherence of his system, and by the elegant manipulation of large-scale concepts than does his English counterpart'.[17] In this passage, the 'French lawyer' seems to be a doctrinal legal writer. The strength of doctrinal legal writing and its centrality in the presentation of French civil law explains this impression in part. As has been stated earlier, it is in the nature of doctrinal writing to seek systematic and coherent treatment of a question, rather than to seek the 'quick fix' to which the judge may be tempted to deal with the case at hand.[18] Equally, the brief legal judgment, with its absence of explanation of reasons for decisions gives an impression of the ineluctable logic that justifies a particular outcome.

13 Serverin, pp 180-181.
14 See Troper and Grzegorczyk, p 131.
15 More generally, see J Bell, 'English Law and French Law – Not so different?' [1995] CLP 63, 76-80.
16 Above, p viii.
17 In Harris and Tallon, *Contract Law Today*, p 389.
18 Above, pp 72-74.

But it is possible to study French law in a different way, and, indeed, Nicholas notes only shortly after the passage quoted that:

> A realistic appraisal of [English and French legal systems] must also take into account the tendency within any legal system for judges to balance the use of traditional concepts with their intuitive feeling of justice. The foreign observer will note that the French judge is adept at this process. [19]

When one considers how judges decide individual cases, then the law seems to take a more pragmatic turn. If one asks how a specific problem is handled in French private law, then it is possible to see the way conceptual categories are manipulated pragmatically in order to produce practical solutions. Whittaker[20] provides a good illustration in relation to the English doctrine of anticipatory breach, ie a deliberate and pre-announced breach of contract. The French do not have an equivalent doctrine and this represents a difference in legal policy – an emphasis on performance, rather than on compensation. But there are ways in which the problem can be met, both procedurally (by application to court for termination after breach and a rapid use of référé) and substantively (a different rule on damages for deliberate breaches). A similar position is noted by Ogus and Tallon in relation to remedies for breach of contract.[1] It is clear that clarity in the use of concepts plays an important part in a sense of the right way to argue a legal point. All the same, the illustration of defective goods shows the way in which French doctrine and case law is willing to manipulate the concepts radically in order to achieve satisfactory solutions. This analogy-based, gradualist approach allows judges (as well as doctrinal writers) to react to the cases which present themselves. The relative absence of major legislation on many aspects of substantive civil law provides scope for this, more pragmatic approach to develop.

The true position may be that French law is not so conceptually driven than might first appear from some of the more elegant, civil law doctrinal legal writing. Rodolfo Sacco certainly argues that, even among doctrinal writers, there is a curious mix of conceptualism and pragmatism in the way concepts are developed:

> ... the French model, compared with other Romanist models, does not appear to be the standard-bearer of the rationalist and systematic spirit. Definitions are made in order to be contradicted by their applications; important conceptual differences are not respected; different definitions are not always coherent in relation to one another. The interest of the French jurist turns towards the practical and axiological aspects of problems, rather than to the conceptual systems.[12]

This emphasis on the practical is, of course, much more common among the notes d'arrêt than in textbooks, since the former have the ambition not only of explaining the place of a decision within the system of principles and rules, but also commenting on

19 Harris and Tallon, p 389.

20 S Whittaker, 'How does French law deal with Anticipatory Breaches of Contract?' (1996) 45 ICLQ 662.

1 Harris and Tallon, ch 6.

2 R Sacco, *La comparaison juridique au service de la connaissance du droit* (Paris 1991), p 139.

the practical merits. The writers of these notes also are frequently engaged in work as an avocat or in consultancy in the field.

One might conclude from this that, though doctrinal writing is more important than in the other branches of law studied (and more than in the common law). Its conceptualism affects above all the presentation of the system to the outside world, and has only a limited impact on the operation of decision-making. Doctrine offers the voice of rationality. But that is not the only voice to be heard by the system. Maybe, even in the citadel of the classical model of French law, some so-called distinctive features are exaggerated.

Chapter 4

Criminal law

Conventionally a distinction is drawn between adversarial and inquisitorial systems and this is seen as a key determinant of a legal culture.[1] The French system clearly is used as a stereotype for the inquisitorial system, even if the French point to the more mixed nature of the French criminal process. The culture of a criminal justice system, broadly understood, involves features such as penology, social education, diversion practices and policing. These set out the purposes for which the law exists and how it will operate. There is clearly much debate on these areas within France. As in most countries, there are fashions in penalties, the use of imprisonment, preventative measures, and the importance of retribution and social rehabilitation. Many of these tasks are carried out by administrative bodies or agencies. This chapter takes a narrower and more classical perspective and concentrates on the organisational features of the French criminal justice system, which are operated by the lawyers and which shape the public functioning of the system. The argument in this chapter will be that the culture of the French criminal legal system is marked by the process of choosing the person to criminalise, rather than by the process of setting and developing standards of behaviour. More recently, especially with the European Convention on Human Rights, the French have had external benchmarks for their criminal procedure to which both judges and legislators refer. The French are seeking to maintain the best features of their own tradition whilst striving to achieve the highest standards in compliance with internationally recognised protections of the rights of the accused and of victims.

A. THE ACTIVITY OF CRIMINAL LAW

(1) The tasks of criminal law

Criminal law is the branch of law that has the highest public profile. The reasons are well known and common to all Western legal systems. As Pradel remarks:

1 See Mirjan R Damaska, *The Faces of Justice and State Authority. A Comparative Approach to the Legal Process* (New Haven 1986).

> ... whereas civil procedure and civil law only involve private interests (most often only financial) criminal procedure and criminal law bring into question both the social order disturbed by the offence, and private interests very often of the highest importance: freedom, honour, even life, and not only financial interests.[2]

In all legal systems, criminal law has a number of functions and France shares in this multiplicity. All the same, there are certain distinctive aspects of the tasks of French criminal law, which shape the culture within which it operates.

(a) Substantive functions

Criminal law has the function of both setting normative standards and organising the appropriate punishment of individuals. The setting of standards serves to encourage certain types of behaviour, but also to send out signals about what society values to the law-abiding as much as to the potential offenders. The symbolic function is carried out both by the declaratory function of publishing legal texts, and by the form of procedure adopted (the majesty of the law). France has a distinctive approach to using criminal law for administrative and medical faults.[3] As will be seen, especially in the 1980s and 1990s, administrators and politicians have increasingly become the subjects of criminal investigations and prosecutions. The use of the criminal law is thus much wider than in other legal systems. As a former minister of Justice, Toubon, remarked, laws are often passed in order to give a political signal.[4] The recent debate on the criminal penalties to which elected officials should be subject also reveals the importance of stigma. The Massot Report notes that between 1989 and 1999, while the number of prosecutions in the courts had remained fairly static, the number of criminal offences rose from 8,805 to 10,029. In practice, 98% of crimes are accounted for by only 500 of these offences.[5] That report recommended a moratorium for a year on the creation of new offences in order to sort out whether a *criminal* penalty is appropriate for the kinds of misdeed. Certainly for that report, the increasing sense of 'penalisation' lies more in the increase in offences than in the number of prosecutions.[6] (Though it would be true to say that there have been a number of very high profile cases in recent years.)

In relation to punishment, Pradel notes that in 20th century French doctrinal writing, there has been a movement from defining criminal law as the totality of rules concerned with the exercise of repression by the State to a more general definition which focuses on the reaction of the State towards offences and offenders. Such a definition includes scope for the re-education and rehabilitation of the individual, not just punishment.

2 *Droit Pénal: tome II Procédure pénal* (8th edn 1995), p 16.

3 See the cases of Contaminated Blood and the Furiani Stadium, below, p 107, as well as the Massot Report (below, pp 128-129) on administrative fault and also J Penneau, *La responsabilité du médecin* (Paris 1992), pp 99-103.

4 In *Justices 2000*, p 26.

5 *Groupe d'étude sur la responsabilité pénale des décideurs publics* (Report to Minister of Justice, 16 December 1999) (hereafter 'Massot Report'), p 46.

6 Denis Salas complains of a move towards *pénalisation* in France (*Le tiers pouvoir*, pp 77ff): also A Garapon, *Le gardien des promesses* (Paris 1996), ch 4 where he talks of the 'préférence pénale'.

This leads him to define criminal law as 'the law of the offence and the social reaction to it'.[7] As in many countries, there have been debates on general penal policy, and France has developed its own distinctive schools such as the 'social control school', long dominated by Marc Ancel who was a leading academic, editor of one of the leading criminal law journals and president of the criminal chamber of the Cour de cassation.

The discussion of alternatives to the criminal justice system is of great significance.[8] There is a balance to be struck between securing an appropriate punishment and effectiveness in disposing of cases. The increasing emphasis on alternatives to trial as a resolution of criminal cases does not represent an abandonment of punishment as an objective, but rather a willingness to achieve a less than maximum solution in return for a speedy clear-up. In a sense, this has always been part of the criminal justice system, but it has come to the fore in recent years. Crawford[9] questions whether the recent development of mediation in criminal law is very French. He is right to stress that a resolution other than by a formal judicial decision has not been the French way of resolving cases, and the models used are borrowed from abroad. But classement sans suite as a form of decision when the juge and the procureur consider this to be sufficient is fairly traditional. One may reach the decision not to prosecute because of the effort involved and the sense that the very process of investigation has achieved a deterrent effect.[10]

(b) Procedural functions

Procedural fairness: The idea of fair procedure focuses also on the individual offender. Because the symbolic and punishment consequences of a criminal conviction are socially (and physically) so important, it is essential that the penalties are imposed on the right people and with a community sense that the process is reliable. Criminal procedure has been the major battleground since the French Revolution. The secretive lettres de cachet which authorised detention without trial, a secretive investigation and the absence of legal representation were among the deficiencies of the Ancien Régime. The following two hundred years have seen various attempts to establish a fairer system, whilst retaining certain key features of the French way of doing things. The role of the investigation process conducted under the control of a judge (either the parquet or, in more serious cases, the juge d'instruction) and the place of the file are important features of the French conception of procedural fairness during the investigation. The questioning of the accused and witnesses on the basis of the pre-trial file and, in the most serious cases, the use of a jury which sits with judges, are

7 *Droit pénal général* (10th edn 1995), § 1.

8 See J Pradel, D 2000 Chr 1 at pp 2-3 where he talks of the 'third way' between prosecution and closing the file on a case, by which he means the various processes of non-judicial diversion or 'composition pénale' (paying a fine instead of prosecution).

9 A Crawford, 'Justice de Proximité – The Growth of 'Houses of Justice' and Victim/Offender Mediation in France: A Very UnFrench Legal Response?' (2000) 9 *Social and Legal Studies* 29.

10 See for instance the fictional case of businessman, M Richard, in C Samet, *Journal d'un juge d'instruction* (Paris 2000), ch VIII, where a compromise of the parquet and the juge decides on a limited charge, but to use *détention provisoire* as a way of making a point which will have as much effect as a subsequent trial to a man of his standing.

important features of the French conception of a fair trial. While French notions are having to be revised in the light of the European Convention,[11] the French are attached to many of the central features of this model.

Procedural effectiveness: The organisation of procedure needs to ensure that it leads to an efficient pre-trial and trial process. The emphasis since 1522 on the investigation at the expense of the interests of the accused betrays a concern for effectiveness. Indeed this is a recurring feature. The procedure needs to be efficient in that it leads to timely decisions about whether there should be a trial, and that the trial comes to the correct result in a reasonable time at a reasonable social cost. The performance indicators would be that it identifies offenders and comes to conclusions with reliability.

Indicators[12] suggest some success in this respect. Most reported offences cannot be pursued by the police for lack of information. Thus of the 4,566,988 offences reported in 1998,[13] 7.2% did not constitute an offence and 66.7% had insufficient information to be able to give rise to a prosecution (typically because the author was unknown). Although formally decided by the prosecutor, the decision in such a case is really taken by the police. Of the remaining 26.1% of cases (1,193,994) which were prosecutable, These then divided into two groups. In the first, some 416,841 cases (34.9%) were not proceeded with (classés sans suite), for the most part (in 53.4% of cases) because the matter was too unimportant to warrant a prosecution. Such a decision is taken by the prosecutor. In the remaining 777,153 cases, there was some form of judicial action. In 163,799 some alternative action to a prosecution was taken in the form of treatment, warning or agreed compensation. Such action would be agreed by the prosecutor before classement sans suite. Thus only 51.4% (613,354 cases) of all prosecutable offences led to a prosecution. Of these offences, only 40,362 were referred to the juge d'instruction. Thus he dealt only with 3.38% of all prosecutable offences, representing 6.58% of all offences actually prosecuted. It can be seen from these figures that the prosecutor is the most important figure in deciding whether offences are prosecuted, and whether alternative action is acceptable.

There is a very high success rate for prosecutions in all courts.[14] The main problem is delay with the instruction, which takes over 16 months on average to complete. The drive for effectiveness is in tension, however, with the need to respect the rights of the suspect (and increasingly of the victim). In a sense, during the 1990s the process has increasingly become a legal vehicle for realising the legitimate expectations of individuals and groups about the behaviour of officials and other people.[15] As the rights of direct and indirect victims, as well as the suspect, become an increasing part of the process, so the structural features focused on an efficient prosecution become subordinated to the need for the hearing before the judge.

11 See below, pp 130-131.
12 Draw from the criminal justice statistics in the *Annuaire statistique de la Justice. Edition 2000* (Paris 2000).
13 See *Annuaire statistique*, pp 96ff
14 See above p 27 below, p 112.
15 See V Wright, 'The Fifth Republic: From *Droit de l'Etat* to the *Etat de droit*' (1999) 22 West European Politics 92 at p 109.

In summary, one may conclude that France shares many of the tasks identified above with other western legal systems. It is the conception of the procedure for implementing the criminal law which is the most distinctive – how the process is conceived, who is involved, and how the issues of effectiveness and fairness are balanced within the process. At the same time, the relationship of the State and the individual in the trial, and the State and society in lawmaking is distinctive compared with other branches of law. In an important sense, the State is acting as the spokesperson of society, much more than as the subject who is controlled, as in administrative law. As in private law, the individual is the person controlled.

(2) Criminal law as a forensic process

While the norm-setting role of the law is important, criminal law should be conceived as essentially a *forensic* process. As Alain Minc suggests, for the French:

> ... the penal ritual remains the expiatory ceremony of modern societies, with its liturgy: press rumours, accusation anticipated by the media, photographs, placing a person under investigation, leaks to journalists, witnesses, incitement, branding with a hot iron, becoming bogged down, the neglect of and indifference to the final decision.[16]

Clearly the procedural side of criminal law is about the way in which one comes to a trial and how it is conducted. Equally, the trial and the statements of judges at the beginning of the judicial year[17] make use of the forensic process to communicate and reinforce normative statements. As in many countries, the individuation of punishment comes through the forensic process in France. Garapon suggests that 'the criminal trial has also value as a rite of passage before the social status of the accused is formally devalued'[18] But the symbolic and normative debate also occurs in other *fora* not least the legislature and the lawmaking process.

Pradel makes the point that procedure lies at the core of criminal law in a way that is untrue for other branches of law:

> ... criminal procedure is indispensable to the application of criminal law. The trial is in reality the necessary link, the inevitable feature uniting the offence with the penalty. By contrast, in civil, commercial or administrative cases, the trial remains an essential and accidental feature, only several institutions always giving rise to a trial (for example, divorce).[19]

Both normative and procedural dimensions are common to many branches of law. In the case of norm setting, the criminal law carries with it a stronger sense of 'shaming' and therefore a stronger power. But in the criminal law, the symbolic and procedural dimensions take on added significance. The trial has a symbolic importance because of the social significance attached to the decision, and it thus communicates

16 A Minc, *Au nom de la loi* (Paris 1998), p 15.

17 See J-C Farcy, *Magistrats en majesté. Les discours de rentrée aux audiences solonnelles des cours d'appel (XIXe- XXe siècles)* (Paris 1998), pp 362-378 for an analysis of the language and ideas used on such occasions.

18 A Garapon, *Bien Juger. Essai sur le rituel judiciaire*' (Paris 1997), p 110.

19 *Droit Pénal: tome II Procédure pénal*, p 15.

expectations in a public way. The point is well made by a procureur. He argues that, by the time a case gets to trial, his job is done. All the evidence is there and in the vast majority of cases, the judge will convict. But the trial is important, since it is the public confirmation of the investigation's results. As Carbonnier notes, 'Criminal law is the most theatrical of all branches of law.'[20] Administrative law with its emphasis on improving the administration, and private law with its focus on individual dispute resolution are, in practice, less public and dramatic. Even constitutional law, though it is very much in the press spotlight, affects a relatively small group of people directly. So there is a difference in the social role of the criminal law.

The reporting of high profile cases demonstrates this attention to the theatrical character of the trial. To take an example, the prefecture in Corsica authorised the rapid rebuilding of the stadium of Sporting Club de Bastia in time for the cup quarter-final match with Olympique de Marseille.[1] There were no written contracts or designs. The newly constructed stand collapsed before the match on 5 May 1992 leaving 15 people dead and 2,177 injured. Eighteen people, including the president of the French football league, the constructors, the prefect at the time and the head of the prefect's office, were charged, though it was decided eventually only to bring 13 of them to trial. Not surprisingly, with the victims and their families as parties civiles, there was much interest in the trial for manslaughter and indifference to endangering life in January 1995. In the press reports, there are quotations from the oral arguments of the avocats for the civil parties and the defence made by the accused.[2] The scenes at the actual decision in the case demonstrate the theatrical dénouement of the proceedings. On 2 April 1995, the court delivered its verdict. After the president had read it out and had acquitted a number of the civil servants, the victims' families were reported as shouting out 'murderers', 'it's a disgrace', 'you have an interest in protecting them'.[3] By contrast, the reporting of the appeal court decisions is more sober and simply summarises the decision of the court and the submissions made to it.[4]

Even more dramatic was the 'contaminated blood' case which involved the prosecution of doctors in 1992 and then of ministers (including a former Prime Minister) before the Cour de justice de la République, a court which exists for trying ministers. Further trials then followed against another 30 officials and doctors in proceedings where the instruction file covered 134 volumes.[5] On 9 March 1999, for the first time in the history of the Republic, a minister, the former minister of health Edmund Hervé, was convicted of manslaughter by negligence for failing to introduce heat treatment for blood in order to prevent the spread of the HIV virus, even when the treatment was available and shown to be effective. As a result, France had a significantly larger number of people affected with HIV from contaminated blood than other countries in Europe. *Le Monde* took the unusual step of publishing the entire judgment.[6] The

20 J Carbonnier, *Droit et passion du droit sous la Ve République* (Paris 1996), p 135.
1 The details of the events in question are well summarised in *Le Monde*, 3 January 1995, p 8.
2 See eg Maurice Peyrot, *Le Monde*, 21 January 1995, p 11, and 27 January 1995, p 11.
3 Maurice Peyrot, *Le Monde*, 3 April 1995, p 22.
4 See *Le Monde*, 15 December 1995, p 14 (cour d'appel de Bastia) and 26 June 1997, p 12 (Cour de cassation).
5 *Le Monde*, 22 May 1999, p 8. On other cases before this Cour de Justice de la République, see Michel Degoffe, 'Responsabilité pénale et responsabilité politique du ministre' Rfdc 1996, 385.
6 See *Le Monde*, 11 March 1999, p 13; and for a general review of the case see Franck Nouchi, *Le Monde* 1 January 2000, supplement.

involvement of public figures enhances the public interest in the criminal process and reinforces values such as equality before the law.

Both the procedural and normative functions of criminal law pass through the criminal pre-trial and trial processes as a primary focus of attention. The specificity of the French system lies in the nature of that process and the actors who are involved. It is in the construction of the criminal process that the key features of the culture of criminal law can be found.

B. THE INSTITUTIONAL SETTING

(1) The basic structure of the criminal process[7]

In terms of procedure, the specificity of French law lies in the close connection between the processes of investigation (*enquête*), preparation (*instruction*), and trial (*jugement*). This involves a separation of personnel and a distinctiveness of the process, but, unlike many systems of law, for centuries there has been a deliberate continuity between the three phases.

French criminal justice involves a combination at the pre-trial phase between the police, the parquet and the juge d'instruction, which may at first seem strange. Despite the well-developed institutional roles, the procedural values do not attach to the difference between *people*, but rather to the separation of the functions of enquête and instruction.[8]

(a) The enquête

The enquête is the initial process of investigation begun either by the police themselves or as the result of a complaint made to the procureur. During the enquête, the French system grants different powers to the police and judges depending on the nature of the offence involved. In the ordinary procedure (enquête préliminaire), the police have limited powers. They can neither arrest nor search without instituting a judicial inquiry (enquête judiciaire), ie involving the procureur or the juge d'instruction who have wider powers, but the police are then constrained to act on their authority. By contrast, in the flagrant procedure (enquête flagrante), there are wide police powers in the early days of the inquiry, albeit under control of procureur, but the juge d'instruction must be brought in to take over the case as soon as feasible. During this enquête phase, the procureur typically exercises supervisory roles, authorising action, but not directing it. He is informed immediately on any arrest. After 24 hours of detention after arrest by the police, the procureur can authorise an extension of detention for a further 24 hours, and this process can be conducted either over the telephone or by personal interview with the accused. (A personal interview is necessary in the case of minors. Such an interview may well include encouragement to the detained person to cooperate with

7 See generally, Bell, Boyron and Whittaker, pp 122-136. There is an excellent flow-chart on p 93 of the *Annuaire statistique*.

8 T Renoux, 'Le Conseil constitutionnel et l'instruction pénale: juges ou magistrats?' (1998) 10 *Justices: La Justice pénale* 75, at p 82.

the police and to make admissions, if indeed the person is guilty.) Since 1993, the person detained has had the right to see a lawyer after 20 hours. The loi of 15 June 2000 gave the right from the beginning of the detention period and at various stages thereafter. The interview is in private and is limited to 30 minutes. The lawyers are not present at police questioning, or at questioning by the procureur. Article 14 of the loi of 15 June 2000 introduces the videotaping of questioning by the police of minors. Further extension of detention has to be under the process of mise en examen led by the juge d'instruction. Special provisions exist for cases involving drugs (for which a 72-hour detention is provided) and for terrorism. The provisions on drugs are very important, since many offences are related to drugs and so the provisions are, in practice, frequently invoked.

In more recent years, the practice of *traitement en temps réel* has been introduced.[9] Under this, there is an office within the parquet, which is permanently staffed by a procureur and a greffier. The police fax the notice of arrest giving the basic reasons. They will then telephone to report on progress, perhaps to ask for instructions or to ask for an extension of detention. They may also initiate a conversation on cases where they may, in future, need warrants or action. This situation enables the procureur to probe what is going on and either to instruct or advise the police about what should happen next. The procureur may consider that a case is sufficiently advanced to justify moving to a prosecution. In such a case, the police may be told to bring the accused to the parquet for an interview. The interview with the procureur will serve as an equivalent of a process of charging the accused. In many simple cases, it may be possible to proceed to comparution immédiate (immediate appearance) before the court. Courts now have a chamber that is able to judge such cases in the late afternoon and into the evening. Thus, in one case which I witnessed, the person was arrested for theft about 11 am and taken into custody by the police, admitting the offence. He appeared before the procureur just before 3 pm, and was interviewed. It was clear that he had eleven previous convictions and did not contest the case. He was then sent downstairs to the court, where he would be seen by the duty avocat, since he did not have his own lawyer. I was told that he was likely to be tried by the tribunal correctionnel that afternoon, and, given the previous convictions, could well be starting to serve his jail sentence that evening.[10]

This process of managing the enquête may involve a procureur intervening in forty cases a day. (In busy courts, there will be several such duty procureurs). The level of control I observed here was varied, and was bound to vary according both to the personality of the procureur and the confidence which he has in the police officers on the case.

In most cases, the police investigation is thus in conjunction with the procureur and he decides how it will proceed – whether it is sent directly for trial and how this

9 For a description and criticism of 'justice en temps réel', see D Salas, *Le tiers pouvoir. Vers une autre justice* (Paris 1998), pp 103-110.

10 Lawyers report that they may only have 15 minutes to read the file as a duty lawyer before the case comes on: see E Hauser-Phélizon in L Gratiot et al, *Art et techniques de la plaidoirie aujourd'hui* (Paris 1995) at p 89. *Comparution immédiate* typically involves duty procureurs, duty lawyers and duty judges with a danger that everything becomes too routine: see the interviews with a judge and lawyers in ibid., pp 83ff.

needs to be done.[11] In principle, the procureur interviews the accused, but, in many minor cases, there may be no interview. The police will telephone the procureur and he will give a date for the accused to attend for a trial hearing. This comparution par procès verbal enables a person not to be held in custody. This process was used in just over 50% of prosecutions in 1998. As an alternative, where the person is in custody, but the case is straightforward, the procureur may order a comparution immédiate in which case, the accused is sent for hearing as soon as possible. In other cases (typically contraventions), there may be a simple summons (citation directe) to appear in court on a particular day. In serious cases (especially rape, murder and violence to the person) or more complex investigations, a more prolonged judicial inquiry is interposed between the police enquête and the trial, this is the instruction. But the procureur retains the direction over this process by the requisition he gives to the juge d'instruction.

(b) The instruction[12]

The basic task of the instruction process is to decide in serious cases whether there is a sufficient case to answer to warrant committal of the suspect for trial. In serious cases, the job of the juge d'instruction is to have the power of investigation in order to be at the service of the victim and the accused. The juge d'instruction is seised of a case by the requisition from the procureur.[13] This defines the ambit of the subject matter of the investigation, and the juge will need further instructions from the procureur to deal with new offences turned up in the course of the investigation. A person will come to a juge d'instruction either as a témoin, a mere witness to answer questions or as a suspect. If the juge considers there are serious indications that the person has committed the offence under investigation, then the person is put under investigation (mise en examen).[14] In other cases, a particular person may have been named in a complaint as the perpetrator of the offence and so that person is given special protection as a témoin assisté, a witness who is allowed to be legally represented at any interview (a status created in 1987). It may well be that only after interview and investigation will the témoin assisté be formally put under investigation.

The tasks of the juge d'instruction are specified in article 81 of the Code of Criminal Procedure (C pr pén): 'the juge d'instruction undertakes all investigating acts which he judges necessary to the revelation of the truth'. These acts will include gathering evidence, for example by ordering expert tests or reports, such as about ballistics, by reconstruction of the crime, or by directing further police investigation.[15] They will

11 For comparison with Italy and Germany, see E Mathias, *Les procureurs du droit* (Paris 1999), pp 153-161.

12 See generally M Delmas-Marty, 'The Juge d'instruction: do the English really need him?' in B Markesinis (ed.), *The Gradual Convergence* (Oxford 1994), pp 46ff; L Leigh and L Zedner, *A Report on the Administration of Criminal Justice in the Pre-trial phase in France and Germany*, Royal Commission on Criminal Justice, Research Study No 1 (1992).

13 The nominee may be removed on grounds of the good administration of justice where the *procureur* or one of the parties requests, but reasons must be given for such a decision (art 84 C pr pén).

14 This was formerly called mise en accusation, but that nomenclature was considered too prejudicial and was dropped in 1993.

15 For an account of these processes, see C Samet, *Journal d'un juge d'instruction*, chs IV and VII.

also involve formal questioning of witnesses, either by taking formal statements from them one by one or even staging a confrontation of witnesses to elicit truth. Most importantly, the juge d'instruction will question the suspect. Apart from the first formal hearing, a lawyer will be present and the purpose is to get to truth, and may involve challenging the suspect on statements by witnesses. The juge may also question witnesses directly. The juge d'instruction then produces a report which sets out his or her own view on what should be done and instructs the procureur about the next steps to be taken in the case.

In numerical terms, l'instruction is receding in importance. For the last 40 years, it is only relevant to about 6%-8% of criminal cases, compared with 33% in 1830. The juge d'instruction dealt with 65,860 persons mises en examen in 1998, 9,587 for a crime and 56,250 for a délit, these represented some 42,196 separate cases. The cases against some 11,557 individuals were then dropped. The average decision time was 16.2 months from the date of the start of proceedings. In 1998, 9317 cases did not involve anyone being mis en examen and so a significant number of prosecutions occur without passing through this stage.

Given the length of the instruction process, the question of detention is a serious issue. The length of detentions, which can amount to nearly half the French prison population, has been a matter of criticism both by external commentators and by the European Court of Human Rights.[16] In 1998, some 24,512 remand decisions were taken on cases finishing in the year, which approximates to some 37% of all people investigated. While the average period of détention provisoire was 5.9 months, the average for those sent for trial by the cour d'assises was 13.7 months.[17] But, even with the reforms of 2000, the expectations about custody before trial are significantly different from the common law. In her introduction to the debate on the 2000 reform, the Minister of Justice suggested that remand in custody should not exceed two years for offences carrying a penalty of under 20 years and three years for longer penalties.[18] In all investigations, the juge d'instruction decides whether to recommend that the suspect is remanded in custody (détention provisoire). In the 1808 Code, there was a separation between the juge d'instruction and a body of three judges who decided on detention, but this was abolished in 1856. From then, the juge d'instruction took remand decisions. Following the Delmas-Marty report, an attempt was made to restore a separate body to review detention in a loi of February 1993, but it was quickly repealed in August 1993. The loi of 15 June 2000 removed questions of remand from the juge d'instruction and created a new role, the juge des libertés et de la détention. The juge d'instruction can decide questions of bail and conditions for that (contrôle judiciaire).

In a further set of changes, the loi of 15 June 2000 has changed the procedure at the end of the instruction. In the past, the file was remitted by the juge to the procureur for onward transmission. Where a case was to be sent to the cour d'assises, the file would be sent on to the Chambre d'accusation which consisted of judges who would examine the file and see if there was a case to answer (essentially a committal stage). As will be seen, the Chambre d'accusation also had a role in supervising the work of the juge and dealing with appeals from his decisions (mainly on remand in custody, but also in

16 See Leigh and Zedner, pp 52-53 and *Tomasi*, below, p 130 note 1.
17 *Annuaire statistique*, p 107.
18 Exposé des motifs of the loi, March 1999 from Ministry of Justice web site.

relation to the nullity of measures taken during the instruction). This body has now been renamed as the 'Chambre de l'instruction' under art 83 of the loi. The juge d'instruction now simply sends a case directly to the cour d'assises by an ordonnance de mise en accusation under the revised terms of art 181 C pr pén.

(c) The trial

Depending on the seriousness of the offence, criminal trials take place before differently constituted courts. There are three levels of offence: contraventions or regulatory offences, which typically carry fines, délits that carry a penalty of imprisonment, and crimes, which are very serious offences. Contraventions are tried before a single judge in the tribunaux de police. Délits are tried by the tribunaux correctionnels,[19] composed of either a single or a panel of three judges. The average length of time from offence to trial was 9.3 months. By contrast, crimes are tried by the 99 cours d'assises, a court compsed of three judges and a jury of nine people. These only dealt with 3,364 cases in 1998 of which only 4.6% were acquitted. The length of time from offence to trial was 49.8 months, with condemnations in absence taking as long as 73.5 months.[20]

There are a number of accounts of the French trial, which offer a reader helpful insights into the distinctive process. The essential feature of the hearing phase, as the French call it (l'audience), is that this is public and the key issues are presented to a fresh judge from the person involved in the investigation. That said, there is a radical continuity between trial and pre-trial processes, which explains the use made of the trial by all concerned. The importance of the instruction is clear from the centrality of the file and the relative lack of oral debate, which most common law observers have noted.[1] For the most part, especially outside the small number of cases in the cour d'assises, heavy reliance is placed on the file and statements made by witnesses in it. As McKillop observed, even if witnesses are heard, no transcript is made of their statements, so any appeal will have to refer back to the statements of witnesses actually on file.[2] In such trials, witnesses are rarely called upon to attend and give evidence in person. In one case I observed, even a conflict between the facts alleged by witnesses and the accused was resolved by the trial judge simply by comparing the written statements of the witnesses on file and the oral statements of the accused. Observers, notably McKillop,[3] stress the importance of re-enactment and confrontation of witnesses prior to trial. If there is a conflict of testimony, this is likely to have been tested by lengthy confrontation between the relevant people in the office of the juge d'instruction, and is not a matter to be sorted out at trial. (Since the lawyers for the

19 *Annuaire statistique*, p 111.
20 *Annuaire statistique*, p 109.
1 See B McKillop, 'Readings and Hearings in French Criminal Justice: Five Cases in the *Tribunal Correctionnel*' (1998) 46 Am Jo Comp Law 757, 777-778. B McKillop, 'Anatomy of a French Murder Case' (1997) 45 Am Jo Comp Law 527, who gives lengthy accounts of trials at different levels within the system. A. Sheehan, *Criminal Procedure in Scotland and France* (HMSO Edinburgh, 1975), pp 82-85 and Appendix 8 gives an account of the trial at the cour d'assises. This is confirmed by accounts given by English judges who have observed cases and by the author's own observations. See also A Anton, 'L'instruction criminelle' (1960) 9 Am Jo Comp Law 441, below, p 116.
2 'Anatomy of a French Murder Case' at p 566.
3 'Anatomy of a French Murder Case' at pp 570-572.

accused have had access to the file, they have had ample opportunity to ensure that it is correct.) As a result, the hearing may well be brief. Only before the cour d'assises will there be an oral rehearing of witnesses.[4] The reason for this is that the jurors have had no access to the information contained in the file and have not the experience of using it.[5] All observers note the importance attached to confessions, described by some as 'la réligion de l'aveu'.[6] Now all these features of a case depend on work done before trial. Confession is not a feature of the trial, but of pre-trial questioning. Although the French do not accept a guilty plea, the presence of an admission of guilt serves much the same function, but does not dispense the investigating court from satisfying itself that there is sufficient evidence to support a conviction,[7] and the trial court will review the issue again.

Observation of the trial suggests that the questioning of the accused by the judge is in language which seeks to explain the wrong which has been done and, in advance of a judgment, to make the person appreciate the extent of the wrong done, as well as for the judge to understand the reasons why the offence was committed. Pre-trial interviews of the procureur or juge d'instruction with the accused often adopt a similar approach. Since most cases involve an admission of guilt, this search for explanation has a more important role than the checking of the facts. In cases where guilt is not contested, the evidence is led by the judge from the file in the questioning of the accused, and the witnesses are not expected to be present.

At the trial the procureur will represent the public interest as well as the prosecution. Placed at the same level as the judges, rather than as an equivalent of the defence lawyer, he is seen to be representing the law and the State, rather than being the adversary of the accused, even if the questioning that he directs and the arguments he make are in favour of a conviction. Before the tribunal de police, the role of parquet is normally taken by the commissaire de police, unless the procureur wishes to intervene.

(d) Appeals and Miscarriages of justice

Appeals lie to the cour d'appel from the tribunal de police and the tribunal correctionnel. Appeals from the tribunal de police are very restricted, especially in cases involving fines of under 5,000F. The chambres des appels correctionnels decided 28,361cases in 1998, of which 3006 (10.6%) led to acquittals.[8] Until article 81 of the loi of 15 June 2000 has introduced an appeal against the decision of the cour d'assises, the French had clung to the idea that the jury was infallible. Appeal now lies to a different cour d'assises composed of three judges and twelve jurors. In all cases, the appeal takes the form of rehearing on the merits. In the cour d'appel, the relevant chamber will base its decision predominantly on the file. The appellant (either the convicted person or the partie civile) will be asked to address the court first and explain the grounds of appeal and will then be questioned by

4 See Sheehan, pp 211-215 and J Godard video 'The Criminal Process in France and Scotland'.
5 The ritual of the public trial in these very serious cases (mainly serious sexual offences such as rape and incest) also has an important symbolic function.
6 Judge Eva Joly cited in Truche Commission, Annexes, p 269.
7 See, for example, the Caroline Dickinson case where the confession of one person asked was subsequently found to be unreliable in the face of DNA evidence which excluded him from being the rapist: see *Le Monde*, 8 August 1996, p 20.
8 *Annuaire statistique*, p 119.

the judges. Indeed, the lawyers will often only have a role of speaking at the end of the proceedings in support of their client's case. In my observation of such appeals, it was clear that the questioning of the convicted person by the judges, based on the evidence contained in the file, was the most important part of the case and the lawyers had little opportunity to rescue an appeal if the convicted person adopted a ridiculous line of defence, eg by admitting that he was driving a stolen car but saying that he did not know how he had come to be sitting in it!

Civil parties and the ministère public can also appeal. In most appeals, the sentence of the lower court can be increased, but this is not the case on an appeal against the cour d'assises under the new arts 380-3 and 380-6 C proc pén.

The Cour de cassation deals with points of law, rather than fact. As such it has a limited role in the day-to-day operation of the criminal justice system. It does not hand down guidelines on sentencing, but concentrates on ensuring a degree of uniformity in the application of the law by the different regional courts. Much of the work of the Cour de cassation is spent in ploughing through the large body of cases which are not going to succeed. It meets in two parts, either as a formation restreinte (with the rapporteur, avocat-général and the president) in the morning to decide a large body of very straightforward cases, and then as a Chambre in the afternoon to deal with the more contentious cases. On a routine hearing day, a section of the Chambre criminelle will dispose of 80 cases. Even in the public session of a section of the Chambre, as opposed to the full chamber, it can frequently happen that no lawyers are present, and the court moves to deliberate on over 20 cases within half an hour. Only the full Chambre, dealing with difficult points of law or cases of public notoriety will attract pleadings from lawyers. In such hearings, fewer cases are listed and as many as four out of five may be the subject of short pleadings by the lawyers. Since the avocats à la Cour de cassation have experience in presenting written arguments (and are thought by judges of the Cour to do this well) and since they will know the basic arguments of the avocat-général, they will know whether it is worthwhile to turn up or just bow to the inevitable.

Miscarriages of justice are handled predominantly by appeal. Since 1895, there has been a procedure of *révision* under which a commission within the Cour de cassation reviews cases and may order either a retrial or the quashing of a sentence.[9] This is a rare procedure. Since the procedure was revised in 1989, there have been some 500 cases of *crimes* investigated by the commission, but the commission has only remitted three to the Cour de révision for decision.[10] In total, only six convictions for murder have been quashed as a result of this process in a hundred years. There is a reluctance to admit mistakes by the jury system. There were considerable doubts about the confessions of an educationally subnormal youth, Patrick Dils, to the murders of two children in 1986, notably arising from the admissions made by another man in 1992. Although these were new facts, the Cour de révision only quashed the conviction in April 2001 after ordering further investigation. Furthermore, it ordered a new trial.[11] There seems a desire to be certain about the real cause of the crime, rather than to focus simply on the uncertainty of the conviction.

9 See J Bell, in C Walker and K Starmer (eds), *Miscarriages of Justice.A Review of Justice in Error* (London 1999), ch 17, esp p 368.

10 See *Le Monde*, 20 May 2000, p 12; also *Le Monde*, 29 January 1999, p 9, and C Prieur, *Le Monde*, 30 June 2000, p 10.

11 Crim, 3 April 2001, *Le Monde*, 5 April 2001.

(2) The central role of judges

From the above account, the process of investigation is central to the development of the French criminal procedure. There are two key figures, the juge d'instruction, and the parquet. The juge d'instruction (originally called the Lieutenant criminel) is inherited from Francis I in the ordonnance of Villiers-Cotteret 1539. His function is to take charge over the police investigation of serious cases. This investigative process has gradually given way to defence rights. The roles of the juge d'instruction thus pull in different directions. As Samet puts it:

> [The very character of the role of the juge d'instruction] thus surprises and misleads, and it has become common to ask oneself whether the juge d'instruction is Salomon or Maigret, judge or investigator, defender of rights or pursuer of wrongs.[12]

But the fundamental idea of a judge who investigates and who also judges is very distinctive in the French form of criminal process (and remains unchallenged by the European convention).

The second feature is the separation of investigation and prosecution. Here the second judge, the procureur, comes into play. Created by the Edict of Blois 1579, the 'king's advocate' came to have the monopoly of leading prosecution. The result was that the avocat was removed from the investigative process altogether and performed a role predominantly of defence,[13] though they may perform a quasi-prosecutorial role in representing the civil party, particularly where this is an association seeking nominal damages. This contrasts with the role of lawyers in England who may perform both prosecution and defence roles at different times in their work.

The third judge is the trial judge, especially the president of the court who will read the file and determine the questioning of the accused and of the witnesses. Although there is a separation of functions and of individuals, the unity of the process is encapsulated in the notion that, from very early on, the criminal process is a judicial process. However, some procureurs express the view that they are more like the avocat of the State and the increasingly adversarial character of criminal proceedings reinforces this.

A related feature is the relative unimportance of the jury, around which much of the procedure of the common law has developed. Adopted only by the Revolution in 1791, the jury has had a limited role in the most serious crimes and has frequently been under State control or influence. It does not have the standing of the English or American jury as the bastion of liberty. We thus have a process which is dominated by the pre-trial and the legal actors involved in it – the juge d'instruction, the procureur, the defence avocat and sometimes the avocat of the civil party. Each of these has a much more politicised role than in England.[14]

12 *Journal d'un juge d'instruction*, p 33.

13 See L Karpik, *French Lawyers* (Oxford 1999), p 26.

14 Ibid, chs 3, 6 and 7; V Wright, 'The Fifth Republic: From *Droit de l'Etat* to the *Etat de droit*' (1999) 22 West European Politics 92 at p 95 who talks of the period before 1958 where there seemed to be 'the requirement that prosecuting magistrates become electoral agents for the regime and keep a close and punitive eye on the "enemies" of the regime.'

(3) The role of the file

A major consequential feature of the French system is the continuity between investigation and trial, especially in the development of the file. To a common law eye, it is striking that French criminal procedure is essentially written. Materials used to establish guilt are collected in the file (dossier) built up in the pre-trial phase and used by trial and appellate judges alike. Indeed, as Anton put it:

> The comparison between the French and Anglo-American trials is misleading for it is only a slight exaggeration to say that, while in England or in the US a *man* is on trial, in France it is a *dossier*.[15]

The existence and use of the file is both a safeguard for the accused and a permanent record of what is said. It will be about the content of this file that most debate turns in the pre-trial stage, and it is used by the trial judge. The items in the file are built up over the months of the investigation by the procureur or by the juge d'instruction.[16] The file is brought to the prosecutor by the police at the first meeting with the accused and will contain all the custody records, as well as statements made to the police. The prosecutor and the juge d'instruction will then add their own contribution. Materials are not edited or removed from the file. Rather, the accused, the civil party and those in charge of the investigation will add elements to it. It is this document which is used at the different stages of the process. Observations of interviews before the prosecutor at the beginning of the investigation (to authorise an extension of police detention) and before the juge d'instruction (a confrontation between a témoin assisté and the civil party) confirm the significant use which is made of the file by all present as the basis of questioning. Knowledge of the content of the file is essential to the role of the lawyer in assisting the client.

The information that the file contains becomes the basis of information on which the trial judge(s) will proceed, even if there is also a jury. As a result, the trial is not

15 A Anton, 'L'instruction criminelle' (1960) 9 Am Jo Comp Law 441 at 456. For an account of the importance of the file in a trial, see C Johnson, 'Trial by dossier' (1992) 142 NLJ 249 and A Sheehan, *Criminal Procedure in Scotland and France*, ch 5. For instance, in the appeal of the police officers accused in the 'Irishmen of Vincennes' incident, witnesses were not heard despite defence protests on the ground that the cour d'appel of Paris considered that it was 'neither useful nor necessary' to go beyond the file. (The case concerned allegations that weapons were planted on members of the IRA in Paris and these individuals were then charged with gun-running: *Le Monde*, 25 June 1991 and 26 September 1991. For a general account of the incident, see J Holland and H McDonald, *INLA: Deadly Divisions* (London 1994), ch 11.)

16 Since 1993, the procureur, the juge d'instruction, or the defence can apply to the Chambre de l'instruction (previously called the chambre d'accusation) to strike out such items from the file during the course of investigations. Although some texts specifically impose the penalty of nullity for breach of procedural rules in the gathering of evidence, eg where a search has been conducted of a lawyer's office without regard to the safeguards established by law. In most cases, however, it is up to the court to decide if the breach of procedural requirements is serious enough to justify the nullity of evidence gathered for breach of public policy or of the rights of the defence. Article 171 C proc pén provides that a nullity is only pronounced where there has been a prejudice to the person concerned.

really the instantaneous moment of the Anglo-Saxon system, but a process in which information is gathered, sifted and, if need be, challenged outside the courtroom and then presented in packaged form to the trial court.

C. ILLUSTRATIONS OF CRIMINAL LAW ACTIVITY

(1) The criminal process and its audiences

In many ways, the relative secrecy of l'instruction process captures press attention more than the public trial. There are clear indications both from writings and interviews that the secret de l'instruction is violated in a number of cases. Publicity is at the heart of the symbolic and deterrent functions of the criminal law, but it conflicts potentially with individual rights, especially the presumption of innocence. Given the importance of the pre-trial process and the low acquittal rate at trial, publicity at the pre-trial phase is central to the activity of the major actors. The press serves both as an interested participant and as a tool which is manipulated by the legal actors.

(a) Media reporting of the criminal process

Criminal proceedings, by their very nature, are a subject of public interest and attract the attention of journalists. They provide stories in already packaged forms, which are designed to engage the interest of a public audience. Indeed, presentation in the media is merely an extension of the public spectacle, which is the trial. The media thus function to support the dissemination of the public message that the criminal prosecution presents. In criminal law, much more than civil or administrative law, the message is directed to the general public, both potential criminals and law-abiding citizens. The collegial decision of the courts represents the majesty of the law.

If reporting of individual cases is integral to the functioning of the system, the pre-trial process is an area of important ambiguity. The process of instruction and building up the file (*dossier*) is not peculiar to criminal law, but is found in different ways in administrative law and in constitutional and civil law. But the process by which it is constructed is different. The nature of criminal law involves much more questioning of individuals and confrontation of witnesses. In the other fields, there is far greater reliance on the inspection of written documents. The process of instruction is thus much more amenable to reporting as it goes along. The scheduled and formal meetings between the prosecutor or judge and the accused or witnesses enable the process to be seen and logged. There is natural conjecture on why people are being questioned, what they are saying, and how far this is leading to the resolution of the crime. Television reporting is greatly assisted by the visual spectacle. As a result, the process of instruction is more apparent and reportable than in any of the other three branches of law. Given the nature of the subject matter and the 'human interest' character of most serious crime, the instruction attracts attention to itself in its modern configuration.

There are two types of case, which attract press interest. On the one hand, many cases discussed later concern public figures. On the other hand, many crimes attract the attention of the press and public because of their seriousness or the character of their victims.

An illustration of the second is the rape and murder of Caroline Dickinson, a 13-year-old Cornish schoolgirl, who was killed as she slept on the floor of a dormitory in a youth hostel in Pleine-Fougères in Britanny. She was killed in the night of 17-18 July 1996 and a man of no fixed abode, Patrice Padé, was arrested and made a confession. However, the only local juge d'instruction, Gérard Zaug, ordered a DNA test which revealed that he could not possibly have been the rapist, but he was only released when he appealed to the chambre d'accusation.[17] Only then did the juge d'instruction go back to the statements of the girls in the dormitory and launch new investigations. The children were interviewed by the British police on video, but then the French authorities took months to transcribe and translate the tapes. The failure to demonstrate efficiency and produce results led the chambre d'accusation of Rennes on 14 August 1997 to withdraw the case from Judge Zaug and assign the control of the investigation to a very experienced juge d'instruction, Renaud Van Ruymbeke from that court.[18] This move had been made formally at the request of the victim's father after a strong campaign, particularly in the British press about the conduct of the investigation. Immediate and dramatic action was ordered by the chambre d'accusation, the DNA testing of all men aged 15 to 35 in Pleine-Fourgères, and the new juge d'instruction held a private meeting with the dead girl's father. Given that Van Ruymbeke was well used to dealing with the press, and was well known by them, one can see in subsequent press accounts a deliberate 'charm offensive' on his part.[19] Apart from dramatic and public steps in the investigation process, there was clearly an attempt to present a picture of a judge advancing the investigation and passing the blame for initial failures in the investigation on the first juge d'instruction.[20] Although, at the time of writing, the investigation has not produced any prosecution, the role of the judge in constructing a public image of the investigation was an important part of his role in that situation.

This type of case differs from that of Little Gregory Villemin where the press coverage indirectly led to both the murder of a suspect and pressurised the inexperienced juge d'instruction.[1] Four-year-old Gregory was found dead on 16 October 1984. On 7 November the juge d'instruction, Jean-Michel Lambert, charged Bernard Laroche, a cousin of Gregory's father, but had to release him for lack of evidence on 4 February 1985. The boy's father killed Laroche on 29 March 1985 because the press coverage had convinced him that Laroche was guilty. Pressed to find the real killer, Lambert charged the boy's mother, Christine Villemin, on 5 July 1985, remanding her in custody for eleven days. The chambre d'accusation of Dijon required further information and eventually dropped all charges against her on 3 February 1993. In this sort of case, treating a prosecution as a scoop tends to blur the line between treating someone as a suspect and declaring him or her guilty.

17 *Le Monde*, 8 August 1996, but he was only released after a formal decision was made on 10 October 1996 by the chambre d'accusation that there was no case to answer.

18 *Le Monde*, 16 August 1997, p 5.

19 He was the investigating judge in the Urba affair, below, p 122.

20 See two articles presenting accounts of the investigation and the judge's latest suspicions: *Le Monde*, 14 February 1998, p 11.

1 See C Samet (ed) *Justice, transparence, démocratie*, pp 29-37.

It must be made clear, however, that media investigation and reporting serves ends that are distinct from those of the judicial investigation. In some cases, for example in the Furiani case,[2] the media are present at the beginning and direct their own enquiries in parallel to the administration and the judiciary. As a result, they produce their own hypotheses and suggest who might be investigated.[3] The circumspection that characterises the judicial process was there criticised as slowness and inefficiency.[4] The media acts as self-appointed spokesperson for the public and has its own conception of what is just, and this may well conflict both with the way in which investigation is conducted and equally with the trial.[5]

Media reporting will also need to adopt a style that is appropriate to the medium. There is thus the image of the juge d'instruction or the parquet as an individual crusader fighting against corruption among the powerful or against other vested interests.[6] Such an approach provides good copy, but is in danger of exaggerating the power and role of those key individuals in the criminal process. All the same, the fact that the processes of investigation and trial can be reported in these ways clearly affects the pressures under which individuals work. The individual juge d'instruction or procureur is likely to be telephoned by journalists looking for a story or wanting to check their facts, and this over a considerable period of an investigation.[7] The use of media interest by others adds to the pressure to talk. Most of the juges who I interviewed were firm in their insistence on the traditional approach, but there is a pressure to change this aspect of the culture, and it is not always respected.

(b) Restrictions on the press

The French press is restricted in what it says about matters under investigation and instruction by controls on the information it is given, by a duty not to exert undue pressure on parties to the proceedings, and by its general duty since 1993 to publish a retraction if a person is finally acquitted.[8] This has been strengthened by the loi of 15 June 2000, art 91, to empower the juge d'instruction to order a correction to be printed where a person is depicted as guilty of crimes which are currently under investigation.

Article 11 C proc pén stipulates that the proceedings during the instruction are to be secret, unless the law provides otherwise, and that all who 'collaborate in' the instruction to respect the professional secrecy of the process. This includes not only the judge and parquet, but also officials involved in the process. Avocats must also refrain from communicating documents obtained in this way.[9] It is not an obligation,

2 Above, p 107.
3 See for example *Le Figaro*, 22 July 1992 asking why the prefect of Corsica had not been accused of an offence arising from the Furiani stadium disaster.
4 See Garapon, unpublished ENM course, 22-26 November 1993, p 7.
5 See reporting of the blood transfusion criminal trial of Dr Garetta, *Le Figaro*, 21 July 1992, which clearly takes the side of the victims.
6 Garapon 1993, p 11.
7 C Grellier in Greilsamer and Scheidermann, 159 at p 164 describes this as 'harassment' and this account of the extent of pressure was confirmed by interviews with current juges d'instruction.
8 See generally M Chesterman, 'Contempt: In the Common Law, but not the Civil Law' (1997) 46 ICLQ 521, esp pp 539-541.
9 P Chambon, *Le juge d'instruction. Théorie et pratique de la procédure* (4th edn, Paris 1997), paras 56-58.

thus, on parties to the proceedings, including the civil party (usually the victim). Breaches of such a rule do not in practice give rise to prosecutions.

The press is essentially restricted by art 38 of the loi of 29 July 1881 on the press which prohibits the publications of decisions in criminal proceedings before they have been read in a public hearing. The ordonnance of 1958 punishes actions bringing 'discredit' on the courts or tending to put pressure on judicial institutions.

In terms of press conferences, the commentary at art C23 C proc pén suggests that 'the practice noted sometimes these days of holding a press conference during the enquête or the information should be strictly forbidden.' But there are certain limited situations in which it is permissible for the procureur or the juge to speak to the press. In 1985, the 'Cotte' circular from the Director of Criminal Affairs and Pardons (now incorporated in art C23 C proc pén) stipulated that:

> The procureur of the Republic can, if he thinks necessary, provide to the press a written communiqué concerning the facts which have justified a prosecution ... so as to put an end to the circulation of rumours or falsehoods resulting most frequently from the use of fragmentary or, perhaps, insufficiently verified information.

Judicial practice sometimes extends this to press conferences or interviews held by the procureur or juge d'instruction. There are clear problems here with a judge presenting views on the case before trial. Noël has argued that 'one must recognise that in certain cases, the proceedings "speak" so strongly that it becomes necessary to accompany them with an explanation, there being a real risk that it will not be understood and will appear as fortuitous, accidental, the fruit of an arbitrary decision by a judge'.[10] Others argue that the media is so much a part of life that the juge cannot avoid having relations with it.[11]

Noel also argues that the attention of the press changed from the 1970s with the birth of the Syndicat de la Magistrature which used information provided to the press as a means of raising its own profile and that of its campaigns. From this one had the first set of 'judges who speak', ie judges who talk about their work outside the courtroom. This position of the leftwing judicial union led to media attention which turned the juge d'instruction into a 'star' and created the image of the 'crusading judge' (*juge frondeur*).[12] The real issue is how the juge lets himself be involved in publicity (passively) or is active in courting it. The press will produce short biographies of individual judges in the news, and the juge d'instruction in a high profile case is likely to be one of those. Certainly some individuals go further and court publicity. In the investigation of the murder of a woman at Bruay-en-Artois in 1972, a scandal was caused by the interview which the juge d'instruction gave to a journalist in his office, with the papers and evidence from the case lying around.[13] More recently, Eva Joly, one of the two juges d'instruction in the Roland Dumas financial corruption investigation, gave a long interview to *Le Monde* about her life and complained about

10 Garapon 1993, p 5.

11 Jean-Louis Brugière in Greilsamer and Schenidermann, p 82; P Lyon-Caen, noted in C Samet, *Justice, transparence, démocratie*, pp 182-184.

12 Garapon 1993, p 6, citing Jean-Marc Théolleyre, former legal affairs correspondent for *Le Monde*, in April-June 1994 Revue juridique de l'Ile de France.

13 See P Chambon, para 61-3.

the material conditions in which she had to perform her work. She was, however, careful to avoid any discussion of the case in question.[14] The danger of the individual juge d'instruction becoming a media star is real.

(c) The juge d'instruction and the media

The traditional view of the secrecy of l'instruction was stated by the advocate-general at the Cour de cassation, Dupuich, in 1955: 'judges do not need the approval of their fellow citizens, but only that of their conscience when it comes to ensuring the law, justice and truth are respected'.[15] In terms of the instruction, the judge would claim that his words only have importance in the courtroom.[16] The traditional view, supported by the judicial establishment is that the case should not be the subject of comment, and even if lawyers talk to the press, the *juge* should remain silent.[17] But the development of investigative journalism in the 1980s and the media attention to the criminal process has made this less sustainable as a position. Observers note a decline in attention to the trial, and an emphasis on the earlier phases where the journalist can appear to be more investigatory and less a chronicler of events.[18] Thus former Minister of Justice, Albain Chalendon, remarked:

> The 'secrecy of the instruction', safeguard of the presumption of innocence, flies out of the window as soon as the press is actively interested in the case. The scope of mediatisation which makes the press the competitor of the juge d'instruction, and the trial a spectacle, created very often by complicity between the judge and the journalist, in which each seeks to manipulate the other. At a stroke, the instruction is being conducted in the public forum.[19]

To be fair, the description of the secrecy of the instruction as an 'open secret' goes back a long way, and was the description given by Professor Garraud in 1912.[20]

In rare cases, the judge uses the press to reinforce his independence with relation to superiors, particularly politicians.[1] The impact of the judicial use of the media in the cases concerning political corruption is attested by the views of Henri Nallet who was minister of justice at the time. In the Urba case,[2] a consultancy company was created to which payments were made by companies in payment of invoices for 'services rendered' and the profits were paid to the Parti Socialiste. The services were fictitious and the scheme was a way of evading restrictions on the funding of political parties. On 13 April 1991, the juge d'instruction at Le Mans who uncovered the scheme, Thierry Jean-Pierre, took a number of steps in the investigation which were unorthodox and which breaches conventional practice, eg by driving up to Paris to catch the

14 See *Le Monde*, 3 June 2000, and also E Joly, *Notre affaire à tous* (Paris 2000); *The Guardian*, 3 February 2001, Weekend supplement, pp 8-15.

15 C Noël, 'L'image des magistrats dans la presse et dans l'opinion en France', IHEJ conference on Justice et médias, Nantes 4 November 1994, p 1.

16 See *juge d'instruction* Serge Portelli (1994) cited ibid, p 3.

17 See P Drai (former Premier Président of the Cour de cassation) in L. Greilsamer and D. Schneidermann, *Les juges parlent* (Paris 1992), 125 at p 134.

18 Garapon 1993, pp 7-8.

19 Evidence to the Truche Commission, Annexes, pp 23-24.

20 See H Leclerc, *Un combat pour la justice. Entretiens avec Marc Heurgon* (Paris 1994), p 318; also C Libman (avocat) in C Samet (ed), *Justice, Transparence et Démocratie*, p 189.

managing director of Urba on a Sunday and to search at his head office, or by summoning a director of Urba at 10 pm on a Saturday night and then arresting him. The prosecutor in Le Mans was minded to request that the juge d'instruction be removed and consulted officials in the Ministry of Justice. These then consulted the minister, Henri Nallet, who agreed to the request for removal. The president of the Tribunal de grande instance of Le Mans acceded. But judge Jean-Pierre then went to the press and became a folk hero.[3] Writing in the following year, Nallet reflected:

> In taking this decision, justified in law, I made a mistake on the level of political judgment. I was not paying enough attention to the suspicion which had been aroused in public opinion and to what a body of judges felt the moment it concerned Urba. The net outcome of the affair was disastrous.[4]

The apparently unauthorised actions of judge Jean-Pierre were upheld by the chambre d'accusation of Angers on 21 April 1991and the Cour de cassation refused to intervene by a decision of 27 June 1991.[5] The subsequent juge d'instruction on the case, Renaud Van Ruymbeke, though more discreet and less of a media star, had to make some concessions to the press and, eventually, to bring about the successful prosecution of the former treasurer of the Socialist Party, then the president of the National Assembly, Henri Emmanuelli. The Minister of Justice was forced to renounce any involvement by his ministry in giving instructions on the conduct of investigations to procureurs in political financing cases. 'It was', Nallet remarked, 'the judicial institution itself, supported by the media, which managed to paralyse any action by the Ministry of Justice in the political-financing cases.'[6]

Other judges in charge of high profile cases have used the press to support their attempt to flush out high profile crime. For instance, Eric Halphern is said to have connived at leaks to the press, which enabled them to follow him to Xavière Tiberi's doorstep when he was conducting a search of the house of the wife of the Mayor of Paris.[7]

1 See for example H Haenel and J Arthuis, *Justice sinistrée: démocratie en danger* (Paris 1991), pp 47-48: 'The role of the press in justice has become almost institutionalised and some judges do not hesitate to confide papers from the file to chroniclers defying in this the most strict principles of the secrecy of the *instruction* and of judicial ethics, the photocopier becoming thus a surprising assistant to a legal system which they consider to have gone astray.'

2 On the Urba case and the judicial investigation, see John Ardagh, *France in the New Century* (London 1999), pp 48-49; C Samet, *Justice, Transparence et Démocratie*, p 24.

3 He explained his taste for the media had followed the protest which he and some colleagues led in Le Mans in protest against the amnesty voted in their own favour by members of parliament for electoral irregularities and of a minister, Nucci. The protest consisted of freeing some petty crooks: see his interview in L Greilsamer and D Schneidermann, *Les juges parlent*, 237. He was elected as a member of the European Parliament in the 1994 elections.

4 H Nallet, *Tempête sur la Justice* (Paris 1992), p 120. The book is an account of his tenure of the office of Minister of Justice.

5 C Samet, *Justice, Transparence, Démocratie*, p 24

6 Op cit, p 123.

7 See J Ardagh, *France in the New Century*, p 51, and see also pp 45-46 and 315 on this case. Mme Tiberi was subsequently tried for corruption, but acquitted on the ground that the evidence had been obtained unlawfully: see *Le Monde* 16 December 1999 and 17 January 2001, though verdict on a separate corruption charge is now pending. See also, C Samet, above note 2, pp 27-28.

The complexity of the relationship of criminal justice to politics and the media is nothing new. Salas recounts the case of Cailleux at the beginning of the 20th century in which politicians were involved in stifling a prosecution for fear of the repercussions on financial markets.[8] But the more modern problem has arisen because of the direct attack on politicians for their own corruption. As Salas remarks:

> From the moment that the kinds of case handled by the criminal justice system affect the governing elites, this power, formerly 'invisible and null' – according to the wishes of Montesquieu – becomes at the same time visible and unacceptable.[9]

During the investigation of Bernard Tapie, a government minister, for match rigging in the case concerning Olympique de Marseille, the juge d'instruction, Eric de Montgolfier, used to hold press conferences shortly before the evening news broadcasts, arguing that he was concerned to prevent the case being buried by political pressure.[10] A Sofres opinion poll of January 1994 found that 57% of those questioned thought the judges had been wrong to communicate with the press in this way and only 25% were in favour.[11] Although the opinions expressed may be coloured by the public's perception of whether the press has done a good job in reporting the case, the opinions reported give an indication of public expectations about the role of the juge d'instruction.

(d) Defence lawyers and the media

Unlike judges, the parties are unrestricted in publicising their own contribution to the investigation. It has become an increasing tactic, especially in high profile cases for the accused's lawyers to provide statements to the press about what occurred during the interview with the judge in order to construct a favourable image of their client.

To give a concrete example, Jean Tiberi, Mayor of Paris, was accused on 28 June 1999 of complicity in misuse of influence in relation to the Office HLM de Paris of which he was president. The basic allegation was that he used his public office in relation to the award of public contracts in ways that enabled funds to be channelled fraudulently to his political party, the RPR. Tiberi was interviewed with his lawyers on 19 July 1999 by the juge d'instruction, Eric Halphen. The report carried in *Le Monde* on 21 July gives a very detailed account of the proceedings.[12] The report contains a number of questions and answers. For example, when asked 'why did you not sack the managing director [of the Office]?', he is reported as replying 'I had not

8 D Salas, *Le tiers pouvoir*, pp 41-43. P Chambon, para 61-62, notes that the press interest in the murderer Vacher in 1898 was so intense that the juge d'instruction fled to America!

9 Ibid, p 57.

10 On Mongolfier see C Samet (ed), *Justice, transparence et démocratie*, p 182; cf Edith Boizette a juge d'instruction investigating Tapie at the same time: Greilsamer and Schneidermann, pp 54 and 66.

11 A Garapon, unpublished ENM course 22-26 November 1993, p 10. A June 1994 poll for the Ministry of Justice finding 49% in favour of judges talking to the media and 46% against is roughly similar to that of the Haenel-Arthuis study of 1991 which found 47% thinking that it was 'acceptable that a juge should have consistent relations with the press' and 49% against.

12 See Hervé Gattengo, *Le Monde*, 21 July 1999, p 6. See also the reporting of the interview between Xavière Tiberi and the juge d'instruction, *Le Monde*, 25 July 2000.

formed a judgment on the behaviour of Mr Pérol'. The judge is also reported as asking Tiberi why monthly sums of 25,000F to 35,000F were paid by the RPR into his bank account between 1992 and 1996. Then, as a supplementary question, and suspecting a cash payment, the judge raises a 'deposit' of 500,000F on 19 November 1993. Tiberi is described as 'disconcerted' by the question and unable to offer an immediate explanation. Nevertheless, he undertakes to provide the relevant information within 48 hours. The interest of the story is not just that it involves an alleged fraud for political ends by a high profile politician. It reveals very clearly the way in which the instruction becomes a focus of attention for constructing an account of what is going on before trial. Unlike committal proceedings, which had the function of testing out the prosecution evidence, this approach is to construct a picture of the accused and to provide his side of the story without chance of reply from the judge. The purpose is to build up an alternative picture of the accused's situation in the minds of the public to counter the opinion that the formal accusation by a judge will create.

A similar situation was shown in the case of the investigation and prosecution of Roland Dumas, president of the Conseil constitutionnel and a former minister of foreign affairs. As a result of revelations by his ex-mistress, Christine Deviers-Joncour, he was accused of receiving illegal payments from the president of the French petroleum group, Elf-Aquitaine. It was alleged that these were used to acquire a flat in Paris as a 'love nest' for Dumas and his mistress. The press stories contained the allegations against Dumas and noted that he had replied in a radio interview on Europe 1.[13] We thus have the picture of leaks to the press between accused enabling rival pictures to be established. The press then sought out (unofficial) clarification of the state of the investigation from the judges involved. Thus, *Le Monde* reported:

> Hesitating to relaunch investigations following the previous statements of Mrs Deviers-Joncour relating to the incident involving the statuettes, the Paris prosecutor's office has now hardly any option but to request further information, several judicial sources were already indicating on Thursday.[14]

The judges were obviously only clarifying formal matters, rather than commenting on the file, but we do have the spectacle of an investigation becoming fought out almost in the press.

Now such a tactic of the avocat is not universally approved, though most have been willing to pass information. As Leclerc suggests, many feel they have to do it in some cases:

> ... it is necessary to defend oneself against rumour, against the false opinions that become entrenched. I don't like that because I know full well that these statements falsify the game and that what I am going to say will lead to other revelations.[15]

13 Hervé Gattengo, *Le Monde*, 20 March 1999, p 8. See more generally, J Ardagh, *France in the New Century*, pp 53-54.

14 Ibid.

15 H Leclerc, *Un combat pour la justice. Entretiens avec Marc Heurgon*, p 318 and more generally ch 14.

(e) Conclusion

Media reports not only show the relationship of legal actors to the media, but also record the relationships between each other. In an opinion survey conducted among judges and other legal professionals in 1997, they argued that the law and the press define key ideas such as the openness of the legal system in different ways.[16] For the lawyers, openness involves a public court hearing. This is the moment when the legal system opens itself for inspection. On the other hand, the press sees freedom of information as the key idea in openness. Thus the idea of secrecy in the instruction until the trial becomes a point of conflict between the two conceptions of transparency. The gulf between press and judicial perceptions was confirmed in evidence to the Truche Commission. The press argued for greater transparency in the process with a proper flow of information which could be appropriately balanced, but which would require the judicial authorities to provide the information[17] In a sense, the length of the *instruction* process makes the need for this essential. It is hard for the press to refrain from commenting for the many months in which an investigation is being conducted.

One feature of the publicity of the instruction process is that it focuses on judges who are identified as individuals, rather than as part of an anonymous bench. As was stated earlier, the procureur or the juge d'instruction works on their own and is known by name. Unlike in most French judicial proceedings where there is a collegial decision, here one has individuals making decisions on their own and being publicly identified for their individual contribution. The culture of criminal procedure develops thus this focus on individual responsibility not just within a collegial team, but with regard to the media and the public. It is therefore not surprising that the judge himself is prepared to act positively in using the media to portray a particular image of the proceedings and of the judge's conduct. All the same, judicial training in the use of the media is rather under-developed, so that the actual use of the media by judges is very uneven.

(2) Law making

The reforms of criminal procedure in 1998-2000 provide a test case of how the criminal law develops. In particular, one is concerned with the issue of who drives the agenda for reform and the influence exerted by legal as opposed to other actors.

(a) Procedural reform: the protection of innocence

In evidence to the *Truche Commission* in 1997, Albain Chalandon took the view that society is structured around the law:

> In a society where cultural and moral values are diffused and conflicting, the role of the judge is to hold onto the unifying principle of the law, the only point that brings people together.[18]

16 'L'opinion des Français sur la justice' conducted by the Institut CSA in 1997 and published by GIP Mission de Recherche Droit et Justice on http://www.msh-paris.fr/gipjustice/ActualitSondage.htm at p 12.

17 See Truche Commission, pp 283, 290, 293, and below p 126.

18 *Rapport de la commission de réflexion sur la Justice* (Paris 1997) t II, p 20.

Law is, in this view, seen as a focal point for the structuring of ideas and debates about how society should be governed and how people should behave. This may be an exaggeration, but it reflects the centrality of debate on law and the legal process as part of the political process.

Unlike England, there is no standing Criminal Law Revision Committee or Law Commission. If the Conseil d'Etat does operate like a think tank on many issues of law reform, technical matters of civil and criminal law are not within its competence, although its advisory functions will include examining any proposed legislation in the field which the government brings forward. Significant reviews of the 1808 Code de l'instruction criminelle were conducted just before the Second World War by a commission chaired by Paul Matter, procureur général at the Cour de cassation, which reported in 1938 and led to a number of reforms implemented by the Vichy Regime. After the War, a more thorough review was undertaken by a commission chaired by Professor Henri Donnedieu de Vabres. This proposed in 1949 to abandon the separation of prosecution and instruction and to put the instruction essentially under the procureur.[19] This led to criticism and was abandoned. A less ambitious project was finally produced, leading to the Code of criminal procedure of 1959. A further enquiry was made necessary by increasing concerns over the impact of the European Convention on Human Rights. The reforms proposed in 1990 by the Commission headed by Professor Mireille Delmas-Marty[20] were equally radical in suggesting a single procedure of investigation under the procureur and conducted by the police under which the parties would be able to contest the process as it evolved and where the judge dealt with liberty and similar matters. In the end, this was dropped and a more limited focus on the rights of defence and greater protection of the suspect by a separation of the investigation from decisions about custody of a suspect. A further commission was set up by President Chirac in 1997 under the First President of the Cour de cassation, Pierre Truche.

Reflecting after the report in 1999, Truche – himself a member of the Delmas-Marty commission – was foreseeing the eventual abolition of the role of the juge d'instruction.[1] All the same, this is not the vision of the government with a ringing endorsement of the existing process by the Minister of Justice, Mme Guigou:

> The accusatorial procedure is by its nature unequal and unjust. It favours the strong at the expense of the weak ... The system we have is better both in relation to efficiency and also in relation to individual freedom. I prefer, and I say this clearly, an independent judge, who gives instructions from start to finish to policemen who alone carry out substantial part of the investigation without judicial supervision.[2]

As a result, some changes were made in relation to both the access to a lawyer and to the control over the remand in custody of the accused. But a further committee was then required to deal with increasing concern (notably among politicians) of the independence of the juge d'instruction.

19 See H Donnedieu de Vabres, 'La réforme de l'instruction préparatoire', RSC 1949, 499.

20 *La Mise en Etat des Affaires Pénales* (Documentation francaise 1991).

1 *Le Monde*, 29 June 1999, p 32.

2 Speech to Senate 15 June 1999, from Ministry of Justice web site.

The composition of committees is interesting. For the most part, they are made up of senior judges, officials of the Ministry of Justice and some other public figures from within the administration. Very few academics are included. The Truche commission had 21 members, six of whom were academics, but only one a professor of criminal law, and six judges (plus two members of the Conseil d'Etat). This contrasts with the Delmas-Marty commission whose 12 members included two professors, two members of the Conseil d'Etat and three judges. Responses to the Delmas-Marty consultation paper were predominantly from institutions with a low number of law faculties directly responding, though a number of law professors responded on an individual basis.[3] Only a few law professors were invited to make submissions to the Truche commission and, surprisingly to a foreigner, all were the grand old men of French academic life, none of whom was under 70 and none of whom taught or wrote on criminal law. One is led to conclude that individual academics may have some influence on law reform, at least in generating and channeling the debate. But much of the outcome of law reform involves a series of political decisions taken by ministers in the light of their judgement of political needs.[4] Such political decisions are influenced not only by elected representatives of the political parties, but also by lobby groups, notably the judges.

The influence of certain key lobby groups on the agenda of law reform can be seen by the contrast between opinion polls taken at the same time as the Truche commission was meeting in 1997. While the public was relatively unconcerned that the presumption of innocence was under threat, it was concerned about the press reporting of cases in progress.[5] Both the Truche commission and the subsequent reforms nevertheless took the general question of the presumption of innocence as central. By contrast, the hierarchical subordination of the procureur to the Minister of Justice was something which the public wished to see changed. This view was argued strongly by the judicial unions. The President of the Republic also put down a marker that the commission should examine this issue and suggest whether the parquet should be separated from the Minister of Justice.[6] However, the past Ministers of Justice and the past directors of the Criminal Affairs in the Ministry were strong and unanimous that the decision to prosecute was a discretionary exercise of power which should be subject to political control and should not be left to the independent action of an unaccountable group of prosecutors.[7] The difference in view might almost seem to reinforce the public's perception that criminal justice was under the thumb of politicians and top civil servants. In the 1997 Sofres opinion poll, 82% of those asked considered that criminal justice was under the political powers, with 73% thinking that it was more indulgent towards politicians compared with ordinary citizens and 69% thinking the same in regard to higher civil servants. In 1990, the figure was only 60% thinking that criminal justice was under

3 See *La Mise en Etat*, pp 322-325.

4 This was most obvious in 1993 where the first (Socialist) follow-up to the Delmas-Marty report involved the creation of a special court to deal with orders to remand suspects in custody, but this was dropped before it was implemented by the incoming right-wing coalition in August 1993: see S Field and A West, below p 134 note 4.

5 See Sofres opinion poll, *Le Monde*, 31 January 1997, p 1.

6 See *Le Monde*, 14 December 1996, p 7, but note the critical editorial in *Le Monde* of 6 March 1997, p 14, criticising the President's interventions in the Conseil Supérieur de la Magistrature where his preferred candidate was not supported by the judicial unions.

7 Truche Commission, Annexes, pp 19-118. 71% in the Sofres poll favoured parquet independence.

political power and the 1999 figure was 62%.[8] The various opinion polls identify a much higher number of people in favour of abolishing the right of the Minister of Justice to give directions to prosecutors in individual cases (67% in 1999) compared with the potential loss of a general penal policy (53%) or absence of political involvement in prosecutor's career promotions (46%). The Sofres poll of October 1999 reveals a strong sense of cynicism across all political parties. The real concern of the public is with the slowness of the legal system, both among those who have been involved as litigants and those who have not, with two-thirds dissatisfied overall and much higher numbers among litigants than among those who have not used the system.[9] The concern that there are secret (and illegal) instructions given to prosecutors would undoubtedly fuel concern about political involvement.[10] But, though some significant reforms were to be voted in the *loi* of 8 July 2000, the reinforced guarantees for the judiciary and the procureur which were to have resulted from a constitutional amendment were dropped when a conflict arose between politicians and the judiciary.[11]

(b) The liability of the elected officials and administrators

The issue of the liability of elected officials and administrators had become a significant problem in recent years. The Furiani stadium case had been one in which liability of administrators for multiple deaths had turned on the failure to follow proper procedures. But more generally, there was a concern that officials were the subject of criminal actions for breach of regulatory legislation, eg in the area of environmental law, and that these would be instigated by associations who could constitute themselves as civil parties. A major new area of prosecutions was for breach of open competition legislation in the award of public contracts. Originally designed to avoid corruption in the wake of the Urba scandal, the legislation quickly led to prosecutions of elected officials, eg the mayor of a town, for breach of the competition rules. Whereas there were no prosecutions in 1994, there were 12 in 1997 for this heading alone, out of a total of 14 prosecutions in the period 1995 to 1999. Of 65 civil servants against whom proceedings were started between 1992 and 1999, 58 were in the préfecture and only one of these had led to a successful conviction.[12] There was a clear concern among these influential individuals that criminal prosecution, with all the attendant distress and publicity was being used in ways that were inappropriate. At the same time, this issue was being raised against a background of nearly a decade of investigations into criminal offences associated with the financing of political parties.

The Massot committee was set up in June 1999 by the Minister of Justice. This followed a public debate in the Senate on 28 April 1999 on the subject.[13] Its composition

8 *Le Monde*, 1 February 2000, p 16.
9 See ibid, article by P Chriqui.
10 See A Chemin, *Le Monde*, 31 January 1997, p 8.
11 Contrast the views of the judiciary on the Truche reforms (that they did not go far enough in establishing the independence of the parquet): *Le Monde*, 11 July 1997; p 9, 3 December 1999, and contrasts the objections of the RPR, 'Justice: Michèle Alliot-Marie explique le "non" du RPR', *Le Monde*, 13 January 2000, just at the very moment that several of their leaders were being investigated for illegal financing of the party.
12 Massot Report, annex 5 and tables therein.
13 See the Ministry of Justice press release (*Courrier de la Chancellerie*) announcing the creation of the committee, 21 June 1999, available on the Ministry of Justice web site.

reflected the involvement of key interests: a senior member of the Cour des comptes, the president of the association of mayors, a president of region, a prefect, and a president of one of the judicial unions, as well as a leading member of the parquet at the Cour de cassation, and presided over by the President of the Finance Section of the Conseil d'Etat. It both reflected all the key interests to discuss policy, but was able to be a technical body to produce reforms of the Code pénal. The solution proposed was to reduce the scope of criminal liability for negligence. Since 1912, the Cour de cassation had held that the criminal and civil standards of non-intentional fault should be the same. The committee recommended a higher standard for criminal law.[14] The Cour de cassation approach produced rather extensive criminal liability and needed to be corrected. In the view of the committee, the recent developments in prosecution of elected officials and administrators for negligence was an unforeseen by-product of various pieces of legislation on substantive areas, such as the environment and public contracts, and procedural reforms, such as increased standing for associations and the requirement for a more speedy beginning to the process of mise en examen.[15] There was also a concern to avoid the use of the criminal law as an alternative form of political protest by the interest groups able to becomes parties civiles in fields such as the environment.[16]

The committee held a number of hearings. It is interesting to note that those who were heard or who made submissions were predominantly from the administrations and local authorities affected, or were practitioners (judges of various courts and lawyers). No academic was heard formally or made submissions on an individual basis.[17] Very few of the works cited in the bibliography in appendix 4 of the report are academic writings. Most are official reports from Parliament, the Conseil d'Etat and the Cour de cassation or other public services, or reports of colloquia held by such bodies.

Given the political momentum behind the inquiry, it is not surprising that the legislative response was swift. The report was submitted on 15 December 1999 and legislation to implement the main proposed changes in the Code pénal were enacted by the loi of 10 July 2000, which reproduces all the main changes proposed in chapter 1 of the report. The function of the loi is to restrict criminal liability to clearly deliberate breaches of duty or involving some form of moral fault, while retaining and enhancing the possibilities of civil or administrative law compensation for the victims. It represents a clear effort at decriminalising administrative mistakes. In order to avoid any criticism that this constituted a 'self amnesty', the amendments of the criminal code apply to the criminal liability of individuals in general.

(c) Influences on law reform

Law reform is very much a political matter for Parliament, politicians and lobby groups. Law and order, and the means of securing this, have always been a matter of significant

14 In practice, in the intervening period, the civil concept of fault had been reduced to an objective standard involving little moral fault: see Bell, Boyron and Whittaker, pp 360-361 and Cass ass plén 9 May 1984, D 1984, 525 note Chabas holding a child liable in fault for carelessly crossing the road.

15 Report, pp 8-11.

16 Report p 41; speech of Minister of Justice, Mme E Guigou, to Senate, 27 January 2000, p 9.

17 See Report, annex 3, pp 118-120.

concern. Recent events merely reinforce the point that an even greater political interest is taken when the politicians (or those who threaten them) may be the subjects of criminal investigation. Senior judges have always had a role in suggesting, if not drafting, law reform measures. The membership of the recent commissions is just part of that pattern. Judicial decisions play a lesser role in law reform, though they play more of a role in the area of criminal procedure. Doctrinal writing is important in debating criminal policy and in establishing a climate for discussion more than in making direct inputs into law reform. It may be that leading academics like Ancel, Donnedieu de Vabres and Delmas-Marty contribute to these general debates, but it is far less clear that doctrinal legal writing contributes significantly to the adoption of specific changes in the law, either by the legislator or by the judge. The influence is more indirect. As a result, one distinctive aspect of the criminal law is a difference in relationship between judge, doctrine and legislator, compared with the civil law. Criminal law is not 'Professorenrecht'.

(d) European Convention

In criminal law and procedure, perhaps more than in other branches of French law, it is important to recognise that the law is no longer a purely national matter. Especially in the last 10 to 15 years, criminal procedure has been reshaped in the light of the European Convention. To bring French law into line with the Convention was precisely the mission conferred on the Delmas-Marty commission. As Pradel suggests, the 'wind from Strasbourg is blowing increasingly strongly' and the Cour de cassation is increasingly basing decisions on it.[18] Delmas-Marty argues persuasively that Europe offers an example of both common standards and legal pluralism in the sense of multiple sources of standards in criminal law.[19]

France only ratified the Convention in 1974 and allowed individual petition in 1981. In the 1990s, there was an acceleration in individual petitions and between 31 March 1998 and 9 November 1999, there were a dozen condemnations of France in criminal law.[20] Indeed of 70 decisions against France between 1986 and 1999, 30 were in criminal procedure. The European Court of Human Rights has been concerned with a number of aspects of French procedure. A major concern has been the period which individuals spend in custody.[1] A further concern has been the fairness of trials and appeals for the accused, both in questioning witnesses[2] and in conducting an unrepresented defence.[3]

In a number of areas, the Chambre criminelle of the Cour de cassation has sought in some cases to anticipate the European Court[4] or at least to follow it, even before the

18 J Pradel, 'La procédure pénale française à l'aube du troisième millénaire' D.2000 Chr 1.

19 See M Delmas-Marty, *Pour un droit commun* (Paris 1994), pp 226-252.

20 See J-P Marquénaud, 'La dérive de la procédure pénale française au regard des exigences européennes' D 2000 Chr 249.

1 For example, ECHR 27 August 1992, *Tomasi v France*, Application 12850/87, Ser A, No 241-A, (1993) 15 EHRR1 where the person spent five years and seven months in custody before being acquitted. For further examples, see Bell, 'The French Pre-Trial System', at p 365 note 35.

2 Eg ECHR 19 December 1990, *Delta v France*, Application 11444/85, Ser A, No 191, (1993) 16 EHRR 574.

3 See ECHR 8 February 2000, *Voisin v France* D 2000, 651, above, p 63.

4 Eg the decision in Crim 12 January 1989, *Randhawa*, Bull Crim no 13 anticipated the decision in *Delta*, above.

legislator has intervened. A good example is the area of telephone tapping. The Cour de cassation permitted telephone tapping without a judicial warrant in 1989. But within three weeks of the condemnation of France in *Kruslin and Hervig* in April 1990, the Cour de cassation set out additional requirements for the conduct of telephone tapping and the use of evidence – there must be no artifice in conducting the telephone tapping and the results must be open to comment by the suspect and any other party, as would any other feature of the file.[5] The legislator then followed with further safeguards in a loi of 10 July 1991.

Marquénaud[6] notes that the Chambre criminelle has not always been willing to follow the European Court. In *Poitrimol* in 1993,[7] the applicant had fled at the time of judgment in the trial and so was condemned in his absence. Rules rendered a pourvoi to the Cour de cassation inadmissible in such cases. The European Court of Human Rights declared that the denial of an appeal was a disproportionate penalty, given the importance to be attached to the rights of the defence. In three cases in 1994,[8] the Chambre criminelle continued to apply the old rule and this led the European Court to give a decision of the full court in 1998,[9] reaffirming its view that the rule violated the Convention. At which point the Cour de cassation backed down by a decision of 30 June 1999. All the same, in *Papon* on 21 October 1999, the Chambre criminelle applied a similar rule where the accused had failed to surrender himself into custody on the eve of the hearing by the Chambre criminelle, as rules of procedure required. This resistance, based on a clash between what the French take to be sensible principles of traditional criminal procedure and the European Court's view of the requirements of the Convention, represents a traditional attitude of French courts towards precedents of superior courts. They see no objection to principled resistance, as long as the lower court complies with a final and reconsidered view by the solemn formation of the highest court.

It is important to note how important the European Convention has become for the everyday practitioners of the system. Observation of the procureur, the juge d'instruction, trial judges and appeal judges in the spring of 2000 noted the way in which the Convention was cited as a natural and ordinary point of reference, either in argument or as raising issues to which attention had to be paid. Lawyers and judges are only too aware of the opportunity of the Strasbourg court as effectively the fourth level of court within the system. France has recently introduced a procedure for revision of cases where the European Court of Human Rights has condemned the process in its courts.[10] This signals a gradual assimilation of the European dimension into the routine of French criminal law.

5 See Ass plén 24 November 1989, D 1990, 34; ECHR 24 April 1990, *Kruslin and Hervig*, Application 11801 and 11105, Ser A, vol 176-B, (1990) EHRR 528 and 547; Crim 15 May 1990, *Bacha Baroudé*, JCP 1990 II 21541 note Jeandidier; Crim 17 Nov 1990, D 1990 IR 221. Generally, Bell, 'The French Pre-Trial System' at p 360. A further condemnation still intervened in this area in ECHR 24 August 1998 *Lambert*, D 1999 Somm 271.

6 Op cit, at pp 253-254.

7 ECHR 23 November 1993, D 1994 Somm 187.

8 Crim 19 Jan 1994, *Guérin*; Crim 7 Feb. 1994, *Omar*; and Crim 15 February 1994, *Coquin*, D 1994, Somm 187.

9 ECHR 29 July 1998, *Omar and Guérin*, D 1998 Somm 364.

10 See loi of 15 June 2000, art 89.

D. THE CORE VALUES OF CRIMINAL LAW

The institutional setting suggests that, though sharing many general features with other legal systems, the specificity of French criminal law lies in the way the normative and procedural tasks are performed. In terms of normativity, we have a predominance of the legislature in setting substantive norms, and thus a displacement of the debate on substantive norms away from the forensic process. In terms of procedural norms, however, the work is more evenly shared between the abstract and general decision-making by the legislature and more concrete adjustment of norms to the needs of individual cases. In this section, one is concerned with what are the core values and how are they set.

The standard definition of criminal law is found in Donnedieu de Vabres: 'Criminal law is the totality of legal norms that regulate the recourse by the state to criminal sanctions'.[11] The process of developing these norms has long been the province of the legislator.

(1) Normative values

The central normative values of French criminal law are legality and proportionality. Article 7 DDHC provides that 'No individual may be accused, arrested, or detained except where the law (loi) so prescribes.' This principle was a deliberate contrast to pre-Revolutionary France where criminal offences were largely defined by customary law determined by the courts. The principle legality (*nulla crimen sine lege*).[12] It is clear that the French courts cannot create new offences, nor can they extend penalties by way of induction.[13] They cannot exceed the penalty set down.[14]

An old example can illustrate the principle of légalité. Under the 1810 Code pénal, theft, larceny and embezzlement were punished under art 401, but the acts had to be accompanied by some seizure or taking (*soustraction*) by the offender, as defined by art 379. If an individual without pretence ordered a meal at an inn without the money to pay for it, there was no taking of the food without consent. This did not amount to theft and there was no fraudulent manoeuvre to constitute embezzlement, and the Cour de cassation refused to extend the application of the Code to it.[15]

11 *Traité de droit criminel et de législation pénale* (3rd edn, Paris 1947), p 1.

12 For example, the principle of legality provides the first section of Marc Puech's *Droit pénal général* (Litec Paris 1988), Titre I. For others the purpose of criminal penalties comes first and the issue of legality provides the first section of the more doctrinal part, eg H Donnedieu de Vabres, op cit., pp 52-56; J-H Robert, *Droit pénal général* (2nd edn, Paris 1992), p 53.

13 H Donnedieu de Vabres, op cit, p 54. Crim 22 March 1955, *Barbier*, D 1955. 418.

14 Crim 15 July 1964, *Valleix*, D 1965.60 note Bouché.

15 See Crim 5 November 1847, *Varnoux*, D 1847.IV.510; Crim 10 December 1869, *Jamot*, DP 1870.1.441. Also Crim 3 March 1934, *Fiollet c Ministère Public*, DP 1934.1.33 concl. Caous, note H Donnedieu de Vabres: an employer who fails to hand on employee social security contributions to the Caisse does not commit a breach of trust under art 408 C pén, even though this is committed in bad faith. Also Crim 7 May 1969, *Court*, D 1969,481 where it refused to extend the offence of putting a room 'at the disposition of a prostitute' (art 335-6 C pén) to the case where the landowner leased it to her.

Principles of interpretation are thus relatively strict. This was recently reiterated by the Cour de cassation when it quashed a decision of the Cour d'appel of Lyons which had held that a doctor who accidentally caused the abortion of a healthy foetus of 20-24 weeks was guilty of involuntary homicide in that, outside voluntary abortion legislation, 'human life' should be treated as commencing at conception.[16] All the same, the French judge is not totally passive. As Pradel suggests, 'in criminal law, as elsewhere, case law is at the same time both educative and creative with the only reservation that the judge does not enter into conflict with the rule of legality'.

In the first place, the courts will apply common sense to obvious errors of drafting. The much-cited example is art 78 of the decree of 11 November 1917 which forbade passengers 'to board or to alight [from a train] other than in stations, stopping places or halts or other stopping places dedicated for the purpose and when the train is completely stopped'. As Voirin noted, in a literal sense it only seemed to permit passengers to board or alight from trains in motion! The Cour de cassation nevertheless upheld a conviction for alighting from the train in motion at a station on the ground that the text 'had to be interpreted as forbidding passengers from boarding or alighting from carriages before the train had completely stopped'.[17] In fact, the interpretation was not very bold, since a correction to the decree had been published in the *Journal Officiel* four weeks before the offence was committed.

Second, the courts will adopt an 'ambulatory' or updating interpretation of texts. A good example is the inclusion of a record within the concept of 'publication' in art 24, para 3 of the loi of 29 July 1881, even though the phonograph had only just been invented in the United States in 1878 and would not have been known to the French legislators.[18] A further example is the case of theft under art 379 of the Old Criminal Code of 1810 which was interpreted in 1912 to cover abstraction of electricity, a solution confirmed by art 311-2 of 1994 Code.[19]

Third, the courts will use the scope for interpretation given by the imprecision of many terms used in legislation to penalise improper behaviour. For example, in the case law relating to driving and taking away of motor vehicles, older case law had held that to keep a hired horse longer than the stated period could not amount to theft.[20] But in relation to cars, the courts distinguished between merely abusing the property of another, and where a person behaves as owner, even for a moment – which could amount to theft. So taking a car for a ride and then returning it to within several hundred metres of the place whence it was taken could amount to theft within art 408 C pén.[1]

Proportionality also originates in the arguments of Montesquieu and Beccaria in the 18th century. Article 8 DDHC provides that 'The law (loi) may only create penalties

16 Crim 30 June 1999, D 1999, 710 note D Vigneau, quashing CA Lyon, 13 March 1997, D 1997, 557 note Serverin.

17 See Crim 3 February 1923, *Procureur-général c Bonhour*, DP 1926.1.229 (apparent accidental repeal); Crim 8 March 1930, DP 1930.1.101.

18 Crim 14 January 1971, *Le Pen*, D 1971,101 concl. Chapar. As a result, Le Pen was convicted of war crimes for the presentation of Nazi songs on the record without any reference to the war crimes committed.

19 Crim 3 Aug. 1912, S 1913.1.337 note Roux.

20 Crim 10 December 1869, *Jamot*, DP 1870.1.441.

1 Crim 19 February 1959, *Theveny et Lancereau*, D 1959, 331 note G. Roujou de Boubée.

that are strictly and evidently necessary.' This has long been applied in the individuation of penalties. Thus the Cour de cassation has accepted that a fine should be proportionate to the resources of the offender, even before this was enshrined in art 41 of the C proc pén by the loi of 11 July 1975.[2] The Conseil constitutionnel has insisted that criminal sanctions should be proportionate to the offence. Thus in 1987, it decided that a *loi* that imposed on any person (for example, a journalist or an official) a tax penalty equivalent to the income of a taxpayer whose details he had disclosed in breach of obligations of confidentiality was potentially disproportionate and excessive.[3]

This limited norm-setting role for the courts is emphasised by the importance of ministerial circulars on the interpretation of some new legislation. Such circulars were important in the introduction of the New Criminal Code, which came into force in 1994 and also in relation to various legislation on reforms of criminal procedure.

(2) Procedural values

If the setting of normative standards is a matter for the legislature, the judge has a more important role in contributing to the shape of the procedural rules that they operate. As the 'exposé des motifs' of the loi of 1993 on the reform of criminal procedure makes clear, 'the texts governing the phase preparing for the criminal trial has developed by taking into account two partially contradictory imperatives: to guarantee a better protection of the rights of individuals and to ensure an increased efficiency in the search for the authors of *crimes* and *délits*'. The history following the Revolution has involved, with some comings and goings, a gradual move to increase the rights of the defence and to make the process more transparent. Naturally, this has involved a significant intervention from the legislature. The Code de l'Instruction Criminelle (CIC) of 1808 was a legislative act and this could only be amended by subsequent legislation. For example, significant reforms were introduced in 1897 to allow the defence lawyer to be present at interviews in the office of the juge d'instruction and then in 1921 for the civil party to have similar rights. Since the new Code of Criminal Procedure was enacted in 1958, the subject has been a matter of intense legislative interest, notably in the 1980s and 1990s (especially when politicians themselves became the subjects of investigation). For example, two lois on this subject were passed in 1993 establishing different procedures for reviewing détention provisoire.[4]

This has not prevented the courts taking a significant role in developing general principles of criminal procedure. For example, the 1808 Code had very little on the use of the commission rogatoire, by which the juge d'instruction delegates powers of investigation and interviewing witnesses to the police judiciaire. But the courts have authorised it. Similiarly, the courts have allowed the juge d'instruction and the procureur

2 Crim 26 June 1958, GP 1958.2.137. See also CC decision No 78-97 DC of 27 July 1978, Rec 31 that there could be different penalties as long as all prisoners fulfilling the same conditions had a right of access to the same treatment regime.

3 CC decision No 87-237 DC of 30 Dec 1987, *Finance Law for 1988*, RFDA 1988, 350; Bell, *French Constitutional Law*, pp 145-146.

4 See S Field and A West, 'A tale of two reforms: French defence rights and police powers in transition' (1995) 6 Criminal Law Forum 473.

to decide that a set of facts, which could be classified as a crime and thus sent to the cour d'assises, might be treated as délit to be judged by the tribunal correctionnel.[5] The purpose of the procedure was to ensure that prosecutorial practice kept the law in line with contemporary thinking. Thus there were many offences classified in 1808 as crimes that were subsequently not seen as really serious.

The development of general principles of procedural law has been enhanced in more recent years by the advent of the European Convention on Human Rights. There has been a gradual process of developing the rights of the defence (*procédure contradictoire*); protection for the presumption of innocence, and a greater focus on the victim of crime.

E. LEGAL ACTORS

The distinct structure of the French criminal process involves not only structures and procedural steps, but also the roles assigned to a number of key individuals and groups.

(1) Le parquet

The role of the parquet has always been difficult to grasp. On the one hand, the parquet is subordinated to the Ministry of Justice because it is carrying out criminal law policy[6] and, until recently, this involved a right for the Ministry to give instructions on the prosecution of individual cases. The minister gives his orders through the procureurs généraux[7] who in turn then keep the minister informed of important cases. There are two main limits to this subordination. First, the head of each parquet can give any orders freely and it would be even possible to give orders contradictory with the wishes of the government, though disciplinary sanctions might follow. Second, any juge du parquet is free to plead according to his convictions, even if those are contrary to the governmental guidance.[8] However, the written submissions must conform to the wishes expressed by the government. This role of the parquet and his relationship to the government is one of the current matters of controversy arising from the political prosecutions of the 1990s.[9] There is thus a freedom of action, which is now reinforced by the voluntary withdrawal (in practice

5 Pradel, *Droit pénal général* p 181.

6 The Ministry of Justice publishes numerous circulars on criminal policy: eg those cited in its document, *La Justice partenaire des contrats locaux de sécurité*, pp 9-10.

7 There is a ministère public at each level of the court system: tribunal de grande instance, cour d'appel, Cour de cassation. The ministère public is headed by a procureur général in the cour d'appel and the Cour de cassation. In the tribunal de grande instance, it is headed by a procureur de la République. His orders from the government come through the procureur général in charge of the district.

8 See further E Mathias, *Les procureurs du droit*, pp 197-205.

9 Jean Pradel and Jean-Paul Laborde, 'Du ministère public en matière pénale. A l'heure d'une éventuelle autonomie?' D 1997 Chr 141 who argue that independence is 'a great necessity of our times' (p 141).

if not in law) of the Ministry of Justice from giving instructions in individual cases. Michèle-Laure Rassat argues that, at the heart of the complexity of the parquet's role, is a confusion between the parquet as representative of the Nation, of the sovereign power, and as representative of the Executive.[10] In truth, as the Truche committee found, there is an inevitably mixed role. The status of the parquet as a judge is also significant. The Conseil constitutionnel considered that the extension of detention by the parquet was perfectly permissible, given that 'the judicial power, which under art 66 of the Constitution ensures respect for individual liberty, includes both the magistrats du siège and the parquet'.[11]

In criminal law cases, the role of the procureur, the juge du parquet, is central to the proceedings; first, the ministère public decides when to prosecute (though the juge d'instruction may decide not to prosecute). Second, the procureur represents the State and the public interests by presenting arguments and requesting a particular sentence against the accused. So as to assure fulfilment of these duties, a number of principles regulate the work of the juge du parquet: he is independent from the parties, and from the juges du siège (they cannot give him any order or have him removed from a case).

Increasingly the procureur is a state official with a broad responsibility for criminal policy. A good example is the role now performed by the procureur as one of the three main signatories of the 'contrat local de sécurité' together with the mayor and the chief of police.[12] In terms of agreements on the general pattern of prosecutions, this is very important for dealing with routine crime, particularly in relation to juvenile delinquency. The procureur acts with the president of the TGI to create a maison de justice which serve as locations for alternative treatment of offenders. Such agreements cover the way in which victims will be informed, how (in general) offences will be policed and prosecuted with and so on. Acting on behalf of the State, the prosecutor becomes, in such circumstances, leader of a team of justice officials who are engaging with the community over justice.

The most important manifestation of the role of the procureur as head of a justice team comes with the search for alternatives to trial. The loi of 23 June 1999 authorises different alternatives to criminal prosecution, viz 'rappel à la loi, sending the offender for health, social or professional treatment, corrective action by the offender, and payment of compensation for damage caused'. These four measures can give rise to classement sous condition. Usually these solutions are brokered through médiation pénale established by the procureur. This may either be through a Maison de Justice et du Droit (MJD) of which 100 are expected to be in place by 2001 or through delegates of the procureur, of whom there are soon expected to be 500. Both the brokering of local criminal strategies and organising alternatives to trial makes the procureur more

10 Conference speech, Nancy November 1997, 'Indépendance du Parquet, opportunité des poursuites' to be found on http://jurispole.univ-nancy2, p 5 of the report. A similar comment was made by an avocat interviewed for this research.

11 CC decision No 93-326 DC of 11 August 1993, Rec 217, considérant 5. See further, T Renoux, 'Le Conseil constitutionnel et l'instruction pénale: juges ou magistrats?' (1998) 10 *Justices: La Justice pénale* 75.

12 A description of these contrats locaux, can be found in Ministry of Justice, *La Justice partenaire des contrats locaux de sécurité*.

than simply a prosecutor of crimes.[13] Dalle has noted the way in which these kinds of developments have pushed the procureur in the direction of becoming 'préfet de la justice'.[14]

(2) Le juge d'instruction

> The investigating magistrate is a figure from the Jacobin State because he is close, in reality and in the imagination, to a functionary bearing the authority of the central State, able himself to investigate and to judge as did the criminal lieutenant and the intendant [of the Ancien Régime] in the past...The ideal of the investigating magistrate is of the man alone, empowered to manage a judicial situation, a search for the truth and a procedure, as a unity. By contrast, the accusatorial procedure emphasises the search by way of a process, the two-sided debate, the equality, at least in theory, of arms between the prosecution and defence.[15]

This description, given by leading criminal judges, brings out the peculiar position of the investigating magistrate within the French system. The juge d'instruction is a single individual appointed by the president of the tribunal de grande instance. Numbers are not large. In 1998, there were 565 and the numbers had not risen for some years. Since they are divided over the country, they are as few as 5 in some towns, but some 60 in Paris, of whom 30 would work in the financial crime unit on the rue des Italiens.[16] The nominee may be removed on grounds of the good administration of justice where the procureur or one of the parties requests, but reasons must be given for such a decision.[17]

Being a juge d'instruction would normally be one phase in a judicial career. In her study of judges involved in political scandals of the 1990s, Roussel did not identify any distinctive social or political background that marked them out from the bulk of judges.[18] It would suit some temperaments to work as a lone individual. For some judges interviewed, this position had become almost a career in its own right. It is more usual for judges to spend a period of perhaps five to seven years in this function, though longer periods are more common in Paris, where scope for mobility while remaining in the same locality are more restricted. All who had performed the task or were currently in post stated that they had undertaken the position as a matter of interest. For those in search of status and promotion, the career at the parquet has higher standing. Being a juge d'instruction is more of a vocation. One of the attractions of the function is that the juge exercises a significant amount of personal discretion.

13 This emphasis on pre-reference activity is part of the Ministry of Justice's strategy: see L le Mesle, Sous-directeur des Affaires Criminelles et des Grâces, Ministry of Justice, in Nancy Conference November 1997, 'Justice et Police: Quels Rapports?', p 9, where he argues that the parquet should focus more attention on activities 'upstream' of referring cases to judges.

14 H Dalle, 'Juges et procureurs: une évolution divergente' in *Justices 2000: Ce qui a changé dans la justice depuis 20 ans* (Paris 2000), p 62.

15 P Bellet, H Calvet, and D Soulez-Larivière, Libération, 10 Dec 1990.

16 For statistics, see *Annuaire statistique de la Justice*, p 103.

17 Art 84 C proc pén. For examples, see the Urba and Dickinson cases, above pp 122 and 118.

18 V Roussel, 'Scandales politiques et transformation des rapports entre magistrature et politique' (2000) 44/45 *Droit et Société* 13.

The instruction process is a rather solitary one for the judge. Despite the publicity given to the criminal 'affaires' in the 1990s, the research conducted by Roussel[19] suggests that there was little contact between judges dealing with similar kinds of issue and that the principal cause of contacts was when superiors caused files to be removed from one juge d'instruction and handed to another. The lack of concerted effort by the judges in such high profile cases is surprising. But the attention to individual criminals, rather than the causes of criminality, provides some explanation for this. Certainly, interviews with individual juges d'instruction suggest that they adopt a very individualised approach.[20]

Unlike the trial judge or the judge in a civil case, the juge d'instruction has to maintain an ongoing relationship with the accused, his lawyers and witnesses over many months. This development of a personal relationship is closer to the juge des enfants and the juge des affaires familiales, but is unlike the role of other judges. As Garapon points out, this kind of office-based, bureaucratic justice is not neat and clear-cut in reaching a decision at the end of a debate between parties, rather it is a process of coming to a decision on the basis of a more fluid set of inputs. He talks about the difference between this justice du cabinet and the justice de l'audience.[1]

The freedom of the juge d'instruction is limited by the fact that he must act on a referral made by the procureur. There is no power to act on his own. Even when seised of a case on a non-criminal matter, eg sudden death, the juge cannot undertake a criminal investigation without a reference from the procureur.[2] The public reputation of the juge d'instruction comes from the fact that he or she is not subordinated to the Ministry of Justice, unlike the procureur, and can be seen as a more impartial champion of the rights of the individual, as well as of the public interest.

Although the chambre de l'instruction (previously called the chambre d'accusation) is his superior, it can intervene in an investigation only in a few situations. First, where the juge simply is inert and fails to deal with a case in good time. Administratively, its president receives brief summaries of progress on files each quarter. If the juge does not seem to be progressing the matter adequately, then the chambre can withdraw the file from him and give it to another juge or to one of its members.[3] Under art 221-2 C proc pén, after four months since the last action in the instruction (two months in the case of a person in detention), any party to the proceedings can refer the matter to the chambre de l'instruction which can issue requests for further information, or can withdraw the file from the juge.[4] Second, the case may be handled promptly, but may be badly managed. On receipt of the juge's report, the chambre here can itself ask for a supplément d'information and charge one of its own members with this.[5] The juge

19 V Roussel, 'Le complot des juges' in (1999) *Justice* No 162, 3. This reports the findings of her thesis: *Les magistrats dans les scandales politiques 1991-7*, Univ Paris X 1998.

20 See, for example, the interviews with Edith Boizette and Jean-Louis Brugière in Greilsamer and Schneidermann, pp 41ff and 69ff.

1 *Bien juger*, pp 257–259.

2 P Chambon, *Le juge d'instruction. Théorie et pratique de la procédure* (4th edn, Paris 1997), paras 43-44. On the general requirement for a réquisitoire introductif, see ibid, paras 71 and 73.

3 The parties may also raise the issue of apparent bias (suspicion légitime) on the part of the juge d'instruction: for an illustration of an unsuccessful case see *Le Monde*, 14 June 2000, alleging the juge met the partie civile at a dinner party.

4 Chambon, para 82-2.

5 See for example the Caroline Dickinson case, above, p 118.

could be removed from the case and the case transferred to another juge, but this is rare (and indeed a slap in the face). More usually, there will be a request for further information from the juge himself. But the Chambre's powers are limited. Thus if the juge does not want to put a person en examen, the Chambre can ask him for further information, but cannot order him to place the person en examen.[6]

(3) The jury

The jury is not a central part of the French legal system. It only exists in serious criminal cases and it is of relatively recent origin. It was imported by the revolutionaries through the loi of 16-29 September 1791. The idea was to provide a popular control over a rather remote judiciary and it coincided with attempts to make the judicial appointment process more democratic through electing judges.[7] The excesses of the Revolutionary jury mean that it has never enjoyed the reputation of the common law jury as a bastion of freedom. Rather it serves the function of widening the experience of a bureaucratic judiciary. Under the system that has prevailed since the loi of 25 November 1941, three judges sit with the jury to decide on both guilt and sentence.[8] Since 1959, there are nine jurors. The jury only sits in the cour d'assises, which deals with a small number of the most serious crimes. In 1998, it heard only 2954 cases (0.52% of the 561,452 offences tried before all criminal courts). The jury does not, therefore, have the kind of substantial role in terms of numbers of cases played by the English jury. Most cases involve violence to the person (74.6%) and the rest are mainly cases involving serious attacks on property (22%) or some drugs cases. The cases are thus of a high profile, but will not include many of the cases, such as délits on political corruption, which would go before a common law jury.

The jury is rather a popular element to legitimate the imposition of the harshest penalties by the State. That said, it has been noted that the procedure by which the judge sits with the jury has radically reduced the rate of acquittals. In 1901, the rate was 30%. In 1985-89, the rate was 7.3% in Paris and as low as 3.1% in Lyons[9] The jury is reserved for serious cases where a particular solemnity is required.

Unlike in the common law, it is the pre-trial structuring of the file, rather than the way information is presented to the jury that shapes the criminal law and the law of evidence.

Despite the public and media interest that the jury trial attracts, it could be considered a predominantly symbolic element of the criminal law culture in France. Although,

6 Crim 25 June 1996, D 1997, 62 note Pradel.

7 See JP Royer, *Histoire de la justice en France* (2nd edn Paris 1996), pp 289-300, noting that there was originally both a jury of presentment and a trial jury. Also R Munday, 'Jury trial, continental style' (1993) 13 LS 204 at pp 204-208.

8 Before then there had been a number of different relationships between judges and jury. During the period 1808 to 1869, the jury first deliberated alone, but then might be required to have a further deliberation with the judge present. The number of jury members has also varied with the present number of nine only fixed by the Code of Criminal Procedure of 1959: see Munday, 'Jury trial', pp 208-209 and note 29.

9 R. Munday, 'What do the French think of their jury?' (1995) 15 LS 65 at 75.

according to the observations of Munday,[10] the jurors appear content with their role, he also notes the critiques of authors like Pradel who is very grudging in his acceptance of the jury role.[11]

(4) The trial judge

The trial judge in the different courts will play different roles. In the tribunal de police, the judge will be on his own. He will have the file, but in many cases when there is an immediate appearance, he will have had very little time to read it. He will depend on the prosecutor (normally the commissaire de police) to lead on the case. In the tribunal correctionnel, again in comparution immédiate cases, the judge or judges will have had little time to digest the file, but they will use the key documents to go through the facts with the accused (at a pace which is probably easier for him to comprehend than in cases of a more lengthy preparation). In other cases, one of the judges will have prepared the case and will lead off the questioning. This judge can also have determined whether there are not further issues which need to be sorted out before the case is ready for trial. (The role of one of the trial judges acting as a reporter in preparing the case acts as an equivalent of a pre-trial review, even though it will not normally involve the lawyers, unless there is a problem.)

The president of the Cour d'assises has not only the role of presiding at the session, he also has to conduct a training session for jurors at the beginning of the assises period. He will also use the file to review the evidence and make sure that the case is ready for hearing.[12] The key role for which the president or judge needs to have the file is to question the accused. The purpose is to make the events explicable, without too much introspection. The judge needs to have prepared the questions well, but must not reveal any opinion about the culpability of the accused – the approach is described as 'un interrogatoire distancié', leaving the parties to intervene with more partisan questions.[13]

(5) The victim

The victim is the bridge between the criminal and the civil process. In its criminal aspects, the victim is seeking punishment and denunciation. Many will not want to take on this role as individuals, even in relation to offences like rape. In the trial's civil aspects, he is seeking compensation, like any civil party, though this may well be nominal. The balance between these aspects will differ. The doctor whose car has been damaged by the cleaner he had just dismissed will want the cost of repair. The grandmother whose possessions were stolen by friends of her grandson whom he had invited into the house will predominantly want the cost of buying replacements. By

10 Ibid.

11 *Procédure pénale,* (8th edn 1995), paras 41 and 42, especially the latter where he comments that the reforms of 1959 have made the jury 'moins mauvais'.

12 See P Le Quinquis, 'Le Président de la cour d'assises' (1998) 10 *Justices: La justice pénale* 99.

13 Ibid, p 106.

contrast, the hunting association as civil party in the prosecution of poachers will be seeking to punish the individuals and warn off others.

Since the ordonnance of 1670, the victim has had to constitute himself specifically as a civil party and pursue a civil action.[14] The victim has to justify a clear, personal loss, which is actual and has already happened, following directly from the crime under investigation.[15] A request for substantial damages is not necessary, since the fact of being a victim gives a person a sufficient interest. The increasing role of the victim in criminal proceedings is an important part of the symbolic process of modern justice: a re-evaluation of the victim and a reduction in the importance of the State.[16] The notion of victim has undergone a significant change particularly since the 1970s. In 1913, the Cour de cassation rejected as inadmissible the claim by an association for the moral protection of youth to be a partie civile, just months after it had accepted such an action by a trade union.[17] This was modified in the 1970s sometimes by *ad hoc* judicial decisions on actions brought by particular associations,[18] but mainly by legislative intervention. Legislation has now extended the right of associations to be civil parties in criminal actions in a whole host of areas, including anti-alcoholism, tobacco and drug abuse, child abuse, sexual violence and prostitution, protection of the family, consumers, defence of women's rights, sex and race discrimination, and protection of the environment, hunting and fishing. Although the Delmas-Marty Commission suggested introducing some order into the situation, this has not been done.[19] Commentators note the impact that this has had on the criminal process. To allow so many associations to bring criminal prosecutions inevitably limits the freedom of the procureur who will be only too aware of the agenda of a relevant association. In a high profile case, such as the prosecution for crimes against humanity of Klaus Barbie in 1986, an association was able to have the indictment quashed and a more serious crime prosecuted.[20] Such prosecutions manipulate the tarnishing effect of a prosecution, even before a conviction occurs (and even if it does not).[1] Such associations are effectively able to represent their sectional interest as that of the general interest.[2] The criminal action can thus take the form of a major piece of social debate and not just a discrete prosecution. Represented in the pre-trial and trial phases, the victim can not only claim damages, but can add a different voice to the discussion of the wrongdoing in question and its social consequences.

In the past, criminal law was seen predominantly as an offence to the State with the central actors as the procureur and the judge, and with a very limited role for the victim.[3] The increasing importance of the individual in society has given the victim more of a place in the criminal process, and also in mediation procedures where a settlement with the victim has become a justification for the procureur not to proceed

14 See P Chambon, *Le juge d'instruction*, para 101.
15 Ibid, para 104-1
16 Garapon, *Bien Juger*, p 246.
17 Crim 18 October 1913, S 1920.1.321 note Hugueney.
18 See Crim 14 January 1971, *Le Pen*, D 1971, 101 rapport Champar.
19 *La mise en état des affaires pénales*. Rapport, pp 154-157.
20 Crim 20 December 1985, D 1986, 500 note Chapar.
1 A Garapon and D Salas, *La République pénalisée* (Paris 1996), pp 23-25.
2 Ibid, p 27; and see Pradel, *Procédure pénale*, p 264.
3 See Garapon and Salas, p 17.

with a prosecution. Victim-offender mediation, albeit under the aegis of state officials, has reduced the interest of the State in punishing crime as an offence against its authority.[4] As Bonafé-Schmitt remarks, the outcome of this movement is a change in the normative system with individuals and groups participating more in creating the norms that will govern their lives, a form of devolution of power from the State.[5] Others would suggest that the State is predominantly taking advantage of the emotional power of the situation of victims to reinforce its own action – it does not replace the victims, but identifies itself with them.[6]

(6) The lawyers

The nature of the French criminal justice system since the 16th century has left the *avocat* as predominatly focused on the role of defender of the accused. The instigation of the inquisitorial and secret system of criminal prosecution by the Ordonnance of Villiers-Cotterets of 1539 and the creation of the King's prosecutors by the Edict of Blois of 1579 left no place for the avocats as part of the prosecution process.[7] This was reinforced by the investigative function of the juge d'instruction. The avocat performs a number of tasks for the accused. The first is of adviser during investigation, a role which has gradually developed. It is only during the course of the instruction in the 20th century that the avocat was able to play a significant role during the long judicial investigation of an offence, especially since 1897 when he gained access to the file. All the same, it was only after the loi of 31 December 1996 that the suspect could be given a copy of the court file by his avocat. Until then it was a document which remained in the hands of the court and the avocat was really the principal intermediary.[8]

The second role was in orchestrating the public opinion of the client. In the 18th century, the Paris Bar became involved in writing tracts published to draw attention to miscarriages of justice and for the defence of individual defendants (which made up for the lack of oral pleading by avocats in serious criminal trials). This polemical role was particularly important in political cases in both the 18th and 19th centuries, in which the avocats were leaders in the development of liberal opinion in France.[9] This tradition of close association with the client, both before and during trial ensured that the lawyer was not just the mouthpiece of the accused during the hearing, but performed a wider role as spokesperson that is continued today.[10] It is not unusual that, in high profile cases, the avocat is interviewed by the media outside the court or the office of the judge to explain the development of the case and to put the client's perspective. Since the

4 See J-P Bonafé-Schmitt, 'La médiation sociale et pénale' in J-P Bonafé-Schmitt et al, *Les médiations, la médiation* (Paris 1999), 15ff.
5 Ibid, p 80.
6 Garapon and Salas, op cit, p 22.
7 See L Karpik, *French Lawyers* (Oxford 1999), p 26.
8 See J Pradel, 'Centenaire de la loi du 8 décembre 1897 sur la défense avant jugement pénal: essai d'un bilan' D 1997 Chr 375. Note that the lawyer is required to pay for the photocopy and so many won't bother: *Le Monde* dossier May 2000.
9 Karpik, p 77 and ch 6.
10 The role is much closer to that of the solicitor of an accused in Britain than their barrister, who has a relatively short-lived relationship with the client in most cases.

avocat is not bound by the secret de l'instruction to silence about what his client said, then this role of one-sided transmission of information can be useful to the client in a protracted investigation. The revelations can take place either as formal interviews (often on the steps of the court) or as off-the-record meetings.[11] As Merle explains:

> When a case has a certain public reputation, the *avocat* cannot restrict himself to his office and to the corridors of the courts. If he wants to defend the cause of his client fully, he must necessarily play the game, give interviews, reply to attacks, correct mistakes. But he is obliged to respect the secrecy of the *instruction*, to observe the deference to which he is bound with respect to the judges.[12]

The third role was conducting and pleading the case in court. Until the revolution, this role was confined to minor offences. In serious cases, the accused was not allowed a lawyer to speak for him, though practice ensured that the accused did have some advice and support from a lawyer.[13] Now with the growth of newspapers in the 19th century, a packed courtroom was an ideal public forum for the lawyer as a political and social actor. With prosecutions conducted by a State employed procureur, the avocat could consistently appear as the defender of freedom against the State. The court thus served as a political, as well as legal forum.[14]

The role thus created for the avocat is one that is completely separated from that of the judge and which can, thus, lead to mutual incomprehension.[15] The traditional role of the avocat as defender creates an antagonism stronger than in systems where the lawyer can sometimes plead for the prosecution and at others for the defence.[16] Interviews with both juges and avocats for this research suggested that this sense of antagonism had been accentuated in recent years. One potential cause was that judges are no longer required to have spent a long period as stagiaire in an avocat's chambers and so have less of a feeling for what the avocat is trying to do. There is a sense that both sides view the other as 'the enemy', the obstructive party to the process.[17] Research on French avocats notes that there are two strategies, the strategy of *rupture*, where the avocat sets himself up as defender of the client against the system and is almost a revolutionary in the cause of right, and the strategy of *connivance*, where the lawyer is respectful of the judge and tries to secure benefits for the client by working with the system. This is not a new phenomenon.[18] The modern situation perhaps exaggerates this.

11 See D Soulez Larivière, *Lettres à un jeune avocat* (Paris 1999), p 93.
12 R Merle, 'Défense pénale' (1998) 10 *Justices* 91 at p 93 and a similar view is expressed by M. Arnold in L. Gratiot et al, *Art et techniques de la plaidoirie aujourd'hui*, p 56.
13 JP Royer, *Histoire de la justice en France* (2nd edn, Paris 1996), p 153.
14 Karpik, pp 132-133. This role declined after the Dreyfus scandal of the turn of the 20th century, and the *avocat* was replaced by the intellectual as the representative of liberal society: ibid, pp 308-309.
15 See the criticism of Henri d'Armagnac, representative of the Fédération nationale des unions de jeunes avocats, in Truche Commission, p 214.
16 See Karpik, p 296.
17 See for example P-A Sadon (then avocat-général at the Cour de cassation) in Greilsamer and Schneidermann, 475 at p 494 where he suggests that some lawyers view themselves as a counter-power, the barrier who blocks procedures. The conflicting views on appropriate attitudes between judges and lawyers is seen in L Gratiot et al, *Art et techniques de la plaidoirie aujourd'hui*, pp 84, 88 and 113.
18 See R Merle, p 93-94; and the unpublished research of Field and West funded by the ESRC.

Among the avocats, there is a clear group of penal lawyers, though nearly all lawyers also perform different functions. In his reflections on the differences between criminal lawyers and other members of the profession of avocat, Leclerc emphasises the importance not so much of knowing the substantive law as knowing the procedural law and how to operate it: 'It is not enough to know the law, you must have the knack [of using it].'[19] While he notes that he has civil work to make the criminal work pay and a criminal lawyer needs to know something about press, tax, customs and business practice, his presentation is of a distinctive work practice and set of knowledge. A similar comment is made by a juge d'instruction, Cathérine Samet:

> For the competent generalist *avocat,* precise knowledge of the facts, of the procedure followed, of the personality of the client. For the *avocat* specialist in délits and crimes, is added the skill of the game, that practice of exchange, of strategy for the future hearing, accentuating or attenuating the replies of the client, refuting all or at least a lot, contesting the validity of the proceedings, going as far as to break with the judicial system, as Maître Vergès has allowed himself to do sometimes.[20]

In addition, of course, there is the role of pleading.[1] In civil and administrative cases, most of the skill in court relates to the preparation of written pleadings and brief summaries of key points before the judge. In criminal cases, one moves from assistance, when first called in, to advocacy at the various stages. This is distinctive, not only with regard to those who engage in the juridique rather than in the judiciaire work, but also from the civil practitioner of judiciaire. This view of the distinctiveness of the criminal lawyer is supported by the broader research on the avocat by Lucien Karpik.[2] He identifies different tasks which avocats may be involved in and how these are distributed among different forms of practice. Unlike corporate lawyers, criminal lawyers are generalists. Karpik identifies a number of specific groupings of subject areas with which an avocat practising in one branch of law might well combine. Criminal law is linked to labour, personal injury and landlord-tenant law, in contrast to more commercial firms.[3] For him this work focus leads to a different form of knowledge (knowledge of people rather than of business or 'intermediate knowledge') and this relates to different kinds of client and thus different strategies of social mobility.[4] There is certainly a sense from the literature that the criminal lawyer, predominantly reliant on legal aid and processing routine cases has a distinctive place within the legal system.[5] Given that the client will be the principal person questioned directly by the juge d'instruction in

19 H Leclerc, *Un combat pour la justice. Entretiens avec Marc Heurgon*, ch 10 at p 198. See also R Merle, p 91.

20 C Samet, *Journal d'un juge d'instruction*, p 17.

1 See generally L Gratiot et al, *Art et techniques de la plaidoirie aujourd'hui*, p 12 which argues that oral argument puts life into the rather abstract file, and lawyers argue, esp p 88, that the function of oral argument is to focus on the human being, rather than on the abstract 'criminal' that appears from the file and the procedure.

2 L Karpik, *French Lawyers*, ch 10.

3 Karpik, p 219.

4 Ibid, p 220.

5 See *Le Monde*, 17 May 2000, p 15: 'Le sacerdoce des petites affaires' recounting the experiences of several lawyers involved in this kind of work: the typical correctionnel case will be paid at 700F a file, while the work of the civil and commercial lawyer proceeds at a more sedate pace: see *Le Monde*, 18 May 2000, p 16.

investigation or the presiding judge at the trial, French works on pleading note the importance of this preparatory activity which is distinctive to criminal law.[6]

Thus, although there is not a tightly definable group of specialist criminal practitioners, there are a significant number of lawyers for whom this kind of work predominates. The writings and comments from lawyers, other practitioners and observers suggests that practising crime is distinctive. It is distinctive because of the pre-trial preparation, notably the contribution to the construction of the dossier and the assistance of a person mise en examen.

(7) The police[7]

The whole prosecution system in France depends heavily on the police. Leigh and Zedner expressed concern in their study that the period of garde à vue where the person arrested is without legal assistance was a situation where pressure (if not brutality) could be used to force a confession.[8] Although some changes have been made in the loi of 15 June 2000, the basic situation of the individual facing police questioning alone for 24 hours (or 72 hours in drugs cases) does give the police much power. The regulation two sandwiches a day (or food brought in by the family or friends) provide limited breaks for the suspect. It has been argued that the increasing use of traitement en temps réel increases the power of the police. They act as the first filter in terms of arrest and action. They notify the procureur and discuss initial steps on the telephone. Depending on the way the case is presented and the presence of mind of the prosecutor, there will be more or less analysis of the case presented for consideration. The procureur may well not ask enough questions and feel compromised, forced to defend the choices he made on the telephone rather than speaking objectively as representative of the law and guarantor of the legal procedure.[9]

It is noted by a number of observers and commentators that the procureurs and the juge d'instruction are only involved in a limited way in controlling the police.[10] Hodgson suggests that the procureur will not visit the police except in limited circumstances and so cannot conduct effective supervision.[11] In most less serious cases, the police come to the prosecutor when they have something sufficiently concrete to report and need some authorisation (to detain or search) or wish to institute proceedings.[12] Modern

6 See L Gratiot et al, *Art et techniques de la plaidoirie aujourd'hui*, pp 56, 88 and 144.
7 See Bell, Boyron and Whittaker, pp 124-125.
8 Op cit, pp 12 and 21.
9 Dalle, op cit, p 58.
10 See, for example, AS Goldstein and M Marcus, 'The myth of judicial supervision in three "inquisitorial" systems: France, Italy and Germany' (1987) 87 Yale LJ 240; JH Langbein and LL Weinreb, 'Continental criminal procedure' (1978) 87 Yale LJ 1549. The lack of real judicial control over the investigation was noted by the Delmas-Marty report (Commission Justice Pénale et Droits de l'Homme, *Rapport sur la mise en état des affaires pénales* (Paris 1991), p 38.
11 J Hodgson (2001) 41 British Journal of criminology 342; also H Haenel and J Arthuis, op cit, p 51.
12 See B McKillop, 'Readings and Hearings in French Criminal Justice: Five Cases in the *Tribunal Correctionnel*' (1998) 46 Am Jo Comp Law 757, 777-8. B McKillop, 'Anatomy of a French Murder Case' (1997) 45 Am Jo Comp Law 527, 567-568 notes the way in which the commission rogatoire is used also to give the police a fair scope of action. The extent of such practices was confirmed in interviews.

procedures of traitement en temps réel permit a fairly continuous dialogue between the police who have to notify the procureur of any arrest and the procureur. My own observation of the process suggests an interchange is fairly common. The police are keen to present things as they see them and to obtain a rapid conviction, but the procureur is keen to ensure a sustainable case is presented. In addition, there is the use by the juge d'instruction of the commission rogatoire, which effectively confers very substantial powers on the police to conduct the investigation formerly under the authority of the judge. The importance of this has to be judged in the context of an ongoing relationship between the local procureur and the local police. There is a working sense of what the procureur is likely to want and when it is necessary to trouble him and when he would like to know what is going on. As has been noted in relation to the Netherlands, it is not so much the close supervision of the police that is relied upon, but the diversity of inputs into the criminal file, which are central.[13]

The training and continuing education for judges and police are distinct, and they are under different ministries, and this keeps them distinct, except for the more recent roles in relation to the contrat local de sécurité.

(8) Doctrine

It would be fair to say that doctrine in criminal law has received less attention than that in private law or in administrative law. There is, however, a long history. There have been journals that digested and disseminated case law, especially of the Cour de cassation since 1829. Journals since the 1890s have tried to go beyond this and offer more critical comment on criminal policies and practices with a comparative dimension. Thus the *Revue internationale du droit pénal* and, from 1936, the *Revue de science criminelle et de droit pénal comparé* have commented on both criminal law and criminal policy. These have proved to be an outlet for both academics and practitioners, although Poncela notes that after 1970, there has been a marked decline in the proportion of articles published by judges and avocats.[14] The academic interest has been heavily in the fields of criminal policy and penology. All the same, with editors such as Marc Ancel who was both an academic and a judge of the Cour de cassation, there has been quite a dialogue between the practitioner and academic writers. The extent of influence is, however, much less well documented than in other branches of law. The doctrine of the procureur-général is also of some significance, as in administrative law. However, the rate of publication of the *conclusions* of the procureur-général is lower than that for administrative law.

On the whole, the influence of doctrine is less dominant than in private law. In part, this is because so many cases before the Cour de cassation are on matters of fact or require little judicial research. Interviews suggest that judges frequently need to do no more than consult the major legal encyclopaedias. The *Juris-Classeur* was described

13 See S Field, P Alldridge and N Jörg, in C Harding et al, *Criminal Justice in Europe. A Comparative Study* (Oxford 1995), 227 at p 246.

14 See P Poncela, 'Pour une histoire d'une revue de droit pénal' in A-J Arnaud, *La culture des revues juridiques françaises* (1988) 29 Quaderni fiorentini per la storia del pensiero giuridico moderno (Il Mulino, Milan 1988), 31 at p 35.

as 'the real manna' on which members of the Cour de cassation thrive. Only in the few choice cases is it felt necessary to branch out into the major doctrinal works of monographs and classical journals. Such observations seem supported by examining the references which are contained in the (few) published rapports in criminal law. For instance, in Souppe's rapport in a case involving the issue of the retrospectivity of criminal laws, no specific references are made to doctrine at all.[15]

Doctrine is clearly read and can be an argument for reform. Commentaries on cases give a clear sense of doctrinal and judicial debate.[16] In addition, recent first presidents of the Chambre criminelle have organised colloquia involving judges and academics on issues of the moment. Furthermore, there is typically an academic serving as a conseiller of the Chambre. A range of judges in different courts commented that they did not think that there was a strong body of academic writing in criminal law. They would typically mention the same two or three leading authors, but did not consider that there was the same number of good scholars compared with branches of the civil law. All this builds into a picture where doctrinal writing does not, in general, have a very major influence on judicial decision-making. It also seems to have a limited place in the other forms of lawmaking.

F. THE CULTURE OF CRIMINAL LAW

To review what has emerged thus far, the argument has been that the centre of gravity of the criminal law system lies in the pre-trial process which shapes the activities and relationships between the various legal actors, even when it comes to the trial itself. A further important point would be that the discourse of justification relates to a number of different audiences in a rather particular way, and this shapes attitudes to the function of the law and criminal procedure. The caricature of the French legal mentality as code-based, deductive and formalist fails to capture the dynamics of the criminal law system.

(1) The centrality of the pre-trial

Within the French criminal process, the pre-trial process plays a central role. As Spencer notes, the period between when a suspect is charged and the case coming to trial has little significance in English law, but the French situation is 'entirely different'.[17] The accused is interviewed, the witnesses are questioned and the accused will be able to put his side of the case to a person independent of the police. The process itself is a focus of attention, and its product, the file, influences the course of the rest of the

15 See Crim 12 June 1989, D 1989, 585 rapport Souppe: art 94 of the loi of 30.12.1985 brought it into force on 1 January 1986 and abolished previous offences; under the civil code, lois come into force one full day after they have been deposited in the local préfecture (here 6 January 1986). The issue arose whether there was no offence in force from 1 January to 6 January.

16 See eg Pradel and Varinard, pp 283-284, 379 and 408.

17 See JR Spencer, 'French and English Criminal Procedure: A Brief Comparison' in B Markesinis, *The Gradual Convergence*, 33 at p 43.

stages through which a case will go. The character of the process is that the police, the procureur, the juge d'instruction (in some cases), the person 'mise en examen' and the victim all make contributions to building up the file in private. But at the same time, there is a process of public debate in which the accused tries to build up a public face.[18] The continuity between the pre-trial and trial in terms of the information means that the instruction process is central. The experienced avocat will begin preparing his lines of argument for the trial already during l'instruction, and strategies begun at that stage can be continued during the trial.[19] Furthermore, the process defines the major actors in criminal law and their roles. Though many official reports have pointed in the direction of removing the juge d'instruction and moving to a more accusatorial process with the procureur more clearly marked out as the public prosecutor, the inquisitorial process remains firmly defended by judges and politicians alike.[20]

The pre-trial process is important, among other things, for the way it shapes distinctive career paths among judges and lawyers. Within the judiciary, the separate functions of procureur, juge d'instruction, and trial judge are distinct, even if they may all be performed at different periods within a single judicial career. The first two are specifically dedicated roles, whereas the last may well be combined with the functions of a trial judge in civil matters. In appellate courts, once again there will typically be specialisation on criminal matters, rather than a mixture of functions. In this way, the criminal law offers a distinctive and readily identifiable aspect of the possible activities of judges. In interview, those who were currently involved in it and those who were now engaged in other activities were able readily to identify criminal law as different. It had 'a greater focus on social reality'; it was 'at the heart of social problems'; it involved conflicts between individual liberty and a certain conception of society; it establishes personal responsibility and determines penalties; it involves dynamic relations with actors outside the judicial sphere – the police, social workers, and so on – much more than in conventional civil and commercial law. The sense of engagement and active involvement were among the most common features highlighted as attractive by those who were, or who had been, involved in it. The dynamism required was one reason for people wishing to move on, though the repetitive character of many situations was also a motive. The distinctiveness of the issues and processes in criminal law generate distinctive sessions for continuing professional development which can help to reinforce a sense of solidarity between the different judges involved in the criminal process and their sense of distinctiveness.

Any sense of how French cases are prepared for trial must give an important place to the procureur. He acts as gatekeeper and supervisor to the police. He decides when cases, as they are presented, can be taken forward and can give instructions on what is necessary to enable the police to obtain a successful prosecution. Within legal limits, he also controls the flow of work to the juge d'instruction. Finally, at trial, he will represent both the public interest and the law in the arguments presented to the trial judge(s) and thereby influence the outcome. As has been seen, both generally and in relation to specific cases, he is the public face of the criminal law system in its concrete

18 See Tiberi case, *Le Monde*, 22 July 1999, p 6.
19 See M Arnold, in L Gratiot et al, *Art et techniques de la plaidoirie aujourd'hui*, p 56.
20 See Francis Casorla, 'L'approche du magistrat' (1997) 68 International Review of Penal Law 83; J Pradel, 'La procédure pénale française à l'aube du troisième millénaire' D 2000 Chr 1.

application. The préfet de police will be able to defend law enforcement in general, and the procureur cannot speak for what the courts will eventually decide. But he is called upon to defend and explain the system in general and sometimes in particular cases to the media. As a judge, the procureur also makes a number of decisions in relation to the suspect and will interview him, often trying to make him understand the wrong which has been done. The juge d'instruction will also develop relationships with the police and the suspect, but, in theory at least, much less with the media.

The importance of the instruction undertaken by the procureur or the juge d'instruction is clear from the centrality of the file and the relative lack of oral debate which most common law observers have noted.[1] These observers, notably McKillop, also stress the importance of re-enactment and confrontation of witnesses prior to trial and on the importance attached to confessions. Now all these features of a case depend on work done before trial. Confession is not essentially a feature of the trial, but comes about during pre-trial questioning. Although the French do not accept a guilty plea, the presence of an admission of guilt serves much the same function, but does not dispense the investigating court from satisfying itself that there is sufficient evidence to support a conviction.[2]

All the same, the detailed processing of cases remains important. It sets the tone for the system and decides what can be left to more rapid processes, secure in the knowledge that instruction sets the standard for the quality of work which needs to be presented to a trial court.

With more rapid processing by the procureur, there is an increased emphasis on the trial as the moment when the various pieces of evidence are put to the test. Certainly since 1973, there have been a number of attempts to process less serious or obvious cases as rapidly as possible, without the heavy weight of the instruction process. But because of the character of offences to which the process before the juge d'instruction applies, it has an important influence both on the public perception of criminal justice, and also has helped to develop the rules on handling the file.

It needs to be recalled that both the juge d'instruction and the procureur are members of the judiciary (magistrats), but the latter are not juges in the sense of taking judicial decisions. Since the French do not consider that all offences must be prosecuted, both procureur and juge d'instruction have discretionary power to take decisions about the merits of a prosecution, and in this they have a political judgment to make in the wide sense of the term 'political'.[3] In particular, the Convention has reinforced moves to extend the rights of the accused to challenge evidence, to be free from detention and to have a decision within a reasonable time. The balancing of these imperatives is of public importance and helps explain the media interest in their activity, over and above the 'human interest' character of the matters under investigation.

The character of the pre-trial process shapes the activity and the qualities required of lawyers. As has been seen, though few avocats are exclusively involved in criminal law, there are a number who perform the work on a regular basis. These develop the

1 See McKillop above, p 145 note 12.
2 See, for example, the Caroline Dickinson case where the confession of one person asked was subsequently found to be unreliable in the face of DNA evidence which excluded him from being the rapist: above p 118.
3 M Troper, *Le Monde* 19 November 1999, p 20.

skills and approach which are seen as necessary to managing the relationships pre-trial with the client, the procureur and the juge d'instruction, as well as both attending interviews and monitoring the file. At trial, they are involved in preparing the client to be questioned by the judges, adding appropriate elements to the file as final submissions, and making brief but eloquent pleading to the court in final argument. In the many cases in the lower courts where the file has not been managed by the lawyer in the pre-trial phase, the lawyer has limited room to influence the course of events. This is even more the case on appeal, where the content of the file will be the basis on which the case is reviewed.

As common law observers have noted, the 'day in court' in a criminal case is often a disappointing event, and even more so the appeal. The dialogue between bench and accused rehearses the key elements in the file, but it is much more a public affirmation of guilt and a determination of sentence than a dramatic exchange between lawyers and witnesses.

Attention in the criminal law process focuses on confirming facts and establishing the right description of the personality of the offender, rather than focusing much on questions of law. This is because, even with alternative procedures, the pre-trial and trial are processes through which the criminal law has to be carried out, unlike the subsidiary role of such processes in other branches of law. With limited scope for judicial lawmaking in this branch of law and a more restrictive scope for creativity in interpretation (the principle of legality), the central place is given not to standard setting, but to the application and proclamation of community standards established elsewhere.

For the wider public, criminal law is something which affects and involves them in a distinctive way. As victims, jurors or just as concerned citizens receiving media coverage or attending the courts, the criminal law offers a process that gives the public a role, as an action of its society. The French situation of each of these roles is distinctive with respect to other legal systems, in that the roles of victims and jurors are not the same elsewhere. In relation to the media, it is more who engages with it, and thus what the citizen receives, which is distinctive compared with the reporting of criminal proceedings in other countries. The kind of involvement both active and passive which this creates is distinctive compared with other branches of law, where the general public is a passive and typically absent spectator.

(2) An inquisitorial system?

Although the control over the pre-trial process by the procureur and the juge d'instruction makes the preliminary phase inquisitorial, the increasing role of the avocat in the more serious cases does attenuate the inquisitorial character of the process. Even in other cases, the procureur will have to anticipate the tactics of the defence in deciding whether a case is ready to be brought to trial. In observation, I noted that there was a reluctance to rely entirely on confessions without corroborating evidence, lest the accused withdraw the confession at trial or his lawyer challenged the circumstances under which it was given. At the same time, the active role of the pre-trial judges (however reliant they may be on the police) and their direct role in confirming points of fact with the suspect and witnesses makes the process necessarily inquisitorial. The French would demur from the description of their system as 'inquisitorial' in relation to the trial. The fundamental value of the presumption of innocence, reinforced by the new drafting of art 1 C proc pén arising from the loi of 15 June 2000, means that the burden of proof of guilt lies with the prosecution. The prosecution and the defence have equal opportunities to state their case and to be involved in the questioning in court. The fact that the presiding judge begins by examining the accused (and expects answers) is not seen as derogating from that. After all, most of the relevant information is already in the file to which all parties have had access. The function of the questions is not to extort new admissions or information from the accused, but to confirm what has been said before, but this time in a public forum, and to probe more the personality of the accused, to obtain explanations, and thus to have better information for decisions on sentencing. In that sense, the trial has significant accusatorial features. The attitudes required of the presiding judge, notably impartiality, reinforce this.

(3) Orality

Criminal procedure is much more oral than civil or administrative law. Although there is a file which forms the basis for questioning and decisions at all stages from arrest to trial, there are a whole series of face-to-face meetings between the procureur or the juge d'instruction and an accused, a partie civile or witnesses. The first two will be assisted by lawyers, both there and at trial. Creating impressions through oral argument and questioning will be as important as what goes down on paper. A one-hour confrontation may be reduced to a two-side summary signed by those present, but it will have shaped the perceptions and future actions of all concerned. Once it comes to trial, the hearing, though brief in most cases, will be oral with individuals present. As we will see, this shapes the form of justification and argumentation involved. Thus, despite the emphasis on the file and the written items of the procedure, orality retains a major importance in the criminal trial, an importance that is seen by judges and avocats. In business crimes, the file will be more important, leaving a limited space for oral argument.[4]

(4) The character of legal reasoning

The formally published judgments and decisions in criminal cases reflect the traditional characteristics of French legal style. Given the number of decisions that a typical trial or appeal court will hand down in any one day, the formal statement of reasons for the decision is necessarily brief. It will recall the main facts, set out the legal rule, and summarise the key decision reached. Because most decisions turn on issues of fact, the most attention is paid to characterising the facts in terms of the legal categories necessary to establish the offence. From this, the rule of law and its application follow readily. The sentence is a matter of discretion, but will not usually have much justification. Decisions of the jury in the cour d'assises are not reasoned, but the questions put to the jury are formally produced by the president of the court and can be the subject of subsequent challenge. The length of a judgment is likely to be greater

4 See L Gratiot et al, *Art et techniques de la plaidoirie aujourd'hui*, pp 140-142.

where the judges disagree with the procureur than when they agree, but this is more a matter of internal comity among the judges, rather than to provide added clarity for the outside observer.

That laconic form of decision does not stand alone, but forms part of several dialogues which constitute the justification in the criminal process. In relation to the appeal court and to the lawyers involved in the case, the short judgment is rather like an 'executive summary' against which the file of the case can be read. The lawyers can go back and examine how far it reflects accurately the elements deposited on file. The appeal court will also have the file and can review the decision in the light of this, as can the Cour de cassation. In relation to the accused and the partie civile, as one judge interviewed explained, the justification is given by the *tenue de l'audience*, the way the hearing is conducted. In both pre-trial phases before the procureur and the juge d'instruction and in trial and appeal hearings, I was clearly able to observe a pedagogic function in the manner and language of the relevant judge interviewing the suspect/ accused/convicted person. Most judges used everyday language and tried to make sure the person understood why the actions under investigation were wrong and, thus, why the person could expect a conviction or to be imprisoned. The distinctive feature of the criminal process is that the procureur, juge d'instruction or court is dealing with the relevant people present before it. There is scope to explain face to face in a way that is seldom possible in administrative and civil cases. Only at the level of the Cour de cassation does this not happen. Finally, there is a dialogue with the media that can be direct or indirect. The Cour de cassation may directly explain its decisions by way of a press release in significant cases, and other courts may ensure that the press has appropriate access to decisions as and when they are handed down. This form of commentary supplements the impenetrable language of the legal decision itself. Given that the press may well have followed a case at earlier stages, the formal decision may indeed provide sufficient information. There is no 'lecture from the bench' to the miscreant, which it is easy to report, and the decision is sometimes handed down some days or weeks later. But the context of the pre-trial will enable the press to understand what is going on, as well as the kinds of question which are led at the public hearing.

The dialogue in relation to the file, the dialogue with the people present, and the dialogue with the media can each be found in other aspects of the French legal system. The distinctiveness of the criminal legal process is how these dialogues are conducted and the frequency with they happen and are combined.

The French culture of criminal law is not static. It has undergone change over the past centuries, not least in an increased emphasis on the rights of the accused. In this area, there have been borrowings from abroad, eg the jury, which have been developed into a home-refined institution. In very recent times, the European Convention has called into question traditional French practices. It has reinforced the arguments of some internal tendencies for reform, and this is where it has been strongest. It has also encouraged an opening to comparison with other countries. That said, there has not been an uncritical adoption of the Strasbourg case law. French criminal legal culture is undergoing change, but by way of adaptation and in a way which will retain what the French consider significant advantages of their system.

Chapter 5

Administrative law

Administrative law is distinctive by virtue of its core task. It has to balance the operational effectiveness of the administration with protection of the rights of the citizen, both fundamental rights and those accorded by law. French administrative law is distinctive in terms of the people to whom this task is entrusted and some of the values that they have sought to incorporate into law. The separateness of French administrative courts, their personnel, their procedures and their rules make it relatively easy to identify a distinctive organisational culture to which lawyers and litigants have to relate. But the distinctiveness of administrative law lies not only in the organisation and personnel, it also lies in an organic body of law, how it has emerged and how it is sustained. At the same time it has to be recognised that the activities and values which have been the traditional core of administrative law are subject to change.

A. THE CORE ACTIVITIES

French lawyers (like their German, Italian, and other Latin counterparts) distinguish between 'administrative law' (*le droit administratif*) and 'administrative litigation' (*le contentieux administratif*). This has a deeper importance than the English law distinction between 'administrative law' and 'judicial review of the administration'. Le droit administratif covers not only the rules governing specific administrative activities, but also the principles which legitimate these activities and which should guide their performance. Concepts of good administration are part of the French sense of government according to law. Le contentieux administratif focuses on the remedies available to the citizen when something goes wrong. It is this whole structure of procedures and principles of judicial control over administrative action that provides the protection for the individual.

In 1974, Debbasch set out the tension between the dual objectives of administrative law:

> A system of administrative law can attempt to achieve two different objectives. It can seek to make the action of the administration as effective as possible in order to enable it to

> protect the public interest in the best way. It can, by contrast, aim to ensure the greatest possible protection to the administered in the face of the activities of the administration.[1]

In his view, the classical law erred on the side of protecting the citizen, while he considered that administrative law in the 1960s and 1970s was leaning more towards the efficiency of government, as the administration tried to take an active role in directing the public good.[2] A similar analysis was shared by Loschak:

> Administrative case-law is not liberal, if one means by that term that it is simply preoccupied by the defence of civil liberties. It is certainly incontestable that the administrative judge has contributed to the guarantee of the rights of citizens against encroachment by the authorities, and that, in this sense, it remains one of the cornerstones of a liberal regime. But this is only one aspect of its case-law. For the judge is also too aware of the requirements of administrative action, and too imbued with 'a sense of the State' to accept that the protection of individual interests can be made to the detriment of the public interest.[3]

In her view, 'the administrative judge who, despite his independence, remains close to power, is willingly to pay attention to the problems which the government encounters in sensitive and serious situations'.[4]

(1) Advancement of the public interest

Administrative law in a primary sense defines the administration and identifies its proper sphere of action. It provides the cement which can join different administrative actions. But, given that the administration exists as a social entity and its actions are the product of political or administrative requirements, the function of the law is both to authorise and legitimate what the administration undertakes, and to set out the framework within which those actions ought to occur. As Heymann-Doat and Loschak wrote:

> Administrative law, in particular, occupies a central place in the way legitimacy is conferred on the apparatus of the State – both by its very existence, which attests that State action is not exercised arbitrarily, and by the impact it has on the collective imagination.[5]

It is natural that the law should be seen as conferring legitimacy on the administration, since laws confer powers on it and authorise actions. The distinctive character of administrative action is usually described as 'exorbitant du droit commun',[6] exceeding what is normally conferred on individuals. The private individual or firm normally

1 C Debbasch, 'Le droit administratif face à l'évolution de l'administration française', *Mélanges Waline* (Paris 1974) vol II, 343 at p 344.
2 Ibid, p 345.
3 D Loschak, *Le rôle politique du juge administratif français* (Paris 1972), p 237.
4 Ibid, pp 241-242.
5 A Heymann-Doat and D Loschak, 'Les fonctions du droit administratif' in P Alliès, *L'administration dans son droit* (Paris 1985), ch 4 at p 151.
6 LN Brown and J Bell, *French Administrative Law* (5th edn, Oxford 1998) (hereafter 'Brown and Bell'), p 132.

needs some form of contract or agreement that permits him to act in a way which interferes with the rights or interests of another. The distinctive feature of the administration is that it is empowered in certain circumstances to act unilaterally, on the basis of its sense of the public interest. On this traditional picture, there is a twofold dynamic – action which is unilateral to interfere with the individual, but a justification which lies not in the private interests of officials, but in the advancement of the public interest. Public law is thus concerned with defining the situations in which the public interest requires such intervention. In modern times, social solidarity requires the State also to act positively to benefit individuals in society. The State is authorised to act to confer benefits, often in the exercise of discretion, and so the efficiency in achieving these benefits is important. Social solidarity also explains the bridge between these two forms of State action: the duty of the State to pay for interference with individual rights in the name of the public interest.

Now such a description of the broad functions of administrative law is not peculiar to France. Most modern states could aspire to a similar description. The distinctiveness of the French approach lies both in the clarity of the conceptual structure within which the missions of the administration are articulated and in the structures through which this is achieved.

(2) Protecting the administered

French legal terminology already gives a flavour of the hierarchical or concessionary nature of the French State. Rather than talking of 'citizens' in the terminology of the 1789 Revolution, those affected by the administration are described as 'the administered' (les administrés) or as 'users' (les usagers) of a public service. It is only with the loi of 12 April 2000 that the term 'citizen' has come to be used to describe those with whom the administration deals.[7] The law acts first of all to define the permissible actions and objectives of administrative action: who can act as the administration and for what purposes. The French conception of 'l'Etat de droit' becomes significant in this context. In a second feature, there are the rights and entitlements of the administered, and finally there are remedies.

(a) L'Etat de droit

For a French public lawyer, 'L'Etat de Droit, c'est avant tout le règne de la loi' ('the rule of law is, above all, the rule of statute').[8] The principle is thus more typically expressed in terms of the 'principe de la légalité' which means than an action 'conforms to *la loi*'.[9] The subordination of the legal system to the legislator has been a traditional ideal of France from the Third Republic until the late 1980s. Of course, there are other values,

7 See P Ferrari, 'Les droits des citoyens dans leurs relations avec les administrations' AJDA 2000, 471.

8 See J Rivero, 'Etat de droit, Etat du droit' in *L'Etat de droit Mélanges en l'honneur de Guy Braibant* (Paris 1996), 609. See also J-L Autin, 'Illusions et vertus de l'état du droit administratif', in D Collas, *L'Etat de droit* (Paris 1987), p 149: 'Sovereignty of *la loi* and sovereignty of the people are inseparable in French public law.'

9 See Vedel and Delvolvé (11th edn 1990), pp 442-443.

not least the accessibility of law, but the fidelity to the legislator has been a traditionally important value. Submission of the administration to the law was one way in which this idea of the 'rule of law' could be achieved. Now this was very much a positivist approach and the role of the Conseil d'Etat has very much been to supplement the rules laid down by the legislator, as well as to undertake more overtly political roles, eg in playing the role of pacifier in the political and religious quarrels at the beginning of the 20th century.[10]

Rivero argued that the Conseil d'Etat's strength law in subjecting the administration to standards which it had created for itself. In that sense, the role of the Conseil is both to create and enforce standards. Although the legislature has created many rules which define and govern the activity of the administration, 'what makes administrative law is that it remains in origin case-law'.[11] Jèze suggested that the progress of administrative law had been made possible only by the absence of an administrative code.[12]

(b) Rights and entitlements of the citizen

Administrative law developed essentially during the Third Republic. During this period, there was a very limited content to the Constitution. In particular, there was no statement of constitutional rights, and no desire on the part of politicians to set any rights above the legislature.[13] The political process defined the positive law and the entitlements and duties of the citizen. Although much of the early administrative law was concerned with control against the arbitrariness of the administration in sensitive areas such as the freedom of religion, the case law of the Conseil d'Etat gradually distilled a set of general principles of law which formed a kind of proto-type of fundamental rights. These rights, though not able to be set against statutes did provide a schema for strong interpretation. Many of the rights were procedural in character and have been extended both by the legislature and by the external institutions defining rights.[14]

(c) Redress[15]

French legal language does not have a concept of 'remedy', a substantive measure of corrective justice. It has a procedural conception of redress (recours) and certain specific actions (sanctions, compensation, orders) which can be taken by the person or body from whom redress is sought.

10 See M Waline, 'L'action du Conseil d'Etat dans la vie française' *Le Conseil d'Etat. Livre Jubilaire* (Paris 1952), 131.
11 R Chapus, *L'administration et son juge* (Paris 1992), p 22. Also Giscard d'Estaing, Speech 24 March 1979, EDCE 1979-80, 277: 'The essential contribution of the Conseil d'Etat is to have succeeded, without the intervention of the legislator, by the sole merit of a slow and judicious development of case law, in imposing on the French administration a sense of legality, that is to say, a respect for the law, then progressively to instill that sense in it.'
12 G Jèze, *Livre Jubiliaire*, 347.
13 See Bell, *French Constitutional Law*, pp 23-27.
14 For an extended discussion, see Brown and Bell, pp 216ff.
15 See generally J Waline, 'L'évolution du contrôle de l'administration depuis un siècle' RDP 1984, 1327.

Administrative redress is essentially through the recours hiérarchique, an appeal to superiors to intervene. Either there is within a specific administration an administrative superior, or there is a supervisory authority (autorité de tutelle) which lies outside the particular administration, such as the Prefect in relation to a local authority.

Judicial remedies emerged from this basic structure of administrative redress. The Conseil du Roi and then the Conseil d'Etat served as representatives of the head of state's role as autorité de tutelle. At the end of the last century, it was hierarchical control that was seen as the most important, and judicial control merely as a part of it.[16]

While the Conseil d'Etat has an important role in giving advice, the focus of the lower administrative courts is essentially that of providing redress for grievances. Those interviewed expressed the opinion that, increasingly there is less a sense of protecting the State and more an ambition to give redress to the administered. It has been noted by writers and judges that there seemed to be a reluctance to award compensation against the administration lest this interfere with good administration. This reluctance has been reduced in areas like the award of pain and suffering damages, the reduction of the requirement for faute lourde and the expansion of no-fault liability. To this extent, as one of the interviewees put it, there has been a growing closeness between the conception of justice in the administrative courts and that in the private law courts. Certainly at a local level, there is a sense among all practitioners that the difference in approach between administrative and civil courts is reducing. The unwillingness to issue orders to the administration was finally broken by the loi of 16 July 1980 which empowered the administrative courts (initially the Conseil d'Etat, but from 1995 the lower administrative courts) to issue an astreinte to ensure performance of an order. But it took until 1997 for such an order to be made against the government.[17]

In more recent years, a number of alternatives to judicial redress have been put in place. Administrative courts have as a primary task the resolution of disputes before them. Although conciliation is a prescribed function of administrative courts, the structure of the procedure does not make it easy for the judge to sit down with the parties and try to conciliate them. Although judges were obliged to conciliate in 1986, most conciliation happens in groups of similar actions, where the effort is made to apply one solution to them all. In other areas, notably in tax cases, there are specific bodies charged with securing conciliation and which do actually reduce considerably the number of cases coming to the administrative courts.[18]

B. THE INSTITUTIONAL SETTING

(1) Involvement of judges with the administration

The integration of administrative courts with the administration provides a very distinctive feature to confidence with which the administrative judges can engage in developing the law. In the first place, the judicial activity is hierarchically integrated.

16 Ibid, 1329-1331.

17 CE 28 March 1997, *Fédération des familles de France*, Rfda 1998, 1165 issuing an *injonction* to revalue family allowances: see Brown and Bell, pp 115-117.

18 See J-M Le Gars, 'Conciliation et médiation en matière administrative' AJDA 2000, 507.

Comments in interviews from judges at different levels within the administrative court system recognised the priority of the Conseil d'Etat. Where the law needed changing, the initiative needed to come from the Conseil, which was seen as unhappy about initiatives coming from the bottom.[19] The Conseil has institutional mechanisms for understanding the problems of the lower courts, and their sources of information about what the others are doing pass typically through the Conseil.

Talking of the Conseil d'Etat, President Odent stated in his lectures that:

> ... the interpenetration of administrative and litigation functions is fortuitous: if administrative judges were isolated from the active administration, if they ceased to be in constant contact with the needs and constraints of administrative life, they would lose their specific character: instead of building a law adapted to the necessities of the public service, they would be inspired by a fossilised law bearing no relationship to the realities of active administration. Administrative judges must have an administrative training, and they have to sustain it to retain an understanding of administrative life.[20]

Certainly, observation of court processes would suggest that familiarity with particular administrations helps the judge to understand how problems arise and what the impact of particular rules would be. In private deliberations among the judges, if a set of facts or a result seems curious, then they will seek to explore the reasons for the action of the administration. A similar kind of discussion takes place in order to assess the impact of a decision. In a procedure where there are predominantly written submissions, the possibility of gaining understanding by direct questioning is less. So prior understanding is often essential. Furthermore, there are examples of the Conseil overturning its previous case law when a particular rule proved to be administratively unworkable.[1]

Within the Conseil d'Etat, there are procedures to ensure the continuing connection between administrative and judicial functions. In the first place, many members are attached to both an administrative and a judicial section. It is not unusual for a member to perform both functions in the same afternoon. (Indeed the author did observe one conseiller come down in the lift from a judicial hearing to attend part of the meeting of an administrative section and then go back in the lift to return to judicial business.)[2]

19 A good example would be the rejection of the idea of 'confiance légitime' (legitimate expectation) from the TA Strasbourg, see below, p 182. But cf some of the case law on blood transfusion and medical negligence: CE Ass plén 10 April 1992, *V*, AJDA 1992, 365; Cass Ass plén, 9 March 1993, *MG*, Rfda 1993, 583.

20 R Odent, *Contentieux administratif* (Paris 1981), pp 746-747. The point is repeated by Mme Questiaux, [1995] PL 247 at p 255 that the generality of powers conferred on the administration requires that judges who review the exercise of discretion 'do not drift too far away from the experience of the administration'.

1 H Le Berre, *Les revirements de jurisprudence en droit administratif de l'an VIII à 1998 (Conseil d'Etat et Tribunal des Conflits)* (Paris 1999) (hereafter 'Le Berre'),p 447: allowing the challenge to decisions of the Prefect to refer decisions of the local authorities to the administrative court.

2 J Massot and T Girardot, *Conseil d'Etat* (Paris 1999) (hereafter 'Massot and Girardot') p 31 note that, in 1998, 97 members were fully attached to judicial sections and 48 were partly attached to administrative sections, while 43 were almost fully occupied with administrative roles.

This sensitivity to the problems of the administration is often counter-balanced by a robust attitude to maladministration. In decisions which I observed, there was an overt expression by judges of the need to maintain the standards of good administration, and of the desire to use the decision in the instant case to teach the administration to behave properly. For example, the concept of 'manifest error in evaluation' would be applied to strike down administrative decisions where English judges would not have been willing to intervene.[3] In such situations, the difference between a hierarchical control over the lower administration and the judicial review of legality becomes blurred. The judge's experience as an administrator or a Prefect gives him or her a surer sense of what was bad administration and what was a legitimate exercise of discretion than would be available to an outsider. Although there may not be a great difference in the skills and attitudes of mind required to control the subordinate administration and to reach judicial decisions, the parameters within which those different types of activity occur are of course distinct. The departmental official is concerned to evaluate actions in terms of ministerial policy; the judge in terms of legally imposed rules and objectives. However, once it comes to standards of good administrative practice – the justification of decisions, giving hearings, communicating documents – then hierarchical superiors and judges will have similar viewpoints. Common ideas on such matters within the French administration, transmitted through ENA and the Conseil d'Etat ensure realism and effectiveness in their implementation. As will be seen, there certainly seem to be great similarities in standards applied within the Conseil between its administrative and judicial sections.

(2) Procedure in administrative courts[4]

(a) Judicial preparation

Under the classic procedure developed by Conseil d'Etat and adopted by the lower administrative courts, a judge is designated as rapporteur at the end of the written submissions of the parties. That judge then prepares the file for hearing. It is then passed to a senior member of the sous-section who acts as réviseur, reviewing the text, and to the commissaire du gouvernement. In the Conseil d'Etat, there is a séance d'instruction at which the rapporteur presents the case and a proposed solution, and this is then discussed by the whole sous-section. Only after this is the case set down for judgment.[5] The Conseil has different formations for judging cases: a sous-section

3 See J Bell, 'The Expansion of Judicial Review over Discretionary Powers in France [1985] PL 99, at pp 110-112.

4 See generally Brown and Bell, ch 5. For a description of the internal workings of the Conseil d'Etat which is lively and has still some currency, see CJ Hamson, *Executive Discretion and Judicial Control* (London 1954), ch 3.

5 The Conseil d'Etat does not consider that it is improper for the rapporteur to be part of the formation of the court sitting in judgment on the case, since he does not originate the case (unlike the *juge d'instruction*) nor does he undertake investigatory measures himself, but essentially he prepares the case for judgment: see CE Ass 3 December 1999, *Didier*, Rfda 2000, 584 concl Seban (dealing with similar roles in the Conseil des marchés financiers). The Conseil does also not consider that the report should be made available to the parties: see CE Ass 3 December 1999, *Caisse de crédit mutuel de Bain Tresboeuf*, Rfda 2000, 574 concl Combrexelle (dealing with the similar procedure in the Commission nationale informatique et libertés).

on its own, sous-sections judging together, the Section du Contentieux, bringing together the presidents of sous-sections, or the Assemblée du Contentieux, bringing together the presidents of all Sections of the Conseil. The appropriate formation depends on the complexity of the case and the degree of change in the case law which is to be introduced by the decision. The séance d'instruction is a feature of the Conseil d'Etat and, in a limited form, also exists in the Cours administratives d'appel,[6] but is not replicated in the tribunaux administratifs. These too have inherited the procedure of a rapporteur, réviseur, and commissaire du gouvernement, with a collegial decision. But the pressure of cases is introducing less elaborate and collegial approaches. The tribunaux administratifs are now authorised to sit with a single judge but the commissaire du gouvernement continues to have a role. In the Cours administratives d'appel, the size of the formation of judgment is quite large (as many as seven, including a judge from another chamber in a multi-chamber court). But again this elaboration is under pressure. By contrast, the loi of 8 February 1995 permitted single judge courts in the tribunaux administratifs, sitting only with the commissaire du gouvernement. There is no automatic requirement that cases of disagreement between them be submitted to a larger formation of the court, so the single judge can prevail over the commissaire du gouvernement whose role is advisory.

Unlike in the civil courts, it is considered a principle of administrative law procedure that the commissaire du gouvernement provides a reasoned opinion in all cases.[7] This forces an element of collegiality which is significant.

(b) *An inquisitorial process?*

Although the administrative court procedure is frequently described as inquisitorial,[8] this needs qualification. The procedure is more directed by the judge than in civil procedure. The written character of proceedings enables the rapporteur to operate at his own pace and he controls the progress of the case towards decision. But the process is not really like an administrative inquiry to the same extent as in the Conseil constitutionnel or the juge d'instruction in criminal law.

Like the civil judge, the administrative court is limited by the grounds raised by the applicant. The judge cannot decide for himself the best basis on which the facts can be judged. Unlike the procureur working with the juge d'instruction or the Conseil constitutionnel, the administrative court has cognizance of a requête, a complaint, rather than an entire situation of fact or a loi which can be examined as the judge sees best. The pleadings will define the issues at stake. To a limited extent, the judge may have some limited scope to interpret the grounds from the way a case is presented, particularly by an unrepresented litigant. It may be possible to read the requête as raising some issues, even if this is not done explicitly. Observation of courts suggests that they bend over backwards to find that an appropriate ground of review was

6 The séance d'instruction in the Cour administrative d'appel is composed of the rapporteur, réviseur, and commissaire du gouvernement.

7 CE Sect 13 June 1975, *Adrasse*, AJDA 1975, 477; N Rainaud, *Le Comissaire du gouvernement par le Conseil d'Etat* (Paris 1996), pp 52-56.

8 Brown and Garner, *French Administrative Law* (3rd edn, London 1983), p 57, but cf Brown and Bell, pp 99-101; R Chapus, *Droit du contentieux administratif* (6th edn, Paris 1996), no 718.

raised. (They seem less inclined to do so where the litigant was represented by a lawyer.) But too bold an interpretation might well be challenged subsequently as a distortion of the applicant's submission. In addition, as in civil law, the judge has the power to invoke a moyen d'ordre public, where a public interest ground exists.[9]

That said, there are a number of ways in which the judge can direct the process. In the first place, the judge can decide that it is necessary to order an expert's report or a site visit. The parties will then be involved in designating the expert, commenting on the report, or in being present at the site visit. As in most of the French system, the judge does not seek to resolve the facts directly, but seeks to obtain an expert opinion which is then the point of reference for further submissions between the parties. Second, the judge may make some informal inquiries. For instance, the rapporteur may telephone the administration to check whether relevant evidence had been sent or to explain its absence, especially if the administration is dilatory in responding to formal requests. Informal site inspections might take place to see whether it is worthwhile to have a formal inspection. Again conciliation might be handled by informal steps, for instance by the *rapporteur* in a tribunal administratif telephoning the tax authorities to see whether there is a way of sorting out the tax affairs of the litigant. The key feature of the process is that the judge decides when the case is ready for trial, not the parties, and thus the judge has a responsibility to decide whether there is enough information already gathered.

As in all French courts, the general principle applies that *curia novit legem*, the court will find out the law. Even if the parties and their lawyers submit references to cases, the judge and the commissaire du gouvernement will search out the law on a topic, either personally or relying on the service de documentation in each court. Within each court, there will be archives which may be of use – unpublished decisions and unpublished *conclusions*. These are likely to be more extensive than the lawyers can gain access to. Particularly in the lower courts, the lawyers may not be particularly expert, so the researches on the law performed by the court will be more extensive. The involvement of a number of judges in a decision will also ensure that 'folk memory' can supplement published materials (though, increasingly, cases are available on CD-ROM).

Daniel Rowland has compared the 'internalised' approach of the Conseil d'Etat to the resolution of disputes to the 'externalised' approach of the common law adversarial system.[10] His observation of the internal procedures of the Conseil d'Etat led him to describe the process as essentially 'delawyered' and 'deoraled'. Whereas the lawyers will be able to view and challenge the factual information and legal submissions of the other side prior to the clôture de l'instruction, they are not able to see or comment upon what happens next. The judge will produce his own cases and the draft opinion will form the basis for an internal discussion in the sous-section and then at judgment. The legal discussion is away from the glare of the lawyers. Only in the conclusions of

9 See Chapus, op cit, no 665, Brown and Bell, p 240; C Debuy, *Les moyens dans la procédure administrative contentieuse* (Paris 1981). The ground must be based on an imperative text without which the case cannot be decided, and this may now include binding European Union law: CE Sect, 11 January 1991, *Morgane*, AJDA 1991, 111 and 149.

10 D Rowland, 'Lessons and insights from the procedure of the Conseil d'Etat in France', AIAL Forum, Sydney, 11-12 April 1996, pp 17-18.

the commissaire du gouvernement does the lawyer have a chance to challenge what has been presented. The skill of the lawyer is to make good written submissions, not to dialogue with the bench. The only opportunity for such a riposte comes with the chance to pass a note en délibéré after the conclusions of the commissaire have been read (and about which he may have obtained prior notice).

(c) Written and oral stages

In administrative courts, the principal role of lawyers is to make written submissions. In certain areas (claims for compensation or contracts) there is a requirement to have your case presented by an avocat, but in others (such as tax and requests to annul administrative decisions) this is not necessary. Oral hearings are not a pure formality (unless no parties actually turn up), but they serve a different function compared with other parts of the French legal system. Given the written character of procedure, the oral hearing serves a limited function. The rules permitting the parties to express themselves before the court are formally in place, but give a misleading picture.[11]

There is a significant difference in function between the tribunaux administratifs and the appellate courts. In the tribunaux administratifs, the judges may still come to the hearing with questions in their minds. The public hearing at which the parties address observations to the court may help to clarify these. Although many lawyers or unrepresented parties may simply refer the court to their written submissions (or may not turn up at all), some give substantial arguments. The presence of an unrepresented applicant may be particularly valuable. Given that the initial request will often not be clearly structured around the legally pertinent issues, the oral hearing may give the judges the chance to ask a few questions and form a clearer picture of what happened. In one case I observed, a schoolgirl complained that she had been asked questions in an oral for the baccalaureat which were off the syllabus and sought the quashing of her failure. The oral hearing enabled the court to understand more clearly what had gone on in the viva, and enabled them to form an impression of the truthfulness of the applicant. In the end, her case was believed. It would not be unusual to see the commissaire du gouvernement hastily re-writing parts of his prepared conclusions in the light of what he has heard at the oral hearing.

Before the appellate courts, oral argument is much less common, not just for reasons of geographical remoteness, but because everything useful has been communicated in writing.[12] In the Conseil d'Etat, the avocats au Conseil d'Etat et à la Cour de cassation are specialists and are more likely to prepare files in proper form and thus make the life of the Conseil easier. Usually, the lawyers will refer to their written submissions. They will listen to the conclusions of the commissaire du gouvernement (of which they may well have advance notice) and may take the opportunity of submitting a brief note en délibéré to focus the court's attention on issues where they disagree with what has been presented.

11 See J Barthélemy, 'Le rôle de l'avocat devant la juridiction administrative' *La Revue Administrative, numéro spécial: Les juridictions administratives dans le monde: France-Allemagne*, 1999, 117.

12 A rare example I observed was CE Ass 16 April 1986, *Cie Luxembourgeoise de télévision* AJDA 1986, 328.

(3) Relations between the administrative courts

The relationships between the administrative courts are essentially hierarchical, rather than lateral. The local character of the tribunaux administratifs and the Cours administratives d'appel has meant that they are well embedded in their regions. The President of the local Cour administrative d'appel will probably have some relations of an informal kind with the presidents of the tribunaux administratifs in her area, but this is not organised on a systematic basis. Much will depend on personalities. As with much of the French system, there is a willingness to collaborate, but each president of court is fiercely independent and would not like to feel that the president of the Cour administrative d'appel is able to dictate to him how he should run his court.

The Presidents of Cours administratives d'appel meet together in Paris on the occasion of formal annual meetings of the heads of courts in the Conseil d'Etat. The informal meetings of the Cours administratives d'appel presidents on this occasion can then lead to further networking in the course of the year. The formal meeting provides an opportunity for discussion of difficulties and for the Conseil d'Etat to present what it is doing or is about to do. Given that the presidents of Cours administratives d'appel are conseillers of the Conseil d'Etat (though not always of long standing), this helps to secure the corporate spirit among a relatively small number of people (there are, after all, only seven presidents of the Cours administratives d'appel, compared with the 33 presidents of the civil cours d'appel).

The Conseil d'Etat retains further control by three mechanisms. In the first place, an Assistant Secretary-General is responsible for the budget and functioning of the lower administrative courts. This enables the Conseil to engage in investment, such as information technology and databases, and to oversee the organisation of the courts. Promotions and movements of judges are also managed through the Conseil, as will be seen later.[13] This is then reinforced by the longstanding role of inspection, where a team from the Conseil d'Etat will visit the court on site for a short period, and will talk with its members. On a less structured basis, the Vice-President of the Conseil will have opportunities to visit various courts in the course of the year. Thus the Conseil d'Etat retains direct links with all the administrative courts and does not use the Cours administratives d'appel as an intermediate administrative layer. If there are problems about case law, then this is likely to be relayed up to the Conseil d'Etat directly.

In terms of case law, the Conseil d'Etat provides the courts with access to electronic versions of its cases. There has been a long tradition of communicating summaries of cases to the lower administrative courts. Equally, there has been a long tradition of the lower administrative courts submitting to the Conseil their leading decisions which are then transmitted among the members of the Conseil d'Etat . Whereas the system is strong on vertical communication, it is rather weak on horizontal communication among the lower administrative courts. On the whole, everything relies on being passed through the Conseil d'Etat.

The relationships between the administrative courts suggest a pattern of centralised supervision and communication. The administrative courts are more strongly connected than the civil courts and this is predominantly the result of the work of the Conseil d'Etat.

13 Below, p 194 and above, p 42.

(4) Alternative controls over the administration

(a) Independent administrative agencies

Outside the administrative courts a number of independent bodies have been charged with supervising the administration and offering redress. In terms of exercising public power to protect individual freedom, like most countries, France has seen an increase in independent public bodies acting apart from the State. Agencies such as the Conseil supérieur de l'audiovisuel and the Commission Nationale de l'Informatique et des Libertés (CNIL) have both regulatory and disciplinary power and this calls into question traditional conceptions of the State as a hierarchically integrated organisation.[14] The former is a supervisory agency over the providers of a public service, who are private bodies for the most part. The CNIL has a general mission of supervising data protection and individual liberties against the public and private sectors. These provide redress before individuals need to consider court action.

(b) The Médiateur

Since 1973, the *Médiateur de la République* has been the French Ombudsman covering central government, local government, and some public sector services, including nationalised industries. The intervention of this office is concerned with the dysfunction of the administration that leads to injustice in the individual case. Such an approach differs from the judge and his function is only to recommend to the administration a solution, rather than constrain it to act to redress the grievance, an act of moral, rather than hierarchical or legal authority. As a result, he has less problem with concepts such as 'legitimate expectation' as the basis of giving relief.[15] In 1999, the Méditeur received 51,189 complaints, an increase of 12.2% on 1998.

(c) Parliamentary committees

Parliamentary committees have had less impact, partly because of size and partly because of the lack of sanctions.[16] As a result, there is not the same resort to a parliamentary committee of inquiry to deal with governmental misconduct as in some other countries.

(d) The Cour des comptes

The Cour des comptes has been an independent body since 1320. It judges public accounts and holds accounting officers responsible for spending. It also produces an annual report to the President of the Republic. In 1999-2000, it examined the accounts of 931 bodies and the Chambres régionales des comptes those of a

14 See J Chevallier, 'Réflexions sur l'institution des autorités administratives indépendantes' JCP 1986 I 3254; A Stevens, *The Government and Politics of France* (2nd edn, London 1996), pp 149-150, Brown and Bell, pp 25-26.

15 See generally http://www.mediateur-de-la-republique.fr; Brown and Bell, pp 32-34.

16 See Stevens pp 196, 208-209.

further 71,050. The Cour des Comptes produce reports which have a significant impact as criticism of government.[17]

C. NORMS AND CONCEPTS

Administrative law is composed of a set of rules and principles which determine who is allowed to act, what activities they are allowed to undertake, for what objectives, and with what consequences (both for appropriate and inappropriate action). There is no general administrative law framework, but rather specific rules for particular administrative bodies and for particular activities. There are specific rules concerning the president and other rules for the powers of a mayor. There is a 'code' (collection of rules) on planning and another 'code' on the administration of public land. These different rules do not form a single code and have not been systematised by the legislator. There is no law on administrative procedure, as exists in Germany. Any coherence comes from judicially developed principles. A number of these are distinctive, compared with other branches of law.

(1) Sources of authority to perform tasks

Unlike German or English law, France starts with the premise that, by virtue of its position and function, the State has certain inherent powers to act. The notion of unilateral or special power has been taken in the past to be one of the determining features of French public law, whereas private law is based on powers conferred predominantly by agreement.

For example, the administration has been recognised to have inherent legislative power – the power to issue decrees in certain areas without the approval of the legislature – in three areas: public order, public emergency, and the internal functioning of the public service.[18]

(a) Public order (ordre public)

Although constitutions have not spelt out the powers of the President of the Republic to make decrees in order to 'maintain public security, tranquility, and health',[19] these have been long recognised. Most famously, presidential decrees of 10 March 1899 and 10 September 1901 promulgated a Highway Code and instituted a requirement for driving licences. The legality of these measures was upheld by the Conseil d'Etat[20] These powers have been held to have survived into the Fifth Republic by both the

17 For example the critical annual report of 2000 on the government's attempts to hide the budget surplus.

18 See J Bell, *French Constitutional Law* , pp 82-84, and Materials 2 and 5, as well case Decision 9.

19 Duguit, *Traité de droit constitutionnel*, 728.

20 CE 8 August 1919, *Labonne*, Leb 737; translated in Bell, *French Constitutional Law*, pp 287-288.

Conseil d'Etat[1] and the Conseil constitutionnel.[2] All the same, the scope left for such inherent public order powers is limited by the need to use a loi in the areas affecting fundamental rights set out in art. 34 of the Constitution of 1958.[3]

(b) Public emergencies

Post-1830 constitutions did not explicitly confer on the head of state powers to deal with emergencies (other than specific legislation in 1849 on the state of siege). But, in a case concerning the suspension of statutory rights of a civil servant against dismissal, the Conseil d'Etat recognised the inherent power of the administration to take steps to deal with emergencies.[4] Within the 1958 Constitution, the state of emergency is regulated principally by art 16 and so there is little scope for recourse to inherent powers.

(c) Public service

The regulation of the public service has been a traditional royal prerogative which has carried over into post-Revolutionary France. Such powers are almost an inevitable consequence of the legal personality of the State as administration, and it is for this reason that no explicit authorisation seems required. The Conseil d'Etat established this in *Babin*, where commissaire du gouvernement Romieu stated:

> ... it is in principle, the executive power that regulates the internal organisation of public services and the conditions for their operation, which do not affect the rights of third parties. In particular, it fixes the rules of the contract between the administration and its agent, their recruitment, promotion, discipline, dismissal, etc. ... [T]he executive power has full authority to decide on, and can freely fix, the terms of this contract, except on those matters which the legislature has, by way of exception, made its own by regulating them itself.[5]

The State has always had power to make règlements d'administration publique. The power of the head of a service to take regulatory or individual measures relating to the organisation and operation of a service has long been recognised, and was formally enshrined by the Conseil d'Etat in *Jamart* in 1936.[6]

(d) Completing details in legislation

These traditional areas are less important than the widespread discretion conferred on the administration to carry out legislatively sanctioned policies of the welfare state

1 CE 17 February 1978, *Association dite Comité pour léguer l'esprit de la Résistance*, Leb 82; CE Sect, 22 December 1978, *Union des chambres syndicales de l'affichage et de publicité extérieure*, Leb 530.

2 CC decision No 87-149 L of 20 February 1987, *Protection of the Countryside*, Rec 22; translated in Bell, *French Constitutional Law*, pp 288-291.

3 See *French Constitutional Law*, p 96.

4 CE 28 June 1918, *Heyriès*, Leb 651.

5 CE 4 May 1906, S 1980.3.110, conclusions Romieu; translated in Bell, *French Constitutional Law*, p 280.

6 CE 7 February 1936, S 1937.3.113 note Rivero. See generally R Schwartz, 'Le pouvoir d'organisation du service', AJDA special number 20 June 1997, p 47.

and of the regulatory state. Article 34 of the Constitution only gives parliament authority to legislate on the principles of many branches of law, leaving the administration inherent legislative power under art 37 to prescribe the details by decree, a process that in no way involves Parliament.[7] The Prime Minister also has power under art 21 to decide on the implementation of lois.

These rules on inherent powers of the administration convey a tone for the way in which administrative law approaches the powers of the administration. If you like, it operates a distinction between the 'natural' powers of the administration to perform traditional governmental functions and the 'additional' powers, ie those which are specifically allocated by the legislature for a particular time or set of policy reasons.

(2) Organising concepts and values

(a) The public interest (l'intérêt général)

The fundamental value underlying the distinction between public law and private law is the public interest (*l'intérêt général*). The idea of 'public utility' as the hallmark of the public sector goes back to Ulpian.[8] The public interest replaced 'the common good' (le bien commun) in the 18th century and has dominated French political and legal culture ever since. Whereas some liberal societies see the State as essentially the guardian of individual freedom, the French, voluntarist tradition sees the State as guaranteeing the sovereignty of the general will. In the recent report of the Conseil d'Etat on the public interest, the authors note that in the French tradition:

> The existence of a public law and a State provided with its own judge essentially translates the conviction that the public interest could never be fully served by private law.[9]

The whole conceptual structure of administrative law relates to the concept of the public interest. Public service (service public), public property (domaine public), a public work (ouvrage public), public works (travaux publics) are all defined by reference to their service of the public interest. The public interest also justifies the actions of the state, eg expropriation, and its special powers (pouvoirs exorbitants). A former president of the Section du Contentieux argued:

> If you want to find what is most fundamental in the culture of the administrative judge, you have to turn towards the notion of the common good or the public interest, much more than towards a principle of fairness.[10]

For Truchet, who has made a long study of this concept in administrative law, the public interest serves as a standard for judging administrative action, a norm for

7 J-L Autin, 'Illusions et vertus de l'état du droit administratif', in D Collas, *L'Etat de droit* (Paris 1987), p 152.

8 Digest 1.1.1.2: 'The study [of law] has two approaches, public and private. Public law is that which concerns the Roman state; private law is that which concerns individual advantage, for there are certain things useful for the public and certain things useful for private life.'

9 'Réflexions sur l'intérêt général', Conseil d'Etat, *Rapport public 1999*, 239 at p 266.

10 M Combarnous, cited ibid, p 307.

control by the courts, and a justification offered by them.[11] In essence, it informs the various grounds of review of administrative action and the administrative courts are called upon in this process of review to refine the concept further. At the same time, the explanation given by the Conseil d'Etat of what is the public interest is limited – it often amounts to no more than an affirmation of what appears to be 'common sense'.[12]

French doctrinal writers differ as to the key organising values of administrative law, and especially the principles that distinguish public law from private law. For M Waline, it was public utility, for de Laubadère and Duguit, it was public service, for Vedel it was public power and for Rivero, it was the existence of special prerogatives (pouvoirs exorbitants).[13] Although public utility is broader than public service, the two are linked and so are handled together. The existence of special powers flows from both public power, the traditional prerogative powers of the administration (les pouvoirs régaliens), and public service, which encompasses more welfare and regulatory state activities. The presentation simplifies a complex debate to highlight some key distinctive values in the way French administrative law is organised.

(b) Public power (la puissance public)

One of the original justifications for the special position of the administration was the special power which it exercises in the public interest. It is traditional to suggest that this concept justifies a number of prerogatives of the state – the power to take unilateral decisions, the power to regulate public order and safety, the power to requisition, and the power to enforce automatically certain decisions. The power to decide unilaterally is in the nature of the authority of the administration, though these days the procedures prior to such decisions being taken typically require consultation and notification. The powers of regulation (les pouvoirs de police administrative) are traditional, both in areas of public order and public health. Increasingly such powers are subject to control in terms of necessity, proportionality and, more recently, the principle of precaution.[14] These developments demonstrate the point made by Chevènement that 'the prerogatives of public power embody the dialectic between individual liberty, the freedom of citizens and the freedom of the sovereign'.[15] As Picard explains, the Declaration of the Rights of Man and of the Citizen of 1789 justifies the need for public power in art 12 by reference to its role in safeguarding fundamental rights.[16] The increasing constraints imposed in order to establish an adequate protection of the individual rights affected by actions taken in the public interest essentially seek to redress this balance.

The power to requisition is a further example of the kinds of power which the administration needs to deal with public emergencies. There are a variety of such

11 D Truchet, 'L'intérêt général dans la jurisprudence du Conseil d'Etat: retour aux sources et équilibre' Conseil d'Etat, *Rapport public 1999*, 361 at 362.

12 Ibid, p 170.

13 See L Favoreu, 'L'évolution de la doctrine depuis 1945' *La Revue Administrative 1997: numéro spécial: Le Conseil d'Etat et la Doctrine*, 18 at p 20; Brown and Bell, pp 134-135.

14 E Picard, 'L'impuissance publique en droit' AJDA numéro spécial July 1999, 11 at p 15.

15 Ibid, p 8.

16 Ibid, pp 18-19.

powers,[17] but an important example is art 10 of the loi of 22 July 1987, which allows the State or the Prefect to requisition private means of assistance. For example, in January 1997, it was invoked to justify the requisition of lodging for those affected by violent storms, and in 1996, the State used it to requisition petrol stations during a strike by lorry drivers so that it could secure supplies to public service vehicles and other priority professions.[18]

The power of the administration to implement its decisions on its own authority has been a traditional feature of many branches of French law. In some cases this has been connected to a requirement of urgency and, in areas such as expulsion of foreigners and the exercise of public order powers, this is becoming seen increasingly as the main reason why the administration should not have to seek authorisation from a judge.[19] As Romieu put it in his conclusions in 1902, 'when the house is burning, you do not seek the authorisation of a judge to send in the fire brigade'.[20] Thus, while recalling that the Conseil d'Etat had reaffirmed as recently as 1982 that the executory character of administrative decisions is a fundamental rule of administrative law, the Vice-President noted in 1999 that it is difficult for administrative authorities to undertake automatic enforcement on this basis, and that recourse to a judge to give the necessary authority was becoming increasingly necessary.[1]

(c) Public service (le service public)

The centrality of the public service in French administrative law is clear from the remark of Guy Braibant that 'Whatever the new solutions and the changes to come, French administrative law must not lose its soul: the public service.'[2] Although it would be an exaggeration to say that public service is the sole rationale for administrative action, it has to be recognised as one of the principal objectives of the administration and as a major explanation for the special position it enjoys.[3] Public service is a concept that has grown up later than the emphasis on sovereign power and is linked to ideas of social solidarity. It leads to a view that there should be 'a State for whom the law is not only an instrument of public power, but also an instrument for realising the missions which it has confided in the service of the community.'[4] There are certain activities that are justified by this idea. On the one

17 For a list see J Quastana, AJDA numéro spécial July 1999, p 25.

18 P Levaye, 'Les pouvoirs de réquisition' AJDA numéro spécial July 1999, 22-23. M. Sapin, ibid, p 24 notes that the powers may not always be used but may serve as a threat to encourage a settlement.

19 See CE 28 February 1919, *Dames Dol et Laurent*, S 1981-19. 3.33 note Hauriou; on recent trends see P-L Frier, 'L'exécution d'office: principe et évolutions' AJDA numéro spécial July 1999, 45 and R Errera, ibid, at p 52.

20 TC 2 December 1902, *Société immobilière Saint-Just*, Leb 715. Normally, he expected a judge to authorise the enforcement of a decision.

1 R Denoix de Saint Marc, AJDA numéro spécial July 1999, 56, citing CE 2 July 1982, *Huglo*.

2 G Braibant, 'Du simple au complexe, quarante ans de droit administratif (1953-1993)', (1993) 45 Études et documents du Conseil d'État 409 at p 420. Also *Le service public* (Report of a commission chaired by R. Denoix de St Marc; presented to the Prime Minister March 1996), p 13.

3 See G Braibant and B Stirn, *Le droit administratif* (5th edn, Paris 1998), pp 136-137.

4 M Long, 'Service public, services publics: déclin ou renouveau?' Rfda 1995, 497.

hand, the administration has inherent authority to regulate the public authorities itself and its collaborators. It has not required explicit authority to issue circulars, to regulate employment. There are certain core values that are central to the French conception of the public service (solidarity towards collaborators, priority of demands of service). The French are aware that their conception of 'public service' is distinctive and have sought to defend it in European fora, notably in the negotiations leading up to the Treaty of Amsterdam.[5] The interesting feature of the concept is that it has been developed essentially by case law, with *la doctrine* coming in at a later point to offer some rationalisation and direction to the law in progress.[6] It offers a good example of the interplay between administrative and judicial branches of the Conseil d'Etat.

(i) The concepts of 'public service' and 'public services' The definition of what is a public service is a matter of academic and doctrinal discussion.[7] Many writers would focus on the idea of a 'bundle of indicia' to establish the existence of a public service. There is certainly no established list of what is a public service. In brief, 'the public service is a legal process by which satisfaction is given to a public interest need'.[8] As such, it is a principal of legitimacy for state actions, as well as a principle which informs the conduct of government and the organisation of its activities. There are thus four crucial elements: the purpose for which an activity is undertaken (the public interest), the institution which decides it ought to be undertaken (the State or another public body), the mechanism by which this is undertaken (the use of public power: la puissance publique) or contract, and those who are involved in providing the service (the civil servants or private persons).

The distinctive character of French law is to see the intrinsic connection *in nature* between the regulatory and operational functions of the State, while being able to separate the *organisation and performance* of the different functions between the various organs of the State and between central and local administrations.[9] It is, however, clear that the easy move from the conception of public service to the need for specific public services and then on to specific organisations which deliver these services (public service organisations) is now under challenge. For the French the essential activities that come within the public service are network services (water, gas, roads etc). This is because they provide the infrastructure for everyday life of the community.[10] There is obviously a distinction between *administrative public services* which at most seek to be self-financing, eg tourist offices or universities, and the increasingly

5 For instance, the prime ministerial circular of 26 July 1995 begins with the phrase: 'The Government is determined to defend the French conception of public services, assuring to all, over the whole territory, the benefits which the citizens of a developed democracy have the right to expect.' (Rfda 1996, 191, para 1.1)

6 See P Jourdan, 'La formation du concept de service public' RDP 1987, 89.

7 This is usefully summarised in R Chapus, *Droit administratif* (9th edn, Paris 1995), vol 1, pp 515-525; D Linotte, A Mestre, R Romi, *Services publics et droit public économique* (3rd edn, Paris 1995), Part I, chapters I and II find the search for criteria elusive.

8 Conclusions Corneille, CE 7 April 1916, *Astruc*, RDP 1916, 364.

9 See A-S Mescheriakoff, *Droit des services publics* (Paris 1991) (hereafter 'Meschariakioff') p 21.

10 See *Le service public*, p 14.

fewer *industrial and commercial public services* (les 'SPIC') which provide services similar to a private company (and may even be structured as private companies with State shareholding).

As the State moves from areas essential to society's own survival (defence, public order, public health) and moves into areas where it makes available opportunities and services for the public, the State is less the commander as the entrepreneur ensuring the provision of basic services. The French, however, wish to draw a line between the situation where an activity is privatised (ie taken out of the public sector altogether) and situations where the delivery of a service (as opposed to its general planning) is delegated to a private contractor.

The area of privatisation offers a good example of the kind of distinctive discussion which the French concept of public service engenders. Where a public corporation, eg a television station, is to be privatised, the French would be inclined to ask 'Is this still going to be a public service when it is privatised?' A recent illustration is the decision of the Conseil constitutionnel on *France Telecom* where it was happy to conclude that the activity of a privatised company which could engage in profit-making activities was nevertheless part of the public service because of the organisational and policy framework within which it operated.[11] For the French, it makes sense to say that an activity is a public service, an activity in the public interest which is subject to a special legal regime, even if it is operated by private companies. English conceptions of privatisation often fail to be clear on this point.

In recent years, all aspects of administrative action have been subject to change in the light of contemporary concerns among liberal governments and in the light of European commitments. The State is increasingly less a monolith. Public services are very often organised, but not run by the State. Meschariakoff notes that in 1991, 90% of transport, 87% of urban heating, 71% of funeral services and 60% of refuse collection were run by the private sector, while other services such as 84% of swimming pools, 79% of museums, 79% of street cleaning and 70% of public spaces were publicly operated. The arrangements for gas and electricity have also become more open to competition due to European Union law.

(ii) Consequences of an activity being considered a 'public service' The public interest gives rise to a set of values, the *Rolland principles*: continuity, adaptability, and equality, to which neutrality is usually added.[12] *Continuity* requires that the service will be made available at all times. The French take this principle further than many countries. Under the *Dehaene* decision, since reinforced by the Conseil constitutionnel, the right of public sector workers to strike can be limited in order that continuity of the public service is assured.[13] This usually means that a minimum service must be maintained, even on strike days. But the principle also justifies the duty of the State to pay compensation to a contractor who meets unforeseen circumstances under a government contract that would otherwise make it impossible for him to continue (the doctrine of imprévision).[14]

11 CC decision No 96-380 of 23 July 1996, AJDA 1996, 694.

12 See Meschariakoff, pp 133-135; D Truchet, 'Unité et diversité des "grands principes" du service public', AJDA special issue 20 June 1997, 38.

13 See Bell, *French Constitutional Law*, pp 160-164.

14 See Brown and Bell, pp 208-210.

Adaptability requires that the public authority must be able to change the specification of a service as the needs of the public interest change. For example, the State does not have to obtain the consent of the contractor to change the requirements of a public service in the public interest (even if it must pay compensation where the concessionary of a public service suffers as a result of changes).[15]

Equality of users is an aspect of the general constitutional principle of equality before the public service.[16] If an activity is done for the good of the whole public, then all relevant categories of the public must have equal access to that service and equal treatment by it. Thus in the leading case, one orchestra could not be denied a chance to broadcast on the radio when others were permitted.[17]

Neutrality reflects the way a liberal state, unlike a private individual, does not seek to impose its ideas of the good life on citizens, rather it facilitates the choice of a diversity of lifestyles. This neutrality principle has particular application in two areas. In the first place, the French State is secular (art 2 of the Constitution of 1958) and so it respects all religious beliefs. It cannot impose unreasonable restrictions on the expression of religious opinions.[18] The second area is in relation to political opinions. Clearly a public authority cannot select those who will be allowed to benefit from its services on the basis of their political opinions. Nor can they support particular political causes, eg railwaymen's strikes or the left-wing government of Nicaragua.[19]

D. ILLUSTRATIONS OF ADMINISTRATIVE LAW ACTIVITY

(1) Advisory roles

In terms of ensuring good administration, an important feature of French administrative law is the advisory function of the administrative judge. Costa argues that the advisory function has more practical importance for the government and the administration than the judicial function.[20] The close connection between such advisory and judicial functions within the Conseil d'Etat ensures that the law is created and interpreted within an environment of dialogue with the administration. This kind of relationship is not found in all legal systems that have a separate administrative court. As Mme Questiaux, a former President of Section and Government Minister, remarked:

> The Conseil d'Etat is ... in a position to supervise all the diverse, specialised forms of administrative action. It is able to anticipate the problems which could arise in litigation while dealing with so far uncontested texts. Last, but not least, it holds a somewhat discreet but central place in the network of national institutions, and from this it derives a special sense of responsibility.[1]

15 CE 10 January 1902, *Compagnie nouvelle du Gaz de Deville-les-Rouen,* S 1903.3.17 note Hauriou; Brown and Bell, p 207.
16 Bell, *French Constitutional Law*, pp 210-211.
17 CE Sect, 9 March 1951, *Soc. des concerts du Conservatoire*, S 1951.3.81.
18 See the discussion below p 175 on the chadour.
19 CE 11 October 1989, AJDA 1990, 112; CE 23 Oct. 1989, AJDA 1990, 119; cf *Wheeler v Leicester City Council* [1985] AC 1054.
20 J-P Costa, *Le Conseil d'Etat dans la société contemporaine* (Paris 1993), p 49.
1 N Questiaux, 'Administration and the Rule of Law: The Preventive Role of the French Conseil d'Etat' [1995] PL 247 at p 254.

The advisory roles in relation to the administration are threefold.[2] In the first place, the Conseil d'Etat gives its advice on all projets de loi before they are presented to Parliament. Indeed, this role essentially involves helping with the drafting of the text, as well as commenting on any text produced by the administration. Since 1945, this consultation of the Conseil d'Etat has become compulsory.[3] Since the constitutional reform of 1992, art 88-4 of the Constitution requires the government to pass to the Assemblée Nationale and the Senate, 'proposals for Community decisions containing provisions having a legislative character'. This has been expanded by constitutional amendment in 1999 to include proposed decisions of the European Union (in its second and third pillars). These requirements have to be interpreted, and so the government passes the measures to the Conseil for advice on which ones must be transmitted to Parliament. In the five years up until 1 January 1998, some 2,531 requests for advice on European legislation, just over half of which were related to taxation.[4] The second function of the Conseil is to provide advice at the request of specific government departments. Article 52 of the Constitution of 1799 allowed the government to consult the Conseil on 'difficulties which arise in administrative matters' but this is understood to apply essentially to technical legal questions. Ministries regularly ask the Conseil for advice on questions about the interpretation of legal, much as it might be sought from the law officers in the United Kingdom. This establishes and reinforces relationships between the 'active' administration and its judge.

The role of adviser in the Conseil goes beyond issues of strict legality to take account of the concern for effective administration. The point made by Letourneur and his colleagues was that the Conseil has a wider remit than just to be a legal adviser. As such, its role is much closer to that of the Attorney-General than parliamentary counsel:

> The Conseil has always recognised its duty not to limit itself to the role of legal adviser in the strict sense, but to be an adviser in the fullest sense, guided by its multifarious experience of the administration which arises both from its knowledge of the life of many government ministries and the concrete experience of its members.[5]

In relation to fundamental rights, a proper concern of a judge, the Conseil's function is to remind the government of the principles of fair procedure, such as the right to a lawyer, the right to reasons for decisions and to equal treatment, as well as proportionate penalties which may have a lower priority with the administration. In contrast to the public embarrassment of censure by the Conseil constitutionnel or by the European Court of Human Rights, the Conseil d'Etat offers the government a private session of

2 See LN Brown and JS Bell, *French Administrative Law* (5th edn, Oxford 1998), pp 64-67.

3 See J Bell, 'What is the Function of the Conseil d'Etat in the Preparation of Legislation?' (2000) 49 ICLQ 661.

4 J Massot and T Girardot, pp 75-76. For illustrations of the *avis* given in relation to draft legislation and to legal questions, see ibid., pp 86-91. See generally, B Stirn, 'Le Conseil d'Etat et l'Europe' in *L'Etat de droit*, 653 at pp 660-665.

5 M Letourneur, J Bauchet and J Méric, *Le Conseil d'Etat et les Tribunaux Administratifs* (2nd edn, Paris 1970), p 181. A similar comment is made by M Rendel, *the Administrative Functions of the Conseil d'Etat* (London 1970), p 231. See generally N Questiaux, 'Do the Opinions expressed by the Conseil d'Etat in its capacity as legal advisor to the Government influence policy?' (2000) 49 ICLQ 672.

advice and a chance to retreat. In relation to its role as adviser on legal questions, it is easy to see that legal questions predominate. The role of the Conseil d'Etat in second-guessing the approach of these other courts is increasingly part of its value as an advisor, and that is very much legal advice.[6] In relation to the Conseil constitutionnel, it is noted that the physical proximity of buildings and the presence of some members of the Conseil d'Etat in that institution ensures that there is communication between the two. The advice of the Conseil d'Etat given before the bill is presented to Parliament is sent systematically to the Conseil constitutionnel that judges the constitutionality of the bill which Parliament has passed. Informal conversations may also occur before the Conseil d'Etat gives its view.[7]

But the Conseil is also concerned to ensure that a measure will be workable. The function of the Conseil d'Etat as general adviser to the government allows it to raise questions not just about technical effectiveness in law, but also about the merits of a proposal. This broad scope of advice is widely recognised in writings of members of the Conseil.[8] The Conseil feels competent to make such comments because its members have a wide experience of the administration, even if they do not discuss the merits of proposals. Costa argues also that the collective activity of the Conseil in this area ensures that individual political views of its members do not influence the non-partisan advice which the Conseil is expected to give.[9] Letourneur also argued that the Conseil could take full liberty with the text submitted, provided it does not trespass on the political merits of the proposal:

> In practice, the administrative sections have always recognised for themselves the same powers in relation to the text submitted to them as the minister who formulated it. They can therefore completely overturn its presentation and even its structure, returning it to the government as lacking merit or, more simply, on the ground that the amendments made have destroyed the internal coherence of the text.[10]

The Conseil may well ask whether legislation is necessary at all. For example, in order to prevent illegal immigration, one might argue that, instead of imposing criminal penalties on illegal immigrants, the government should be looking to improve administrative action in the exercise of existing powers. Such questions do not question the political objective of preventing illegal immigration, but they probe whether the chosen means are really going to work.[11]

6 Costa, op cit, pp 49 and 118-119.
7 N Questiaux, [1995] PL 247 at p 256 suggests: 'Relations with the Conseil constitutionnel depend on a common desire to avoid contradiction and inconsistency. This is facilitated by the physical proximity of our buildings.' See more generally Y Gaudemet, 'Le Conseil constitutionnel et le Conseil d'Etat dans le processus législatif', in *Conseil constitutionnel et Conseil d'Etat* (Paris 2 colloquium 1988), 87.
8 For a clear summary and references, see Massot and Girardot, pp 82-83; see above p 173 note 4.
9 Op cit, p 49.
10 Op cit, pp 75-76. Cf M Rendel, op cit, p 231: 'The Conseil d'Etat, in its work of drafting, is concerned with legality in the widest sense of conformity with law, with desirability and with efficacity'.
11 The recent requirement that ministries produce impact assessments for bills makes this kind of comment easier: see circulars of 21 November 1995, 18 March 1996 and 26 January 1998: Massot and Girardot, pp 69-70.

The impact of the advisory function is well acknowledged. If the Conseil has given advice on proposed legislation or on a question referred to it by the government, then it is conventional that only the highest judicial formation of the Conseil can depart from that opinion.[12] Since the advisory consultation will have been in abstract, it is not unsurprising if specific concrete fact situations make the Conseil see legal rules in a different light. The more normal situation is of a continuity between legal advice and judicial decisions. This is well illustrated by the issue of the Islamic head-dress worn by girls in schools. Article 2 of the Constitution proclaims France as a 'secular' republic. The increasing number of Muslims in France and a greater strictness in the religious practice among some of them led to conflicts between school authorities seeking to enforce the secular character of State schools and pupils seeking to conform to religious requirements. In order to diffuse this politically live issue, the Minister of Education, Lionel Jospin, sought an avis from the Conseil on the rules which schools could adopt. In a sage decision,[13] the Conseil interpreted the law as permitting freedom of expression, but with three limits which were traditional in the operation of public services – the protection of public order, respect for the freedom of others, and the protection of the proper functioning of public services. Pupils thus could not wear religious symbols in an aggressive or proselytising manner, nor could they interfere with the proper operation of the school. In its judicial capacity, the Conseil subsequently annulled sanctions imposed on girl pupils by schools for wearing the chadour which were not adequately justified.[14] All the same, where the wearing of the chadour interfered with the operation of the school, eg making physical education instruction unsafe, then the school could take action.[15]

The third area of the advisory roles of the Conseil d'Etat is the 'think tank' function of the Section du Rapport et des Etudes. Not only does it engage in regular review of the operation of the Conseil d'Etat and the administrative courts in the annual report of the Conseil, the *Etudes et Documents du Conseil d'Etat* which have been produced since 1945, it also sets up working groups to consider particular issues and to report on them. Thus in recent years, reports have been produced on the internet and computer networks (1998), a review of bioethics law (1994 and 1999), and compulsory purchase in planning law (1999). Members of the Conseil also chair or are members of external committees on law reform, eg Massot on the reform of the law on the criminal liability of elected officials.[16]

(2) Lawmaking

The rules of administrative law are predominantly contained in lois and decrees. If one takes any specific activity, be it planning, public works, the organisation of local

12 Massot and Girardot, pp 84-85. For an account of the solidarity of 'the house' as an institution, see P Sabourin, 'Un Persan au Conseil d'Etat' AJDA 1993, 515.

13 Avis of 27 November 1989, *RFDA* 1990; 6, *Grands Avis*, No 33. See J Bell, (1990) 2 Education and the Law 121 and C Wiener, 'Les foulards noirs et la République', in *L'Etat de droit*, 761.

14 See CE 2 November 1992, *Kherouaa*, Leb 329; CE 27 November 1996, *Khalid and Sefiani*, Leb 460; Massot and Girardot, pp 180-182.; Avis of CE Ass 3 May 2000, AJDA 2000, 602.

15 CE 10 March 1995, *Aoukili*, Leb 122.

16 See above, p 128-129.

authorities, taxation, you will find a wealth of specific texts. Below this level, there are many internal circulars that guide the relevant administration on the application of these rules and on which the citizen can rely.[17] It is true that administrative law does have a constitutional foundation, as Vedel stressed,[18] but the basic principles of public law and civil liberties are few and general, compared with the body of detailed law which exists. In this respect, administrative law is much like any other branch of law, though with perhaps more specific legislation than in civil law. But in two aspects, it is conventional to distinguish administrative law as judge-made: in relation to general principles of law, and in relation to the principles of judicial control of the administration.

Nearly fifty years ago, Bernard Schwartz commented:

> ... the development of a system of administrative law to help minimize [the danger of arbitrariness] has been, in France as in the common law world, largely the handiwork of the judge. In this respect the *droit administratif*, unlike most other branches of French law, bears a ressemblance to the kind of law prevalent in the Anglo-American system. The French administrative lawyer, like his confrere in the common law world is accustomed to derive the basic principles of his system inductively from the decided cases ... [But] in the common law world the basic principles of administrative law have been worked out by the ordinary courts by analogy from the principles of private law. In France, on the other hand, the law courts concerned with the dispensation of justice between individuals have played only a minor part in the field. ... The *droit administratif* is based on the existence of a special law for cases involving the administration and of special courts to decide them.[19]

This kind of distinctiveness requires further analysis.

(a) Codification

In the first place, it has to be recognised that the Revolution of 1789 did not attempt any systematisation of the rules and principles of administrative law similar to that attempted in the codes on criminal, civil and commercial law. Indeed, at this point, the distinctiveness of administrative law was only slowly being recognised.[20] Despite the existence of principles inherited from canon law, the droit savant, and the Parlements, Mestre identifies the principal legacy of the Ancien Régime as predominantly institutional. There were no treatises like those of Pothier on administrative law, nor principles produced by the legislator such of those of Colbert on commercial law.

The second point is that the institution of the Conseil d'Etat was viewed with suspicion during the Restoration (1814-30) and its membership was purged because of its political affiliations at a number of points.[1] While there was a lot of continuity of

17 CE Ass 29 January 1954, *Notre Dame du Kreskier*, Rec 64; CE Sect 11 December 1970, *Crédit Foncier de France*, RDP 1971, 1224 note Waline.

18 G Vedel, 'Les bases constitutionnelles du droit administratif' EDCE No 8, 21; G Vedel and P Delvolvé, *Droit administratif* (11th edn, 1990), vol 1, Part I, ch 1.

19 *French Administrative Law and the Common-Law World* (New York 1954), pp 2-3.

20 J-L Mestre, *Introduction historique au droit administratif* (Paris 1985) p 175. The term 'droit administratif' seems to date from 1798 and was first used in official documents in 1807, but it took some time to distinguish this idea from 'le droit civil dans ses rapports avec l'administration publique'; J-L Mestre, 'Le "Cours de législation administrative" de Portiez de l'Oise (1808)' Rfda 1993, 239 at pp 244-245.

1 See generally *La Revue Administrative 1997: numéro spécial: Le Conseil d'Etat et les changements de régime politique* (1998).

membership during the 19th century, despite these periodic purges, this did slow the development of a distinct set of administrative law principles. Although many of the ideas were developed piecemeal during the Second Empire (1852-70), it is only with the Third Republic and after the purge of 1879 that we get the strong development of principles. Equally within the universities, the teaching of public law was only gradually recognised, and there was no separate aggregation until 1895. The material conditions for what Schwartz describes as a traditional picture really emerged only in the 70 years before he was writing. As Mestre notes, institutional factors have enabled this distinctive picture to emerge, and these centre around the Conseil d'Etat as first (and later final) judge of the administration, as elaborator of doctrinal ideas and as interlocutor of the administration.

The description of administrative law as case law goes back to the beginnings of modern administrative law writing. The two foundational texts of the discipline, Edouard Laferrière's *Traité de la juridiction administrative et des recours contentieux* (1887) and Maurice Hauriou's *Précis de droit administratif* (1893) both consider that the administrative judge makes law through his case-law.[2]

The making of case law was a slow process. In the first place, the decisions of the Conseil d'Etat were not reported until 1821, and even then they were so brief that they were barely comprehensible to the outsider.[3] Only in the works of the early doctrinal writers (themselves members of the Conseil) was it possible to gain a sense of the law which was being developed. Macarel's treatise of 1852 ignored case law in three of its four volumes, and it is really after 1872 that one gets a real sense of direction through the case law of the Conseil. The lack of a proper Constitution in the Third Republic led to the lack of a posited framework for the control of the administration outside parliament, and to the lack of thought about the principles which should govern this control. As a result, the gap was filled by the Conseil and the Tribunal des Conflits, but on a case-by-case basis. Aspects of the case law were then systematised gradually.

This form of influence is important, but has limitations. In the first place, the drafting of decisions by the Conseil follows a similar laconic and brief form to that of the Cour de cassation. As a result, it is not always easy to identify the decision reached in terms of principles of law, let alone the reasons for it. Thus it may not be clear to the reader whether there has been a reversal in the established case law or not.[4] Although the drafting of leading decisions is undertaken with great care, the production of a decision by a very large group of people will often be brief, the lowest common denominator necessary to achieve the decision.[5] Occasionally, there may be 'authorised commentary' by members of the Service de documentation of the Conseil, who publish a regular review of recent decisions in AJDA since 1962, and this can serve as a kind of briefing for the wider public. Rather than relying on the format of reasons, the skilled interpreter

2 See J Hardy, 'Le statut doctrinal de la jurisprudence en droit administratif français' RDP 1990, 453 at pp 458-459.

3 T Fortsakis, *Conceptualisme et empiricisme en droit administratif français* (Paris 1987) (hereafter 'Fortsakis'), pp 55 and 58-60.

4 See Le Berre, pp 279-280, 284-287. An often-quoted example of changing established case law is CE Sect 27 July 1990, *Bourgeois*, AJDA 1991, 346, concerning whether the plaintiff prove faute lourde in order to find the administration liable outside contract in certain difficult services (eg tax, medical treatment).

5 See J Bell, 'Reflections on the procedure of the Conseil d'Etat' in G Hand and J McBride, *Droit sans frontières* (Birmingham 1991) (hereafter 'Bell, 'Reflections''), 211 at p 226.

is forced to rely on certain institutional practices. Le Berre notes that the internal practices of the Conseil may be a good indicator – if a decision is taken by the sous-sections réunies, then it will not be intended to overturn established case law, since that function is reserved to the more solemn formations of the Section du contentieux or the Assemblée.[6] Since the Conseil controls the publication of its own decisions, this process is also used to signal whether the decision is making an important development in the law, or merely is a routine decision or one confined to its facts. The absence of publication of a decision can minimise its importance.[7] Finally, the publication of the *conclusions* of the commissaire du gouvernement makes available a further source of information. For, even if the court has not followed his views, the commissaire will have drawn up arguments in full knowledge of the reasoning of the rapporteur and will explain the reasons why he agrees or disagrees with them. From this information, one can construct the probable reasoning of the court. In all these, the Conseil d'Etat serves as the first line in interpreting the importance of its own decisions. There is a self-disclosure and internal self-control over its lawmaking power.

While the creation of case-based principles is important, lawmaking also occurs through interpretation. Bernard Gény wrote in 1950 that:

> ... public law offers several examples of cases where the judge, breaking out from his usual constraints, has not hesitated to draw from a legislative provision effects apparently contrary to its text, and has lined up solutions whose justification, from a literal point of view it must be said, require the most refined skills of dialectic.'[8]

(b) Influences on lawmaking

The influences on the decision-making of the Conseil d'Etat are interesting:

(i) The private law and courts To begin with, public law was not taught to a significant extent in the universities and recruits to the Conseil d'Etat were trained at the university law faculties. As a result, their initial exposure was to private law and private law concepts.[9] As Jèze remarked:[10]

> Until the first years of the 20th century, French administrative law was inspired by principles and theories from civil law. The judges of the Conseil d'Etat, and also the professors from the Faculties of Law, were imbued with private law; the texts of Roman law had formed them in their youth. They were convinced that Roman law was written reason and that the Civil Code gave the solution to all problems – it sufficed to give a slight adaptation to meet new needs. The terminology employed by the judgments of the Conseil d'Etat and in the works of professors reproduced that of private law.

6 Le Berre, p 297; Bell, Reflections, p 229.
7 Le Berre, pp 298-9, citing as an example CE Sect 7 July 1982, *Commune de Guidel c Mme Courtet* RDP 1983, 1439 which allowed a recours pour excès de pouvoir against a contract, but which was side-lined by non-reporting in *Lebon.*
8 B Gény, 'De la méthode et de la technique du droit privé positif à celles du droit administratif', *Livre Jubilaire* 277 at p 280.
9 Fortsakis, p 335.
10 G Jèze, 'Collaboration du Conseil d'Etat et de la doctrine dans l'élaboration du droit administratif français', *Livre Jubilaire* 347 at p 348.

The development of more specific administrative law terminology and ideas came later. If that provides an historical explanation of the influence of private law, it remains true that a number of problems and issues are remarkably similar in the issues facing administrative and civil courts. Not only are there matters such as motor cars and more recently competition regulation which have been passed to the private law courts in order to give coherence to the case law.[11] In other topics such as employment, contracts and liability, similar issues arise in the public and the private sectors. Often rules are laid down in private employment law, but not in public law. To remedy this, the Conseil has developed public law in parallel through 'general principles of law'. For example in *Dame Peynet*, the Conseil developed a principle preventing the dismissal of a public employee on grounds of pregnancy similar to that already adopted in private law by the legislator.[12] On the construction of public buildings, the administrative courts apply similar rules to the civil law on construction and monitor civil case law. Chapus in his 1953 thesis demonstrated the reciprocal influences between civil and administrative case law in the area of liability.[13] The concepts and vocabulary of civil law is accessible to the Conseil d'Etat.[14] For example, in the case of blood transfusions, patients receiving infected blood from private associations were able to recover without proof of fault, whereas those receiving infected blood from public hospitals had to prove gross fault. The Conseil d'Etat aligned its case law in *Epoux V*. More recently, the liability for failure to inform patients of the risks of medical treatment has been alligned.[15] Dellis also notes that in the area of penalties, where the administrative courts operate a kind of criminal sanction against those who obstruct the highway or interfere with public works, they borrow principles from the ordinary criminal courts, although the administrative nature of the issues may lead to significant adaptation of the original rules.[16]

That said, there may well be principled disagreement between the two supreme courts. The most infamous of these was the disagreement between 1975 and 1989 on the priority of European Community law over national lois.[17] Observation of decision-making would suggest that civil case law is taken seriously and that divergence is for a reason, either a matter of principle in relation to the appropriate outcome, or a difference in objective to be pursued, eg liability based on égalité devant les charges publics, rather than on risk.

(ii) Constitutional law In more recent years, the Conseil constitutionnel has played a significant role in influencing the decisions of the administrative courts. It produces

11 Brown and Bell, pp 145-146.

12 CE Ass 8 June 1973, Leb 406; See also Le Berre 396 and 414-416, discussing CE Ass 5 May 1976, *SAFER d'Auvergne c. Bernette* D 1976, 563 note Sinay and CE Ass 29 December 1978, *Darmont*, AJDA November 1979, 45. For illustrations of citation of decisions of the Cour de cassation in conclusions of the commissaire du gouvernement before the Conseil d'Etat, see A Bernard, 'Aperçu sur l'oeuvre juridictionnelle des commissaires du gouvernement durant la seconde moitié du XIXe siècle', *Livre Jubilaire* 299 at p 300-301.

13 R Chapus, *Responsabilité publique et responsabilité privée* (Paris 1954).

14 Le Berre, p 391. On civilian influence in liability law see Odent, cited ibid p 395.

15 CE Sect. 5 January 2000, *Assistance publique- Hôpitaux de Paris*, AJDA 2000, 182.

16 G. Dellis, *Droit pénal et droit administratif* (Paris 1998), p 414.

17 CE Ass, 20 October 1989, *Nicolo*, Rfda 1989, 812 concl Frydman; *Grands Arrêts*, No 106 which discusses the origins of the change; also above, p 59.

'reservations of interpretation' and these are strongly influential in the interpretation of the loi thus approved. More generally, the Conseil constitutionnel may set a tone for legal developments. The trigger for the *Nicolo* decision in 1989 lay in the decisions of the Conseil constitutionnel of 3 September 1986 and 21 October 1988 on the interpretation of treaties. In the latter case, an election decision deferred to the priority of the European treaties in an area which had such close parallels with the work of the Conseil d'Etat that the latter could not ignore the direction. On the other hand, there are examples of the Conseil d'Etat influencing the Conseil constitutionnel.[18]

(iii) European law More recently, the case law of the European Court of Justice and the European Court of Human Rights have become very strongly influential.[19] Even before *Nicolo*, it was said authoritatively that the Conseil d'Etat tried to follow the Luxembourg case law as much as possible.[20] Principles such as the respect for family life[1] and the concept of a fair trial[2] have influenced the development of the Conseil's case law. Other ideas have also come from international courts. Thus the concept of *erreur manifeste* came from the case law of the International Labour Law tribunal in which one of the senior members of the Conseil sat.[3] On the other hand, it is apparent that French administrative law influences these courts. In the case of the European Court of Justice, the influence is well documented both in terms of the borrowings in procedure (eg the advocate general modelled on the commissaire du gouvernement) and in substantive law.[4] The European Court of Human Rights also borrows. In a recent case (against France), it made use of a French concept of participation in 'puissance publique' to identify a group of civil servants whose disciplinary procedures were not subject to the requirements of art 6 § 1 of the Convention.[5]

Flauss argues that the European Convention is perhaps more present as an influence on rules and theories of administrative law and thus as a vector for Europeanisation, than European Union law which has an influence on specific sectors of administrative law, rather than on its general principles.[6] Fields such as competition law and public services, as well as public employment are now significantly affected by European legislation which has not respected traditional French concepts and values. The free market concepts at the core of the Single Market idea clash with the French tradition of defining the public service in terms of the national public interest.[7] But in terms of procedure, then it is the European Convention which has predominated.

18 See cases on peines correctionnelles: Bell, *French Constitutional Law*, pp 99-102, and 291-292.
19 On the reciprocal relations between these institutions and the Conseil d'Etat see B Stirn, 'Le Conseil d'Etat et l'Europe' in *L'Etat de droit*, 653; J-F Flauss, in J Schwarze, *Administrative Law under European Influence* (London 1996), 31.
20 J-C Bonichot, Rfda 1989, at 601.
1 See CE Ass 19 April 1991, *Belgacem*, AJDA 1991, 553.
2 CE Ass 14 February 1996, *Maubleu*, Rfda 1996, 1186 concl Simon (rights to a hearing in the discipline of avocats).
3 On the origins of the concept in the ILO, see X Philippe, *Le contrôle de la proportionnalité dans les jurisprudence constitutionnelle et administrative françaises* (Paris 1990), pp 52-53.
4 See Brown and Bell, ch 10.
5 ECHR 8 December 1999, *Pellegrin v France*, Application 28541/95, paras 65 and 66.
6 Flauss, op cit, p 101.
7 See, for example, J Bell, 'The Concept of Public Service under Threat from Europe? An Illustration from Energy Law' (1999) 5 European Public Law 189; Flauss, pp 53-62 (public services) and 34-46 (civil service).

In his very substantial study of the influence of the European Convention on French administrative law, Braconnier has identified a very substantial number of influences from the Convention.[8] In sheer numerical terms, the development is remarkable. In 1981-83, the Conseil d'Etat referred to the Convention in its judgments on 24 occasions, but in 1996 it did so on 851 occasions.[9]Articles 6 (fair trial) and 8 (family life) have been particular influences. There have been recurrent condemnations for delay in coming to decision in administrative cases and these have encouraged reforms in administrative court procedure. In substantive law, there have been changes in case law to provide better rights to a hearing in disciplinary cases[10] In relation to art 8, it has been applied to influence the decision to deport foreigners if the family is already established in France.[11] All the same, Bracconier notes that there is a persistent tension between the role of the Convention as guardian of individual liberty and the role of French administrative law and its courts as guardians of the public interest. There is a marked tendency for the French administrative courts to give a higher priority to the public interest and public policy in justifying administrative decisions than the Court in Strasbourg is willing to admit. [12]

A significant feature of both the European Union and the European Convention is that they do not respect the French conception of the distinction between public and private law.[13] What appears to the French as 'natural' has to be justified to an external audience and occasionally re-adjusted to meet both economic and human rights objectives. All the same, the common influence from the outside has undermined fairly well entrenched rules. For example, in 1990, the Conseil d'Etat overturned the practice adopted since 1823 that, when it was faced with an issue about the interpretation of a treaty, it asked for an opinion from the Ministry of Foreign Affairs and applied its interpretation.[14] The conclusions of the commissaire du gouvernement in the case compare the approach of the European Court of Justice, the practice of courts in other Member States, and the interpretation of art 6 of the European Convention.

In this respect, the development of administrative law by legislator and judge is not isolated from currents of opinion amongst national legislators and courts or among supra-national courts. For the most part, the Conseil has chosen its own moments to act, whether in relation to European Community law or in relation to national legal developments. It has found the arguments from consistency and conformity irresistible in some cases, so much so that some commentators have argued that the balance of initiative has moved from the Conseil to other courts, especially the Conseil constitutionnel and the courts of Strasbourg and Luxembourg.

8 S Bracconier, *Jurisprudence de la Cour européenne des droits de l'homme et droit administratif français* (Brussels 1997).

9 Ibid, p 28.

10 Eg CE Ass 14 February 1996, *Maubleu*, Rfda 1996, 1186 concl Simon and CE Ass 17 February 1995, *Marie*, AJDA 1995, 420.

11 See CE Ass 19 April 1991, *Belgacem*, AJDA 1991, 551. It should be noted that the Conseil d'Etat and the European Court of Human Rights did not take identical interpretations of the requirements of art 8 in this field: Bracconier, pp 168-169.

12 Braconnier, p 514, and also, for example, pp 169, 215, and 307.

13 Ibid, pp 359ff; Flauss, p 115.

14 CE Ass 29 June 1990, *GISTI*, AJDA 1990, 621 concl Abraham.

(iv) Social trends In terms of relating to wider administrative and social trends, the Conseil has always prided itself on its ability to keep up-to-date. The claims were well stated by Latournerie:

> ... closely involved in the life of his century, much more than the civil judge, and, often even, in different forms, in the management of important interests of the country, he puts at the service of the latter, in his judicial functions, the clear-sightedness which this experience gives him about the deepest needs of his epoch.[15]

For this reason, it is necessary for the administrative judge to retain close and concrete links to the life of his contemporaries.[16] Clearly, there are social movements, such as inflation or equality of sexes to be detected and taken into account.[17] Furthermore, the administrative advice given to the active administration itself influences the development of the judicial work.

There is institutional autonomy, but a recognition that one court has to adapt to the surrounding environment. Thus Latournerie wrote that contemporary morals could not be ignored, but directly only played a modest role in legal argument in public law.[18] To this extent, one can see that one corps has to adapt informally to the roles of the others. At the same time, the Conseil chooses its own moments and does not approve of other administrative courts seizing the initiative. Interviews with members of the lower courts made it clear that they considered that initiatives from their part would not generally be welcomed, and this seems borne out by the attempt by the TA of Strasbourg to introduce the idea of 'legitimate expectation' into French law.[19] The existence of a distinct corps which is quite close-knit and communicates within itself on a formal and an informal basis enables a direction and cohesion to emerge. There are also institutional mechanisms to ensure this. The presence of the *troika*, the president and presidents adjoints who assist at meetings of the sous-sections réunies and discuss the cases pending, ensures that there is an awareness within the institution of what is happening in its different branches. The internal hierarchical pyramid for decisions depending on the seriousness of cases also facilitates cohesive decision-making. As has been said, there are also informal mechanisms for the Conseil to learn of the concerns of the lower courts.

(v) The influence of doctrinal writing[20] Doctrinal writing shows the centrality of the corps of the Conseil d'Etat to the development of administrative law. Hardy argued that:

> French doctrinal writing is more practitioner than academic. It is more preoccupied with the good administration of the law than concerned to produce an academic theory about its

15 R Latournerie, 'Essai sur les méthodes juridictionnelles du Conseil d'Etat', in *Livre Jubilaire*, 177 at p 241 (hereafter R Latournerie).
16 Ibid, p 262.
17 Le Berre, pp 434-435.
18 R Latournerie, p 202.
19 TA Strasbourg 8 December 1994, *Freymuth,* AJDA 1995, 555, reversed by CAA Nancy, 17 June 1999, Rfda 2000, 254; Brown and Bell, pp 235-236.
20 M Deguergue, *Jurisprudence et doctrine dans l'élaboration du droit de la responsabilité administrative* (Paris 1994) (hereafter 'Deguergue'), p 18 defines 'doctrinal legal writing' as any writing on law which is a work of reflection. The need for critical comment, rather than apologetic, was made by Jèze RDP 1914, 314.

> genesis. This task is abandoned to the 'related disciplines' and permits doctrinal writing to fulfil its function of 'legal policy'. The role which it has given to case-law is a particularly visible indicator of this.[1]

The function of analysing legal policy and trends has necessarily focused on analysis of the case law of the Conseil. Although it has been said that the doctrinal writers have become more empirical and engaged in exegesis of the decisions of the Conseil,[2] it is clear that more theoretical writing focusing on general principles has been needed in greater measure in some periods than in others. Fortsakis rightly notes that the first generation of writers in the 'golden age' were involved in creating the first principled synthesis of case law, albeit based on earlier compilations of law. In the period 1887 to 1927, Laferrière, Hauriou, Duguit and Jèze developed the founding principles of French administrative law by analysis of case law in the light of principles which gave a specific orientation to the law in their lights.[3] Their role was as reformers and as exponents. In the period just after the Second World War, especially in the 1950s and 1960s, Latournerie, Chapus, d'Amselek, Vedel and de Laubadère all helped to review inherited ideas and re-arrange principles to meet new conditions, notably in the light of the principles set out in the 1946 Constitution.[4]

The relative position of doctrinal writing and case law in administrative law is well expressed by Gaudemet in his seminal work on legal method:

> The situation is very different ... for doctrinal writing in private law, whose activity has, to a great extent, to be exercised through an understanding and evaluation of the substantial and established written law; now, faced with this written law, doctrinal writing found itself, in a manner of speaking, on equal footing with the judge. By contrast, the commentary on administrative legislation has always been shown, except in certain specific fields, as a fastidious task and above all of limited value; a true doctrine of administrative law was only able to prosper through the study of case-law.[5]

Rivero noted that one consequence of this situation was that, whereas private law doctrinal writing and case law corresponded to two groups which were professionally distinct – the professors and the judges, in public law the roles are more closely connected. From the very beginning 'the judge writes and the judge teaches'.[6] Historically, the first writers on administrative law were members of the Conseil d'Etat

1 J Hardy, RDP 1990, at p 467.

2 Fortsakis, p. 130; J-J Bienvenu, 'Les origines et le dévéloppement de la doctrine' *La Revue Administrative 1997: numéro spécial: Le Conseil d'Etat et la Doctrine*, 13.

3 See Deguergue, pp 16-19.

4 Fortsakis, pp 129.

5 Y Gaudemet, *Les méthodes du juge administratif* (Paris 1972), p 148; E Laferrière (*Traité* (1st edn 1887), p XII, cited in Deguergue, p 5) noted the importance of case law:

> ... case-law is one of the essential sources for doctrinal writing because it alone can separate between the permanent principles and the contingent provisions, establish a hierarchy between texts, redress their silence, their obscurity, their insufficiency, inspired by general principles of law and justice.

Vedel also noted (cited ibid, p 7) in 1954 that 'to declare the law is, for the administrative judge, above all in large part to create it'.

6 J Rivero, 'Jurisprudence et doctrine dans l'élaboration du droit administratif', EDCE 1955, 27 at p 29.

who engaged in teaching and published their courses as texts, in much the same way as the professors of private law published their courses. The earliest administrative law writers, Macarel, Cormenin, Aucoc and Laferrière, were members of the Conseil. Aucoc's text was his course at the administrative training school, the Ecole des Ponts et Chausées, and Laferrière's text was his doctoral course at the Faculty of Law in Paris. More recently, the treatises of Odent and Braibant were courses given by leading members of the Conseil d'Etat at the Institut des Sciences Politiques in Paris, the preparatory school for the ENA concours. (It has been a tradition for members of the Conseil to teach at Sciences Politiques since its creation in 1871.) As Rivero remarks,[7] it was necessary to read case law in order to understand administrative law. Doctrine served to systematise this case law, and so it could be said that administrative law doctrinal writing 'was born on the knees of case law'. But does not of itself explain why this continued. It seems more plausible to attribute this to the influence of both judges as doctrinal writers and the role of the commissaires du gouvernement down to the present day. Although the judge is inevitably empirical in his approach, the judge as doctrinal writer shares with the professor the concern to introduce order and system, an ambition shared from the earliest days by both Laferrière and Hauriou. At the same time, the preoccupations of the judge are reflected in his doctrinal writing.[8] Whereas Letourneur criticised the 'faiseurs de systèmes' as engaged in too abstract an activity, Rivero was able to counter correctly that the search for general principles was not seen as an abstract activity, but rather doctrine in administrative law tried to perform the task similar to codification in private law.[9]

The influence of doctrinal legal writing can be both formal and informal. In formal terms, the influence of writings can be traced into the conclusions of the commissaire du gouvernement. As Deguergue notes in her thesis,[10] conclusions at all periods have cited authors. Stirn notes that the conclusions of the commissaire du gouvernement has the dual function of both providing an explicit link between the judicial decision and doctrinal writing and also contributing directly to the latter.[11] Where the author is a member of the Conseil, he is likely to be cited by name. Where the author is an academic, then this is not always the case. Famously, Romieu adopted in a leading case the arguments of Professor Hauriou by saying 'on a proposé …'[12] The long discussion of case law, writings and principles in the conclusions of the commissaire du gouvernement is the nearest equivalent to a common law judicial speech and offers a focused effort to persuade the court to develop the law in a particular direction. It has

7 Ibid, p 30.

8 Ibid, p 31. See also B Genevois, Rfda 2000, 1207.

9 Ibid, p 35 and also J Rivero, 'Apologie pour "les faiseurs de systèmes"' D 1951 Chr 99.

10 Deguergue, pp 729-730. Gaudemet, pp 151-161 offers a number of examples of how there has been borrowing from doctrinal writing in coming to judicial decisions in administrative law.

11 B Stirn, 'Les commissaires du gouvernement et la doctrine' *La Revue Administrative 1997: numéro spécial: Le Conseil d'Etat et la Doctrine*, 41.

12 CE 6 February 1903, *Terrier*, S 1903.3. 26 at p 28. M-A Latournerie notes in her article 'La doctrine vue par le Conseil d'Etat' *La Revue Administrative 1997: numéro spécial: Le Conseil d'Etat et la Doctrine*, 46 that:

> I could say that, according to the epoch, the *commissaires du gouvernement* know that it is more or less appropriate to lay weight on quotations from doctrinal writing in their *conclusions* and that, to carry conviction with the judging court, it is sometimes preferable to be more allusive and less exhaustive in doctrinal references in their *conclusions*.

the ambition to survey the law, but also to offer a personal perspective. It is clear that personality counts here much more than in other aspects of the work of the administrative courts.[13] For this reason Deguergue assimilates the commissaire du gouvernement to doctrinal legal writers.[14] Unlike the judge who has to come to a decision in the particular case, albeit with an eye to consistency and coherence,[15] the commissaire takes part in the exercise of systematising and drawing principles from the case law. But as a judge, the commissaire du gouvernement has the power of initiative, to select cases that emerge and dictate the pace of legal change to some extent. The professor is influencing first the members of the Conseil and then avocats who may decide to bring cases to the administrative courts or to construct their arguments in a particular way. (In this sense, the importance of the professor as consultant to avocats cannot be disregarded).

An important feature noted by Gaudemet[16] are the informal contacts which exist between doctrinal writers and judges. Certainly among key writers, there are numerous contacts and, in cases such as Jèze, some writers have even become members of the Conseil d'Etat, though this is rarer than in the civil courts. Several professors were among the committee which drew up the recent *Code de la juridiction administrative*, which illustrates a further form of connection between doctrinal writers and administrative judges.

(3) Legal reasoning

Administrative courts produce short judgments and follow the style of the Conseil d'Etat, which is very similar to that of the Cour de cassation. Any discussion of the legal mentality which these reveal has to take account not only of the style, but also the purpose of judgments, which are often taken to be the principal evidence on which theories about legal mentality are based.[17]

(a) The evidential base

Legal reasoning is about how lawyers think. As Zweigert and Kötz point out with their concept of 'style', reasoning is not only a matter of what is said and the forms of argument used, but the concepts that are used to express it and the ideology or values which inform it.[18] Underpinning the whole activity of administrative law in France is the pervasive ideology that public law is different. Legal reasoning reflects this in decisions reached and reasons given. But there is also a difference from private law in the place of judicial reasoning as a model of legal thinking and how this is constructed.

13 See the articles by A Bernard and F Gazier in the *Livre Jubilaire* pp 299 and 303 on the work of the commissaire in the 19th and 20th centuries, and the discussion of the work of one of the leading commissaires Romieu by G Cohen Salvador, op cit, p 323.
14 Deguerge, pp 731-732 and 738.
15 Bell, 'Reflections' pp 225-226
16 Gaudemet, p 158.
17 See above, pp vi and 15.
18 Zweigert and Kötz, pp 67-72.

We have seen that, in administrative law, the reasoning of the judge, principally the Conseil d'Etat, provides the paradigm of good legal reasoning – it is the influence on the rest of the system. It is clear in most cases what the Conseil d'Etat has decided in terms of the rule of law it has laid down. But the evidence for how the Conseil itself justifies this is less obvious. This section relies on three main sources. In the first place, there are the judgments themselves, laconic though they may be. They use careful language and have a purpose. Second, there are the conclusions of the commissaire du gouvernement which are long discussions of the issues in the case and the state of the law in which the issue has to be decided. Because they are arguing towards a particular outcome, they are clearly justifications of legal solutions, rather than general doctrinal expositions of the state of law. Unlike in the civil cases, the rapport is not published and is not available to the members of the lower administrative courts, though the commissaire du gouvernement has seen it before he produces his argument. It is thus not possible, as in the civil and criminal chapters, to compare the style of argumentation in the rapport of the reporter judge and the conclusions of the avocat-général. Since the court may not agree with the commissaire, his conclusions do not necessarily explain the decision of the court, nor do they summarise the justifications on which the decision relies. All the same, they offer an illustration of the kind of style of persuasive reason that is acceptable in the court. The third source of information is based on personal observation. In 1985–6, I was privileged to be able to attend for some six months the séances d'instruction in the Conseil d'Etat and hearings in some tribunaux administratifs. On one or two occasions, I was permitted to be present during the délibéré. I did in some cases read files and was thus able to read the rapport and compare it with the draft conclusions, as well as hearing them in the court sessions I observed. My comments were then discussed with members of the courts at the time.[19] Interviews in 2000 have confirmed that nothing substantial has changed since the original observations. Given the confidentiality of these hearings, opinions of individual judges cannot be attributed, nor can information be given such as to identify the judicial decisions about which the observations are being made. It is thus not possible to present evidence in a way which will offer the reader the chance to present independently his or her own analysis of the facts observed. The observations do, however, offer some correlation for the analysis that could be made on the basis of published conclusions.

There are three distinct forms of legal reasoning. The conclusions and observations of avocats and litigants are examples of legal *argument* – an attempt to persuade the court of a particular point of view. That oral activity, however supported by written documentation, necessarily will have embellishments to retain the attention of the audience and will perhaps contain arguments of fairness as well as technical legality. The observations of the séance d'instruction and court deliberations provide examples of legal *debate* – an exchange of views and attempts to persuade in an oral and relatively unstructured setting. Hidden from the public and from any public record, a more conversational style is exhibited in the reflections of individuals who will try out arguments, as much to come to their own opinion on the issues as to persuade others. Such debates illustrate the kind of legal issues that are considered relevant, but do not show how the different legal considerations fit together into a coherent justification, unlike the judgment or the conclusions. The judgment and the conclusions in different

19 For a fuller account, see J Bell, 'Reflections'.

ways illustrate legal *justification* – which reasons demonstrate the correctness of the legal solution adopted. The judgment demonstrates a logical connection between a rule of law (which may have been formulated during this case) and the decision reached. The judgment does not contain the reasons why it might be convincing to formulate the rule in that particular way or to make use of that rule in this particular case. These are only available in the indirect sources – the rapport and the conclusions.

(b) The content of reasoning

Analysis of both the conclusions of commissaires du gouvernement and observations of judicial deliberations suggest that all the kinds of justification which would be familiar to a common law audience and which are discussed in classic texts such as Neil MacCormick's *Legal Reasoning and Legal Theory.*[20] Reasoning is not deductive. Not only in argument, but also in justification, support is sought for a solution from consequences, coherence and consistency.

Consequentialist arguments appear both in the published conclusions of the commissaire du gouvernement and in the oral deliberations. Gaudemet argued, 'consequentialist reasoning has the first place among the modes of reasoning which the administrative judge uses'.[1] For example, the Conseil d'Etat had to consider whether the lower administrative courts should ask for an avis from the Conseil d'Etat on the interpretation of European Community law or whether they should make an immediate preliminary reference to the ECJ under art 234 TEU. To resolve this, the conclusions of Guillaume Goulard focused on the practical difficulties of separating questions of French law and Community law.[2] These are what Rudden[3] calls the 'in-built consequences' of a rule, but the courts also speculate on 'behavioural consequences'. For example, where a customer was challenging a telephone bill (in the period in which this was a matter for the administrative courts), upon whom should the burden lie to prove that the telephone apparatus was working normally – the customer or the administration as public service provider? It might be argued that to allow a person to succeed in challenging the telephone bill without showing a malfunction in the apparatus would make the job of the administration too difficult if it sought to justify the bill. On the other hand, since the apparatus was under the control of the service provider, the consumer might find it impossible to prove a malfunction as the pre-requisite for challenging a bill.

Arguments of coherence and consistency abound. Consistency can simply be related to rules of law established by the legislator or by the European Union.[4] But there is also consistency between decisions of the administrative courts, an aspect of precedent, and between the decisions of the administrative and the civil courts, an aspect of comity.[5]

20 Oxford 1978.

1 Y Gaudemet, *Les méthodes du juge administratif* (Paris 1972), 67. An example would be the case law on public sector strikes.

2 Avis, CE Sect 4 February 2000, *Mouflin*, AJDA 2000, 554 at p 558. For further examples, see Bell, 'Reflections', p 225 and esp note 27.

3 B Rudden, 'Consequences' 1979 *Juridical Review* 193.

4 See the discussion in the conclusions in the *Mouflin* case of the consistency of a rule of French civil service pensions law with art 119 EC in relation to sex discrimination.

5 See generally Bell, 'Reflections', pp 224-227 and 229-230.

Consistency and coherence is not only secured through the pleadings of the lawyers, the researches of the commissaire du gouvernement and the rapporteur, and the internal debate within the deliberating formation of the court. There are also institutional mechanisms that ensure consistency at least over the recent past and the current period. At the judgment stage in the Conseil d'Etat, a key role is played by the présidents adjoints who preside over the deliberations of joint subsections. They will see what happens in other subsections and in the higher formations of the Conseil, and can draw attention to recent decisions in those formations. They will also report the decision to the *Troika* (the President and the three présidents adjoints) which meets weekly to review decisions taken. This meeting may lead to a request for the modification or reconsideration of a particular decision. Consistency is also assured because the President will see all proposed judgments before publication, and he also can request changes. In the lower administrative courts, a similar role is played by the President who may use the plenary session of the court to ensure a resolution of conflicts. At present in the Cours administratives d'appel, the court will sit in several chambers and there is cross-membership of chambers to ensure consistency. The service de documentation may also occasionally spot issues, especially if a member is asked to take notes of a deliberation.

(c) Precedent

Both lawyers and judges rely heavily on case law to justify their arguments, and precedents of the Conseil d'Etat in particular will be abundantly cited in submissions, in the rapport of the rapporteur and in the conclusions of the commissaire du gouvernement. The names of cases trip off the tongue of a French administrative judge, or a lawyer dealing with administrative law litigation with a similar frequency to that of a common lawyer. The databases and documentation services available to administrative judges support the importance of using case law. Textbooks are also cited, but, as in England and more so than in the civil law, judicial precedents are the major forms of authority cited both as a source of general principles and for interpretations of lois and decrees. In tax law, where all the decisions of the Conseil d'Etat are published in the *Revue de la jurispudence fiscale*, the judges complain of being particularly constrained by precedents. A previous decision, even of a single subsection, will be flourished by an avocat to support an argument in a subsequent case. The rapporteur and the rest of the court will be bound to consider the precedent case and to use techniques of distinguishing or not following it, should it prove inconvenient. Naturally the judgment will not state that the case has been distinguished or not followed, but this should be clear from the *conclusions* of the commissaire (and from the unpublished report of the rapporteur). In addition, it may well be considered necessary to convene a formation of the court hierarchically superior to that which decided the precedent case.[6] *Stare decisis* may not exist formally, but it is possible to observe a very strong sense of the hierarchy of legal authority so that the lower formation must follow the decisions of a higher formation of the Conseil, or at least

6 See above, p 160.

press it to change its mind. Judges of the tribunaux administratifs talk among themselves about being 'bound' by the case law of the Conseil. While a single, isolated decision might not be considered authoritative, except from the Section or Assemblée of the Conseil, established case law was treated in much the same way as in the common law. A president of a sous-section in the Conseil d'Etat said in interview that it was more or less a principle that the line of case law should not be changed for at least ten years, unless there were compelling reasons. In other words, the stability and certainty of the case law, as well as the orderly functioning of the judicial hierarchy had a place in the justification of the respect for precedent comparable to that in the common law.

The practice of drafting judgments shows a special respect for precedent. The French style of judgments is very precise in its formulations. Rapporteurs are told to reproduce a precedent word for word unless they intend to depart from it. There is no question of following the common law judicial habit of paraphrasing a precedent, but meaning the same thing. If an expression different from the precedent is used, this indicates a change in the case law. For example, in dealing with requests for naturalisation, the Cour de cassation had ruled that the applicant had to demonstrate 'an actual residence presenting a permanent and stable character and coinciding with the centre of family attachments and professional activity'. In order to permit greater flexibility in assessing which aspects of an applicant's lifestyle evidenced a permanent and stable residence, the Conseil merely required that the applicant show that he had established in France 'in a stable form the centre of his interests'.[7]

More generally, it can be said that precedents are a natural reference point in any bureaucratic procedure. Legal certainty and respecting legitimate expectations which may have been built on past practice both support a degree of consistency. At the same time, respect for the law also requires judges to make the right decision and to correct injustices. French administrative judges do feel able to reverse previous lines of case law when they think it appropriate. But they will have to await a suitable case and there is a procedure to be followed. As a result, the practice of distinguishing does in fact happen. Where a decision has been reached by the plenary formation of a tribunal administratif or a Cour administrative d'appel or by the Section or the Assemblée du Contentieux within the Conseil d'Etat, members of those courts consider themselves bound to respect it, unless it is so wrong or obsolete that a major change is necessary. Even then, they must await the right moment to reverse it. For example, the *Nicolo* decision on the priority of Community law over national law followed a long period when many members of the Conseil wished to overturn the *Cohn-Bendit* decision.[8] But it was not opportune to present a case to the Assemblée for a number of years to achieve this effect, not least until there had been a change in senior personnel within the Conseil. There was no question that either within the Conseil or in the lower courts, judges could have ignored this precedent which had deliberately set out to resolve an issue. Judicial caution and incremental change are as much a feature in the administrative courts as they are in the common law.

7 CE Sect 28 February 1986, *Akhras and Bouhanna* AJDA 1986, 320 concl Denoix de St Marc.

8 CE Ass 20 October 1989, *Nicolo*, Rfda 1989, 812, concl Frydman; CE Ass 22 December 1978, *Cohn-Bendit*, D 1979, 155 concl Genevois.

(d) The function of the reasoned opinion

Because the categories of legal reason deployed are so varied, this makes the style of the reasoned opinion look curious. Respect for art 12 of the loi of 16-24 August 1790 that judges must not lay own regulatory decisions is observed more in form than in substance. Everyone in administrative law knows that, in appropriate areas, judges make the rules. But the format of the decision of an administrative court is deductive in style and exiguous in justification, which might suggest a timidity in the exercise of judicial lawmaking power. As Gaudemet suggests 'The drafting of the decision cannot be simply the written transposition of the work of reflection and reasoning of the administrative judge.'[9] The explanation lies in considering the function of the text of a judgment.

As a previous President of the Section du Contentieux helpfully explained in interview, the Conseil's judgment is meant only to indicate the framework ('charpentre') of the court's reasoning – to give the essential points, but no more. He indicated two qualities of mind that were essential for the judicial task in this context: conciseness and the ability to identify key arguments. The rapporteur has to sift through all the arguments presented by the parties and all the researches that he and the commissaire du gouvernement have conducted, and to distil the grounds of application or appeal and formulate the legal response to them in clear and concise terms. If one point will resolve the case, then there is no need to bother with the rest of the arguments. A two-line judgment is quite possible. When discussing a draft judgment, the question 'do you need these phrases?' crops up frequently in discussion, and adjectives are kept to a minimum. As Ducamin put it:

> [T]he adoption of this style is not simply an attachment to an historical tradition, but from a twofold concern: that of respecting the mission of the judge, and that of acting with caution. By definition, a specific problem is referred to the judge within a precise framework and he has to reply to an argument as it stands. He does not have to resolve for the future questions on which there has been no argument from both sides and about which he does not have precise information. It follows that the Conseil d'Etat considers that, in its decisions, it should settle only those questions which are necessary for the result and should avoid as much as possible to resolve inadvertently questions which have not been addressed to it. That is what appears frequently in our deliberations when we seek to reject formulations which would make possible a reasoning *a contrario*.[10]

Apparent *obiter* are there for a definite purpose and do not represent the ramblings of a judicial argument. The purpose of the text is to give a clear ruling that can be adopted by the administration, lawyers and lower courts. These expectations are reflected in judicial reasoning. In one deliberation I noted the remark 'parce que nous sommes en plénière (fiscale), faites un considérant qui éclaire le problème' ('since we are in the (fiscal) plenary session, write a considérant which will clarify the issue'). The succinctness is that of a letter from the tax inspector who tells you how much you owe and the basic steps in reaching that assessment, but no more, in precise and technical

9 Op cit, p 95.

10 B Ducamin, 'Le style des décisions du Conseil d'Etat: les réactions d'un public cultivé', EDCE 1984-5, 129 at p 135.

language. The object is to tell you the result, rather than persuade you that it is right. You have to go away and talk with a professional to see whether, taking the starting points which have been set out, the result follows logically. Whereas you can ask of the common law judgment, Is it convincing?, the administrative law judgment only permits the question, Is it right? In this aspect, the administrative courts share the practices of the civil and criminal courts. The pedagogical function of the common law judge is performed not by the judgement, but by the *conclusions* and by the semi-official commentaries in the *Actualité Juridique* or in the annual report of the Conseil d'Etat. The communication with the audiences thus takes place in different ways within the administrative legal system as a whole.

E. LEGAL PERSONNEL

(1) Administrative judges

(a) General observations

The administrative courts have always had a distinctive recruitment both within the civil service, but the distinctiveness of careers in relation to the civil judiciary has accentuated in recent years. Whereas in the 19th century, the members of the Conseil d'Etat would have been educated largely in the law faculties, as would civil judges, the patterns have changed.[11] At the beginning of the century, a competitive examination distinct from that undertaken by the civil judges helped to chart a separate educational path. By the 1930s, the Ecole de Sciences Politiques was educating almost all the members of the Conseil d'Etat prior to the entry by competition.[12] In addition, it has to be recognised that recruitment to the civil judiciary has always been more provincial than the Conseil d'Etat which is heavily Parisian. The creation of the tribunaux administratifs in 1953 and in 1989 the Cours administratives d'appel has offered the possibility of a more provincial judicial career similar to that of the civil judiciary. The social role of member of the Conseil d'Etat is considered sufficiently important to feature in studies of social élites in France, but this is not the case for ordinary judges, even in the Cour de cassation.

Despite the closeness of administrative judges to the administration, there are few suggestions that they succumb directly or indirectly to pressures from the administration or are tempted to adopt views too closely associated with it. This effective independence of administrative justice has been recognised as a constitutional value by the Conseil constitutionnel.[13] The value was institutionalised in relation to the judges of the tribunaux administratifs by the loi of 6 January 1986 which makes

11 C Charle, *Les élites de la République 1880-1900* (Paris 1987), pp 109-110. He remarks (p 215) that, at the turn of the 20th century, the Conseil d'Etat was more a 'haven for tired prefects' than a place for jurists.

12 The Bulletin of the Ecole Libre des Sciences Politiques claimed in 1936 that of 124 auditeurs appointed to the Conseil d'Etat since 1900, 121 had come from the Ecole: CE Friedman, *The Conseil d'Etat in Modern France* (New York 1961), pp 50-51.

13 CC decision No 80-119 DC of 22 July 1980, RDP 1980, 1691 and CC decision No 84-179 DC of 12 September 1984, Rec 73.

them unremovable and places their promotion and discipline under an independent national council similar to that which exists for private law judges.

(b) Recruitment

As was mentioned in Chapter 2, the career as administrative judge passes typically through the ENA. It is rare that administrative judges are drawn from groups outside the various corps of the fonction publique. Recruitment is mainly by the concours, though there are some alternative routes.

(i) Concours Since 1945, ENA has become the training college for the civil service of which administrative judges form a part. The typical entrant takes the preparatory course at Sciences Politiques, where the legal courses are often taught by members of the Conseil d'Etat in relatively small groups. The ENA entrance examination is stiff and the numbers of places are strictly controlled by the government.[14] For example, in 1999 there were 55 places for this concours externe (for those coming out of higher education), 44 places for the concours interne (for civil servants of at least five years' experience), and 11 places for the troisième concours, which recruits persons from the private sector under 40 who have at least eight years' experience. But once a student has passed into ENA, then she or he is ensured of a civil service career of some kind. The formation in ENA is generalist taking two years – there is no specialist formation for those who are going to become administrative judges. The training involves a combination of courses in Paris and Strasbourg and placements in various parts of the administration or even abroad or in the private sector. There will be specific courses on public administration and public law. At the end, there is an exit examination that produces a listing of students in order of merit. According to their place in this order of merit, candidates have their pick of the postings available in that year. The Conseil d'Etat, like the Inspection générale des finances and the Cour des Comptes, is chosen by bright and ambitious recruits not merely because of its work, but also because of the opportunities which joining this corps will have for their future career.[15] Those lower down the order might well choose to become members of the corps of the tribunaux administratifs and the Cours administratives d'appel. Whereas to join the Conseil d'Etat is considered to be one of the élite posts, joining the other judicial corps does not have much more prestige than becoming an administrateur civil. Whereas those joining the corps of the tribunaux administratifs will expect to devote their entire career to judicial work, those who enter the corps of the Conseil d'Etat do not necessarily aim to devote themselves to the legal work of the Conseil for their whole life. Indeed, members of the Conseil often complain that this aspect features too little in the ambitions of new recruits.[16] They attribute this in part to the lack of stimulation in legal work and there are alternative attractions.

Thus the recruitment pattern of the young recruits does not establish a 'career judiciary' at the higher levels, equivalent to that seen in the civil side. A closer approximation is the

14 Admission numbers can be found on the ENA website: http://www.ena.fr.

15 Massot and Girardot (p 36 note 55) note that of the 67 *majors* (top of the class) up to 1998, 31 had chosen to belong to the Conseil d'Etat and 30 the Inspection générale des finances.

16 Mind you, Letourneur already commented on this trend in 1970.

ambition of the civil judge who wants to be a procureur or to enter into a ministerial office. (Though, even then, the members of the Conseil d'Etat are less often conseillers techniques and more often occupy policy-making posts.) All the same, those who enter as auditeurs through this route are likely to occupy the senior positions.[17]

(ii) Tour extérieur Particularly since 1983, there has been an effort to supplement the recruitment of young people through ENA with the recruitment of more experienced people at a later stage in their career. Given the cost of financing the preparation year and achieving the appropriate level of education at an early stage, it was unsurprising that a certain social élitism characterises membership of the ENA recruits, particularly to the most senior corps. The tour extérieur is available for entry into the various grades within all corps. There are two major groups recruited through the tour extérieur. The first are members of the corps of the tribunaux administratifs and the Cours administratives d'appel. Since 1985 one post of conseiller in six and one post of maître des requêtes in four is reserved for members of that corps, and indeed since 1992 half the nominations for the tour extérieur as maitre des requetes were filled by members of the lower administrative courts. As a result, there has been a considerable professionalisation of the tour extérieur. The other major group for recruitment to the administrative courts will be those in other branches of the civil service, the administrateurs civils and those in the local government service. At the level of conseiller in the Conseil d'Etat, individuals are likely to have performed at a high level in another civil service corps. Since 1994, the Vice-President of the Conseil has to give a public opinion on all proposed nominations to the tour extérieur except for individuals coming from the lower administrative courts. This is clearly an attempt to put the brake on political patronage which was so important in the past.

In 1998, of 141 presidents and conseillers, only 12 had come in as maitres des requêtes by the tour extérieur, and 31 came in by that route as conseillers (with 8 from the tribunaux administratifs). Among the 137 maitres des requêtes, 27 came in by external recruitment (other than from the lower administrative courts).

In practice, the tour extérieur has been very important for a rapidly expanding corps. In relation to the tribunaux administratifs, there have been a number of exceptional recruitment rounds. Most recruits come from the public service and are aged above 35, so they have a different, but relevant experience of the administration in most cases.

(iii) Service extraordinaire Rather than join the corps of administrative judges, individuals can remain within their original corps, but work en détachement within the various administrative courts for a fixed number of years, usually four. Their own previous experience can help to feed into the experience and knowledge of the Conseil d'Etat or of the administrative courts, though members of those courts consider that these détachés are being formed. Massot and Girardot suggest that most of the external nominees (either conseillers en service extraodinaire or from the tour extérieur) in the Conseil d'Etat are chosen for their technical expertise. In 1998, these included seven from the lower administrative courts, four prefects, three administrateurs civils, three civil judges, two diplomats, two professors and two military officers.[18]

17 See Massot and Girardot, p 37.
18 Massot and Girardot, p 38.

(c) *Initial and continuing education*

While education at ENA will involve some legal subjects (essentially in public law), it will not be the equivalent of a university degree. Thus much of the relevant law is acquired on the job. One former prefect remarked in interview that 'any administrator is presumed capable of knowing the law'. The remark was made in response to questions on why French government departments did not have many legal advisors of their own. Understanding legal rules and applying them is part of many administrative tasks. They require good analysis and precision, which are characteristics which any administrator should have. As one President of Section remarked, analytical training is not peculiar to law. Legal education encourages attention to emphasing major, relevant issues and being brief. Although being involved in litigation and writing reports encourages these, a prior legal training is not the only way to develop the method.

A crucial part of the training of all administrative judges is the *stage* in the Conseil d'Etat.[19] In this period, trainees are not only given lectures (typically by judges from the administrative courts), but they spend several months attached to a sous-section and follow its work. They are also taught to prepare files by way of practical exercises. This common element in formation helps to form links between individuals and encourages a standardisation of approach, achieved in the ordinary courts by the training at the ENM.

The Conseil also undertakes a limited programme of continuing education. The programme is not as large as that offered by the ENA or ENM, but it is run by the central court and focuses on the judges. There is little overlap with the continuing education programme of the civil judges.

(d) *Promotions*

It is only since 1900 that the majority of promotions to senior posts in the Conseil has come from within the ranks of the corps.[20] Before then, most appointments and promotions were made by way of political patronage. The internal promotion system has gradually come to dominate the corps and create a real career track in judicial work within the Conseil, even if many, in practice, will also serve outside as part of their career.

Under the loi of 6 January 1986, there is an independent *Conseil supérieur des tribunaux administratifs et des cours administratives d'appel* on which members of this corps and the Conseil d'Etat are represented.[1] As was noted on pp 42 and 163, this process is managed from within the Conseil d'Etat, and considerable knowledge of individuals is built up by informal means among what remains a relatively small group. The process is less formal and more within the control of judges than the equivalent process for the ordinary judiciary.

(e) *Career development*

A variety of potential career paths for administrators is predominantly relevant to the Conseil d'Etat. The corps of judges of the tribunaux administratifs and the Cours

19 See above, p 42.
20 Massot and Girardot, p 36.
1 Brown and Bell, p 88. See more generally, P Fanachi, 'Les tribunaux administratifs de 1953 à l'an 2000' *La Revue Administrative, numéro spécial: Le Conseil d'Etat avant le Conseil d'Etat* 1999, 115.

administratives d'appel has less prestige and is less called upon to perform wider roles. France has a technocratic government much more than the UK. Ministers cannot serve as deputies at the same time, and many have not served in Parliament. Civil servants, including administrative judges, can have a political activity.[2] If they seek to enter Parliament, they can remain in their corps while campaigning for election, and are put on disponibilité when elected. When they cease to hold elected office, they can apply to end their disponibilité and can rejoin the activity of their corps. Major electoral defeats lead to large numbers of civil servants rejoining their corps while others enter Parliament or Government. Many members of the grands corps have served as minister or prime minister. The Conseil d'Etat has a significant role in this respect with members such as Laurent Fabius serving as prime minister, president of the National Assembly and Minister of Finance.

The grands corps also serve as a platform for other types of career in the public and private sector, often in managerial roles. A judge can also seek a placement within the ministerial office, either in a technical function, as advisor on particular issues, or more generally as a policymaker. Particularly at the higher levels, these are politically sensitive posts and these rely on an individual having some political commitment. Membership of external bodies in a more legal capacity is common, just as it is for common law judges. A member of the Conseil may be asked to chair or be part of a departmental inquiry over problem or issue. Thus Bernard Tricot chaired the inquiry into the Greenpeace affair in 1985-86, and Jean Massot produced the report on the criminal liability of elected officials in 1999. The image of the Conseil d'Etat given by one of its members is that it is a 'resource of personnel for the rest of the administration'. Advisory roles may be as much informal as formal, so that there is a request for advice which comes to people with known expertise. The relatively small number of ENA graduates enables informal networks to be set up.

(2) Lawyers

(a) Avocats au Conseil

The members of the Conseil have a good appreciation of the work of this specialist bar, and there are some informal links with it. Formal links are more limited. Fifty years ago André Morillot described the different skills needed to plead before the Conseil d'Etat compared with the ordinary lawyer:

> Here no forced or exuberant mannerisms, no brilliance, no brilliant elocution, or oratorical flourishes, but precise ideas, developed in a very sober language with the minimum of images and colours. You are attacking the reason and not the emotions of the judge, his legal knowledge and not his sense of fairness. You do not seek to move, but to direct his mind and his reason.[3]

Though rarely noted, there are clear situations of influence of the lawyers in their preparation of a case in developing the case law of the Conseil. The perspective is

2 On the politicising of the civil service, see L Rouban, *Les cadres supérieurs de la fonction publique et la politique de modernisation administrative* (Paris 1994), ch 6.4.

3 A Morillot, 'La collaboration de l'Ordre avec le Conseil d'Etat' *Livre Jubilaire* 367, at pp 368-369.

obviously different: the lawyer has to win the case and use the law as an arm for his client. There is an individual and precisely strategic objective. That said, the avocat aux Conseils is a repeat player and has interest in developing the law in a particular direction for the long-term benefit of his clients and his role as advisor.[4] Barthélemy suggests there are three roles for the avocat au Conseil d'Etat.[5] First, he mediates between the litigant and the Conseil d'Etat in that he explains the rules by which it proceeds, he has access to the file, and he has the monopoly of pleading, helping both to ensure that the case is put in an appropriate way. The second role is that of filter to ensure the proper functioning of justice – to avoid cases which are not serious, by using his independent judgment. Third, he has the role of adapting the law to the individual case. This can include offering an external view of the law from that presented internally within the Conseil and drawing attention to solutions which are inappropriate or obsolete. Thus he has the job of protecting the court and his client.

(b) Avocats in the lower courts

At one point, there were few lawyers who specialised in cases at this level in the system. Now that the cases at first instance and appeal have become more straightforward and local, then greater use is made of this opportunity for litigation by a wider range of lawyers. This means that they are less specialist and more diffuse. While there may be some lawyers who develop regular personal links with members of the local court, there are few formal and systematic efforts to draw them in.

In many ways, it is argued that some of the litigants have become more specialised and able to handle administrative litigation. Particularly in areas such as immigration and planning, there are associations who are regular litigators, often directly rather than just supporting individuals. They have the expertise to present cases in ways judges would find easy to understand.

F. THE CULTURE OF ADMINISTRATIVE LAW

> It would be hardly an exaggeration to say that the edifice of administrative law, that is to say the totality of the solutions given in France to the problem of the relations between man and the authorities (*le Pouvoir*) in so far as he intervenes in his daily life, rests, essentially, on the intellectual tradition and ethic of the *grand corps* which constructed it.[6]

The importance of this remark is the emphasis on the role of the Conseil within the administrative order. We have seen in this chapter that there is a corps of the civil service, the members of the Conseil d'Etat who occupy the commanding heights of administrative law. In the first place, they are involved in its creation, and are often the

4 See B Odent, 'La jurisprudence du Conseil d'Etat dans l'élaboration du droit vue par un avocat aux Conseils', *La Revue Administrative, numéro spécial*: *Les juridictions administratives dans le monde, France-Liban*, 1999, 89.

5 J Barthélemy, 'Le rôle de l'avocat devant la juridiction administrative' *La Revue Administrative, numéro spécial: Les juridictions administratives dans le monde: France-Allemagne*, 1999, 117.

6 J Rivero, 'Apologie pour les "faiseurs de systèmes"' D 1951 Chr at p 99.

originators. In terms of lois and major decrees, they will all pass through the Conseil for advice, and a member of the Conseil will be tasked with the drafting of the text. The advice will not only be on technical matters of drafting and legality, but will be more broader issues of suitability, as long as these do not tread on the areas of political judgment. In other cases, members of the Conseil, if not the Conseil itself through its Section du Rapport et des Etudes, may have recommended the change in the first place. In relation to the general principles of administrative law and the grounds of judicial review and liability, the key principles are judge-made and that means that they were made by the Conseil d'Etat. When it comes to the implementation of the law, the Conseil is present as legal adviser to the administration. Many of its members are out in the administration performing leading administrative (if not political) roles. There is opportunity for dialogue between the active administration and the Conseil in both pre-litigation and litigation roles. Third, as judge of the administration, the Conseil d'Etat exercises control over the operations of the administration in a supervisory role. It is able to interpret the rules to be operated, to guide and control the exercise of discretion and influence administrative behaviour, as well as protecting the interests of the administered. Doctrinal writers play a part, but always respecting the status of the Conseil. Finally, as superior of the lower administrative courts, it is able to control the budget and to supervise the functioning of all administrative courts, and to ensure that it receives intelligence on the issues emerging from them. It is not just a superior court that waits for cases to come to it and sending remote messages to the lower courts. There are ways in which a more active communication takes place.

The Iribarne analysis of corps developing relationships one with another would seem apt to describe the way in which the Conseil positions itself in relation to the rest of the administration, as well as to the lower courts and legal doctrine. Its members are on missions, it engages in supervisory and advisory activities. It is rarely in the position to dictate, but it is able to influence the agenda and to position the rest of the administration in relation to certain tasks. It has been successful in knowing when to pull back and how to adjust. The recurrent purges and the confrontation with the government in 1963 have shown that it is not all-powerful and cannot always get its own way, but it remains there.

Although the personnel is important, administrative law is shaped importantly around certain activities. The distinctive tasks are of setting out criteria for the legitimate competence of administrative action, setting standards for how that competence should be exercised (both procedural and substantive), safeguarding in advance the interests of the administered, redressing grievances as they arise, and providing an effective system for redressing unlawful decisions or giving compensation. There are two aspects here. How far is administrative law a process for achieving that kind of standard setting or remedying grievances? How independently does the administrative legal system operate?

In relation to the former, most of the rules and procedures of administrative law emerge from Government, Parliament or local authorities and other administrations in the form of decrees or lois. These negotiate with the civil service unions and other interest groups, as well as between politicians who seek to get the administration to achieve certain political or administrative objectives. Legal institutions and lawyers have some input, notably the Conseil d'Etat. This involvement ensures that issues of administrative legality and standards of behaviour are kept in mind. The standards of administrative law are one set of obstacles around which the administration must operate. In remedying grievances, there are a number of mechanisms available, many of which are defined by law. Legal redress is merely one form of redress and there is the expectation that other forms of redress will have been used before it. The fact that the administrative courts have not allowed the exclusion of recourse to the courts, and the numbers of cases have increased significantly, demonstrate the importance of judicial redress.

The administrative legal system operates in a curious mix of collaborative and independent ways. There are direct links in terms of personnel and processes between rule-making, administrative implementation, and adjudication. There is a celebration of the connection between the personnel and operations of the administrative courts and the administration. It would be fair to say that the lower administrative courts are predominantly charged with the task of remedying grievances (by decisions on administrative action and the implementation of their decisions). They act with limited contact with the administration of a formal kind. The standards and role of administrative law at all levels makes it distinct.

Chapter 6

Constitutional law

Constitutional law is a distinct branch of public law because it is concerned with the operation of the organs of government and with fundamental rights. In this latter aspect, it has close connections with criminal law and civil law, as well as with administrative law. Because constitutional law defines the competence of the legislator, it is not subordinate to loi and so has a distinctive relationship to sources of law. The basic rules of government are grounded in popular sovereignty, but the Constitution serves to constrain the immediate desires of the popular will.[1] Although constitutional law is a long established discipline, the Fifth Republic has introduced a number of innovations. In particular, the rationalised Parliament and constitutional review through the Conseil constitutionnel have encouraged a movement to recognise the Constitution as a legal document and the role of law in defining and defending it.

A. THE CORE TASK

Constitutional law is predominantly concerned with the interpretation and application of the Constitution, but the process of making the Constitution itself is legally defined in many respects.

(1) Constitution making

The making of constitutional rules is an infrequent process. The process of drafting a text for constitutional amendment is obviously a legal task, but there is also a major process of building a political consensus in favour of the reform. The Maastricht treaty offers a good illustration of the different phases of constitutional revision.[2] The treaty to reform the European Communities was submitted to the Conseil constitutionnel by the

1 See A Peczenik in N Berggren, N Karlson and J Nergelius (eds), *Why Constitutions Matter* (Stockholm 2000), pp 17ff.

2 See S Boyron, 'The Conseil constitutionnel and the European Union' [1993] PL 30. See also the ratification of the Amsterdam Treaty: A Bonnie, 'The Constitutionality of Transfers of Sovereignty: the French Approach' (1998) 4 *European Public Law* 517.

President in March 1992 to ensure its conformity with the Constitution. The Conseil[3] found that a number of provisions were not compatible with the existing constitution. In particular, the provisions permitting EU citizens to vote in local elections would affect indirectly the appointment of members of the Senate. Furthermore, the power to control the currency was considered to be an aspect of national sovereignty that the creation of a single European currency controlled by a single central bank would take away. As a result, it was necessary to amend the constitution through the Congress in June 1992 to insert arts 88-1 to 88-4, which made the ratification of the Treaty possible. A number of members of the opposition challenged the compatibility with the Constitution as revised. This time, the treaty was found to be compatible.[4] This political process allowed debate on the principles to be settled by politicians. But the actual loi authorising the President to ratify the Treaty was put to a referendum on 20 September 1992 which was narrowly won, and which the Conseil constitutionnel claimed to have no competence to review.[5] Although some technical expertise was required to produce appropriate formulations of the constitutional amendments, the principal problem was obtaining the requisite majority first for the constitutional amendment and then for its application in the law on ratification of the Treaty.

Most constitutional law activities will involve the tasks of interpreting and applying the text as the various organs of government try to operate within the framework set by the Constitution. A Constitution is predominantly concerned with procedures: how decisions are to be taken, who is to be involved and what consultations and assents have to be given. Even in the area of fundamental rights, the Constitution sets out what political decisions can be made within the existing constitutional framework. But, as we shall see in relation to asylum,[6] the Constitution can always be amended provided that the right procedure is followed, and after that new policies can be implemented. In a deep sense, therefore, all constitutional law is about the procedure by which particular types of decision can be taken. Of course, such a formulation presupposes that constitutional amendment is feasible. In France, the principal method requires a loi to be passed in identical terms by both houses and then to be approved by a two-thirds majority in a joint session of both houses, the Congress. A riskier procedure has been to submit the proposal to a referendum. De Gaulle lost a constitutional amendment referendum in 1969, Mitterand nearly lost the Maastricht ratification law referendum in 1992, and there was public indifference over the constitutional reform of New Caledonia and the reduction of the presidential mandate to five years in 2000. The ability to make use of a constitutional reform cannot be assumed – it depends on available political circumstances. So for most practical purposes, the fundamental values and procedures laid down in the Constitution set obstacles to political policies.

(2) Constitutional interpretation

The problem with such rules is that they are defined in very abstract terms. They do not really tell politicians concerned with detail what they can do. In the first place, the

3 CC decision No 92-308 DC of 9 April 1992, *Maastricht I*, Rec 55.
4 CC decision No 92-312 DC of 2 September 1992, *Maastricht II*, Rec 76.
5 CC decision No 92-313 DC of 23 September 1992, *Maastricht III*, Rec 94.
6 Below, pp 229-230.

procedures set out in the Constitution are general and contain a number of features that are desirable, rather than practical. Let us take two areas which will be discussed later, parliamentary voting procedure and amendment. In all Parliaments, there is a problem of members not being present to vote. Article 27 of the Constitution provides for a strictly personal vote. But practice for a long time recognised that members might be absent and it was common for the keys used to vote to be given to a colleague (or head of delegation) to vote on the absent member's behalf. When faced with a flagrant situation where a vote had not been personal, but had been cast by a colleague, the Conseil chose to treat the provision as not essential.[7] On the right of amendment, art 44 of the Constitution provides that both members of Parliament and the government have the right of amendment. But this does not specify what counts as an 'amendment' and how late in the proceedings one can be tabled. Interpretation will involve an elaboration of the text.[8]

(a) Priority between constitutional texts

In relation to fundamental rights, there are more difficulties. The 1958 Constitution did not try to set out a new set of rights. Rather it merely took over the statements in previous constitutions. In 1946, there were problems in obtaining popular approval for a new statement of fundamental rights. The eventual compromise was to reaffirm the Declaration of the Rights of Man and of the Citizen of 1789 together with a set of 'principles particularly necessary for our times'. The 1958 Constitution simply adopted these documents. There is clearly a problem of priority between the two documents. The Conseil had to resolve this in relation to the nationalisation of various key industries. Paragraph 9 of the 1946 Preamble provides that:

> Any property or business, whose exploitation has or acquires the character of a national public service or a *de facto* monopoly, should become the property of the community.

This seemed a positive encouragement to nationalisations. By contrast, art 17 of the 1789 Declaration defended the right of individual ownership of property:

> Property, being an inviolable and sacred right, none can be deprived of it, except when public necessity, legally ascertained, evidently requires it and on condition of a just and prior indemnity.

The Conseil constitutionnel used historical arguments to justify the priority of the 1789 text. The first draft Constitution had tried to set down a new statement of rights, but it was rejected by referendum in May 1946. The reaffirmation of the 1789 text by the Preamble to the October 1946 Constitution (confirmed by the Preamble to the 1958 Constitution), duly approved by referenda, showed that art 17 retained its full force. The 1946 Preamble suggested that its own statements of rights were complementary to those of 1789, and this was the appropriate way to construe the provisions.

7 See CC decision No 86-225 DC of 23 January 1987, *Séguin Amendment*, below, p 231. Y Aguila, 'L'interprétation constitutionnelle' (1995) Rfdc No 21, 9 at p 34 suggests that this was a recognition of the practical realities of constitutional life.

8 See *Séguin Amendment*, below, p 231.

(b) Completing the constitutional texts

The Preamble to the 1946 Constitution also states that it affirms 'the fundamental principles recognized by the laws of the Republic'. But it fails to state which laws or, indeed, which republic. It was understood to apply essentially to the fundamental values recognised by the laws of the Third Republic.[9] That Republic did not have a constitutional text and so a number of laws on key issues were passed, eg the press law of 1881, the associations law of 1901. But this concept has given the Conseil scope to augment the corpus of constitutional texts. The decisive decision establishing constitutional review, the *Associations Law* decision,[10] was based on the right to association that was a fundamental principle recognised by the laws of the Republic, notably the loi of 1901. The process of making a decision involves a number of stages. First, the Conseil identifies a text which talks about the value in question. In doing this, the Conseil needs a prior conception of which right is at issue and whether it is possibly fundamental. Typically the authors of the reference will cite texts. The text will either be a whole loi, or even a disparate provision, as was seen in the case of the freedom of education which was 'discovered' in art 91 of the Finance law of 31 March 1931.[11] Second, the Conseil looks not so much at the precise words of the text as at the fundamental value which it expresses, a general principle underlying its specific provisions. Finally, having elicited a principle of general import, like the freedom of association, it has to produce a specific rule capable of resolving the question before it, such as the rule against prior restraint. In performing this task, the Conseil is at its most creative. Apart from the freedom of association and the freedom of education and of conscience, the Conseil has also declared as fundamental the independence of administrative, and the separation of public and private law courts,[12] the rights of due process in legal proceedings,[13] the freedom of teachers in higher education,[14] the freedom of movement and the right of privacy,[15] the continuity of public services,[16] freedom of commerce and enterprise,[17] and human dignity.[18]

In addition to these fundamental principles which leave scope for interpretation, the Conseil has set out a number of 'objectives having constitutional value'.[19] They

9 The Conseil appears to endorse principles adopted in legislation up until the adoption of the 1946 Constitution. Thus in CC decision No 97-393 DC of 18 December 1997, *Family Allowances*, Rec 320; GD No 49, the Conseil was prepared to consider that an ordonnance of the provisional Government from 4 October 1945 and a loi of 22 August 1946 could be the basis for such a fundamental principle.

10 CC decision No 71-44 DC of 16 July 1971, *Associations Law*, Rec. 29; Bell, *French Constitutional Law*, Decision 1.

11 CC decision No 77-87 OF 23 November 1977, *Freedom of Education*, Rec 42; Bell, *French Constitutional Law*, Decision 21.

12 CC decision No 86-224 DC of 23 January 1987, *Competition Law*, Rec 8.

13 CC decision No 89-271 DC of 11 January 1990, *Election Expenses*, Rec 21.

14 CC decision No 83-165 DC of 20 January 1984, *University Professors*, Rec 30.

15 CC decision No 76-75 DC of 12 January 1977, *Vehicle Searches*, Rec 33; Bell, *French Constitutional Law*, Decision 17.

16 CC decision No 79-105 DC of 25 July 1979, *Strikes on Radio and TV*, Rec 33; Bell, *French Constitutional Law*, Decision 23.

17 CC decision No 81-132 DC of 16 January 1982, *Nationalisations*, Rec 18; Bell, *French Constitutional* Law, Decision 2; GD No 31.

18 CC decision Nos 343 and 344 DC of 27 July 1994, *Bioethics*, Rec 100; GD No 47.

19 See B Faure, 'Les objectifs de valeur constitutionnelle: une nouvelle catégorie juridique?' (1995) Rfdc No 21, 47.

are means for implementing constitutional values. As Genevois states, 'the objective of constitutional value appears as the necessary corollary of the implementation of a constitutionally recognized value'.[20] Since these are matters of means, rather than ends, it might be thought that the legislature is free to identify and define these objectives and to pursue their implementation. But the Conseil constitutionnel has been reluctant to leave Parliament with total liberty in this area. If an objective is identified as of 'constitutional value', it has a special status as a means by which the legislature must realise a fundamental constitutional value. The law cannot be changed in such a way as to weaken the constitutional protection afforded to individual rights. In this way, the objectives restrict the freedom of action of the legislature. At the time of writing, the Conseil has recognized the search for criminals and the prevention of threats to public order, especially to persons and property,[1] the preservation of the pluralist character of socio-cultural expressions of opinion,[2] and the pluralism of daily newspapers of political and general information,[3] and the possibility for everyone to have decent lodging.[4] A clear illustration of the way they work can be found in the *Press Law* decision of 1986, discussed below, p 232.

Outside the area of rights, Parliament has added to the corpus of constitutional rules with the ordonnance of 2 January 1959 on finance laws and the loi organique of 26 July 1996 on social security budgets. Because nearly all finance laws are submitted to scrutiny by the Conseil, a well-developed body of interpretation has been created which is concerned not only with the procedure for adopting finance laws, but also with their content. Finance laws (including social security budgets) are governed by separate rules of procedure under the Constitution. The timescale is compressed and the government can effectively impose a budget unless Parliament votes the finance law within the required period. Members of Parliament have very limited rights to make proposals. To counterbalance this severe limitation on the powers of Parliament, the Conseil has been insistent that the procedure is respected, and has annulled the budget in its entirety once because of failure to respect this.[5] In this case, a minority government had tried to force a single vote on the entire budget, rather than respect the requirement in the 1959 ordonnance that the tax receipts be voted in the first part before expenditure is approved in the second part. Additionally, the Conseil has been concerned that provisions, which do not belong properly in a finance law, are not included, since this prevents proper discussion by Parliament. For example, a minister of education sought to include a provision to pay for private school teachers to be incorporated into the civil service before such a policy had been approved by Parliament.[6] The degree of intensity with which such cavaliers budgétaires are scrutinised has varied. In the early years, the Conseil was fairly strict, but in recent

20 B Genevois, *La Jurisprudence du Conseil constitutionnel* (Paris 1988), § 342. He draws a parallel with the *Nold v Commission* [1974] ECR 491 (European Court of Justice).

1 CC decision No 80-127 DC of 19 and 20 January 1981, *Security and Liberty*, Rec 15; Decision 18, § 54.

2 CC decision No 82-141 DC of 27 July 1982, *Audio-visual law*, Rec 48.

3 See the *Press Law* decisions of 1984 and 1986, below, pp 232-233.

4 See CC decision No 94-359 DC of 19 January 1995, *Diversity of Housing*, Rec 176, § 7.

5 Bell, *French Constitutional Law*, pp 129-131; CC decision No 79-110 DC of 24 December 1979; GD 28.

6 Bell, *French Constitutional Law*, pp 132-133; CC decision No 84-184 DC of 29 December 1984, *Finance Law for 1985*, Rec 94.

times, it has been more willing to be laxer at least to the extent of permitting the inclusion of decided policies which might have an impact on the budget in future.[7]

The activity of the Conseil shows how constitutional law has to work. Texts are pitched at a level of generality that requires a great deal of further specification. Furthermore, there is no single and coherent statement of the constitutional principles and values. The texts have to be made into a coherent corpus, and the Conseil constitutionnel is given to talking of 'principles having constitutional value'. This process has been judge-led. Doctrinal writing has followed, offering analysis and evaluation.

B. INSTITUTIONAL SETTING

(1) The interpreters of the Constitution

The activity of 'interpreting' the Constitution is not confined to the Conseil constitutionnel and academic doctrinal writers. A number of other individuals occupy functions which both require them to interpret the Constitution, but also give authoritative rulings on aspects of it.

(a) President of the Republic

As Romi has pointed out,[8] the President of the Republic occupies an important place in interpreting the Constitution. Institutionally, under art 5 of the Constitution, he has responsibility for supervising respect for the Constitution. Since he has the role of making decisions to ensure the proper operation of public authorities, this includes giving interpretations of the Constitution. A couple of examples drawn from the first cohabitation period illustrate this role. The division of responsibilities between President and Prime Minister drawn from different parties was not clear. Mitterand produced a statement which he presented in a message to the opening session of the National Assembly in April 1986.[9] The division of respective areas of competence was not set out in the Constitution, but had to be worked out as a matter of principle, rather than an *ad hoc* political compromise.[10] Later in the same year, the President also refused to sign ordonnances presented to him by the Prime Minister. Now art 11 of the Constitution uses the word 'signe' which could mean either the President 'signs' or 'shall sign'. The President decided that he was not obliged to sign and there was no way in which this could be challenged by the Prime Minister.[11] A similar finality of the President's judgment comes in the use of the referendum as an alternative method of enacting lois, a procedure for which the Constitution makes no specific provision. The Conseil refuses to accept jurisdiction over lois which have not been passed by Parliament, but have simply been

7 See L Philip, (1997) Rfdc No 29, pp 125-126 and (2000) Rfdc No 41, pp 136-137.

8 R Romi, 'Le Président de la République, interprète de la Constitution' RDP 1987, 1265. See also I Richir, 'Le chef d'Etat et le juge constitutionnel, gardiens de la Constitution' RDP 1999, 1047.

9 8 April 1986; Bell, *French Constitutional Law*, Material 1.

10 Bell, *French Constitutional Law*, p 61.

11 See Bell, *French Constitutional Law*, p 107.

submitted to a referendum.[12] How such referendum laws are used remain within the discretion of the President. Thus, in the allocation of duties between himself and the Prime Minister during cohabitation, in determining the scope of the power of the President to appoint ministers, and in these other areas, the President has made a final determination. At best, the activity of the President is controlled by constitutional convention.[13] There is thus a kind of political morality which supports and sanctions the interpretative activity in question. Only in some instances is the Conseil able to comment on the President's view. In the *Séguin Amendment*, the Conseil indirectly supported the President's interpretation. It also approved the President's view that, when the Conseil had annulled provisions of a loi, he could ask for a new reading of an existing text, rather than promoting a new loi.[14]

In a more general sense, the President is guardian of the Republic and has certain powers to ensure this. One such power contained in art. 16 is to declare a state of emergency. In this decision, he must consult the Conseil constitutionnel, but its function is essentially advisory. It operates in this way rather like the Conseil d'Etat, rather than as a constitutional court. All the same, even though the President has the final say, as he did in 1961 and there against the advice of the members of the Conseil,[15] the need to justify himself to an outside audience offers some, albeit limited, constraint on the abuse of power.

(b) Conseil d'Etat

The Conseil d'Etat is very clearly an interpreter of the Constitution. Particularly in relation to the pre-legislative advice,[16] the Conseil will frequently have to examine the constitutionality of what the government is proposing. The ruling which the Conseil d'Etat provides is confidential, but it will be made available to the Conseil constitutionnel. It may also become known more widely. Certainly, it will have some influence on the actions of the government. In relation to general legal advice, the government will often ask questions which have constitutional importance. For example, the question of how far school rules could regulate the wearing of religious insignia, eg girls wearing the chadour, required the reconciliation of the freedom of individual expression in Declaration of the Rights of Man and of the Citizen of 1789 and the principle of the secular state to which the Constitution of 1958 is committed in art 3. The task is clearly one of interpreting the Constitution in a way on which the government was able to rely, essentially publishing the advice as a circular. It is precisely the sort of question which would come to a constitutional court in another legal system. But the absence of a power to refer issues to the Conseil constitutionnel for a declaratory ruling leaves a gap for the Conseil d'Etat to fill. Of course it will also have to make rulings on such matters in its judicial capacity. But it is in its formal advisory capacity that the Conseil d'Etat most resembles a constitutional court.

12 *Maastricht III*, above, p 200; CC decision No 62-20 DC of 6 November 1962, *Referendum Law*, Rec 27; Bell, *French Constitutional Law*, Decision 14; GD No 14.
13 P Avril, *Les conventions de la constitution* (Paris 1997), pp 131-132, 138-139.
14 Decision No 85-197 DC of 23 August 1985, *Elections in New Caledonia*, Rec 70.
15 J Boudéant, 'Le Président du Conseil constitutionnel' RDP 1987, 589.
16 On this function, see above, pp 172-175.

(c) Presidents of National Assembly and Senate

The Presidents of the two assemblies have the task of making rulings on the admissibility of motions and proposals within Parliament. In particular, art 41 gives them the right to make rulings on claims by the government that a bill or amendment proposed by a member of Parliament infringes the government's legislative competence arising either under the Constitution or by virtue of a delegation of powers to it already made by Parliament under art 38. In the event of a disagreement, either the President or the government can refer the matter to the Conseil constitutionnel. This is the sole situation in which a bill can be referred to the Conseil before it has been passed. In other situations, the President may make rulings, but they cannot be challenged until after the bill has completed its parliamentary stages. The President has thus no power to make binding decisions. At most he can make provisional decisions. Nevertheless, through their role as set out in art 41 and in their power to refer bills to Parliament, they are able to act as guardians of the Constitution. After all, it was the reference by the President of the Senate who referred the *Associations Law* to the Conseil, which was the starting point for the role of the Conseil in striking down legislation and in developing the range of constitutional norms. More recently, the President of the National Assembly referred the *Bioethics* law to the Conseil to obtain a ruling confirming the constitutionality of a loi on a very controversial subject. The role of gatekeeper requires some interpretation of the Constitution both to make rulings and to take the initiative, but the role is more limited.

(d) Government

The government has three different roles as interpreter of the Constitution. In the first place, it is guardian of its own prerogatives. Article 41, just mentioned, provides a mechanism by which it can require Parliament to desist from trying to legislate in its field of competence. This particular article has not been used since 1979. In addition, since 1982 the Conseil has not struck down provisions of lois which legislate in areas in which the government was also competent to legislate.[17] More typically, the government will refer various legislative provisions to the Conseil in order to have them declassified so that it can amend them without returning to Parliament. In such a situation, the government makes a preliminary interpretation of the Constitution to decide what it considers might fall within the remit of its own legislative powers within art 37 and then seeks confirmation and approval from the Conseil.

In the second place, the government is a regular interlocutor of the Conseil. Through the Secretary-General of the Government, it will write formal observations on references made to the Conseil. In addition, officials within ministries may well be seen by the rapporteur to provide explanations of various provisions in the bill. It is well documented that many of the reservations of interpretation which the Conseil produces come from the interpretations offered in the observations made by the government.[18] The Secretary-General of the Government is acting here rather like the legal representative

17 See Bell, *French Constitutional Law*, p 90: CC decision No 83-143 DC of 30 July 1982, *Freeze on Prices and Salaries*, Rec 57.

18 See below, pp 217-219.

of the government. Obviously, before he has to engage with the Conseil, he will act more like a legal adviser in either providing or obtaining opinions from lawyers. Since the Secretary-General is drawn from the Conseil d'Etat, he will have legal expertise of his own. All the same, the government does not have its own legal service and so ministries will obtain legal opinions not only from the Secretary-General, but also from members of the Conseil d'Etat (or even formally from the Conseil d'Etat) or from outside lawyers or law professors. Thus in relation to nationalisation in 1981, the ministry obtained an opinion from two eminent law professors.

Third, the government has to apply decisions made. In the case of the administration, a circular of the Prime Minister of 25 May 1988 reminded civil servants of the need not only to respect decisions of the Conseil constitutionnel, but also to anticipate potential breaches of the Constitution.[19]

(2) Procedure and methods of working in the Conseil constitutionnel

Since the Conseil is not formally a court, its procedures are not fully judicial and in many ways resemble those of an administrative inquiry. Outside the area of electoral law, there is no set of procedural rules, other than the exiguous organic law contained in the ordonnance of 7 November 1958.[20] The obligation of secrecy on members of the Conseil about their deliberations has led to an air of secrecy about the way in which it functions, but the procedure has become increasingly 'contradictoire'. The description of the procedure which follows draws on a number of disparate remarks in the literature and upon discussions with members of the Conseil and especially of its legal service.

The procedure before the Conseil varies significantly depending on the task in hand. It is most judicial when dealing with electoral disputes and least judicial when deal with the declassification of lois under art 37 § 2.

(a) *Election disputes*

Acting as an election court for parliamentary elections, the Conseil operates very much like the Conseil d'Etat when it deals with disputed local elections. Here the ordonnance of 7 November 1958 is at its fullest, providing some 14 detailed articles on the procedure to be adopted.

Within ten days from the election result, any candidate or elector for that constituency may present an election petition by way of letter to the Conseil or to the local Prefect or equivalent, setting out the grounds of complaint. The Conseil operates in sections of three members chosen by lot, who are assisted by associate reporters chosen from members of the Conseil d'Etat or the Cour des Comptes on an annual basis. One of these associate reporters is chosen to act as reporter (rapporteur) on the particular petition. His task is to provide the analysis of facts and rules on which the section can

19 See RDP 1989, 436.

20 See D Turpin, *Contentieux constitutionnel* (PUF 1986), p 219:

> The procedure followed before the Conseil constitutionnel is essentially customary in the sense that, outside the provisions relating to time limits or, within the scope of article 61 of the Constitution, to the nomination of the *rapporteur*, there only exist rules relating to the procedure to be followed for disputes about the election of deputies or senators.

prepare a report for discussion by the whole Conseil. This process of *instruction* is closely modelled on the procedure of the Conseil d'Etat. The deputy or senator elected is asked for his or her observations, and he or she is usually legally represented, even though there is not an oral hearing. The process is thus contradictoire in the French sense. The Ministry of the Interior will be asked to provide any relevant information, since it is responsible for the conduct of elections. But third parties are not permitted to intervene in the case.[1] Once the instruction is complete, the report is presented to the Conseil. Only members of the Conseil have a vote, though the reporter may present the case to the meeting. The process is fully legalistic and really like that of a court. Though individuals affected may criticise the decisions of the Conseil as political,[2] this is not the general perception.

The role of the Conseil constitutionnel in presidential elections and referenda is not simply as a constitutional court. It is effectively the returning officer, deciding who are the registered candidates and declaring the results of the election. It also formally recognises the existence of a vacancy for president and sets the process of electing a new one in motion, as it did in 1969 and 1974. Operational decisions are with the ministry of the interior, but more important and contentious matters are with the Conseil. In this, it is hard sometimes to draw a distinction between a judicial function as an administrative court and an administrative function as the electoral returning officer. A former Secretary-General of the Conseil has remarked that, in these matters, 'the Conseil intervenes both as advisor, player and judge in an environment of political tension and high stakes with strong resonance in the media'.[3]

(b) References on organic laws and ordinary lois

All organic laws must be referred to the Conseil. In the case of ordinary lois, a reference depends on the motivation of the interested political groups. There may be some subjects where the opposition may feel too politically embarrassed to make a reference, even though there might be some constitutional issues to be discussed. It was generally thought that the Conseil only had competence to censure a text referred to it. But in a decision of 1999, the Conseil declared as unconstitutional a provision in a loi on which it had already pronounced in 1985 and which it had not declared unconstitutional.[4] This procedure, in a modified form, applies now to the sub-national legislation of New Caledonia, which is referred by 18 members of the assembly or certain officials.[5]

(i) The 'juridification' of the Parliamentary stage A number of authors have argued that questions of constitutionality have led to a 'juridification' (*juridicisation*) of the parliamentary process. As Jan explains:

> To say today that the challenge to the parliamentary majority 'is becoming juridified', is to argue that the parliamentary opposition concentrates its criticism no longer on the level of

1 CC 88-1073 of 3 October 1988, *AN Paris circ 19e*, Rec 142.
2 See Jack Lang criticising the quashing of his election for breach of the rules on electoral expenses: *Le Monde*, 13 December 1993, p 7.
3 O Schrameck, 'Le Conseil constitutionnel et l'élection présidentielle de 1995', AJDA 1996, 3.
4 Decision No 99-410 DC of 15 March 1999, *New Caledonia*, Rec 51 see D Rousseau, 'Chronique de jurisprudence constitutionnelle', RDP 2000, 19 at p 39.
5 See J Bell, 'Devolution: French Style' (2000) 6 *European Public Law* 139.

> political opposition to the texts of the *lois* under discussion, but on their legal validity, seeking to transform its political defeat into a legal victory.[6]

Stone Sweet suggests that there is a reflexive interaction between the legislative process and constitutional court decisions, with the legislator altering behaviour in order to anticipate possible sanction by a constitutional court.[7]

It is argued that this operates in two ways. First, and most importantly, the *exception d'irrecevabilité* is a motion which raises a preliminary point of order concerning the constitutionality of the text. As such, it forms an a priori question which could prevent a discussion of the political merits of the bill in question. Second, there is the reference to the Conseil constitutionnel before the bill is signed by the President.

In terms of importance, the first method, the parliamentary *exception* is the most significant. Formulated as a legal argument, the purpose is to deflect the government from its political option. According to Jan, only one *exception* in three presented in Parliament turns into a reference to the Conseil, but this can be for a number of reasons. To begin with, if the *exception* is successful in either the National Assembly or the Senate, then the bill will have to be withdrawn. This happened, for example, in 1998 to the loi on the Pacte de Solidarité (PACS) which was to permit limited recognition to extra-marital and same-sex unions. But a slightly revised bill was presented a month later and subsequently passed. The Conseil did not consider that this was an abuse of procedure by the government.[8] More commonly, the Opposition may cause the government to amend the bill so that the constitutionality point disappears in the final version of the bill. There is no requirement of a minimum number of members of the parliament for such a motion, unlike for a reference, so groups such as the Communists may be able to use the parliamentary route, but not the reference to the Conseil. All the same, Jan notes that in the 1980s and 1990s, about one reference in two from the socialist group when in opposition continued the argumentation presented first as part of the *exception*. In other words, the necessarily legalistic formulation of the *exception* provides a major indication of the eventual basis for a reference to the Conseil. Indeed, some procedural grounds require the matter to have been raised by way of *exception* in Parliament before the issue can be used as a reference.[9] This thus forms a legalistic feature of *parliamentary* procedure, which requires careful preparation in the *bureau* of the party. Stone notes that the *exception* in Parliament is often supported by very technical legal argumentation.[10]

Stone offers a detailed analysis of the impact of the threat of reference to the Conseil on the Press law of 1984. Opposition deputies raised a number of motions arguing that the bill was unconstitutional. In order to avoid censure by the Conseil, the majority Socialists tabled a number of amendments in the parliamentary committees

6 P Jan, *La Saisine du Conseil constitutionnel* (Paris 1999) (hereafter 'Jan'), p 481.

7 See A Stone Sweet, *Governing with Judges* (Oxford 2000) (hereafter 'Stone Sweet'), pp 194-203.

8 CC decision No 99-419 DC of 9 November 1999, Rec 116; D Rousseau, *Sur le Conseil constitutionnel. La doctrine Badinter et la démocratie* (Paris 1997) at pp 42-43.

9 See, Jan, pp 489-490 and arts 40 and 42 of the budget ordonnance of 1959 and LO 111-3 of the Code de la sécurité sociale.

10 A Stone, *The Birth of Judicial Politics in France* (New York 1992) (hereafter 'Stone'), p 75 discussing legislation on public sector strikes where debates discussed administrative case law in detail.

watering down what they considered to be the constitutionally weak provisions.[11] Stone argues that the existence of constitutional review has given rise to a greater legalism in the parliamentary process. In part, this is simply because the exception d'irrecevabilité, whose use has increased massively since 1974,[12] is in itself a legalistic argument and requires technical expertise to produce.

The level of juridification is conditioned in part by the level of success. In the case of the *exception*, there are a number of cases where the bill has been modified to avoid subsequent challenges. In the case of references to the Conseil constitutionnel after the bill has been voted, analysis of the grounds of reference suggest that nearly 40% have led to some form of partial or total invalidity (mainly partial). The increase in success has come since 1981. But a more precise analysis would suggest that only some 10% of the grounds raised in references are successful. Indeed, of the provisions struck down, some 37.2% came from the initiative of the Conseil and not from the arguments of the parliamentarians.[13] The increased subtlety of the case law has produced a greater corpus of arguments which the parliamentarians can raise. But, at the same time, there is not a marked increase in the success of these kinds of argument. The conclusion would be that there has been a juridification of political arguments, but that this has not significantly hampered the government:

> The reference to the Conseil constitutionnel is a parliamentary weapon in the sense that for those who seise the constitutional judge, in most cases, it continues a battle lost in Parliament on the text. That is why the law remains an instrument of political battles and the reference to the judge is a means of fighting the majority politically rather than being at the service of the law, whether it involves ensuring that the Constitution is respected or constitutionalising new principles. Law has laid hold of politics, but the politicians make use of the law for purposes which are not exclusively legal.[14]

For this reason, Stone prefers to locate the centre of gravity of the Conseil constitutionnel within the political process, as a kind of third chamber of Parliament, rather than within the legal system, an analysis to which I shall return.[15] Jan prefers to consider that there is effectively a dual control over government, by Parliament and by the Conseil.[16]

Jan rightly concludes that parliamentary control remains the most important and cheapest approach, but there is a dual approach available to the politicians to use as they see as appropriate. But once the text has been referred, the matter is out of the politicians' hands and they may find the Conseil has based its decision on grounds which the members of Parliament would not find congenial.

(ii) Procedure within the Conseil The rules on procedure for referring legislative texts are very limited. The ordonnance of 7 November 1958 merely states who should

11 See Stone, Table 7.1, pp 182-183: 26 of 42 articles underwent revision including all on Title II on pluralism and on Title III, the powers of the Commission on the Press.
12 Stone, table 5.2, p 127.
13 Jan, p 506.
14 Ibid, p 508.
15 See Stone, pp 209ff and below, pp 239-240.
16 Jan, p 513.

transmit the text, who should be notified in the case of a reference made by members of Parliament, and that decisions should be reasoned. For the rest, it is a matter of practice and personalities, both of which have changed over time.

Where there is a compulsory reference, the text is transmitted by the Prime Minister in the case of an organic law, or by the President of the relevant Assembly in the case of parliamentary standing orders. Since both have been the subject of a public vote in Parliament or in one of its Assemblies, there is no need to warn anyone that a reference has taken place, nor does the reference have to be based on any specific grounds.

Where the reference is optional, as in the case of ordinary lois and treaties, then notification of the reference is only formally required where it is made by 60 senators or deputies, so that the office-holders, the President of the Republic, the Prime Minister, the President of the National Assembly and the President of the Senate, are made aware of this and can make observations.

Since 1983, the text of the reference letters is published in the *Journal Officiel*, and since 1994 the text of any government reply is also published. But there is no publication of these documents to the other side, as in criminal or civil proceedings. As a result, there is a system of blind pleadings.[17] Unlike in the administrative courts where arguments raised by the court as a matter of public policy must be put to the parties,[18] there is no equivalent in the procedure of the Conseil constitutionnel.

The Conseil must decide within a short period. This is normally one month, though this can be reduced to eight days where the government claims that it is a matter of urgency. The test of urgency is not defined, but, in practice, there is a *gentleman's agreement* not to use the urgency procedure, and the Secretary-General of the Conseil and the Secretary-General of the government come to an arrangement about the time-scale for decision. It is notable that the urgency procedure was not invoked in the case of the *Urgency Law for New Caledonia* in January 1985, when the Conseil took barely 24 hours to make its decision. Equally, at the government's request, the Conseil published its first decision on nationalisations on a Saturday when the Stock Exchange was closed, since the decision was bound to affect dealings in the companies in question.

A reference is usually reasoned, setting out grounds for challenging particular articles of the loi, but, as in the case of the *Associations Law* of 1971, the letter may simply request the Conseil to examine the constitutionality of the whole text.[19] In some cases, such as in a reference on a treaty, the President of the Republic may refer the text without specifying the issues which concern him. These days, however, the references are usually well-reasoned, and are often based on legal arguments drawn up by consultants (often professors of constitutional law). They may, at times, be excessively inventive in argumentation. They may be supplemented by memoranda from those making the reference. This has become particularly common since 1986 when the government's observations have been made available to the authors of the reference.

17 G Carcassonne, cited Jan, p 514. In 1986, Badinter did propose that there be a proper debate before the Conseil, but this idea came to nothing.

18 See Brown and Bell, *French Administrative Law*, pp 100-101.

19 CC decision No 71-44 DC of 16 July 1971; Bell, *French Constitutional Law* Decision 1: there was a subsequent supplementary, reasoned memorandum in this case, but this is not a requirement of a reference.

For example, in the *Hunting Law* case of 2000,[20] there was a memorandum from these authors in response to the government's observations and then a further round of memoranda from each side.

An important feature of all French courts is that they are not confined to the arguments raised by the parties and they reserve the right to raise issues on their own initiative. These moyens soulevés d'office have particular importance in constitutional law. The Conseil constitutionnel takes the view that the whole text is referred to it for review, not merely the specific articles contained in the reference. Since the decision certifies the constitutionality of the loi, the Conseil considers that it has the right to raise issues *ex officio*. It is not trying to resolve a dispute between parties. Jan claims that of the 282 provisions censured by the Conseil since 1974, when members of Parliament were given the power to make references, 37.2% were at the initiative of the Conseil itself, while only 15.8% were at the instance of the members of Parliament.[1] The ability of the Conseil to select its own grounds of review in this way has the potential to make its decisions even more unexpected and more likely to be criticised as political. For example, in the *Feminine Quotas* case of 1982,[2] where the article of the electoral law providing for a minimum of 25% of candidates of each sex on the lists for local elections was struck down as unconstitutional, even though this was not one discussed in the reference. On the whole, issues are only raised *ex officio* where there is an obvious question of unconstitutionality. This practice has become more frequent in recent years. In his study of the question, Di Mano argued that there is developing a constitutional public policy that justifies the use of the moyens d'ordre public.[3] In his view, the function of such grounds is to ensure enforcement of the basic guarantees which the Constitution affords both in relation to fundamental rights and in relation to rights of participation. In this he is supported by a former member of the Conseil, Vedel, and its former Secretary-General, Genevois.[4] We thus have a process which allows the Conseil substantial freedom to choose its own grounds of intervention, and its own chance to develop case law.

The short timescale for deliberation and the limited scope of the argumentation in the reference may require the Conseil to do a lot of work in a short time. Quite sensibly, but unlike a normal court, the Conseil has developed a practice of starting work on a case before it is submitted. When a bill is presented to Parliament, opponents will usually move a motion that it, or some of its articles, are unconstitutional and are thus out of order, and will set out the reasons for this view. The government will provide a reasoned reply to the motion, thus making sure that the basic issues have been aired. Such motions put the Conseil on alert, and the President may well then decide to appoint a reporter from among its members to start work, building up the file on the

20 CC decision No 2000-434 DC of 20 July 2000. All the associated documents can be found with the decision on the Conseil constitutionnel's website: http//www.conseilconstitutionnel.fr.

1 Jan, p 506.

2 Below, pp 226-227.

3 T Di Mano, *Le Conseil constitutionnel et les moyens soulevés d'office* (Paris 1994), esp pp 156ff.

4 See Genevois, pp 169 and 170. On p.170 he cites Vedel talking in 1989 after he left the Conseil:
> Without assigning them a 'supra-constitutional' status, the Conseil constitutionnel appears to make fundamental freedoms and rights into a category of rules whose politico-legal importance is such that the constitutional juge, seised of a *loi* which breaches them, should declare them censured, if necessary of his own motion.

potential reference. The choice of reporter is at the discretion of the President. Attention will be paid to a reasonable distribution of the work-load, but also to the expertise of particular members. Although the identity of the reporter is not officially made public, it is known that Chatenet and Lecourt acted as reporters on European Community matters, Segalat on finance bills, Gros on audiovisual laws, Vedel on a wide range of measures, notably nationalisations (1982) and privatisations (1986), the Competition Council (1987) and the press (1984 and 1986), Mayer on the *Séguin Amendment* (1987), Robert on bioethics (1994).[5]

Depending on the personality and legal expertise of the reporter, the Secretary-General and the legal service may well have an important role in the preparation of the file and in the drafting of the text of the decision presented to the Conseil. (It is not, however, unknown for a reporter to seek legal advice from outside the Conseil's staff.) The file will be built up by the reporter acting usually with the help of the Secretary-General (an expert lawyer) and the small legal service under him. This will consist initially of three elements. First, there are the legal texts (constitutional and otherwise) on this particular area, so as to show the context and scope of the contested provisions. Second, there will be the parliamentary debates, with special attention to the arguments on constitutionality developed at different stages in the parliamentary proceedings (the Conseil is equipped to listen into parliamentary debates at any time). Third, there will be other materials, such as decided case law in the public or private law courts, doctrinal legal writings, or memoranda produced by the legal service to help the reporter (which can be more or less full). The advice given to the government by the Conseil d'Etat on a government bill is not published, but since the 1990s it is transmitted to the Conseil constitutionnel.

Once a formal reference has been made, the reporter will have a precise set of grounds to work from, though they will be almost identical to points made earlier. The text of the reference is sent to the Secretary-General of the Government, who will usually provide observations on it or on the loi in general. The function of these observations is not a full defence. A Secretary-General has written:[6]

> The written observation presented by the Secretary-General of the Government in no way constitute a memorandum in defence. Most often, they remain limited to replying to questions asked by the member of the Conseil constitutionnel designated as reporter during a working meeting held at the Conseil constitutionnel.

The reporter remains master of the procedure. He may consult or listen to whomsoever he likes, and take note of whatever he wishes. It is up to him how much of what he learns in this way is reported to his colleagues when the Conseil meets. The reporter may often consult the reporters of the parliamentary committees which examined the bill. On 3 June 1986, Badinter suggested that this might be formalized and that the reporters might officially be consulted. This proposal was rejected by the Presidents of both chambers on the ground that the committee reporters had no standing to speak on behalf of the whole chamber. All the same, the practice is of some importance.[7] The authors of the reference and the Secretary-General of the Government may well be called to meetings with the reporter, so that he can clarify issues. In addition, others

5 J Boudéant, op cit, at p 615, nn 107 and 108; L Favoreu, RDP 1989, at p 411.
6 R Denoix de St.Marc, *Conseil constitutionnel et Conseil d'Etat* (Paris 1988), p 108.
7 See L Favoreu, *Nationalisations et Constitution* (Aix 1982), 29; Boudéant, op cit, 618.

may be invited to attend, or may seek an audience. Pressure groups may telephone the reporter at home or invite him out to lunch. For example, in the case of nationalisations, some of the directors of the affected companies were seen by the reporter. Interested persons may write letters to the reporter, and he makes such use of them as he considers fit. Rather like an administrator composing a report, the reporter in the Conseil follows up all interesting leads until he considers he has seen all sides of the question.

Reporters work in different ways, some very much on their own, others discussing matters with the legal service, and others discussing with colleagues. Since not all of them are based in Paris, this last may be difficult to arrange much before the decision-making meetings. The President of the Conseil may play an important part. He may keep in contact with a reporter to see how things are going, and may arrange meetings of a few members from time to time. Presidents too have their styles. One President preferred to have lunch with the reporter or with other members of the Conseil from time to time. Other Presidents have left reporters very much on their own. Although not acting as reporter himself, the President may well secure a good sense of how the draft judgment is going to look and may seek to influence its content. But the President is not typically a dominant figure among so many authoritative figures. One former member of the Conseil wrote:

> In truth, important though the role of its President is in the functioning of the Conseil constitutionnel, this is only through the climate which he creates between its members, by the tone which he contributes to deliberations, and by the way in which he conducts these. This role includes no interference with the judgment of each of the Conseil's members. It would be altogether wrong to contrast the Gaston Palewski case-law or the Roger Frey case-law to the case-law of Leon Noel: there is only a case-law of the Conseil constitutionnel whose development is explained essentially by the widening of the grounds on which references are made.[8]

The reporter produces a draft judgment which is circulated to all members of the Conseil at least the day before the decision. These other members may receive a general file from the Secretary-General setting out the legal texts, the parliamentary debates, and other matters which the reporter considers would be useful.

Only members of the Conseil attend the deliberation to reach a decision and no minutes are kept. The report and draft decision are discussed and votes, if necessary, are taken. No time-limit is set on discussion, and some cases take more than one day (hence they have two dates in their official reference). It is not generally known how people vote. It is known that the Conseil split 6:4 on the referendum law decision, and that it split 4:4 in the *Séguin Amendment* decision.[9] In general, it is reliably said that unanimous decisions are common, and that members do not necessarily vote in the way their party allegiance might expect them to do.

(c) Declassifying lois

When the government wishes to legislate by way of decree, using its powers under art 37, it may need to ask the Conseil to declassify a provision contained in a loi enacted

8 F Goguel, RDP 1979, 5 at p 24. N Lenoir, 'Le métier de juge constitutionnel' *Débat* No 114 (2001), 178.
9 Below, p 231.

after 1958 (it does not have to follow the declassification procedure for earlier lois). The procedure is entirely ex parte in that nobody other than the government and the Conseil are involved. The government will submit a list of texts which it wishes to amend or repeal by decree, together with drafts of what provisions it proposes to enact. This last part of the procedure is not necessary, but it helps the government to obtain a useful ruling from the Conseil, in that the latter will try to frame its decision in such a way as to provide guidance to the government in relation to what it has specifically in mind. This process has many similarities with that of obtaining advice from the Conseil d'Etat. Although there are no formal hearings of government representatives, there may well be informal contacts. The substantive issue is for the Conseil constitutionnel to mark out the boundaries of the legislative powers of the government. It is not clear that it requires to have this clearance before it acts, but the activity of the Conseil fits well with the advisory role of the Conseil d'Etat. If there should be any debate, it ought to be with the Parliament, but the Conseil constitutionnel effectively acts as a buffer here. At best, it has been able to interpret the Constitution so that it has become permissible for Parliament to legislate on topics which fall within the competence of the government, provided that the government does not object.[10]

(d) Treaties

A treaty does not have the force of law in France until ratified. Article 54 of the Constitution provides that the President of the Republic, the Prime Minister or 60 senators or deputies may refer a treaty to the Conseil before it is ratified. The Conseil then has to rule whether the treaty is compatible with the Constitution or whether it can only be ratified after a constitutional amendment. The President has invoked the power several times, particularly in relation to treaties enlarging the powers of the European Community (now Union). The Gaullist dissatisfaction with the loss of sovereignty under the Treaty of Rome in 1957 was the reason for this provision in the first place. As has already been noted, this process has had important political consequences, especially in the case of the Maastricht Treaty.

The procedure is often closer to that on the declassification of lois than that of enacted lois. The President can refer the treaty before any bill for ratification has been laid before Parliament. This happened, for example, in the first *Maastricht* decision.[11] The President may simply refer the whole text and not specify any provisions about which he is particularly anxious to obtain a ruling. On the other hand, a reference may be made once the ratification loi has been voted by Parliament. In the second case, the procedure is very much the same as for any other loi passed by Parliament.

The nature of the decision in treaty cases is to determine the rules of engagement in the political game. Where a treaty is declared compatible, for example the signature to the additional protocol of the European Convention outlawing the death penalty in 1985, the President can proceed to have a loi of ratification presented to Parliament. In that case, the process could be completed before the Socialists lost their large majority

10 See CC decision No 83-143 DC of 30 July 1982, *Freeze on Prices and Salaries*, Rec 57, discussed above, p 206; also C Cans, 'La délégalisation: un encouragement au désordre' RDP 1999, 1419.

11 Above, p 200.

in the National Assembly. On the other hand, where it is not compatible, then the very different process of constitutional revision has to take place, and this will usually require some support from the Opposition in order to establish the requisite majority in the Congress.[12] In some cases, such a procedure is not politically possible. For example, the Charter on the recognition of minority languages was held incompatible with the Constitution's requirement that French was the language of the Republic, but it was not possible to obtain a constitutional amendment to permit the ratification of this treaty.[13]

(e) *Parliamentary standing orders*

Any change to the standing orders of the National Assembly or of the Senate must be referred to the Conseil. The text is presented by the President of the relevant chamber. The text will not be specifically justified or criticised. However, the Conseil will have available the parliamentary debates and can see the sorts of issue which have been made. There may also be observations from the government which is concerned to protect its prerogatives. The Parliament has always wished to protect its freedom of action and has resented this subordination since the Fifth Republic was created. For example, the initial standing orders of the National Assembly and the Senate were submitted to the Conseil in 1959.[14] Both had provisions struck down as incompatible with the role of the government in the new constitution. Whereas the National Assembly submitted revised proposals immediately, the Senate refused to submit revised standing orders for over a year to mark its profound disagreement with the Conseil. Since the Conseil is intervening in the self-government of Parliament and its ability to control and block the government, the exercise is fraught with difficulty. Because the Conseil is here a kind of arbiter, its procedure is rather remote from the actors.

(3) Consequences

The Conseil constitutionnel's process produces a rather limited equivalent to a debate in court. First, although the reference has been published since 1983 and the eventual reply of the government since 1994, there is not the kind of public discussion before a court of the arguments for and against a particular solution, such as exists in other countries and in other areas of French law such as criminal law. The lack of a public forum of debate reduces the direct impact of the Conseil. The parties to this process are predominantly the members of Parliament and the government. Second, and as a result, everything hinges on a decision which is directed back to these same people. The role of the Conseil is predominantly locked into the political process. The Conseil can thus be said to operate in three dimensions: the dimension of contemporary political reality, the dimension of contemporary media impact and the dimension of future

12 See Rousseau, p 161.

13 See CC decision No 99-412 DC of 15 June 1999, Rec 71 which was in line with its decisions of 94-345 DC 29 July 1994, *loi Toubon*, Rec 106 and 91-290 DC of 9 May 1991 *Corsica*, Rec 50.

14 See CC decisions Nos 1 DC of 14 May 1959 and 2 DC of 17, 18 and 24 June 1959, Rec 57 and 58.

judicial practice. Because questions are asked of the Conseil abstractly, in real political time, rather than at some distance in time from the political decision being taken, the Conseil is necessarily an integral part of the political process. The question is asked to receive an answer which has political consequences and the Conseil is well aware of this, especially as many of its members have been politicians. That means that the Conseil is not just engaging with the legislature in general, but in the divisions between and within political parties. As such, we have a process where the Conseil has to relate its arguments specifically to the questions which interest a range of contemporary politicians and mark out its position in relation to them. The Conseil is helped in this regard by the fact that it does not have to confine itself to the issues raised by the reference. In this way, it can operate as an independent verifier of constitutionality and distance itself from the partisan concerns of those who make the reference, but, despite this, its decisions will be put to immediate political use.

Formally, art 62 of the Constitution states that a provision which the Conseil has declared unconstitutional cannot be promulgated or implemented. That aspect of the decision effectively binds the President on lois and treaties, the government on proposed règlements, or the Parliament in respect of proposed bills, amendments or standing orders. More widely, the same article states that its decisions 'are binding ... on all administrative and judicial authorities'. It is necessary to examine the informal and formal impact of the decisions of the Conseil.

(a) Interpretation with reservations

The Conseil can make one of three decisions. It can declare that a provision does not conform to the Constitution and thus annul it. By contrast, it can declare the provision to be compatible. But third, it can declare the provision to be compatible, though only if interpreted in a particular way. This was made clear by the layout of one of the Conseil's earliest decisions.[15] Increasingly, a decision will typically contain 'reservations of interpretation' which are directed to the courts, as well as to politicians. These are read assiduously by the courts and commentators.

In his detailed study of this topic, Alexandre Viala notes that in the forty years from 1959 to the end of 1998, some 126 decisions of the Conseil constitutionnel had contained reservations of interpretation.[16] For ordinary lois, reservations are included in about 30% of decisions. Indeed, in some years they have been included in well over half the decisions on lois referred to the Conseil, particularly years with a change of government.[17] The technique is similar to that of the Conseil d'Etat which upholds the validity of an administrative rule or decision while 'extracting its venom'.[18] The Conseil

15 See CC decision No 59-2 DC of 17, 18 and 24 June 1959, *Standing Orders of the National Assembly*, Rec. 58; Bell, *French Constitutional Law*, Decision 13.

16 *Les réserves d'interprétation dans la jurisprudence du Conseil constitutionnel* (Paris 1999), p 8, and see also pp 51 and 162-163.

17 See Viala, p 51 noting that the level of reservations was low before 1981 (10% of decisions), but reached 50% in 1987 and 1996 and even 66% in 1998.

18 On the retrait du vénin, see for example CE 4 January 1957, *Syndicat autonome du personnel enseignant des Facultés de droit*, RDP 1957, 673 note Waline: a ban on the holding of international conferences without the permission of the Minister was upheld provided it was interpreted as applying only to conferences requiring financial support from the administration.

uses this technique to reduce the number of times it would have to annul provisions in legislation. By giving a more specific (and often restrictive) scope to a provision, the Conseil is able to make it compatible with the Constitution. Such reservations can be illustrated from the important decision *Security and Liberty* of 1981.[19] In that case a provision made it an offence, *inter alia*, to use any means to hinder or obstruct the passage of vehicles on the highway. It was objected that this might interfere with picketing or demonstrations connected with the right to strike. The Conseil simply stated that 'there is no possibility that the application of these provisions might, in whatever way, prevent or interfere with the lawful exercise of the right to strike or union action'. It thereby offered an *interpretation* of the text that was consistent with the Constitution. Such interpretations may be accompanied by addressing *injunctions* to the administration about how the law should be applied. Thus in relation to identity checks, the Conseil remarked that:

> ... with a view to preventing abuses, the Legislature has surrounded the procedure for controlling and checking identity which it has created with numerous precautions; as it is up to the judicial and administrative authorities to ensure they are fully respected as well as for the competent courts to punish, where necessary, illegalities which are committed and to provide compensation for their harmful consequences.

This was a strong encouragement to the courts, who are normally reluctant to provide damages for illegal acts by the police. In the case of this decision, the interpretations offered by the Conseil were subsequently incorporated in a ministerial circular.

Viala argues that this technique offers a third way in making decisions by offering interpretations for the courts and directives to the administration, the Conseil is able to control the future application of a loi, even though there is no mechanism for referring issues to it after the loi has been signed by the President. In other countries, such as Germany, which permit the ordinary courts to request a ruling from the Constitutional Court in concrete cases, there is no need for that Court to go to such lengths to control the future application of the law referred to it in abstract, pre-enactment proceedings. The Conseil starts from a presumption that the legislator intends to act constitutionally,[20] and then it tries to ensure this is the case. Whereas the legislator focuses on achieving the specific objectives of the loi which is being passed, the Conseil constitutionnel, like the Conseil d'Etat, seeks to ensure that the law as a whole is coherent, and may therefore offer interpretations which fit the new legislation into the existing law in a way which is constitutionally acceptable.[1]

In drafting its reservations, the Conseil frequently draws on the parliamentary debates and the observations of the government submitted to it in the case. In doing this, it is making explicit what those applying the law might otherwise have to research. For example, in a 1997 decision on immigration,[2] a provision of the loi empowered the police to retain the passports of foreigners illegally resident in France, which the

19 CC decision No 80-127 DC of 19 and 20 January 1981, Decision 17. On the interpretative techniques, see GD pp 460-462 and 620-622.

20 See Y Aguila, 'Cinq questions sur l'interprétation constitutionnelle' (1995) Rfdc No 21, 9 at pp 22-23.

1 Ibid, pp 31-33; Viala, p 247.

2 CC decision No 97-389 DC of 22 April 1997, *Immigration Law*, Rec. 45; Viala, p 204.

Opposition claimed breached the freedom of movement. In its observations, the government claimed that the sole purpose of the provision was to ensure that the foreigner would be in possession of a passport when he decided to leave France. The government explanation was incorporated more or less verbatim in the Conseil's decision in order to demonstrate that it did not violate the right of free movement. The reservations are thus part of a dialogue, if not a form of bargaining, between the legislature and the Conseil. They are certainly part of the legislative process taken in its widest sense, since in their submissions, the members of Parliament may propose reservations of interpretation which they hope the Conseil will adopt.[3]

(b) Relations with the media

In the second dimension, the Conseil's decision is the subject of media interest, if only because of its political implications. The text will be the subject of informed commentary and the lines of the Conseil's judgment will be picked over. There will often be informed articles in the quality press on particularly sensitive decisions. For that reason, the Conseil has to look both in its drafting of the decision and in its wider dissemination to ensure that the right impact is made.

There are some instances where the judgment has been written with one eye to its dissemination. Certainly the length of the decisions, compared with those of the Conseil d'Etat and Cour de cassation, is long and attempts to explain the reasoning for the solution adopted. They do contain the kinds of aside which would not traditionally be seen in the higher courts (but which might be seen in the Cour d'appel). Unlike the ordinary courts where there will be a public hearing at which parties and the avocat général will make public statements from which the kinds of argument raised in the case can be determined, the Conseil will only ever publish the contentions of the parties. There is not even a half insight (such as through published conclusions or a rapport) into the debates and reasoning within the court. There are no public hearings such as would be held by a political inquiry and from which explanations for a final report could be worked out. As a result, the text of the judgment is the sole point of reference to understand the Conseil's decision. Now that the reference is published and the observations of the government, it is possible to see that the Conseil typically replies to each of the arguments raised by the parties. From the combination of these public documents, it is possible to gain a good understanding of the solution which the Conseil is proposing and its reasoning.

On the basis of this fuller argument, there is something on which the media can latch. In more recent years, the Conseil has tried to remedy this by producing its own press release which tries to meet some of the more obvious criticisms that might be made of decisions.[4] In addition, the Secretary-General does brief journalists, particularly from the quality press, and thus is able to give them a better understanding of what is happening. The formal and increasingly informal dialogue with the media is a recognition to which the Conseil has come that it cannot shelter behind the kind of respect for the judiciary which applies to the ordinary courts.

3 See Viala, p 31.

4 See the reference to the press release in the *Regional Council Elections* case, below, p 227.

(c) Application by the ordinary courts[5]

The third dimension is application by the ordinary courts. If the purpose of this kind of constitutional review is to obtain early and authoritative rulings on all aspects of a *loi*, then it is important that the courts adhere to its decisions. But French courts do not have a formal doctrine of *stare decisis* and were initially reluctant to treat as authoritative rulings on abstract points of law coming from what is, formally at least, a non-judicial body, though attitudes have changed in more recent years.

As we have seen, French courts cannot formally make rules for the future and the authority of the decision is thus confined to the case itself. Unlike the ordinary courts, however, the Conseil is not solving particular disputes between parties, but it is ruling in abstract on the validity of a loi that will affect a variety of future cases. Since there can be no further references after the loi is signed, the Conseil recognises its responsibility for giving guidance and creating constitutional doctrine in a field less well-developed than private, criminal or administrative law. In its decisions, the Conseil has tried, therefore, to set out general principles of constitutional law, rather than simply specific rulings related only to the particular loi under discussion. In this way general guidance can be offered to the government, the Parliament and the courts.

The Conseil takes a wide view of the binding force of its own decisions. In *Agricultural Orientation Law* of 1962,[6] it stated:

> … the authority of the decisions [of the Conseil constitutionnel] mentioned by [article 62 of the Constitution] attaches not only to their result [*dispositif*], but also to the reasons which are its necessary support and constitute its very foundation.

In that case, the Conseil had already ruled in two decisions of 1961[7] that the fixing of agricultural prices fell within the legislative competence of the government under art 37. When asked the same question in relation to a different loi in 1962, the Conseil merely replied that it did not require an answer since the Conseil had already ruled on that matter.

The scope of such binding authority extends to any provision having the same effect as one on which the Conseil has already ruled. Thus in the case of the *Amnesty Law of 1989*,[8] a provision was introduced to amnesty and made eligible for reinstatement those who had been guilty of serious fault during industrial disputes. A provision to this effect had already been struck down in the case of the *Amnesty Law of 1988* because it would impose an excessive burden on the victims of the fault.[9] Although the Legislature had tried to modify the 1988 provision by making an exception where an excessive burden would thereby be placed on the employer, the Conseil did not consider this cured the problem, particularly in relation to the burdens which reinstatement would place on the fellow employees. Relying on its previous decision, the Conseil struck down the new provision as 'violating the authority which attaches, by virtue of article 62 of the Constitution, to the decision of the Conseil constitutionnel of 20 July 1988'.

5 Stone Sweet, pp 122-124.
6 CC decision No 62-18 L of 16 January 1962, Rec 31.
7 CC decisions No 61-3 FNR of 8 September 1961 and 61-4 FNR of 18 October 1961.
8 CC decision No 89-258 DC of 8 July 1989, Rec 48; Bell, *French Constitutional Law*, Decision 4.
9 CC decision No 88-244 DC of 20 July 1988, Rec 119; Bell, *French Constitutional Law*, Decision 3b.

After some initial difficulties, the ordinary courts have applied the rulings of the Conseil including in relation to the interpretations it has offered. The Conseil d'Etat has not had to clash with its neighbour. In a decision of 1985,[10] it overruled its own case law on the classification of pollution levies in the light of a ruling by the Conseil constitutionnel in 1982. Furthermore, in 1994 it struck down sanctions imposed by the Conseil Supérieur de l'Audiovisuel because they had not been preceded by a warning as required by a reservation of interpretation expressed by the Conseil constitutionnel when approving the loi which created that administrative body.[11] In that case, the decision of the Conseil constitutionnel is specifically cited in the judgment, which is very unusual in the drafting of Conseil d'Etat decisions.

In more recent years, the Cour de cassation has behaved similarly. Thus, for example, in 1995 and 1996, in cases concerning identity checks by the police, the Cour applied the reservations of interpretation expressed by the Conseil in 1993 when approving the loi authorising such checks.[12]

Consistently with the attitude of all French judges to superior courts, there have been instances where the ordinary courts have rejected the solutions offered by the Conseil constitutionnel. Most famously, in the area of criminal penalties, the Conseil argued that règlement could determine *contraventions* and the penalties applicable to them provided that these did not include measures depriving someone of their liberty.[13] The Cour de cassation disagreed, since one whole class of *contravention* did carry a sentence of imprisonment. The Procureur Général Touffait argued that the proviso relating to measures for the deprivation of liberty did not bind the criminal courts because 'the Conseil constitutionnel has stressed its reasoning by inserting a general principle which in the case was incidental, not to say superfluous'.[14] In this he was followed by the Cour de cassation, and the Conseil constitutionnel eventually overturned its earlier decision.[15] The necessary reasons were only those very directly concerned with disposing of the case before the Conseil, viz. the classification of those provisions submitted to it, and Touffait was followed by the Cour de Cassation in thinking that the proviso did not fall within that narrow category. Equally, the ordinary court may subject the decision of the Conseil to restrictive interpretation. For example, in a decision of 1977, the Conseil constitutionnel held unconstitutional a loi which intended to confer on the police a new unlimited power to search vehicles on the highway even where no crime had been committed and there was no threat to public order on the ground that the imprecise nature of the grounds of intervention by the police threatened individual liberty. The Chambre criminelle of the Cour de cassation held in 1979 that the police had powers to search vehicles belonging to any person under the existing general provisions relating the investigation of 'flagrant offences'.[16]

10 CE Ass, 20 December 1985, *Sté des Etablissements Outters*, RFDA 1986, 513, concl Martin.

11 CE Ass, 11 March 1994, RFDA 1994, 429 concl Frydman.

12 Cass 2 civ, 28 June 1995, *Bechta* D 1996 Somm 102; also Cass crim, 10 October 1996, *Procureur général, CA Toulouse* c *X*, D 1997 Somm 145. See generally GD pp 177-183.

13 CC decision No 73-80 L of 23 November 1973, *Criminal Penalties (Rural Code)*, Rec 45; Bell, *French Constitutional Law*, Decision 10.

14 Conclusions to Cass crim. 26 February 1974, Schiavon, D 1974, 273.

15 CC decision No 87-161 L of 23 September 1987, *Post Office Code*, AJDA 1988, 62; Bell, *French Constitutional Law*, pp 99-102.

16 Crim 8 November 1979, Triganol, D 1980 Chr 102; cf CC decision No 76-75 DC of 12 January 1977, *Vehicle Searches*, Rec 33; Bell, *French Constitutional Law*, Decision 17.

While formally consistent, the latter decision did much to undermine the effect of the decision of the Conseil constitutionnel.

(4) Who influences the Conseil?

In other branches of law, it is possible to discuss the various influences on the lawmaking process – in this case, the process of constitutional interpretation. In other chapters, there has been a discussion of doctrinal writing and the development of ideas by the corps of judges. But in constitutional law, a search for evidence of such sources is more difficult. The procedure described enables us to see the mechanisms by which some of the influence may be exercised. As Stone points out, the process does not lend itself to social science enquiry and French academic writers have not been interested in it.[17]

(a) Members of the Conseil

My own contention would be that members of the Conseil are sufficiently strong personalities that they dominate the shaping of constitutional law. They have reputations and ideas, they are deciding in relative secrecy, and they have little future ambition which depends on the need to please other people. In this way, they are free agents who can't be removed whatever they decide, and yet they are also people with commitments. The sources of information on the way the Conseil has worked are sparse. Much is publicly known about a few individuals, and interviews have been able to give a little more insight into the generality of operations.

It is probably necessary to distinguish the majority of members who have firm views about specific results which they wish to see achieved, and the minority of lawyers who are interested both in the formulation and in developing a body of case law (*jurisprudence*). Among the latter, one might include, for instance, Luchaire and Vedel on issues of public law, Segalat on finance laws, Badinter and Robert on human rights. Others might rely more on the support of the secretariat to provide the consistent legal formulations for the results which they consider appropriate.

With professors such as Vedel, it is possible to compare his published writings, both as an academic and a chair of public committees, and the decisions reached by the Conseil when he was the rapporteur. The most obvious of the coincidences is the area of press ownership, discussed below, p 232. Here Vedel had been chair of a committee set up to review the regulation of the press in 1979, and he was rapporteur in relation to two lois on the subject. In the first in 1984, the Conseil entrenched certain principles which Vedel had earlier proposed as objectives of constitutional value. In the second case in 1986, the Conseil stood in the way of too great a departure from those principles. Indeed, Vedel's views on pluralism and transparency in the media were developed into a series of decisions during his tenure.[18] Other areas in which he had a marked influence were the right to property in the fields of

17 Stone, *Birth of Judicial Politics*, p 116.
18 See Bell, *French Constitutional Law*, pp 166-176.

nationalisation and privatisation, and the constitutional status of the distinction between public law and private law[19] Indeed, Rousseau talks of the 'Vedel legacy',[20] but the same could be true of a number of other members who have been consistent reporters on particular issues.

Dominique Rousseau has made a long study of the influence of Badinter as president of the Conseil in developing a case law on the protection of fundamental rights of the human being.[1] He also notes the coincidence of views on the interpretation given to the right to property in the consultation given to the government by Professor Robert in 1981 and that in the 1989 *TGV Nord* decision[2] by the Conseil constitutionnel of which Robert had recently become a member.[3]

As has been noted, there is sufficient evidence that members of the Conseil do not necessarily divide on votes according to their political allegiance. They have little to gain in terms of future career or external recognition by pleasing political authorities or colleagues. Once they are in the Conseil, with no political future ahead of them, they can act as free agents. In any case, the dynamics of collective decision-making free from public gaze may produce different pressures from decisions in a politicised forum. The dynamics of respect between members of the Conseil will have an important influence on their behaviour. If individuals have personal authority in different ways, this is going to be respected by other leading figures of the establishment, and they will be willing to listen and change their views.

(b) The government

The government is the most regular interlocutor of the Conseil. It will be involved in most decisions especially where the exercise of legislative power is concerned. The channel for this work will be the Secretary-General of the Government. As has been said,[4] the Secretary-General is a member of the Conseil d'Etat and is effectively the head of the government legal service. The Secretary-General will be the point of contact, both formally and informally, with the Conseil. Thus the reporter in the Conseil may contact him, particularly in relation to declassification cases. On the other hand, the Secretary-General of the Government may have an informal conversation with the Secretary-General of the Conseil to discuss possible constitutional questions arising with legislation under discussion and sound him out about his views on the constitutionality of various possible courses of action.[5] This informal contact (typically when both are members of the Conseil d'Etat) helps to establish a degree of mutual understanding between the institutions.

19 Ibid, pp 69 and 176-182. See CC decision No 86-224 DC of 23 January 1987, *Competition Law*, Rec 8: cf G Vedel in preface to the 7th edition of Vedel and Delvolvé, *Droit administratif*, reprinted in 8th edition 1984, pp 26-27.

20 D Rousseau, *Sur le Conseil constitutionnel*, pp 38ff.

1 Ibid, pp 103-134.

2 CC decision No 89-256 DC of 25 July 1989, Rec 53; Bell, *French Constitutional Law*, Decision 31.

3 *Sur le Conseil constitutionnel*, p 169.

4 Above, pp 206-207.

5 Jan, p 484.

(c) *Parliamentarians*

The impact of constitutional law on Parliament can be seen in three main ways. In the first place, the Constitution defines what Parliament can do. The principal objective of the 1958 Constitution was to 'rationalise' the activity of Parliament. Parliamentary competence in legislation and parliamentary procedure were to be subject to control. To that extent, parliamentarians first experienced the Conseil as an interference in their activity, especially in relation to the standing orders of each house.[6] Both were subject to extensive censure from the Conseil as it imposed the spirit of the new constitution on those who had been used to a more parliamentary system in the Fourth Republic. The Senate took umbrage and refused to produce a revised draft for several months. The reaction to decisions such as the *Séguin Amendment* reflect this resentment of being an institution under external control. But, in the second place, the existence of a Council engaged in constitutional review provides an additional weapon for the Opposition. It becomes a way of disrupting the legislative programme of the political majority. Thirdly, as the media case itself shows, the parliamentary process has to include not only concern about policy objectives, but also it has to second-guess the likely attitude of the Conseil to the provisions which members of Parliament wish to include. Stone goes so far as to suggest that the Conseil recasts the policy-making environment, encouraging certain legislative solutions and blocking off others, and even encouraging its solutions to be included in the text of future legislation.[7]

Parliamentarians are thus operators of constitutional law both as they formulate rules of their own procedure and as they seek to interpret the constitutional rules which govern their lawmaking activity. In these senses, interpreting constitutional law is an important parliamentary activity.

While a significant number of members of the Parliament may be able to develop the broad ideas which shape a reference and will contribute to discussion in their party meetings, a much smaller number will be sufficiently versed in the Constitution to formulate a reference to the Conseil or an irrecevabilité motion. These will be supported by the secretariat of the party and by the judges, lawyers and academics who are able to draw up a technically sound submission.

(d) *Doctrinal writing*

Doctrinal writers carry different authority and can influence in different ways. As has been seen, the writing of the reference can often be contracted out to a law professor who may introduce ideas into the text which he hopes will influence the Conseil. The Conseil also may draw directly upon law professors as advisers. Thus Mayer as president had Gicquel as an adviser, and Badinter had Luchaire, a former member of the Conseil and, like Badinter, professor at Paris 1, as well as Duhamel. The informal and confidential dialogue would, one surmises, provide ample opportunity for a strong influence of a well-briefed doctrinal writer. In a similar, and possibly even more powerful way, the Secretary-General of the Conseil will provide legal support and can suggest legal solutions and ways of making decisions of the Conseil more coherent. By assisting with drafting,

6 See above, p 216.
7 Stone, p 203.

the Secretary-General can help in the formulation of the development of the Conseil's case law, even if he cannot, in principle, influence the specific outcome to the decision. Recent Secretary-Generals have also written frequent commentaries in law reviews.

Stone carefully documents the roles played by doctrinal legal writers during the parliamentary debates on the Nationalisations legislation of 1981. The government had sought the opinion of leading constitutional law professors, François Luchaire, a former member of the Conseil, and Jacques Robert, before their bill went to the Conseil d'Etat for its opinion. The Opposition in the National Assembly commissioned three further law professors, Loussarn, Drago and Delvolvé, to produce a memorandum which formed the basis of a motion of irrecevabilité.[8] This case is merely an illustration of the fact that law professors have been used extensively to write references made to the Conseil.[9] The small number of professors in this subject have effectively become a kind of alternative bar. It should be noted that writing on the Conseil on a regular basis has come late, with a regular section of the Revue de Droit Public only appearing in 1985 and a dedicated journal, *La Revue française de droit constitutionnel* appearing only in 1986. In a sense, the work of the Conseil has not simply drawn on the expertise of professors, it has generated writing and scholarly activity which has enhanced the size and importance of this sector of public law.

Furthermore, the absence of established case law in the early period made the writings of doctrinal writers particularly important as a source of inspiration for constitutional arguments. Stone notes how doctrinal writing created the climate for the decision by the Conseil in the *Associations Law* case to recognise the right of association as constitutional and to engage in judicial review of legislation.[10] But the relevant writings are not just in academic works but, importantly, include writings in the quality press. Writers such as Luchaire, Favoreu, Maus, Vedel, Avril, Duhamel, Gicquel, and others frequently write articles in the press commenting on constitutional issues, especially activities of the Conseil. Such writing has an important impact on public opinion, and it indirectly disseminates more scholarly output. The importance of doctrinal writing as a source of arguments is obviously strong where the constitutional writer was himself a member of the Conseil. Thus in the Nationalisations case, the opinions produced for the Opposition drew heavily on the writings of Vedel, who was a member of the Conseil.[11] All the same, Jan notes that the citation of doctrinal writing in references is usually limited,[12] and the citation of Vedel may have been more tactical, rather than illustrating that doctrinal writing is a major source of constitutional argument.

C. DECISIONS OF THE CONSEIL CONSTITUTIONNEL AND THE POLITICAL WORLD

It is clear from what has been said that the Conseil constitutionnel interacts formally and informally with political actors. The very process of abstract constitutional review brings it into the heart of live political issues. As Stone notes, whereas abstract review is a very

8 Stone, pp 145-148, and 153-154.
9 Ibid, p 130.
10 Ibid, p 70.
11 Stone, p 164.
12 Jan, p 483.

minor part of the case-load of most constitutional courts, it represents the bulk of the activity of the French Conseil constitutionnel.[13] This intervention in the political process effectively enables the Conseil to shape political debate. The illustrations given in this section show how the Conseil can be involved in both substantive and procedural constitutional law and political debate. These cases, taken from more recent times when the Conseil has become well established, demonstrate the kind of political debate that its decisions can engender. But the suggestion will be that, whereas the Conseil is able to shape the procedures by which decisions are reached, it is not ultimately able to control the substantive agenda. Of course, procedural obstacles can make the achievement of substantive ends more difficult, but where there is sufficient political will, then the political will to achieve substantive objectives will prevail.

(1) Quotas for women candidates[14]

The idea of ensuring greater representation of women in elected posts has been an issue that has led to a clash between conventional liberal conceptions of equality as formal equal treatment and ideas of equality of outcome. The role of the Conseil has been to force a constitutional amendment that departs from the traditional formal concept of equality set out in 1789.

The slogan of the 1789 Revolution was 'careers are to be open to talents', not to birth or privilege. Accordingly, art 6 DDHC provides that, 'all citizens, being equal [in the eyes of the law], are equally eligible for all dignities, places and public employment, according to their abilities and without any distinction other than that of their virtues and talents'. This is not a simple equality provision, but rather sets out positively the relevant criteria for selection to public office, a pure meritocracy. Other reasons are excluded so that appeal to equality is a way of focusing attention on relevant, constitutionally entrenched reasons for selection.

There is an abundant case law of the Conseil d'Etat applying this principle to entry to the civil service. Although not formally invoked by the Conseil d'Etat itself until the *Barel* decision of 1954, it had been used in arguments by commissaires du gouvernment since 1912.[15] This enabled some advances to be made in securing equal treatment for women in public employment, even before the 1946 Preamble was adopted.[16]

In this light, it comes as no surprise that policies of reverse discrimination have not been allowed. For instance, a parliamentary amendment proposed to modify the election rules for local authorities, requiring that lists of candidates contain no more than 75% of persons of the same sex, thus ensuring a minimum of 25% of women on all lists. In its decision on *Feminine Quotas*[17] the Conseil raised an objection *ex officio* to this provision. Basing itself on art 3 of the 1958 Constitution and art 6 DDHC, it stated in paragraph 6 that:

13 Stone, p 232.

14 Stone Sweet, pp 105-106; N Lenoir, 'The Representation of Women in Politics: From Quotas to Parity in Elections' (2001) 50 ICLQ 217.

15 CE Ass, 28 May 1954, RDP 1954, 505; CE 10 May 1912, *Bouteyre*, D 1914, 3.74, concl Heilbronner.

16 See CE 3 July 1936, *Dlle Bobard*, D 1937.3.38, concl Latournerie.

17 CC decision No 82-146 DC of 18 November 1982, Rec 66; Bell, *French Constitutional Law*, Decision 34 and pp 210 and 349.

> ... from a comparison of these texts it follows that the status of citizen itself gives rise to the right to vote and to be eligible for election on identical terms to all who are not excluded by reason of age, incapacity or nationality, or for any reason designed to preserve the freedom of the voter or of the person elected ...

It is interesting to note that one of the members of the Conseil, Vedel, had written in 1979, before he was appointed, that 'a text which reserved a certain number of places for women ... without doing the same for men ... would be contrary to the principle of equality'.[18] Although the text in 1982 was less obviously unequal, the philosophy of the Conseil seems close to that of Vedel. Substantive arguments in favour of reverse discrimination did not justify inequality. Equality of chances within the law is not favoured, but rather formal equality. It is not without interest that the provision annulled was one which the government did not propose and did not defend with any force in its observations to the Conseil.

Rebuffed in this way, the issue of improving women's representation did not go away, and was particularly strong among Socialist deputies elected in 1997. For the government, the 1982 decision represented an orthodoxy which could not be avoided, and so a text was proposed to Parliament on 18 June 1998 by the government amending art 3 of the Constitution to state that 'loi shall facilitate the equality between men and women'. That text was still being debated in the National Assembly and had yet to be discussed by the Senate when a bill on the election of regional councillors was being passed by Parliament. An amendment was made to the bill on regional council elections to require that party lists should have equal numbers of men and women. In his speech to the National Assembly, the minister in charge of the elections bill, Chevènement accepted the amendment enthusiastically, but argued that it was necessary to keep an eye on the parliamentary timetable to ensure that the constitutional amendment was passed before the electoral law.[19] In the event, the constitutional amendment took much longer than anticipated and was not finally approved by the Congress until 8 July 1999. Although the proposal had the backing of the President and the Prime Minister, the right wing Opposition in the Senate proved obstructive. Unsurprisingly, the provision on parity between men and women in the loi on regional council elections, which was passed on 22 December 1998, was challenged by opposition senators as unconstitutional. They simply referred to the 1982 decision. In reply, the government merely noted that the provisions were different from those annulled in 1982 , but then lamely stated 'It will be for the Conseil constitutionnel to assess if this initiative runs into the same constitutional obstacles as the provision which was at issue in 1982'. In other words, they indicated that they also thought it was unconstitutional. In its decision, the Conseil cited the 1982 decision in its visas and repeated its wording of 1982.[20] The press notice issued by the Conseil made it clear that the constitutional amendment to remove the obstacle to such reverse discrimination was not yet in place, and so the application of the 1982 decision had been inevitable.[1] There had been no serious expectation that the Conseil would overrule its precedent.

18 Cited in JTS Keeler and A Stone, 'Judicial-Political Confrontation in Mitterrand's France', in G Ross, S Hoffmann and S Malzacher, *The Mitterrand Experiment* (Cambridge 1987), at p 171.
19 Parliamentary debate, 23 June 1998: http://www.assemblee-nationale.fr/2/2dossiers.html.
20 CC decision No 98-407 DC of 14 January 1999, *Regional Elections Law*, Rec 21, § 11.
1 See R Ghevontian, Rfdc 1999, 142 at p 144.

The timing of the events is important. The contested amendment started off in the genuine expectation that it would be constitutionally valid by the time the loi was finally approved by Parliament. In the event, the necessary constitutional reform was stalled in December 1998, and the provision was allowed to go forward, as much to put down a marker on the issue as in a real expectation that it would be upheld by the Conseil. A compromise text of the constitutional amendment had been worked out between the President and the Prime Minister,[2] so the Conseil was able to argue in its decision that 'at present' (en état) the provision was unconstitutional, but this would not rule out a future provision after a constitutional amendment. Both in 1982 and in 1999, by annulling the provision, the Conseil was not going against the wishes of the political establishment, even if certain activists were disappointed. Certainly, in 1999, the Conseil did not appear as critical as one of its former members, Vedel, about the vagueness of the constitutional amendment.[3]

Once the constitutional amendment of 8 July 1999 was in place, a loi could be proposed to facilitate equal access of men and women to elected posts, and the new loi was referred to the Conseil constitutionnel in May 2000.The opposition senators argued that the decisions of 1982 and 1999 remained current in that the travaux préparatoires of the constitutional amendment made it clear that this new text was not normative but set a goal to be achieved, and so it was argued that it did not impose any new constraint. The senators argued that the *loi* imposed quotas. They also argued that it was contrary to a constitutional tradition to change the electoral law within a year of the elections. By contrast, the government cited the travaux préparatoires of the constitutional amendment at some length to show that the new loi was precisely what had been envisaged by the constitutional reform. It was these arguments which the Conseil adopted to reject the senators' arguments.[4] They adopted the argument of the government that it was now the province of the legislature to determine the balance between the various constitutional values at issue.

The case illustrates the way in which the Conseil can act as a brake on political developments by channelling the political debate into one on constitutional amendment, which involves some compromise with the opposition in most cases, rather than through the conventional legislative process.

(2) The right of asylum

The strongest clash between the Conseil and Parliament came in relation to the *loi Pasqua* on immigration of 1993. The right-wing majority elected in March 1993 sought to tighten up immigration, in part to steal the thunder from the Front National which

2 See *Le Monde*, 15 December 1998, p 6.

3 See G Vedel, 'La parité mérite mieux qu'un marivaudage législatif!', *Le Monde*, 8 December 1998, p 16.

4 CC decision No 2000-429 DC of 30 May 2000. The decision did strike down one provision of the loi. This applied the loi to districts with a minimum number of electors below that specified in the rules on corruption and on cumulation of elected mandates. These had been fixed by an organic law passed only a few months earlier and which it was not within the competence of the ordinary legislator to alter. In doing so, the Conseil specifically referred to its arguments in the decision on that organic law (CC decision No 2000-427 DC of 30 March 2000).

was drawing away voters. A substantial revision to immigration law consisting of 51 articles was passed by the majority parties in both the National Assembly and in the Senate. Not only had there been criticism from the left-wing parties, there had also been legal concern about a number of provisions. The Conseil d'Etat took the unusual step of extending its deliberations so long that the minister had to delay the expected date for presenting the bill to the Council of Ministers. Though the deliberation was confidential, it was reported that particular criticism was focused on the provisions concerning family reunion and asylum. In the event, these were the provisions that were the subject of censure from the Conseil constitutionnel.[5] In its longest ever decision, the Conseil set out some basic principles to the effect that the legislator had to respect the freedoms and fundamental rights recognised to all people on French territory, whether they were citizens or not. It then annulled eight articles and approved a further ten only subject to strict reservations of interpretation. Among the provisions struck down were those which affected the reunion of families of refugees and students, and provisions on the detention of suspected illegal immigrants. On asylum, the Conseil reaffirmed the right recognised in the Preamble to the 1946 Constitution that there was a right to asylum for those who were persecuted in the cause of freedom, and it also stressed that asylum seekers had rights to which all on French territory were entitled. A particular problem was caused with the proposed way in which the Schengen Convention was to be implemented. Under that Convention, which the Conseil had already ruled as compatible with the Constitution in 1991,[6] a decision to grant asylum in one signatory state was to be recognised in another. This agreement followed from the Dublin Accord of 1990 obliging member states to deal with asylum applications of those arriving on their territory. The Conseil upheld the provisions of the loi which permitted France to apply the asylum decisions made in another member state to those now requesting asylum on its territory, but 'under the strict reservation' that those who claimed to fall within the provisions of the 1946 preamble were entitled to a provisional entry. But, the loi went further and provided that the Prefect could simply apply the asylum decision, and the Office français de protection des réfugiés et apatrides (OFPRA) could not examine their request. The Conseil held this to be unconstitutional as against the rights of defence.

The decision provoked a storm of protest from the government. The minister responsible for the bill, Pasqua, argued 'The Conseil constitutionnel is not infallible. It is an open secret that in the Conseil constitutionnel there are people who have political commitments, as everyone knows, and that this political commitment, for the majority of them, does not correspond with the majority of today.' Furthermore, he said that 'The Conseil constitutionnel makes pronouncements more and more according to the merits and not in relation to the great republican principles which I respect as much as anyone else'. The clear message was that the Conseil, now with a Socialist majority, was seeking to obstruct the newly elected right-wing government for political reasons. For him the annulling of the provisions on administrative detention of refugees and refusing them the right to refer their case to OFPRA were particularly objectionable. The argument was that the government had been seeking to tighten the law on asylum and to implement the

5 CC decision No 93-325 DC of 13 August 1993, Rec 224. See also *Le Monde*, 27 May 1993, p 9.
6 CC decision No 91-294 DC of 25 July 1991, Rec 91.

Schengen Accord. The Conseil had adopted a position whereby asylum decisions made by other EU member states might have to be re-examined because the person claimed to qualify for asylum not under the Geneva Convention, but under the 1946 Preamble as a fighter for freedom. The will of the people expressed by the resounding defeat of the Socialists in the March 1993 elections was being thwarted.

But the criticism was not all negative. Former member of the Conseil, Vedel, challenged the argument made by Pasqua's advisers that the decision violated the sovereignty of the people. He pointed out that sovereignty was now limited by the Constitution and that the people could re-establish their view of what was constitutional by a constitutional amendment.[7] Although the government favoured this approach, some of its own supporters came to the defence of the Conseil. The President of the Commission des lois (and a future member of the Conseil), Pierre Mazeaud argued that the Conseil had merely repeated its reservations expressed in relation to the Schengen Accord in 1991 and that these were right.[8] Others such as the constitutional expert Maurice Duvergier argued that it was inappropriate to use a constitutional amendment to deal with a problem which could be adequately handled by a loi on appeal procedures for asylum seekers.[9] In the view of the Conseil d'Etat in its opinion to the government of 22 September, such a loi would be permissible, but it would not permit a strict use of the possibility given by the Schengen Accord simply to apply asylum decisions made by other member states, which would require a constitutional amendment.[10]

The government pressed speedily ahead with its proposal for a constitutional amendment to achieve the full power to implement the Schengen Accord. A bill was passed by both houses of the Parliament and was approved by the requisite majority in Congress on 19 November.

The whole saga was interpreted by most commentators as a deliberate attempt by the government to teach the Conseil constitutionnel a lesson and to impose its will at the beginning of its term of office.[11] The President was effectively forced to distance himself from the Conseil and leave it isolated. But, even if this case represents a clash of wills which the government won, it did not really deter the Conseil. For within months, it was annulling another major bill. This time, the loi sought to give local authorities discretion in determining the amount of subsidy to be provided to local private schools. As the Conseil had decided in relation to a Socialist loi in 1985, the failure to provide safeguards to ensure equality of provision in relation to the right to education rendered the loi unlawful.[12]

(3) The right of parliamentary amendment

Clashes between the Conseil and politicians are not confined to interpretations of substantive constitutional law. They occur also in matters such as parliamentary procedure. After all, the Conseil was established to police the boundary between

7 *Le Monde*, 19 August 1993, p 7. See also Loic Philip, *Le Monde*, 11 September 1993, p 14.
8 *Le Monde*, 17 September 1993, p 24.
9 *Le Monde*, 3 September 1993, p 2.
10 See *Le Monde*, 25 September 1993, p 11.
11 See D Rousseau, *Sur le Conseil constitutionnel*, pp 80-90.
12 CC decision No 93-329 DC of 13 January 1994, *Amendments to the loi Falloux*, Rec 9.

governmental and parliamentary competences in legislation. The scope of the right of amendment gave rise to a major clash between the Conseil and the parliamentary majority in January 1987.

The cohabitation between President Mitterand and Prime Minister Chirac was becoming increasingly strained. Having obtained a power in July 1986 to make ordonnances, inter alia, on various social matters, the Government proposed to alter the working day and the restrictions on working hours which then existed for women and others. On 10 December the ordonnance proposed by the Minister of Labour Séguin was agreed by the Council of Ministers, but on 17 December President Mitterand said he was going to refuse to sign it because it went back on 'social heritage' of the previous half century. The Parliamentary session was to end just before Christmas and the next would not start until April. The Government simply tabled the 17 articles of the ordonnance as an amendment to a Miscellaneous Social Provisions Bill then in its final stages in Parliament and used the issue of confidence procedure of art 49-3 to ensure it was passed. The Conseil struck the provisions down as exceeding the power of amendment by their scope and content.[13] There had been an abuse of process. Numerous articles of the Labour Code were amended by the Séguin amendment, and there was a major change by breaking the compulsory link between flexibility and reduction in working hours. Effectively the Conseil was saying that a new bill should have been presented, although everyone realised that this would inevitably delay the whole process.

It was widely rumoured that the Conseil split 4:4 on this issue, and, in the absence through illness of Louis Joxe, the Socialist president of the Conseil, Badinter, had the casting vote (indeed, it is reported that the Conseil chose this, more contentious, ground rather than a more clear-cut breach of procedure in that members of Parliament did not vote in person).[14] The presidents of both chambers objected not simply because they were government supporters, but also because the decision represented an interference by the Conseil constitutionnel in what they perceived to be the internal affairs of Parliament.[15]

The Conseil subsequently reinforced this line of argument that the right of amendment is a corollary of the right to initiate legislation, but it is restricted to provisions which have some connection with the text amended and are not excessively large or broad.[16] Indeed, the Conseil has tightened its control over procedure. In the *Hunting Law* case, it prevented the re-writing of previously agreed clauses by amendments introduced in the joint committee of both houses set up to deal with a conflict between them.[17]

(4) Press ownership

The Liberation ordonnance of 26 August 1944 had insisted essentially on the transparency of press ownership, by securing publicity about the proprietor and major

13 CC decision No 86-225 DC of 23 January 1987, *Séguin Amendment*; Bell, *French Constitutional Law*, Decision 15.

14 See Rousseau, p 151.

15 See *Le Monde*, 25-26 January 1987; F Luchaire and G Conac, *Le droit constitutionnel de la cohabitation* (Paris 1989), p 220.

16 See CC decision No 89-268 DC of 29 December 1989, *Finance Law for 1990*, Rec 110.

17 CC decision No 2000-434 DC of 20 July 2000, applying a change in its interpretation which had been made after the bill had been passed: see CC decision No 2000-430 DC of 29 June 2000.

shareholders. In a report presented to the Economic and Social Council in May 1979, the Vedel commission reviewed the law in the light of press mergers of the 1970s. It argued that mergers might well serve to save titles, but that they should be scrutinised by an independent commission to ensure the protection of pluralism.[18] Adopting these recommendations, the Socialist government passed a loi in 1984 to limit the size of groups owning newspapers, to create an independent Press Commission, and to require further publicity on press ownership.

In its *Press Law* decision of 1984,[19] the Conseil rejected the Opposition argument that requiring publicity of transactions was against the freedom of the press or of commerce. It argued that in requiring publicity, 'the Legislature is enabling the readers to exercise their choice in a truly free way and to form their opinion by an informed judgment on the kinds of information offered by the written press'. Furthermore, with regard to the measures on pluralism (restricting holdings to 15% of the market) in the legislation, it stated:

> Considering that the pluralism of daily newspapers dealing with political and general information ... is in itself an objective of constitutional value; as in fact the free communication of ideas and opinions, guaranteed by article 11 of the Declaration of the Rights of Man and of the Citizen of 1789, would not be effective if the public to which these daily newspapers are addressed were not able to have available a sufficient number of publications of different leanings and characters; as in reality the objective to be realised is that the readers, who figure among the essential addressees of the freedom proclaimed by article 11 of the Declaration of 1789, should be able to exercise free choice without either private interests or public authorities substituting their own decisions ...

The flexible interpretation of the constitutional texts is well exhibited here. First, the 1789 Declaration's right *of publishers to publish* becomes *the right of the audience to receive information*. This is in line with art 10 of the European Convention, but has no place within the ideas of 1789 or 1881. Second, the Conseil introduced the notion of 'an objective of constitutional value', a means for giving effect to an explicit constitutional principle, which enabled it to give constitutional status to a value which post-dated the 1958 Constitution. The force of the newly discovered 'objectives' can be seen from the attempt by the Chirac government to amend the 1984 loi in 1986. The Chirac reform wanted to increase the percentage of the market share that an individual could own to 30% (thereby protecting the RPR's ally and benefactor Hersant who was currently facing prosecution for breach of the 1984 legislation). In its *Press Law* decision of 29 July 1986,[20] the Conseil stated that Parliament could always repeal earlier lois and that it was the judge of the merits of such action. But 'the exercise of this power cannot lead to the removal of legal guarantees of requirements having constitutional value'. It repeated the principle stated in 1984 on pluralism and then noted that the new loi did not just modify the rules, but removed existing legal protections of pluralism in the press, which was a 'principle of constitutional value', and so the new provision on

18 Stone, pp 177-178.

19 CC decision No 84-181 DC of 10 and 11 October 1984, Rec. 73, GD No 36; Stone, ch 7. For Vedel's views see already his *Droit constitutionnel* (Paris 1949), p 328.

20 CC decision No 86-210 DC of 29 July 1986, Rec 110; Bell, *French Constitutional Law*, Decision 26.

pluralism was held unconstitutional. Once an objective has constitutional value, it must be pursued by the legislature, though the means for this task are its own choice, provided that existing protections are not weakened. Clearly this suggests a rather State-centred view of the protection of constitutional values in line with the Vedel proposals, which ran contrary to the deregulation philosophy behind the Chirac reforms.

Naturally, the government denounced this interference with the will of the majority by those who were associated with the past majority. But what we actually see is the influence of the European Convention on Human Rights and Fundamental Freedoms slipping in to shape French constitutional law, and an unwillingness of the Conseil to depart from key features of the Liberation. The circumstances of the 1986 loi did not give the impression of considered law reform in the general interest, but decisions to please a political ally. The Conseil was really requiring some further thought about the more fundamental questions of how rights were to be protected.

(5) General observations

The four illustrations which have been presented are of high profile cases. But it would be difficult to find cases of legislation challenged before the Conseil which is not controversial. The Conseil is necessarily operating in a politically sensitive area at a moment where passions are still live. It is attempting to call attention to fundamental values while politicians appeal to their political mandate as the elected majority. A clash is inevitable in such a context, and censure will obviously be resented. But the lack of clarity of the constitutional principles invoked and the unforeseen extent of the Conseil's intervention can cause more resentment among politicians, with the understandable complaint that those nominated by the past majority are trying to block progress by the new majority.

The decisions in the Feminine Quotas cases were not a surprise to those who knew current thought in constitutional law. The loi second *Press Law* case was clearly trying to work round the constitutional principles which the Conseil had recently laid down. The principle of asylum for freedom fighters had been pointed out by the Conseil d'Etat. In each of these cases, there was only a limited element of surprise in the principles invoked by the Conseil. The problem lay rather with the freedom of manoeuvre left by the Conseil to develop new principles. Although the Conseil asserts frequently that it does not enjoy a freedom of decision equivalent to the legislature, it does sanction the excess use of legislative power or, as in the *Press Law* case, the under-use of legislative power to secure protection for fundamental values.

In the areas of substantive law discussed, it is clear that the decisions of the Conseil can always be overturned by a constitutional amendment. The Feminine Quotas and Asylum issues show this. But the former area demonstrates how difficult that process is, and how long it may take to build up a sufficient majority. The *Press Law* cases show that, in the interim, the legislator may be forced to legislate or leave in place legislation that does not suit his political programme. Constitutions are, deliberately, slow moving. The policy of positive discrimination for women encountered the traditional conception of equality as equal treatment, which had been hard won in the Declaration of 1789. The asylum case turned on a value established in 1946. Departing from those entrenched values was necessarily going to be difficult. On the other hand, the *Press Law* decision of 1984 offers an example of an updating construction of the 1789 declaration, which was a substantial change. Whether such a radical revision will be undertaken by the Conseil depends on the broader environment within which the decision has to be set. In that case, there had been a movement more generally in terms of fundamental rights thinking to embrace values of transparency of ownership and pluralism, which had become the new orthodoxy in the light of the 1944 ordonnance and the 1950 European Convention. The political changes desired in the other cases were not well established but were new ideas of the majority of the moment.

By contrast, in the area of procedural law, the Conseil is arbiter between the conflicting interests of government and Parliament. In such a situation, the Conseil's decisions are likely to be hard to overturn. Constitutional amendments to change the workings of Parliament are rare and require a very broad cross-party consensus. The decision of the Conseil on the *Séguin Amendment* offers the situation of the Conseil protecting the workings of Parliament, but to the annoyance of the current political majority. The very substantial case law on the procedure for passing finance legislation illustrates the extent to which the Conseil has been able to set a framework for the operation of political debate, which is designed to serve the right to be heard of the Opposition in Parliament.

The criticism of the Conseil in these cases illustrates both the strength of the political feelings within which it is operating and the limited ability which the Conseil has to defend itself publicly. In more recent years, it has obviously attempted to present its own side of the story to the press and cultivate certain journalists. But it relies on public figures and commentators to come to its defence. Its members keep a discrete silence on its decisions. Since the decision only explains the reasoning to a limited extent, there is obvious scope for others to offer interpretations of the decision which suggest that it is politically motivated. The Conseil tries to behave like a court in this regard, but in a context which is always politically live.

D. LEGAL PERSONNEL

The character of French constitutional law makes it difficult to talk of 'legal personnel' in quite the same way as in other branches of law. As was seen above, the procedure of the Conseil constitutionnel is not a classical judicial procedure, which involves lawyers making representations and giving advice in advance. Rather, there are a series of interventions in the political process first by the Conseil d'Etat and then by the Conseil constitutionnel. The restricted number of parties who are permitted to make references to the Conseil constitutionnel and thus to invoke constitutional questions produces a special context for the operation of constitutional law. It would be best to distinguish three groups of people: the promoters, the advisors, and the judges of the process.

(1) The promoters

The promoters of legislation or legislative amendments will either be the government or members of the Parliament. They will engage in constitutional interpretation before presenting the bill or amendment, during its parliamentary stages, and then in representations to the Conseil. There is only a formal place for the government in these stages. It will have to obtain an advisory ruling from the Conseil d'Etat. Such a reference is prepared within the ministry promoting the bill, but in conjunction with a member of the Conseil d'Etat assigned to work as rapporteur. Ordinary members of the department will represent it before the Conseil. There is not a separate corps of 'government lawyers' as in most countries. The civil service thinks itself competent enough to deal with legal issues or to second individuals as needed to work on a project. On occasion, such as in relation to a process such as nationalisation, which has international repercussions, the government will seek legal advice (eg from one of the large American law firms), but this is unusual. The Conseil d'Etat is the government's legal adviser. All the same, individual ministers may seek out advice on an ad hoc basis. Within Parliament, the commission des lois has its own secretariat, this is drawn essentially from the civil service. It will examine the text both for legal and political issues.

Among the opposition parties, there will be need for legal advice in formulating a reference to the Conseil constitutionnel. Here there is a combination of politicians with experience in drafting references and advisers with legal experience. Government deputies or senators will have to draw on similar sources of advice when they formulate amendments. They will not normally be parties to any reference to the Conseil constitutionnel, and so will have no standing in proceedings. They are more likely to rely on informal channels of communication.

(2) The advisers

Unlike in other branches of French law, there is no special group of lawyers with rights of audience either before the Conseil d'Etat in its advisory capacity or before the Conseil constitutionnel. Constitutional law is not a recognised field of specialism for any avocat. It simply forms a background element in any study of public law. The client base is so specific within the political community, that the choice of adviser will be based as much on political allegiance, as on specialist knowledge. On the one hand, the government will be seeking advice on its bills and then on its response to references to the Conseil constitutionnel, on the other hand, there will be the Opposition.

There is thus not a set of specialised professionals used to make references; there is rather a number of individuals who have the relevant experience and knowledge. They will be drawn from a number of fields. For example, there are professors of constitutional law.

The process by which a reference is made to the Conseil is informal and varies according to the subject matter. One can distinguish four types of issue.

In *electoral matters*, the Conseil constitutionnel proceeds very much like the Conseil d'Etat in relation to local elections. A request will be submitted by an individual who has standing, and will be defended by the member of Parliament or the presidential candidate. The candidate will normally be assisted by an avocat who specialises, among other matters, in electoral law. The personal nature of many of the allegations make this a sensible course of action. There may also be assistance from the political party to whom he belongs.

By contrast, the procedure of *declassification* is not a dispute inter partes. It is more like a request to the Conseil d'Etat for legal advice, though with a more binding decision as an outcome. In the procedure, the request is presented by the Prime Minister, though through the Secretary-General of the Government. The relevant minister and the Secretary-General are involved in making the request for declassification and will present arguments, including some indication of what is intended. In more recent years, this is passed to the presidents of the assemblies for comment, but this does not really join them as parties. The work of preparation is undertaken by the Secretary-General who has the most appropriate legal service.[1]

The third process of *parliamentary reference* is the most common. Here the emphasis is on the work of parliamentary groups.[2] Each party proceeds in its own way, but the Socialist and RPR groups are the most organised. Here it will be the parliamentary group, which will make decisions prepared by its bureau (executive) and secretariat. The political decision on whether it is opportune to make a reference on a particular point is a matter for the political members. But the preparation of legal argumentation, which many references now require, will normally exceed the competence of political advisors. Jan's research suggests that among the legal professionals, avocats, judges and law professors, are the most highly considered.[3] This falls within the confidential phase of the process. The process is different from the public debate by relatively independent lawyers that might appear before conventional constitutional courts in other countries. They are like lawyers appearing for any other client, and may, indeed, appear one time for one party and the next time for its opponent. In France, the legal professionals are typically political sympathisers associated in the process. Where particularly technical arguments will be required, then the reference is 'bought' from a law professor who will draft the request.[4] The process is much like an avocat obtaining a consultancy from a law professor in a civil case. The difference is that the person piloting the case through the court is not the professional lawyer, but the political representative of a party.

Under Badinter, himself a former law professor, a number of colloquia were held both with academics and judges within France, and with associations of constitutional courts from other countries.[5] This was a deliberate attempt to increase the status of the Conseil. They also provided a forum in which the broad direction of the Conseil could be discussed, away from the partisan political debate on specific decisions. But, of course, given the role of law professors, avocats and judges in advice during the preparatory stages of references to the Conseil, the colloquia also provided a forum in which there could be public debate between at least some users of the system and the Conseil members. The fact that members of the Conseil are public figures in any case will ensure that there are informal meetings at which members of the Conseil can have exchanges with others. Those who are members of the Conseil d'Etat will clearly have meetings with other members of their corps from time to time (especially as the buildings of the two Conseils are adjacent). The law professors and politicians will also have opportunities to meet with colleagues from their constituencies. Being a member of the

1 See circular of 30 January 1997, JO 1 February 1997.

2 See M Charasse, 'Saisir le Conseil constitutionnel' in *Pouvoirs* No 13 (2nd edn, 1986), 87 at pp 91-94.

3 Jan, p 483. Only rare cases will these people be publicly associated with a request: ibid, pp 483-484.

4 Jan, p 484.

5 Rousseau, op cit, pp. 90-100.

Conseil does not preclude a number of public activities, including teaching, and so the members are not isolated from their audiences of legal professionals.

A key figure will be the Secretary General. The last three, Bruno Genevois, Olivier Schrameck, and Jean-Eric Schoettl, have been active commentators on constitutional law during their period in office. Both were members of the Conseil d'Etat and had reputations already as commissaires du gouvernement. This enabled them to have outlets for their commentaries well established before they started .

(3) The composition of the Conseil constitutionnel

Because the Conseil was not originally conceived as a court, but as an independent commission, there are no specific criteria established for its membership. All the Constitution lays down is the power of the nominators. The President of the Republic, the President of the National Assembly and the President of the Senate nominate one member each every three years for a fixed term of nine years. Should a member fail to complete his mandate (eg because he dies during it), then his nominator can nominate someone else to complete his term of office. Formally former presidents are also members of the Conseil, but none has sat since 1962, and so convention seems to have made this provision lapse. The ordonnance of 7 November 1958 does set out certain functions which are incompatible with membership of the Conseil, and this will restrict the field of potential candidates. A member of the Conseil cannot also hold a position in government, in Parliament, or on the advisory Conseil économique et social. Thus, in order to take up the position of Prime Minister in 1962, Pompidou had to resign, and similarly Michelet resigned so as to enter the National Assembly in 1967. These prohibitions on occupying major political positions for a period of nine years are sufficient to make membership of the Conseil unattractive to politicians, save at the end of their careers. So, many politicians are appointed well into their sixties or even seventies. For others, this may be less of a handicap. All the same, a rare member of the Conseil to complete her period of office under normal retirement age was Noelle Lenoir in February 2001.

Although there are no formal criteria, some relevant features can be identified. The fields of work include parliamentary procedure and elections, so some experience of Parliament is useful, either as a member of the National Assembly or Senate, or as a member of their secretariats. A further aspect of the work is to control the scope of legislation that the government may introduce and the prerogatives of the government in parliamentary procedure. In this context, experience as a minister or as an advisor in a ministerial *cabinet* will be useful. Of course, the decisions of the Conseil constitutionnel have to be based on law and this will require the interpretation of quite complex legal rules. There will also be the creation of new legal rules. To this end, legal experience is also useful.

When one analyses the 59 appointments from 1959 to 2001, there have been 15 avocats, 16 members of the Conseil d'Etat (including two former Vice-Presidents), three members of the Cour de cassation, two of the Cour des Comptes, one former member of the European Court of Human Rights and one of the European Court of Justice. At some periods, especially since 1986, the majority of members have been lawyers. A number of others had law or political science degrees. Thus legal expertise is seen as valuable, but not a pre-requisite. For example, Mme Schnapper, appointed in

2001, has a doctorate in sociology. Over half the members of the Conseil have served in Parliament as politicians, and others, such as Abadie and Lenoir, have served in the secretariat of the Parliament. In terms of government experience, 19 have been ministers and a further 13 served as advisers in ministerial *cabinets*. As was noted in relation to the appointment of Mme Pelletier in March 2000, the President was fortunately able to find a respected lawyer (an avocat and assessor to the juge des enfants), who had been a minister and political activist, and had voted for him in the presidential elections. Most of all, appointees have to have personal authority. Decisions delivered by a group of political hacks in the midst of active political debate would be resented. Indeed, as has been seen, a number of the Conseil's decisions have been criticised for being political. But the quality of both political and legal members has been such that this has not tarnished the standing of the Conseil as a whole.

The appointment of presidents of the Conseil has been controversial. Mitterand's choices were particularly disputed. In the case of Badinter, the appointment of the then Minister of Justice came a few weeks before the expected Socialist defeat in the March 1986 elections. The then president 'resigned' before the end of his period of office, allowing the President to appoint a nominee for a further nine years and thus prolong his influence on its activity. [6] Even more so, the President in February 1995 appointed an old political friend, Roland Dumas, as President for nine years, just before Mitterand was due to leave office in May 1995. That appointment became a further scandal when Roland Dumas was investigated for corruption as a minister in 1998 and forced first to step aside and then to resign from the Conseil in February 2000. It was an open secret that a number of members of the Conseil had wanted him to resign earlier, but the balance tilted against him when he was formally charged with corruption. Presidents of the Conseil have been former ministers of the President's party until the appointment of Guena to replace Dumas.

Most members of the Conseil have been active politically at some point in their previous careers. Given that the three nominators are politicians and the task is politically sensitive, this is not surprising. Examining the period up to 1988, Stone considers that political affiliation is the single most important criterion.[7] He notes how this became an increasing criterion in the period (though it should be noted that it became less significant from 1989 onwards). It is common to note how the political balance of the Conseil shifts from right to left over different periods. There was a right-wing dominance from 1959 to 1989 and a greater left-wing dominance from 1989 to 1997. But this focus on the political past is not a good basis for predicting decisions. After all, the great activist leap forward in the *Associations Law* decision of 1971 involved an overwhelmingly right-wing Conseil quashing a loi voted by a right-wing Parliament and government to disband left-wing political organisations. Rousseau argues that entry into the Conseil, the intellectual quality of its debates and the more general feature of 'the serenity of old age' limit the importance of past political convictions.[8] This is not to argue that people lose their strong political convictions, but that the common enterprise of coming to decisions on 'the rules of the political

6 For an account, see D Rousseau, *Sur le Conseil constitutionnel*, pp 25-29.
7 Stone, p 52.
8 Op cit, p 42.

game', rather than the merits of specific policies leads to a different focus of attention. Over 30 of the early members of the Conseil had been involved in the drafting of the Constitution. Others were law professors or, like Mayer, Badinter, Robert and Schnapper were strongly involved in human rights campaigning. In such areas, the strength of the arguments on fundamental values do not always follow party political allegiance. Interviews over a number of years conducted by the author, and writings of various commentators stress that political allegiance provides too simplistic a frame of reference to explain the decisions of the Conseil. Personality has a much more important role. In the first place, the work of the reporter is rather solitary. Many members of the Conseil will work on their own, with support from the secretariat, and there will be few meetings with other members of the Conseil prior to the discussion in formal session. Some have been known to work on their own and just circulate a draft decision on a complex piece of legislation the day before the meeting. Thus, second, the ability to participate effectively in the discussions will depend on personal features such as knowledge of the field, prior preparation (often at their own initiative), and general levels of health and concentration. Third, the personal knowledge and authority of an individual may be able to influence the Conseil. For example, Rousseau makes much of the personal standing and argumentative abilities of Georges Vedel, who had been a leading constitutional law professor for over forty years before his appointment to the Conseil.

It is true that the early Conseil was very subservient to De Gaulle. The second President of the Conseil, Palewski admitted that it had acted as 'yes-men' to the President of the Republic.[9] But this was at a period when the Fifth Republic was very insecure and was only just getting established. As Favoreu and Philip remarked, 'In reality, the Conseil of 1977-1980, which one might consider one of the most political (Frey, Monnerville, Peretti, Joxe, Coste-Floret) was one of the most active, least servile, most protective of freedoms and most juridical.'[10] Rousseau argues that the Badinter presidency was very much focused on developing a case law on human rights.[11] As he points out, this conflicted with the populist policies of governments of both left and right.

In many ways one needs to pay attention to the audiences. Vedel was among those who attacked the idea of dissenting opinions on the ground that it relieved the Conseil of making an effort to achieve a text which would gain the consent of all members. That sense of solidarity within the small group of members working together and who have respect for each other is an important dynamic in the process, especially as individual opinions are not published and are rarely leaked.

E. THE CONSTITUTIONAL LAW CULTURE

Observers of French constitutional law differ in their analysis of what is occurring. The leading foreign political scientist, Alec Stone, argues that the institution is best conceived as a kind of third chamber of Parliament when dealing with pending

9 See J Boudéant, 'Le Président du Conseil constitutionnel' RDP 1987, 589 at p 637, also pp 627-632.

10 GD (5th edn, 1989) p 378 (text not reproduced in latest edition).

11 D Rousseau, *Sur le Conseil constitutionel,* pp 107ff.

legislation.[12] For him the constitutionalisation of areas of law is not the central issue. Some areas were well established, such as criminal law and procedure, some were not, such as nationalisations and media law, and the Conseil has expanded the corpus of constitutional texts. But the central feature is the political environment within which the Conseil is an actor. The concrete impact of the Conseil constitutionnel's decisions is on the legislative area, forcing a further deliberation on a text. Most texts considered by the Conseil become lois after some modification, or simply by removing the offending provisions. Passing through the Conseil constitutionnel just becomes almost part of the process of making legislation. In this way, politicians are in charge of the constitutional review process. For him, the Conseil is 'a *Council* of policy-makers which derives its legitimacy from the fact that its composition will eventually "follow" the electoral returns'.[13] To use a less provocative analogy than the third chamber, Stone suggests that the Conseil serves as a kind of legal advisory body.[14] But, even if the political aspect of the Conseil's intervention remains paramount, the Conseil's contribution has been to introduce legal argument into it. Looking at constitutional courts in general, he argues that:

> The regular use of abstract review mechanisms during periods of intense and non-incremental legislative activity leads to a *general* juridicization of policymaking processes. In consequence, constitutional law becomes constitutive of legislative behaviour, and legislative activity becomes a constituent element in the building of constitutional law.[15]

But the uniqueness of this French mechanism is that 'the most effective mode of obstruction available to the French parliamentary opposition is at the same time an effective guarantor that a whole panoply of civil rights and democratic procedures will be essentially terms of legislative debate'.[16]

It is in this view of the political impact and use of the Conseil that Stone is wary of the desire of many French writers to emphasise the judicial character of the Conseil. His analysis focuses particularly on the period 1981 to 1987, in which the Conseil was seeking both to impose certain values during changes of political majority and was being used by politicians with a surge of vigour. Both sides were getting used to the idea of *alternance* and what it implied. At the same time, the agenda of commentators was to demonstrate the legal credibility of this new phenomenon and to emphasise its legal pedigree, perhaps by downplaying the political role of a court and by insisting on the character of the Conseil as a *juridiction*. As Rousseau documents, the Conseil under Badinter continued to develop a body of constitutional principle which could act as a framework within which political debate could operate.[17] Among the leading proponents of the judicial character of the Conseil has been Favoreu who has devoted extensive and detailed writings to show the development of constitutional legal principle in what the Conseil is doing. His theme is the legal coherence of the body of case law which the Conseil has developed, and the increasing judicialisation of

12 Stone, p 139.
13 Ibid, p 219.
14 Ibid, p 109.
15 Ibid, p 245.
16 Ibid, p 220.
17 Rousseau, op cit.

procedure. His writings are perhaps an exaggeration when they suggest that debate is 'pacified' by the decision of the Conseil, but it is true that certain issues are make untouchable for politicians, except by constitutional amendment. He is also right to suggest that the Conseil attempts to establish a set of republican principles which should control and inform the political process, whichever party is in power. For Favoreu, constitutional law has become the foundation for all branches of French law, setting their fundamental principles, and it has also 'laid hold of politics'.[18] Favoreu's approach is situated very much in the French tradition where law and politics are seen as distinct activities, even if many of the actors are the same.[19] Just as there is a desire to stress the clear separation of the judicial and administrative functions of the Conseil d'Etat, so even more Favoreu is arguing that the reasoning involved in the decisions of the Conseil constitutionnel is fundamentally different from political debate. The Conseil's own stress that it does not have the same decision-making power as Parliament emphasises this distinction. From this difference and the Conseil's refusal to enter questions of merits, Favoreu and other legal commentators develop the idea that the Conseil is not engaged in politics.

In many ways, as Stone argues, the debate about whether the Conseil is a political or judicial body is a false dichotomy. Constitutional law is about how politics is conducted and seeks to frame the procedures for and limits upon political activity. These limits are procedural and substantive. Constitutional adjudication is necessarily political and legal. It is political in that it aims to set out a framework within which decisions on the future of society are taken. It is legal in that the justifications given have to relate to constitution principle, rather than to party political doctrine. The legal readings of the constitution are necessarily political, but aim to be different in character from some of the political arguments that are deployed in ordinary political debate. Stone illustrates this in relation to the decisions on press and media pluralism:

> The Conseil not only exercised its veto authority over important legislative priorities, but it also demonstrated its capacity to recast the policy making environment, to encourage certain legislative solutions while undermining others, and to have the precise terms of its jurisprudence written into legislative provisions.[20]

This impact of the Conseil is a deliberate action. The Conseil is consciously trying to shape and channel political debate and action on fundamental issues, or at least to contribute, as Rousseau puts it, to a more deliberative democracy by balancing the rights of Parliament and the government in the procedure of decision-making. To this

18 L Favoreu, 'L'apport du Conseil constitutionnel au droit public' (1986) 13 *Pouvoirs* 17; ibid, 'L'influence de la jurisprudence constitutionnelle sur les différentes branches du droit', in *Mélanges Leo Hamon* (Paris 1982), 235. His view about the foundational character of constitutional law is contested by other lawyers, if only because the ordinary courts cannot refer issues to the Conseil constitutionnel. But this is perhaps too narrow a conception of how constitutional law can inform other branches of law and Favoreu's argument coincides with Vedel's inistence on the constitutional foundations of administrative law: see G Vedel and P Delvolvé, *Droit Administratif*, Introduction.

19 Contrast D Rousseau's plea for a more interdisciplinary approach 'Les transformations du droit constitutionnel sous la Ve République' RDP 1998, 1780.

20 Stone, p 203.

end, the Conseil is made up of people who have an understanding of political life and often of government as well. There are relatively few judges, either of civil or administrative courts, who have been members of the Conseil. It is confined to engaging with politicians on abstract issues of interpretation during current political debates. For that reason, the culture of the Conseil constitutionnel activity, as it impacts on government and Parliament, is strongly political, in the sense of shaping the direction of society. The activity of setting the constitutional norms in this context is different from the way in which the administrative and civil courts have to interpret the constitutional law in concrete cases, when the political passions have died down. In political terms, the role is much closer to the advisory role of the Conseil d'Etat, which also is asked to provide legal advice in controversial political circumstances. But the difference there is that the Conseil d'Etat offers *advice* to the government, which can be rejected and which remains confidential, unless the government wishes to make it public. By contrast the Conseil constitutionnel comes to *decisions* often in disputes between government and Parliament which are public, and thus it establishes itself in a more confrontational position. There are marked differences in these two roles.

What remains clear is that, in terms of procedure, in terms of decision-making context, in terms of the other actors in the process, and in terms of purpose, the Conseil constitutionnel operates differently from normal judicial bodies in administrative and private law. Its reasoning is not drawn from codes, but really tries to construct a constitutional corpus from a disparate set of documents and ideas. The style of its arguments is fuller than the Cour de cassation or the Conseil d'Etat, because it is trying to give guidance and to respond to the arguments of those making the reference. It is as much a constitution maker as the interpreter of an established constitution. Even if constitutional law is not an all-encompassing, foundational subject in the way Favoreu claims, it does offer an attempt to produce some foundational principles of substantive law and procedure for political decision-making. Such principles are produced not by deduction from codes, but by the synthesis of disparate sources and the evaluation of different idea to produce a set of principles that are consistent with both texts and contemporary ideas of basic values. The reasoning requires legal scholarship and knowledge, but the answers are not easily distilled from existing literature or decisions of courts. The work of the Conseil constitutionnel and other constitutional actors is an original work of constitution-making. As Stone Sweet remarks, 'abstract review petitions enable constitutional courts to construct the constitutional law, to extend techniques of control over law-making activities, and (the same thing) to make policy.'[1] Although it does not articulate it, the Conseil has to be working on a politico-legal theory of what is fundamental to French society. In a changing social and political environment, this is inevitably a matter of controversy, and so the Conseil changes some of its approaches in the light of criticism and in the light of changing personnel. It may well be that the Conseil has become more like a court. It is not simply a political diversion, or a substitute for politics by the Opposition, though that is how it is used. Rather, it is an attempt to install a meta-political debate.

1 Stone Sweet, p 55.

Chapter 7

Conclusion

In the Preface to this book, I set out at length the principal characteristics of the French legal style which comparative lawyers have traditionally identified. In the chapters which followed, I hope that I have made it clear that the picture is, in fact, more complex. There are specific features of the different major branches of law studied here which distinguish them from each other not only in terms of their content, but also in more fundamental ways – in terms of their core tasks and the influences which the different legal professionals exercise on their development.

A. THE CLAIMED DISTINCTIVE FEATURES OF FRENCH LAW

In the Preface, I identified seven major features of the legal system that might usefully be reviewed at this stage.

(1) The primacy of loi

The primacy of parliamentary loi is a constitutional principle dating from the Revolution. This principle has been materially altered in three ways since 1958. In the first place, the 1958 Constitution itself has recognised the inherent legislative power of the Executive in art 37. Parliament is no longer omni-competent and the Executive can object to interference in its proper legislative sphere (although it now rarely does so). As long as there is no objection, Parliament can legislate in this sphere as well. But the Conseil constitutionnel's function in declassifying lois serves to legitimate the Executive's independent legislative action. As a result, loi has to be understood as the product of either Parliament or of the Executive, each in their respective spheres of competence. In the second place, the Constitution defines what counts as loi and what it can legitimately prescribe, as well as how it must be enacted. As the Conseil constitutionnel pointed out, loi only represents the general will within the strict respect for the Constitution.[1] Popular sovereignty has been exercised first by the enactment of

1 CC decision No 85-197 DC of 23 August 1985, *Elections in New Caledonia*, Rec 70 at p 76.

the Constitution, and only within that framework can subsequent acts of popular sovereignty (falling short of constitutional amendment) take place. To police this, the legislature and thus loi is under the supervision of the Conseil constitutionnel, whenever politicians choose to bring it into play. In the third place, constitutional amendment in 1992, and judicial decisions before then have stressed the priority of European law over loi. All courts act as European Union courts in implementing the treaties. The Conseil constitutionnel may not give priority to EU law over the Constitution, but it recognises its place in electoral matters. More recently, a similar status is being accorded to the European Convention. As a result, all branches of law have undergone change, though constitutional law is the most prominent in imposing restrictions on loi.

Now these changes of a generalised kind have an impact on the role of the judge. The judge is legitimated in certain respects to enforce higher norms over lois. In acts of interpretation, especially in constitutional law, there is freedom for judicial creativity. All the same, one of the fundamental ideas stated by traditional comparative lawyers remains correct. Within the legitimate sphere of loi, the judges have to give priority to it over their own views of what is right. That basic constitutional principle remains.

(2) Codified law

Codified law is not only written law, it is systematic, complete and principled. It is interpreted teleologically and with some freedom by the judges, as is expected. Now, as we have seen, the extent of codification is radically different in different branches of law. On the one hand, civil and criminal law have substantive and procedural codes. The substantive codes are set out in terms of principle and are systematic, to varying degrees. This enables them to be relatively self-contained bodies of law within which analogies and distinctions can be drawn. The Civil Code is perhaps the clearest example, because it has not been amended to a very large extent, except in one or two major areas, such as family and company law. Criminal law is the subject of much more legislative interest. As a result, the coherence of the law can become broken down into a series of specific instances. All the same, the revision of the Code in 1994 reflects a desire to give it greater coherence. If anything, it is in the area of criminal procedure that the more fragmentary character of the law becomes apparent because of very frequent changes of political policy – a perpetual battle between 'law and order' and 'civil liberties'. By contrast, administrative law has no substantive code. It has grown by case law, supplemented in very many major areas by specific bodies of legislation often now labelled 'codes' in areas like communes and planning, but which are no more than compilations of texts. Even the 'Code de justice administrative' of 4 May 2000 is only a systematisation of administrative court procedure and, because of the way the codification was authorised, it has not been able to give the law the radical overhaul which the Code civil and the Code pénal represent. Equally, the Constitution of 1958 is not really a codification of constitutional law. It offers a foundation document on institutional matters, but in terms of fundamental values, it refers out to the Declaration of the Rights of Man and of the Citizen of 1789 and the Preamble to the 1946 Constitution, as well as to fundamental principles recognised by the laws of the Republic. These are not a structured set of values and it has fallen to the Conseil constitutionnel to elaborate them in a way not too dissimilar to the way in which the Conseil d'Etat developed 'general principles of law'. The point of this contrast is to suggest that codification is not a pervasive feature of French law. The values of structure, coherence and systematic organisation are widely recognised, but they are achieved to varying degrees. Civil law and criminal law had foundation moments in the Revolutionary and Napoleonic periods, where the heritage of the past was reviewed in the light of contemporary values. That has not happened in administrative law. The law has been developed as problems have arisen. There was a serious attempt to engage in a radical restatement of fundamental values as well as organisational principles in the Constituent Assembly of 1945-46. But the product of this deliberation was rejected by the referendum of May 1946 and nobody has tried since to restart the process. The 1958 Constitution was an attempt to change as much as was necessary in a hurry. Codification is, therefore, as much a feature of historical accident as a deep feature of a culture of a particular branch of law. But once there has been a code in place, then the lawyers have learned to work with it, and it is in that sense that it has, in time, come to define the proper way of working and reasoning in a particular branch of law.

(3) Legal authorities: la jurisprudence and la doctrine

The changed status of loi has a significant impact on the role of the judge, and the same is also true for the existence of a code. The branches of law which we have studied lie on a spectrum. At one end, there is administrative law where the basic principles are of judicial creation. The grounds of review of administrative actions, the grounds on which the administration is liable contractually and extra-contractually, the general principles of law which must be respected, are all of judicial creation. Naturally, the judges have drawn on texts within and outside administrative law, but the judicial decision provides the legal basis for the existence of these rules and principles. At the other end of the spectrum lies criminal law, where the substantive rules and the rules of criminal procedure are frequently altered by the legislator, and so the scope for judicial creativity is limited. Furthermore, the fundamental values of legal certainty and *nulla poena sine crimen* restrict the scope for creativity to protecting the rights of defendants, rather than creating crimes to any significant extent. In the middle, there is civil law where the Code sets out very general principles in many areas and, as was seen in the case of defective products,[2] there is significant scope for the judges, through interpretation, in effect to create the rules which govern specific aspects of the law. The legislator often will not intervene and the courts do not feel they can wait. At the same time, the authority of the judge is less than in administrative law, and there is less scope to create new frameworks of principles. The constitutional judge has more flexibility because of the explicitly incomplete character of the Constitution. The development of the fundamental principles recognised by the laws of the Republic, as well as objectives of constitutional value have added to the scope for interpretation in the statements of constitutional values. The values were general and were long considered more to be pious statements of intention, rather than standards which could be legally enforced. As a result, the Conseil constitutionnel has been able to work out its own conception of the Constitution, with the reserve

2 Above, pp 80-81.

power of the legislator to propose and have enacted constitutional amendments. But it has been rare for the constitution to be amended to alter the decision of the Conseil; more often the legislator has been told to change the constitution in order to enact a policy, eg on Europe or on women candidates in elections, and has gone ahead and done so. All the same, there are significant fixed reference points for the principles which the Conseil interprets and there is not the same scope to develop completely unwritten rules as in administrative law.

The place for judicial development of the law has a significant impact on the scope for doctrinal legal writing. In administrative law, the members of the Conseil d'Etat have played a significant role in systematising the law and suggesting ways of developing it, especially through the published arguments of the commissaire du gouvernement. In this situation, it has been the judges who have been among the leading doctrinal writers, in and out of court. University academics have played an important part, but have not always been prominent. Constitutional law also presents a major area of judicial activism. The influence of doctrinal legal writing is less easy to document, although academic writers have played a significant role as consultants to references made to the Conseil and as members of the Conseil. The published doctrinal legal writing has tended to document, publicise and systematise the decisions of the Conseil constitutionnel, rather than play a proactive role. All the same, the lack of commentary by members of the Conseil on their own work has left scope for individual academics and for the Secretary-General to be authoritative commentators on the Conseil's work. By contrast, in civil law, doctrinal legal writing has been influential because of the weakness of judicial doctrine and the lack of involvement of the legislator. Doctrine has served not only to systematise, but also to propose new solutions. The activity of the legislator in criminal law has reduced the scope for innovation by doctrinal legal writers, although they have a significant role in systematisation and critique. Human rights is likely to change this as the Strasbourg case law will have to be married with French legislation and case law in hitherto unusual ways. But up to now, doctrinal writing has not been as prominent, although individual academics have been very prominent in government committees proposing legislative reform.

The pattern of relationships between *jurisprudence*, the legislator and *doctrine* found in civil law is not replicated in other branches of law. The three act as counterbalances. The strength of one tends to have an impact on the scope for action by the others. It would, however, be wrong to suggest that judges have ever been totally passive. In all branches of law, they have the chance to dictate the pace of change, subject to the priority of the legislator. Doctrinal writing has scope to influence publicly through its articles and books and privately in committees, consultations and the activity of its members as judges. Its scope for action depends on the strength of legislator and judges. The weakness of both of these in civil law is not replicated in the other branches of law and this has a significant impact on the role of doctrine.

(4) Legal concepts

The argument of Lawson and Samuel suggests that French law has distinct concepts from the common law and this shapes the frames of reference within which legal problems are discussed. That argument has much plausibility. But the argument can equally be used within French law. It is most clear in the contrast between administrative law and civil law. Each has their own sets of concepts. Administrative law deals with 'the State', 'the public service', 'the general interest'. This provides a basis for liability in concepts such as 'equality before public burdens' and 'social solidarity'. The fundamental relationships are either between the public interest and the individual interest (the 'administration' and the 'administered'), or within the public service, either between administrations or between the administration and its officials, who hold a special status because of their contribution to the general interest. Few of these values are from early Roman law. They are taken in many cases from canon law, mediated through debates in the renaissance period. They, have, however, undergone a radical transformation in the 19th and 20th centuries as the conception of the French state developed, especially under the Third Republic.

Civil law is dealing with different basic relationships. Unlike in public law, in private law the dimension of the State is missing both in terms of concepts and in terms of the fundamental framework of relationships. For public lawyers (and for criminal lawyers), the State is not just another legal person who can have relationships with other legal or physical persons. It is a superior legal entity, which represents the community and whose wishes and status have a higher value. Since the Revolution at least, there is a formal equality between individuals and so the relationships between private individuals is considered as basically equal, though some will need special supervision (minors, prodigals or the mentally infirm). The reciprocity of relationships is then set up around obligations, personal status or property. Relationships are fundamentally voluntary, arising predominantly from choices, rather than from status or the dictation of a superior. Even when dealing with comparable issues – building contracts, employment or property, there will be some important differences between the requirements of the public interest (eg the continuity of the public service) and those of the private interest. Public works cannot be destroyed, public employees have limited rights to strike and have better protection, and public property cannot be easily alienated.

Constitutional law and criminal law concern different versions of the public law framework of relationships. Constitutional law, like administrative law, is about the organisation of public power, especially the powers of government and Parliament. There is, however, a set of values which applies most directly to what public authorities can be allowed to do in relation to citizens or in relation to each other, but these apply indirectly to inform the interpretation of private law. French law has, perhaps, been less prominent in its development of the horizontal effect of fundamental rights than, say, German law. The Constitution and the statements of fundamental rights do not have their origins in Roman or canon law, but in the Revolution and in the 'republican constitutional tradition' as it was developed, particularly in the Third Republic, and, again, in the Fifth Republic. Criminal law principles have yet other origins. Hardly any come from Roman law. A few principles have their origins in canon law, but most have developed more recently, especially in the Revolutionary period at the beginning of the 19th century. There has been a strong utilitarian influence on substantive criminal law, as well as more recent social welfare principles of criminology. Criminal procedure has evolved especially since the Third Republic under the influence of a number of dramatic miscarriages of justice, such as the Dreyfus affair and Vichy, as well as more recently. It is an area that is profoundly influenced by developments in constitutional law and in international human rights law. The procedural aspects of the system have become very important. In criminal law, the method of subsuming facts under a rule performs a very different role than in private law, where the concern is to promote the underlying social relationships, rather than to apply rigid rules.

(5) Rights and remedies

Samuel's suggestion is that French civil law is very much based on rights, rather than remedies. For Jolowicz, the judge is provided with a set of facts and she tries to provide a legal classification that will offer a solution.[3] French civil law is not based around procedural mechanisms, but around rights. Now this feature is substantially true also for constitutional law. The Conseil constitutionnel deals with lois and treaties in abstract and receives the whole text. It is not constrained by the grounds of a reference and forms its view on the constitutionality of any part of the text in question. The availability of remedies is not an issue. Equally, constitutional texts are, in part, explicit in their statement of rights without much statement of remedies for their breach. All the same, procedure does play a significant part in constitutional law. If a loi has been signed by the President, then it cannot be challenged in the ordinary civil, criminal or administrative courts (except in so far as it also breaches binding treaty obligations). This particularly affects private individuals, since they have no way of referring issues to the Conseil constitutionnel. In this way, rights are relative to a procedure.

In the case of administrative law, then one is more clearly in the area where the law works around remedies. The law has been developed around the two basic groups of remedies, the recours pour excès de pouvoirs and the recours de plein contentieux. The grounds of review have been the basis on which the law has been developed on a case-by-case basis. Administrative law does not start from the idea that there are rights of the citizen against the administration. There are general principles of law which the administration should observe, but these need to be activated through specified remedies, each of which has its own rules on time-limits, the obligation to be legally represented and, still to some extent, the jurisdiction of the courts.

Although there are important rights of the accused in criminal law, most of these are procedural, either against the police or in respect of the pre-trial and trial procedures before the procureur or the juge d'instruction. I have argued that criminal procedure, particularly the investigation, lies at the heart of the activity of criminal law. In consequence, it makes little sense to separate rights and remedies. Admittedly, the breach of rights frequently leads to a remedy only at the discretion of the judge, and so evidence obtained in breach of rights may still be admissible.[4] In other words, there is certainly a rhetoric of rights of the accused in the criminal law which is important, but the rights are typically to procedural safeguards, rather than to substantive outcomes.

Therefore, it would be true to say that, with the exception of administrative law, French law is not shaped by the forms of action and can concentrate on the rights of the citizen, but this is not particularly helpful as a generalisation, because procedures for the protection of rights play an important part, especially in criminal law. Samuel's argument is that the French start their legal reasoning with a right and then find a way

3 J A Jolowicz, *On Civil Procedure*, ch 10.
4 Above, p 116 note 16.

of protecting and enforcing it. That stems from the legislative statement of rights, rather than from the construction of the law in terms of remedies before the courts. In this respect, French law is uneven. French administrative law is less rights-based in its approach, and resembles the common law much more. The substantive law was judicially developed through the availability of remedies, and this continues to mark the law. To a lesser extent, this is equally true of constitutional law. Unless the issue has been raised before the Conseil constitutionnel, then it is difficult to raise the issue of a constitutional right against lois. Civil and administrative law do not leave much space for discussing such issues.

(6) Legal professions

The argument of Zweigert and Kötz, cited on p x, was that the *representative lawyer* is indicative of the style of a legal system. For them, the representative figure for France was the avocat, whereas for Germany it was the professor. I think the analysis is helpful, but I consider the conclusion to be wrong. We need to distinguish carefully between branches of the law, especially as there is no single structure of legal professions. In administrative law, the most representative lawyer is probably the commissaire du gouvernement. The leading commissaires have developed the law both in their courtroom speeches and in notes in law reviews, if not in textbooks for their courses at Sciences Politiques. The laconic style of judicial decision and the absence of any published form of the rapport makes the conclusions of the commissaire du gouvernement the principal point of reference for lawyers and doctrinal writers alike, both inside and outside the administrative courts. In constitutional law, then the representative lawyer is harder to discern. He is probably the judge working individually and collectively to produce the judgment. Doctrinal writers and those working on submissions have moulded their work to reflect the kinds of argument that the judges produce. It is a casuistic system that is trying to develop general principles under the influence of some good quality doctrinal legal writers. But they are predominantly following, rather than shaping judicial thinking (except in so far as they act themselves as members of the Conseil or as advisers to its president). In criminal law, there is a tension between two 'representative' lawyers. On the one hand there is the juge d'instruction who is an individual judge who is often able to develop an individual profile in the media and among the professions. The single-minded fidelity to the law and the independence from the powerful in politics or in society constitute the ideal of this judge around which the integrity of the criminal prosecution process is built. On the other hand, the icon for the defence is indeed the avocat. He is able to follow the investigation process and defend his client at every turn. The ideal is not the duty avocat, who is the person most frequently found, and who barely has time to read the file and talk to the client before the case comes on for trial. Rather, as the sparring partner with the juge d'instruction, the ideal is of the avocat who is the guardian of individual liberty against potential oppression by the State and the police. Whereas the juge d'instruction ceases to be involved once the decision to prosecute is taken, the avocat has the theatre of the criminal courtroom to make interventions and defend his client. His interventions will be less dramatic than a common law cross-examination, for the trial judge has centre stage, but the avocat does have a major role in the continuity of the criminal process. Zweigert and Kötz are probably right in respect of civil law that the avocat is a representative figure, but not for the reasons they give. Oratory is not a significant part of the role of the civil law avocat. Civil procedure is written, and the most important role of the avocat is in legal advice. In the setting of advice, the lawyer will wish to produce solutions which distil the rules from the Code and case law and combine this with business and doctrinal analysis of how these apply in contemporary circumstances. Most issues are routine, requiring little legal research, and rely much more on practical judgment. The doctrinal writer producing a *consultation* will operate in a similar way, though with an emphasis on the legal rules, rather than business judgment. In terms of legal reasoning, it will be in the difficult cases that analysis of legal rules becomes important. Here, the lawyers most frequently encountered are the avocat au Conseil d'Etat et à la Cour de cassation and the avocat agrégé. The former will prepare the cases for the highest court and will need to include analysis of case law and doctrine. The latter will do the same, but, as a professor, will be writing case-notes on her specialist field, and then earning fees pleading cases in that area.

I think it is misleading simply to contrast the career judge and the avocat within the legal professions. Their roles are different in each branch of law, because the core activity is different. Each branch of law has judges, avocats and professors, but these may well sub-divide, and they play different roles in different branches.

(7) Court structure and procedures

France does have distinctive court structures and procedures, but these are not uniform. Since 1995, there has been a broadly similar pattern of courts in civil, criminal and administrative law. There are local first instance courts dealing with law and fact, there are regional appeal courts dealing with law and fact, with a single national supreme court dealing with the cassation of appeal court decisions or preliminary references on a point of law. The Conseil d'Etat still has a few roles as a court of first and last instance, but these are residual. The courts are not the same and belong to different hierarchies, a feature that makes France distinctive in Europe. All the same, a gradual convergence has emerged over the past fifty years. The position of the Conseil constitutionnel is idiosyncratic. It is not within the judicial hierarchy at all and cannot deal with references or appeals from the ordinary courts.

As far as procedure is concerned, there is not a single French court procedure, but a form of procedure for each branch of law. There are a number of features around which this issue can be discussed. In the first place, one can differentiate procedures according to whether they are written or oral. On the whole, the French legal procedures differ in their degrees of writing. At one extreme, the procedure in constitutional law is entirely written with no formal oral hearing (although there may be some oral meetings held by the rapporteur as he prepares the file). At the other extreme, criminal law has oral elements both in the pre-trial and in the trial phases. The interviews with the procureur or the juge d'instruction may well involve a detailed examination of the accused and of witnesses, if not also a confrontation of their versions of events. At trial, represented or not, the accused is going to be the first person to speak, even if witness testimony is confined to written depositions. In between, administrative law and civil law have varying degrees of orality. Both rely on written pleadings and evidence with only rare oral questioning of witnesses in a pre-trial phase. Administrative law is more focused on written documentation than civil law, particularly because relations between citizens and the administration is typically conducted or recorded in written form. The administrative courts are less likely to have to talk to individuals to find out the facts, though this can sometimes occur, eg if the issue arises as to whether a question given in an oral examination for the baccalaureat was on the syllabus or not.

A second feature is the contrast between inquisitorial and accusatorial procedures. At the one extreme, the Conseil constitutionnel adopts an entirely inquisitorial approach. There is scope for written debate between the parties in their submissions, but it is up to the rapporteur to adopt whatever procedure he considers appropriate to become fully informed of the issues. The fact that the file is started even before the case begins confirms this proactive judicial approach. At the other extreme, civil law is clearly adversary. Each party produces arguments and information and, on the basis of these the judge will decide. The judge may ask questions and suggest that information is missing, but he will not go and search for it. Even the appointment of experts is agreed by the parties and subject to debate between them. In the middle, administrative law is more inquisitorial than criminal law. Formally, the only information available is that contained on the file, which the judge has requested or which the parties have submitted.[5] The reporter judge may write to the administration (or even informally telephone it) to obtain information. This may be in addition to the material the parties have submitted, though it is for the purposes of understanding rather than to gather fresh evidence. The attitude of being part of the administration and finding out what it does forms part of the culture of the administrative judge. The applicant in an administrative case will often not be represented, and may well not appear at a hearing. The judge therefore has a role of compensating for this in the battle between the litigant and the administration. The lack of form for applications in certain types of proceedings also increases the need for the inquisitorial approach of the court. In the case of criminal law, the procureur or juge d'instruction may well order evidence to be gathered from experts, but then it is open to debate and is transparent, because the accused has access to the file at any time. The expectation that the accused will be represented, if he wishes, leads to a more adversarial atmosphere in criminal proceedings.

A third procedural feature is the presence of a public representative, the ministère public, in the proceedings. This transforms the debate from a bilateral to a formally tri-lateral form – plaintiff, defendant, and public interest. This procedure is compulsory at all levels in administrative law. Even in single judge hearings, the commissaire du gouvernement must enter conclusions. For administrative lawyers, the commissaire du gouvernement is a non-voting part of the judicial team, and is not one of the parties. In civil law, the equivalent is the avocat-général. It is rare that he will make submissions below the level of the Cour de cassation. His position is much closer to that of the European Court of Justice advocate-general. He will have knowledge of the file and be part of pre-hearing judicial deliberations, but he does not take part at all in judicial deliberations on the final decision. In criminal cases below the Cour de cassation, the procureur is clearly a party in that he argues for a conviction in the public interest, even if he also owes duties to the law that may also favour the accused. It is this

5 Article R 611-10 Code de la justice administrative provides that the rapporteur decides the deadlines for transmission of documents, and can request that they produce any documents useful for the resolution of the case.

feature which has led the European Court of Human Rights to criticise the criminal law procedure before the Cour de cassation where the civil model applies, but where it felt the procureur général was more like a party than part of the judicial team. In the Conseil constitutionnel, there is no public representative, as there is no hearing and there are not really any parties.

If anything, the diversity of procedures and court structures is lessening in France. The external model of the European Court of Justice (originally modelled itself on the Conseil d'Etat) has encouraged the development of preliminary reference procedures. The rulings of the European Court of Human Rights on art 6 of the Convention have also moved proceedings along more standard lines, with greater transparency and adversarial debate, and, in the Cour de cassation, a greater similarity in the role of the avocat-général to his namesake in the ECJ.

B. REFLECTIONS

As reflected in Figure 1 on p 22, law is subject to internal and external inputs. In each field discussed, there is crucially a distinct activity, a distinct set of values, and distinct professions establishing relationships between each other; there is also a different history and institutional setting.

(1) Diversity of tasks and diversity of models

The basic argument presented here is that the divergences between the different branches of French law results from a difference in the core task and activity with which they are dealing. The activity of controlling Parliament and the government requires different actors and procedures in constitutional law, which, in turn gives rise to a different way in which the professional legal actors relate to each other and influence the outcomes of the process. But this is also influenced by the normative framework with which they start, arising out of an institutional setting determined by history as much as by the nature of the task at hand.

The core task of each area is different. Constitutional law is concerned to control Parliament and Executive in the interests of the balance of powers and the protection of fundamental values (including the rights of citizens). It is a role of supervision in abstract. Administrative law controls and advises the administration and again is interested in principles on the proper functioning of institutions, as well as the protection of individual interests. Criminal law is concerned to ensure appropriate and effective prosecution and law enforcement balanced against individual rights. Finally, civil law is concerned to resolve disputes between private citizens, when they choose to present them, and thereby to protect individual rights and interests at their request. The public interest is present to different degrees in these tasks and the rights of individuals are also involved, though protection is paternalistic in constitutional law and advisory aspects of administrative law, but more concrete and at the request of the citizen in civil law and, to a great extent, in criminal law.

The institutions created to perform these tasks are different. They are the product of both values and history. In part, they also reflect institutions and professions available at the time the task was initiated or revised. The institutions and professions have grown up at different times. The Conseil constitutionnel was specially created for its task, as was the Conseil d'Etat. Civil and criminal procedures have evolved more incrementally over many years. The Revolution of 1789 provides an important caesura in legal history, but subsequently many things have evolved on a gradual basis, as need has arisen. In particular, institutions have been re-shaped by waves of new values. In particular, the republican tradition created by the Third Republic in the last quarter of the 19th century, and the fundamental rights culture of the last quarter of the 20th century have caused revisions to the values which institutions serve and this had led to changes in the procedure and operations within which tasks are performed.

(2) Diversity of values

The diversity of tasks reflects and implements diversity of core values. The values may not be difficult to reconcile, but they provide a different focus of attention in each area of law. The value of reconciling citizens in relation to each other and whilst respecting their rights, lies at the heart of the civil law. Traditionally administrative law has tried to reconcile the reasonable expectations of the administered with those of the administration. In the past, the complaint was that they proceeded too much on the basis of the efficiency of the administration. Nowadays, the lower administrative courts are moving more closely to the civil model of a litigation as a dispute between parties.[6] Nevertheless, the investigatory process is justified in administrative law by the need to ensure the administration carries out its missions. In contrast, criminal law is concerned with the efficiency of investigating crime and punishing offenders, which is balanced against the rights of the individual. In this balance, the violation of the rights of the accused may not lead to the prosecution being stopped.[7] Constitutional law is involved in protecting the appropriate role of different institutions of government and reconciling these, in some cases with fundamental values, including individual rights. The importance of rights is less in some areas, compared with others.

(3) Legal professional actors

The presence of distinctive legal professional groups is important. But the relationships differ from area to area as a result of their differing roles in the tasks which each field assigns to them, or which they have carved out within it. The analysis of D'Iribarne about the 'honour' of each group explains both their own sense of status, and the continuing relationships between them. In the criminal law, the tension between the juge d'instruction and the avocats reflects their sense of their own special role which the other must not trespass upon. The system works by mutual respect, not by dominance. A similar analysis could be made of the relationships between each of those groups and the procureur. There is a different sense of the proper role of the juge and avocat in the civil case. The limited success of court-based conciliation reflects the sense that this is the role of the avocat and that, if a case has come to court, it is

6 Above, pp 157 and 161.
7 Above, p 116 note 16.

because the avocats need to get a decision from the judge, not further attempts at conciliation. The centrality of the advisory task also brings in the professor as doctrinal writer and *consultant*. Here, the doctrinal writer forms part of the avocat team and is accorded respect. As an influence on the judge, the professor has to compete with other voices from judges and, most of all from the legislator, in lawmaking. In administrative law, the avocats have a less strong role. Their skills in oratory avail little and their filing of papers is under the active direction of the judge. The more bureaucratic juge, who is also knowledgeable about the administration in a way which the avocat is not, establishes a more dominant position which has to be respected. The commissaire du gouvernment plays an important linking role in terms of explaining informally to avocats what he is likely to recommend (and thus what may well happen). There is a far less specialist bar in administrative law than in criminal and civil law, and this sets up different dynamics of respect between bench and bar. The lack of professionals in constitutional law sets up entirely different dynamics. A different group of judges has to relate to politicians, rather than to avocats. The avocat and the professor may form part of the team of politicians and write the submissions, but they do not have the same status that they enjoy in civil law. Others have a central role as the experts and respected groups in the field.

It is clear that each branch of law has its own élites and key professions. Some of these overlap, such as avocats, but others do not. The distinctiveness of professions sets up different circles of critical reflection. There are cross-references from one major branch of law to the others, but this is limited. The distinctiveness of key professionals, notably among the judiciary and academics, accentuates any differences which might be thought to exist between the different branches of law.

(4) History and lawmaking

Each branch of French law originates in a specific combination of several elements – Roman law, canon law, customary law, Revolutionary ideas, modern legislation and the republican tradition of the Third and Fifth Republics. Civil law is very marked by its origins in Roman and customary law, reshaped by Revolutionary law into a coherent code. Administrative law has some distant Roman law and particularly canon law origins in some of its ideas, but it is particularly marked by the republican tradition and modern legislation. Criminal law has origins in royal and canon law, but has been reshaped by Revolutionary ideas and modern legislation. Constitutional law owes its content to the republican tradition above all. The family resemblance may well result from the way the different branches of law dip into this genetic pool which has been evolving for many centuries in different political and social climatic conditions.

The driving force for law reform is different for each branch of law, as we have seen. The centrality of the legislator is acknowledged, but the role of judges and doctrinal writers is more variable.

C. IS THERE A FRENCH LEGAL CULTURE?

This book has argued that there are distinctive cultures within French law. The question arises, however, whether there is a French legal culture as a unified entity in contrast to other legal cultures. It may be true that there is not a uniform French culture. All the same, their may be a 'family resemblance' between the different sub-cultures. Just as two members of a family will probably not be identical, but they will share characteristics which are different one from another, so it is with the legal family. There will be features which a number will share in common, and certainly make them closer to each other than to members of other legal families.

The similarities between different branches of French law lie in the fact they come from a certain social and political context. The rules and principles have been developed gradually within a relatively distinctive society, which has been politically independent. To take an analogy, Coulommiers, Fourme d'Ambert, Munster and Comté are all French, cow's-milk cheeses; but their texture, smell and taste are radically different. In many ways, Fourme has more similarity to English Stilton than to its French companions. Similarly, different branches of French law may have certain similar ingredients, but they end up being significantly different products, because of the process of their creation and operation.

We have seen that there are some similarities between the different branches of French law, which mark them out as distinctively French. The style of judgments is typically laconic and brief. This is less true in constitutional law, but all the same, there is a way of writing judicial decisions which is typically French. Because the law is part of a constitutional system, then certain common values are shared across the system. Among these constitutional values, the respect for loi is central. Although the Conseil constitutionnel may have to exercise control over the legislature, it still is respectful of the freedom of decision which the Constitution affords to it. The Conseil is mainly concerned with the procedure by which legislation was passed, rather than with controlling the substantive law.

The French legal system is not self-contained. The internal constraints, which the Conseil constitutionnel has elaborated, are then complemented by external constraints arising from treaties, notably the European Convention, and from the law of the European Union. These add to the new ideas and values which the legislature and the executive introduce from time to time in particular branches of law. These inputs are by no means synchronised and compatible. The different branches of the legal system have to interpret them and integrate them appropriately. The mere fact that substantial inputs into the different branches of law studied here come from the French legislator is no guarantee that French law will remain distinctive. Many measures, such as privatisation, have brought France into line with other countries, even outside the requirements of EU law. In many areas of law reform, for example in family law, there will be extensive comparative law research to discover the best ideas for France to adopt. Any argument that French law is distinctive cannot rely on the idea that French law is able to remain self-contained. All the same, some of the well-established features of the system are slow to move and change, if only because they appear to work well enough.

My argument would be that French law is distinctive compared with other legal systems for a variety of reasons not all of which apply to every branch of law. A long tradition of independent nationhood, the existence of legal professions and legal practices, such as the juge d'instruction, which have evolved over a long period of time have developed a distinctive way of carrying out legal activities. On the whole, France, and particularly the French legislature and the French public service, has been in control of the pace and direction of legal development, either in leading developments or in responding to social situations as they evolve. The different groups of French lawyers in each branch of law have also been able to be in control of developments. But it has not been the same group in each branch of law, nor has the line of development been the same. Rather there is a congeries of features that makes French law French. When we are comparing the law in France to the law in Sweden or Italy or England, we can recognise its distinctiveness. Its systems of constitutional and administrative justice, its rules on administrative liability, the prosecution and investigation of criminal offences, the career patterns of its judiciaries will mark French law out as distinctive compared with any of the legal systems just mentioned. There will equally be similarities between the legal systems, especially in terms of values.

In this context, I do not think it helpful to talk about a single, uniform French legal culture. There is a tradition of the law in France having a number of distinctive features. Some of these, like the juge d'instruction continue to be embedded even when other legal systems have abandoned their equivalents. Some of them, like the juges consulaires of the conseils des prud'hommes, are being transformed and are becoming less different from other systems. The distinctiveness of French law has been to hold a particular variety of features together, each of which has its own dynamism and culture. Viewed from the outside, like the varieties of French cheese, there is a 'Frenchness' about the diversity and the particular mix of elements. But that is as much a feature of geography and of institutional setting, rather than an inherent similarity of culture. Once we examine particular elements of the system, we become aware of important similarities of content with other systems, where there are similar influences. But we can also see similarities in the dynamics of legal development between common law and French administrative law as judge-made systems, and between codified legal systems in the area of criminal law. To talk simply of a single 'French legal culture' is not much more illuminating than to talk of 'French cheese'. To compare it as a block against other legal systems leads to conclusions which are only partially true and may be distorting.

In debates about legal convergence or divergence, we have seen in the Preface that the concept of 'mentality' is deployed to suggest that there are barriers to convergence. I would not wish to deny that this is an important feature of legal systems which has to be understood. But I would want to argue two things. First, legal actors are educated and operate within institutional settings that change. The reflective process among professional legal actors is matched by reflection among legislators and others. There is therefore a renewal and change among attitudes to legal activities and thus to mentality over time. It is not a rapid process, but it does occur, and the attitudes of French lawyers in the different branches of law towards European Community and European Convention laws provide a good example. Mentalities are not fixed for all time. Second, it is important to recognise that the diversity of legal cultures within a single legal system has as a consequence a diversity of reactions to external pressures, either from the national legislator or from Europe. The extent of any difficulty or willingness to converge will be uneven across the legal system. This has an important impact on research.

D. FRENCH LAW: A CHANGING PICTURE

There are two reasons for change in the traditional cultures of French law. On the one hand, there are changing expectations of the law within France. On the other hand,

France is not immune from external influence. In particular, the various chapters have shown how far European Community and European Convention law are changing the substance and procedure of the law and the attitudes and roles of French lawyers. No culture is static, but these dual pressures are of major importance.

In terms of social expectations, one of the major features has been the heightened role of judges. It has been argued that this current increase in the role of judges results from the social context in which they are placed. Domique Rousseau has argued:

> Since Parliament abstains from legislating or enacts only minimal legislation, judges, faced with concrete cases, have to fill the gap and invent a response, for example, on the wearing of the chadour, surrogate motherhood, the publication of photographs, or the appropriate ways of facilitating the equal access of women to political offices and functions.[8]

He argues that this 'default' role is supplemented by institutional authorisation, in that certain regulatory institutions and roles are being created, and by 'cultural authorisation', whereby the judge has become accepted over the past twenty years as an independent figure in the rise of the rule of law.

8 *Le Monde*, 19 November 1999, p 21.

Select bibliography

GENERAL WORKS

French Law

J Bell, *French Constitutional Law* (Oxford 1992)
J Bell, S Boyron and S Whittaker, *Principles of French Law* (Oxford 1998)
LN Brown and J Bell, *French Administrative Law* (5th edn, Oxford 1998)
B Nicholas, *The French Law of Contract* (Oxford 1992)
JP Royer, *Histoire de la justice en France* (2nd edn Paris 1996)

Legal theory

N MacCormick and O Weinberger, *An Institutional Theory of Law* (Dordrecht 1986), Ch 3
F Ost and M van de Kerchove, 'De la pyramide au réseau? Vers un nouveau mode de production du droit?' (2000) 44 *Revue interdisciplinaire d'études juridiques* 1
JR Searle, *The Social Construction of Reality* (London 1995)
W Twining, *Globalisation and Legal Theory* (London 2000), esp Chs 3 and 7
M Van Hoecke and M Warrington, 'Legal Cultures and Legal Paradigms: Towards a New Model for Comparative Law' (1998) 47 ICLQ 495

PREFACE: DISTINCTIVE FEATURES OF FRENCH LAW

The distinctive features of French law are set out particularly in:
R David, *French Law* (1959, English trans by M Kindred, Baton Rouge 1972)
D Harris and D Tallon, *Contract Law Today* (Oxford 1989), pp 7-16, and Ch 8
H Lawson, *A Common Lawyer looks at the Civil Law* (Ann Arbor 1953)
P Legrand, 'European Legal Systems are not Converging' (1996) 45 ICLQ 52
B Nicholas, *The French Law of Contract* (Oxford 1992), Ch 1
K Zweigert and H Kötz, *An Introduction to Comparative Law* (3rd edn trans T Weir, Oxford 1998), Chs 5, 7 and 9

CHAPTER 1: LEGAL CULTURE

This work draws on both general works on culture and specific writings on legal culture. Among the general works, this book relies in particular on Bauman, Geertz, and Trompenaars and Hampden-Turner. On specifically legal culture, the leading collection of essays is that of Nelken. The works of Legrand, Markesinis and Watson set out some of the key established positions among comparative lawyers. Krygier and Samuel study legal culture in terms of legal theory, most particularly in relation to legal reasoning, an approach also adopted by Bell. Garapon offers a specifically French perspective.

General works on culture

Z Bauman, *Culture as Praxis* (London 1973)
S Bernstein, *Les cultures politiques en France* (Paris 1999)
C Geertz, *The Interpretation of Cultures* (1973, Basic Books edn, London 1993)
GER Lloyd, *Demystifying Mentalities* (Cambridge 1990)
F Trompenaars and C Hampden-Turner, *Riding the Waves of Culture* (2nd edn, London 1997)

Legal culture

J Bell, 'Comparative Law and Legal Theory' in W Krawietz, *Festschrift for RS Summers* (Berlin 1994) 19
W Ewald, 'The Jurisprudential Approach to Comparative Law: A Field Guide to "Rats"' (1998) 46 Am Jo Comp Law 701
V Gessner, A Hoeland and C Varga, *European Legal Cultures* (Aldershot 1996)
A Garapon, *Bien juger. Essai sur le rituel judiciaire* (Paris 1997)
A Garapon, 'French Legal Culture and the Shock of 'Globalisation' (1995) 4 *Social and Legal Studies* 493
M Krygier, 'Law as Tradition' (1986) 5 *Law and Philosophy* 237
P Legrand, 'European legal Systems are not Converging' (1996) 45 ICLQ 52
P Legrand, *Fragments on Law-as-Culture* (Deventer 1999)
B Markesinis, 'A Matter of Style' (1994) 110 LQR 607
D Nelken (ed), *Legal Cultures* (Aldershot 1997)
E Örücü, E Attwooll and S Coyle, *Studies in Legal Systems: Mixed and Mixing* (Hague 1996)
G Samuel, *The Foundations of Legal Reasoning* (Antwerp 1994), esp Ch 3
A Watson, *The Making of the Civil Law* (Cambridge Mass 1981)

CHAPTER 2: INSTITUTIONAL SETTING

The institutional setting can be studied from a number of perspectives, hence the variety of works listed here. A number of works of a general kind are more popular, rather than academic studies, but they offer valuable insights into the law, without detailed footnotes (see, in particular, Carbonnier, Minc, and Salas). On the French professions, the judiciary is carefully studied by Bancaud, Bodiguel and Boigeol from an historical and sociological perspective. A similar approach is adopted by Karpik for the profession of avocat. Kourilsky (-Augeven) offers sociological studies of how the law is perceived by young people. In relation to sources, the two works by Troper and Grzegorczyk are particularly valuable as they are in collections which compare other legal systems. The impact of Europeanisation is studied more in relation to administrative law than in relation to some other branches of law.

French society and government

J Ardagh, *France in the New Century* (London 1999)
A Stevens, *The Government and Politics of France* (2nd edn, London 1996)
V Wright, *The Government and Politics of France* (3rd edn, London 1989)

French social culture

P Bourdieu, *La noblesse d'Etat. Grandes Ecoles et esprit de corps* (Paris 1989)
P D'Iribarne, *La logique de l'honneur* (Paris 1989)

French law in general

Annuaire statistique de la Justice 2000 (Paris 2000)
J Bell, 'English Law and French Law – Not so different?' [1995] CLP 63
J Carbonnier, *Droit et passion de droit sous la Ve République* (Paris 1996)
J Carbonnier, *Flexible droit: pour une sociologie sans rigeur* (7th edn, Paris 1992)
C Kourilsky, 'Socialisation juridique et identité du sujet' (1991) 19 *Droit et Société* 259
C Kourilsky-Augeven, 'Sociologie juridique et modèle culturel. L'image du droit en Russie et en France' *Droit et Société* no 18 (Paris 1996), 19
A Minc, *Au nom de la loi* (Paris 1998)
D Salas, *Le tiers pouvoir. Vers une autre justice* (Paris 1998)

French legal professions

A Bancaud, *La haute magistrature judiciaire entre politique et sacerdoce* (Paris 1993)
J-L Bodiguel, *Les magistrats, un corps sans âme* (Paris 1991)
A Boigeol, 'La magistrature française au féminin: entre spécificité et banalisation' (1993) 25 *Droit et Société* 489
A Boigeol, 'Les magistrats "hors murs" ' (2000) 44/45 *Droit et société* 225
L Greilsamer and D Schneidermann, *Les juges parlent* (Paris 1992)
L Karpik, *French Lawyers* (Oxford 1999)
V Roussel, 'Scandales politiques et transformation des rapports entre magistrature et politique' (2000) 44/45 *Droit et société* 13
D Soulez-Larivière, *Lettres à un jeune avocat* (Paris 1999)

Sources of law

S Belaid, *Le pouvoir créateur et normatif du juge* (Paris 1974)
J Bell, 'Conceptions of Public Policy' in P Cane and J Stapleton, *Essays for Patrick Atiyah* (Oxford 1991), 87
W Dale (ed), *British and French Statutory Drafting* (London 1988)
E Picard, '"Science du droit" ou "Doctrine juridique" ', in *L'unité du droit. Mélanges en hommage à Roland Drago* (Paris 1996), 119

Y Poirmeur et al, *La doctrine juridique* (Paris 1993)
M Troper and C Grzegorczyk, in DN MacCormick and RS Summers, *Interpreting Precedents* (Aldershot 1997), Ch 4
M Troper, C Grzegorczyk and J-L Gardies, in DN MacCormick and RS Summers, *Interpreting Statutes* (Aldershot 1991), Ch 6

The impact of Europe

J-C Bonichot, 'Le droit communautaire et le droit administratif français' AJDA, *Special Issue*, 20 June 1996, 15
S Bracconnier, *Jurisprudence de la Cour européenne des droits de l'homme et droit administratif français* (Brussels 1997)
R de Gouttes, 'La Convention européenne des droits de l'homme et le juge français' (1999) 51 RIDC 7
J-P Flauss, in J Schwarze, *Administrative Law under European Influence* (London 1996), pp 31ff

CHAPTER 3: CIVIL LAW

French civil law is the subject of much commentary. The selection here picks out some of the main themes of the Chapter – judicial lawmaking and the influence of doctrinal writing, the specific case of defective products, and civil procedure and dispute resolution. Among the key works in English on judicial lawmaking are Lasser and Tunc. In French, the study of Serverin and the work of Belaid (noted under Chapter 2) are the most developed. Jestaz and Jamin offer a general survey of the position of doctrinal writing, and Samuel develops the idea of distinctive legal concepts. Beardsley and Jolowicz offer particularly readable studies of civil court procedure.

General

J Gordley, 'Myths of the French Civil Code' (1994) 42 Am Jo Comp Law 459
P Morvan, *Le principe en droit privé* (Paris 1999)
B Nicholas, *The French Law of Contract* (2nd edn), esp Chs 1 and 2
G Samuel, 'Classification of obligations and the impact of constructivist epistemologies' (1998) 18 LS 448
G Samuel, 'Comparative Law and Jurisprudence' (1998) 47 ICLQ 817
G Wiederkehr, 'La culture des revues françaises de droit privé' in A-J Arnaud (ed) (1988) 29 *Quaderni fiorentini per la storia del pensiero giuridico* 9

Doctrinal writing

P Jestaz, 'Déclin de la doctrine?' in *Droits 20: Doctrine et recherche en droit* (Paris 1994), 85
P Jestaz and C Jamin, 'The entity of French doctrine: some thoughts on the community of French legal writers' (1998) 18 LS 415

Judicial lawmaking and methodology

J Boulanger, 'Notations sur le pouvoir créateur de la jurisprudence civile' (1961) 59 RTDCiv 417
F Gény, *Méthode de l'interprétation* (Paris 1919)
L'image doctrinale de la Cour de cassation (Paris 1994)
M Lasser, 'Judicial (Self-)Portraits: Judicial Discourse in the French Legal System' (1995) 104 Yale LJ 1325
JM Portalis, 'Discours préliminaire' in F Ewald ed, *Naissance du Code civil* (Paris 1989), Ch 1
E Serverin, *De la jurisprudence en droit privé. Théorie d'une pratique* (Lyon 1985)
A Tunc, 'The Methodology of the Civil Law in France' (1976) 50 Tulane L Rev 459
A Tunc, 'It is wise not to take the Civil Codes too seriously. Traffic accident compensation in France' in P Wallington and RM Merkin (eds), *Essays in memory of Professor FH Lawson* (London 1986), 71
A Toufait and A Tunc, 'Pour une motivation plus explicite des décisions de justice', RTDCiv 1974,487

Civil procedure

J Beardsley, 'Proof of Fact in French Civil Procedure' (1986) 34 Am Jo Comp Law 459
J-P Bonafé-Schmitt, *Les médiations, la médiation* (Ramonville St-Agnès 1999)
JA Jolowicz, *On Civil Procedure* (Cambridge 2000)

Defective products

F Leduc et al, *La responsabilité du fait des choses. Réflexions autour d'un centenaire* (Paris 1997)
Ph Malinvaud, 'La responsabilité civile du fabricant en droit français', GP 1973.2.463
H Mazeaud, 'La responsabilité civile du vendeur-fabricant' Rfdc 1955, 611
C Larroumet, 'La responsabilité du fait des produits défectueux après la loi du 14 mai 1998' D 1998 Chr 311
G Viney, 'L'introduction en droit français de la directive européenne du 25 juillet 1985 à la responsabilité du fait des produits défectueux' D 1998 Chr 291

CHAPTER 4: CRIMINAL LAW

There are a number of very valuable records of observations made by foreign scholars of the French criminal process (notably Crawford, McKillop and Munday). A lively fictional account is provided by C Samet, *Journal d'un juge d'instruction.* Studies on the development of criminal law and its social function are provided particularly by Garapon, Garapon and Salas, and Pradel.

General

P Chambon, *Le juge d'instruction. Théorie et pratique de la procédure* (4th edn, Paris 1997)

H Dalle, 'Juges et procureurs: une évolution divergente' in *Justices 2000: Ce qui a changé dans la justice depuis 20 ans* (Paris 2000), p 62

Mirjan R Damaska, *The Faces of Justice and State Authority. A Comparative Approach to the Legal Process* (New Haven 1986)

A Garapon, *Bien juger. Essai sur le rituel judiciaire*' (Paris 1997)

A Garapon and D Salas, *La République pénalisée* (Paris 1996)

J-P Marquénaud, 'La dérive de la procédure pénale française au regard des exigences européennes' D 2000 Chr 249

P Poncela, 'Pour une histoire d'une revue de droit pénal' in A-J Arnaud, *La culture des revues juridiques françaises* (1988) 29 *Quaderni fiorentini per la storia del pensiero giuridico moderno* 31

J Pradel, *Droit Pénal: tome II Procédure pénal* (8th edn 1995)

J Pradel, 'La procédure pénale française à l'aube du troisième millénaire' D 2000 Chr 1

Accounts of the criminal process

J Bell, in C Walker and K Starmer (eds), *Miscarriages of Justice. A Review of Justice in Error* (London 1999), Ch 17

A Crawford, 'Justice de Proximité – The Growth of 'Houses of Justice' and Victim/ Offender Mediation in France: A Very UnFrench Legal Response?' (2000) 9 *Social and Legal Studies* 29

L Leigh and L Zedner, *A Report on the Administration of Criminal Justice in the Pre-trial phase in France and Germany*, Royal Commission on Criminal Justice, Research Study No 1 (1992)

B McKillop, 'Readings and Hearings in French Criminal Justice: Five Cases in the *Tribunal Correctionnel*' (1998) 46 Am Jo Comp Law 757

B McKillop, 'Anatomy of a French Murder Case' (1997) 45 Am Jo Comp Law 527

R Munday, 'Jury trial, continental style' (1993) 13 LS 204

R Munday, 'What do the French think of their jury?' (1995) 15 LS 65

Investigation process

A Anton, 'L'instruction criminelle' (1960) 9 Am Jo Comp Law 441

M Delmas-Marty, 'The Juge d'instruction: do the English really need him?' in B Markesinis (ed), *The Gradual Convergence* (Oxford 1994), pp 46ff

S Field and A West, 'A tale of two reforms: French defence rights and police powers in transition' (1995) 6 Criminal Law Forum 473

E Mathias, *Les procureurs du droit* (Paris 1999)

J Pradel, 'Centenaire de la loi du 8 décembre 1897 sur la défense avant jugement pénal: essai d'un bilan' D 1997 Chr 375

JR Spencer, 'French and English Criminal Procedure: A Brief Comparison' in B Markesinis, *The Gradual Convergence*, 33

Attitudes of legal professionals

H Leclerc, *Un combat pour la justice. Entretiens avec Marc Heurgon* (Paris 1994)

H Nallet, *Tempête sur la Justice* (Paris 1992)

C Samet, *Journal d'un juge d'instruction* (Paris 2000)

C Samet (ed), *Justice, Transparence et Démocratie* (Paris 1997)

Law reforms

M Delmas-Marty (chair), *La Mise en Etat des Affaires Pénales* (Documentation francaise 1991)
J Massot (chair), *Groupe d'étude sur la responsabilité pénale des décideurs publics* (Report to Minister of Justice, 16 December 1999)
P Truche (chair), *Rapport de la commission de réflexion sur la Justice* (Paris 1997)

CHAPTER 5: ADMINISTRATIVE LAW

Much of the literature concerns the Conseil d'Etat or is a general doctrinal exposition of the law. There are some records of observations made by visitors (see Bell and Hamson). The most informative studies have been connected with the anniversaries of the Conseil d'Etat. The website of the Conseil d'Etat contains useful information on the operation of the administrative courts and some recent decisions.

General

LN Brown and J Bell, *French Administrative Law* (5th edn, Oxford 1998)
G Braibant, 'Du simple au complexe, quarante ans de droit administratif (1953-1993)', (1993) 45 EDCE 409
G Braibant and B Stirn, *Le droit administratif* (5th edn, Paris 1998)
C J Hamson, *Executive Discretion and Judicial Control* (London 1954)
D Loschak, *Le rôle politique du juge administratif français* (Paris 1972)

Administrative court procedure and interpretation

J Barthélemy, 'Le rôle de l'avocat devant la juridiction administrative' *La Revue Administrative, numéro spécial: Les juridictions administratives dans le monde: France-Allemagne*, 1999, 117
J Bell, 'Reflections on the procedure of the Conseil d'Etat' in G Hand and J McBride, *Droit sans frontières* (Birmingham 1991), 211
B Ducamin, 'Le style des décisions du Conseil d'Etat : les réactions d'un public cultivé', EDCE 1984-5, 129
N Rainaud, *Le Comissaire du gouvernement par le Conseil d'Etat* (Paris 1996)

Conseil d'Etat

Le Conseil d'Etat Livre Jubilaire (Paris 1952)
J-P Costa, *Le Conseil d'Etat dans la société contemporaine* (Paris 1993)
J Massot and T Girardot, *Conseil d'Etat* (Paris 1999)

Advisory role of Conseil d'Etat

J Bell, 'What is the Function of the Conseil d'Etat in the Preparation of Legislation?' (2000) 49 ICLQ 661
N Questiaux, 'Administration and the Rule of Law: The Preventive Role of the French Conseil d'Etat' [1995] PL 247

N Questiaux, 'Do the Opinions expressed by the Conseil d'Etat in its capacity as legal advisor to the Government influence policy?' (2000) 49 ICLQ 672

Authority of doctrinal writing and case-law

M Deguergue, *Jurisprudence et doctrine dans l'élaboration du droit de la responsabilité administrative* (Paris 1994)
L Favoreu, 'L'évolution de la doctrine depuis 1945' *La Revue Administrative 1997: numéro spécial: Le Conseil d'Etat et la Doctrine*, 18
T Fortsakis, *Conceptualisme et empiricisme en droit administratif français* (Paris 1987)
H Le Berre, *Les revirements de jurisprudence en droit administratif de l'an VIII à 1998 (Conseil d'Etat et Tribunal des Conflits)* (Paris 1999)
La Revue Administrative 1997: numéro spécial: Le Conseil d'Etat et la Doctrine
J Rivero, 'Apologie pour "les faiseurs de systèmes"' D 1951 Chr 99
J Rivero, 'Jurisprudence et doctrine dans l'élaboration du droit administratif', EDCE 1955, 27

Influence of Europe

S Bracconier, *Jurisprudence de la Cour européenne des droits de l'homme et droit administratif français* (Brussels 1997)
J-F Flauss, in J Schwarze, *Administrative Law under European Influence* (London 1996), 31

CHAPTER 6: CONSTITUTIONAL LAW

There are fewer general analyses in French constitutional law than on more established branches of law. Many valuable articles are written as annual surveys or case-notes in the *Revue de Droit Public*, the *Revue française de droit constitutionnel* and other public law journals. There are also a number of doctrinal studies not listed here. The major works in English are Stone and Bell. In French, Rousseau offers a comparable approach. The works of Genevois and Favoreu are more doctrinal. The more recent studies of Jan and Viala contain much valuable information and analysis of the practical operations of the Conseil constitutionnel. The Conseil constitutionnel's own website provides reviews of its operation, as well as the text of cases.

General

J Bell, *French Constitutional Law* (Oxford 1992)
L Favoreu et al, *Droit constitutionnel* (Paris 1998)
L Favoreu and L Philip, *Les grandes décisions du Conseil constitutionnel* (10th edn, Paris 1999)
B Genevois, *La Jurisprudence du Conseil constitutionnel* (Paris 1988)
D Rousseau, *Sur le Conseil constitutionnel. La doctrine Badinter et la démocratie* (Paris 1997)
A Stone, *The Birth of Judicial Politics in France* (New York 1992)
A Stone Sweet, *Governing with Judges* (Oxford 2000)

Specific commentaries

A Bonnie, 'The Constitutionality of Transfers of Sovereignty: the French Approach' (1998) 4 *European Public Law* 517
S Boyron, 'The Conseil constitutionnel and the European Union' [1993] PL 30
R Romi, 'Le Président de la République, interprète de la Constitution' RDP 1987, 1265
I Richir, 'Le chef d'Etat et le juge constitutionnel, gardiens de la Constitution' RDP 1999, 1047

Procedure and interpretation of the Conseil constitutionnel

Y Aguila, 'L'interprétation constitutionnelle' (1995) Rfdc No 21, 9
J Boudéant, 'Le Président du Conseil constitutionnel' RDP 1987, 589
P Jan, *La Saisine du Conseil constitutionnel* (Paris 1999)
'Le Conseil constitutionnel' *Pouvoirs* No 13 (Paris 1986)
T Di Mano, *Le Conseil constitutionnel et les moyens soulevés d'office* (Paris 1994)
A Viala, *Les réserves d'interprétation dans la jurisprudence du Conseil constitutionnel* (Paris 1999)

Index

Index of authors discussed